Y0-BRP-745

AN INTRODUCTION TO PARALEGAL STUDIES

DAVID G. COOPER, J.D.
ASSISTANT PROFESSOR, FULLERTON COLLEGE
MEMBER, STATE BAR OF CALIFORNIA

MICHAEL J. GIBSON, J.D.
MEMBER, STATE BAR OF CALIFORNIA

SOUTH-WESTERN PUBLISHING CO.

1 2 3 4 5 6 7 8 9 10 D 02 01 00 99 98 97 96 95 94 93

Printed in the United States of America

Managing Editor: Robert E. Lewis
Coordinating Editor: Barry Corrado
Acquisitions Editor: Betty B. Schechter
Production Editor: Kimberlee Kusnerak
Senior Designer: Jim DeSollar
Production Artist: Sophia Renieris
Marketing Manager: Colleen J. Thomas

PHOTO CREDITS

p. 29 Mike Mazzaschi/Stock, Boston
p. 57 © The National Geographic Society, courtesy, The Supreme Court Historical Society.
p. 83 © Kaz Mori/The Image Bank
p. 217 Bohdan Hrynewych/Stock, Boston
p. 275 Joseph Sohm/Stock, Boston

Library of Congress Cataloging-in-Publication Data

Cooper, David G.
An introduction to paralegal studies / David G. Cooper and Michael J. Gibson.
p. cm.
Includes index.
ISBN 0-538-70729-1
1. Legal assistants—United States. I. Gibson, Michael J. II. Title.
KF320.L4C66 1994
340'.023'73—dc20 92-34609
CIP

PREFACE

Students who are beginning a program in paralegal studies are, quite naturally, filled with enthusiasm. They have been drawn to the field because they have heard that a career as a paralegal can be exciting, challenging, personally satisfying, and lucrative. They have been told that the market for qualified paralegals is rapidly expanding and that few careers offer a more diverse range of job opportunities.

An Introduction to Paralegal Studies is designed to capitalize on this enthusiasm by giving the beginning student a sense of why so many paralegals find the profession satisfying and enjoyable. After presenting the basic knowledge needed to perform the job, the book asks the student to begin practicing the skills that paralegals use every day. By the time students complete the course, they should know not only what paralegals do, but also whether they want to pursue a career doing those things. This practical approach to the profession has something to offer every student and makes this book well suited to any introductory course in paralegal studies.

ABOUT THE TEXTBOOK

An Introduction to Paralegal Studies was written with two goals in mind. The first goal was to create an easy-to-read text that would provide solid, basic coverage of the topics most important for beginning paralegal students. The second goal was to develop a text that would emphasize the practical over the theoretical. The purpose of every paralegal studies program is to train students to become qualified practicing paralegals, and an introductory course is the best place to begin. Accordingly, this book covers such paralegal skills as fact investigation, legal research, legal analysis, and legal writing. An effort has been made to treat even the most theoretical topics, including substantive law and professional ethics, in a down-to-earth manner that emphasizes practical applications.

Organization of the text reflects the dual goals of simplicity and practicality. Part 1 begins with an overview of the paralegal profession itself, followed by an insider's guide to the microenvironment within which most paralegals function: the law office. This is followed by a basic introduction to the American legal system.

Part 2 enables students to build a basic legal vocabulary. Legal terms are introduced within the context of an overview of seven important fields of substantive law. This approach helps students to recognize that in order to understand the meaning of a legal term they must understand how the term fits within the framework of legal rules. Important terms are identified in boldface in the text and are defined succinctly in a comprehensive glossary at the back of the book.

Part 3 focuses on learning about and practicing the basic skills that every paralegal must have. Fact investigation, legal research, and legal analysis and writing are introduced in Chapters 6, 7, and 8, followed in Chapter 9 by a step-by-step introduction to the litigation process that emphasizes how all of these skills are utilized on a day-to-day basis by litigation paralegals. The critical interrelationship of these skills is reinforced by examining the use of each skill in the context of a single fictional case, *Smith v. Lemon Motors*. Each chapter begins with a memorandum outlining tasks that a paralegal might be expected to perform in the course of readying the *Smith* case for trial.

Part 4 discusses legal ethics, with an emphasis on how they apply to paralegals, and addresses the timely topic of paralegals and the unauthorized practice of law. Extensive references are made to guidelines for ethical conduct that have been adopted by professional organizations, including the recently promulgated ABA Model Guidelines for the Utilization of Legal Assistant Services. (The ABA's guidelines as well as those of two paralegal associations are included in the text's Appendix.) Numerous examples illustrate the application of these guidelines to the paralegal's daily experience in the workplace.

Several features have been woven throughout the text to enhance its practical approach. Extensive use is made of illustrations, especially sample documents that typify the kind of work product generated by paralegals on a day-to-day basis. A special effort has been made to point out the role computers can play in assisting the paralegal. ''Pointers'' are scattered throughout the text to emphasize the importance of particular information, to draw attention to the interrelationship of topics discussed in different parts of the text, or to provide additional information that will help the student understand key ideas contained in the text.

ABOUT THE STUDENT RESOURCE MANUAL

For each chapter of the text, the student Resource Manual presents a concise Summary that will aid the process of test review. Each chapter summary is followed by Study Questions to help the student focus on key concepts covered in the text. Discussion Questions—and in some chapters, special Assignments—are included for the purpose of challenging the student to think critically about issues raised in the chapter. Grouped under the heading Test Your Knowledge, a series of exercises in matching, multiple choice, and true/false formats round out the collection of study aids provided for each chapter. Answers to Study Questions and Test Your Knowledge exercises are included at the end of each chapter of the manual.

ABOUT THE INSTRUCTOR'S MANUAL

The Instructor's Manual is also organized in a chapter-by-chapter format. Each section begins with a set of Learning Objectives listing the tasks a student should be able to perform after completing study of the chapter, followed by an Annotated Outline designed to assist the busy instructor with lecture planning. Particular attention is given to the development of legal vocabulary. Outlines include cross-references to illustrations in the text, as well as to Teaching Suggestions that follow chapter outlines in the manual itself. The Teaching Suggestions for each chapter will help the instructor achieve maximum student involvement in both classroom activities and research projects conducted outside the classroom. Special emphasis is placed on cooperative learning activities that allow students to teach and learn from one another. (Transparency Masters are provided at the back of the book for use in classroom lectures and discussions.) Following the Teaching Suggestions for each chapter are guidelines for the instructor's use in evaluating student answers to the Discussion Questions and Assignments in the student Resource Manual. Finally, the Instructor's Manual contains test questions for each chapter in a variety of matching, multiple choice, true/false, short answer, and essay formats. Answers are provided for all test questions.

ABOUT THE AUTHORS

David G. Cooper holds a Juris Doctor degree from the University of San Diego School of Law. He earned his Bachelor of Arts degree at Loyola Marymount University, where he was inducted into Alpha Sigma Nu. Currently an assistant professor teaching paralegal studies and business law at Fullerton College, Mr. Cooper was the first director of Fullerton's paralegal studies program.

Michael J. Gibson holds a Juris Doctor degree from the School of Law of the University of California, Los Angeles. He earned his Bachelor of Arts degree at Loyola Marymount University, where he was named Alpha Sigma Nu Scholar of the Year. Mr. Gibson is currently engaged in private practice in the Los Angeles area, where he specializes in both commercial and real estate transactional law and commercial and real estate litigation.

ACKNOWLEDGMENTS

The authors wish to thank Elizabeth C. Richardson, J.D., who served as consulting editor for this project, for her expert advice and invaluable assistance. We would also like to thank Joyce Birdoff of Nassau Community College and Faith O'Reilly of Hamline University, whose comments and suggestions during the manuscript stage of development contributed greatly to the finished product. We wish to acknowledge and thank our colleagues, students, and friends for their many contributions. Finally, we wish to express our heartfelt thanks to our families—Ann and Samuel Cooper and Shawn, David, and Kevin Gibson—for their patience, understanding, and support.

David G. Cooper
Michael J. Gibson

SUMMARY OF CONTENTS

CONTENTS

1 WHAT IS A PARALEGAL?

Welcome to an exciting, challenging, and dynamic new career field! After reviewing over 500 occupations, the U.S. Department of Labor recently predicted that paralegal will be the fastest-growing occupation of the 1990s.[1] This prediction has inspired tremendous curiosity about the profession, yet most people have only vague ideas about what a paralegal is and what a paralegal does.

Chapter 1 will introduce you to the paralegal profession. After studying this chapter, you should be able to answer the following questions:

- What is a paralegal?
- What are the differences between paralegals and lawyers?
- What has caused the dramatic growth of the paralegal profession?
- To become a paralegal, what abilities, personal characteristics, education, and training will you need?
- Who employs paralegals?
- What areas of specialization are available to paralegals?
- How much do paralegals earn?

ATTEMPTING TO DEFINE PARALEGAL

A **paralegal** is a professional who performs legal tasks under the supervision of a lawyer. An experienced, well-trained paralegal working under the supervision of a lawyer can perform many of the tasks that the lawyer would otherwise have to perform. Together, lawyer and paralegal function as a team that provides legal services to clients.

Formal Definitions

Let's begin by taking a look at how lawyers and paralegals themselves define the position. In 1986, the American Bar Association (ABA) adopted the following definition:

> A legal assistant is a person, qualified through education, training or work experience, who is employed or retained by a lawyer, law office, governmental agency, or other entity in a capacity or function which involves the performance, under the ultimate direction and supervision of an attorney, of specifically-designated substantive legal work, which work, for the most part, requires a sufficient knowledge of legal concepts that, absent such assistant, the attorney would perform the task.[2]

Notice that the American Bar Association uses the term "legal assistant" rather than "paralegal." Legal assistant and paralegal are synonymous and interchangeable, just as the terms lawyer and attorney are.

In 1984, the National Association of Legal Assistants (NALA) developed this definition:

> Legal assistants* are a distinguishable group of persons who assist attorneys in the delivery of legal services. Through formal education, training, and experience, legal assistants have knowledge and expertise regarding the legal system and substantive and procedural law which qualify them to do work of a legal nature under the supervision of an attorney.[3]

The footnote to "Legal assistants" reads, "Within this occupational category, some individuals are known as paralegals."

In 1987, the National Federation of Paralegal Associations (NFPA) provided the following definition:

> A paralegal/legal assistant is a person, qualified through education, training, or work experience to perform substantive legal work that requires knowledge of legal concepts and is customarily, but not exclusively, performed by a lawyer. This person may be retained or employed by a lawyer, law office, governmental agency, or other entity or may be authorized by administrative, statutory or court authority to perform this work.[4]

Defining Paralegal in Terms of Tasks Performed

As you can see, no single definition of paralegal is accepted universally. Bar associations and paralegal associations have formulated definitions that vary from one another in subtle ways. One reason for this difficulty is that paralegals perform such a wide range of legal tasks. To a large extent, the tasks of a given paralegal depend on the particular area of law in which the individual specializes. A paralegal who works mostly on trial-related matters has duties very different from those of a paralegal who specializes in shareholder agreements and employee benefit plans. Each holds the title paralegal, yet the two jobs are not the same. Therefore the term paralegal should be defined in relation to a particular specialty area. We will illustrate by considering the specific duties of paralegals specializing in two distinct areas, litigation and Social Security disability law.

Example 1: Litigation. Many paralegals specialize in **litigation**, the process through which a dispute is settled in the courts. Litigation paralegals draft documents such as complaints, cross-complaints, and answers that are filed with the court. They also draft documents designed to obtain information about a lawsuit: interrogatories, requests for admission, and requests for production of documents. (The exact nature of these litigation documents and how paralegals prepare them is discussed in Chapter 9.)

Litigation paralegals may also perform investigative functions such as examining accident scenes, locating witnesses, and searching government records. (Investigation is discussed in Chapter 6.)

Another important function of litigation paralegals is summarizing the sometimes overwhelming volume of material associated with a case and organizing the material to enable easy access by the supervising lawyer. This can be especially important at trial, when the lawyer needs to locate materials quickly. One of the paralegal's main functions at trial is to provide the lawyer with materials and exhibits precisely when they are needed.

Example 2: Social Security Disability. Now, in contrast to the duties of a litigation paralegal, let's look at the duties of a paralegal who works in a law firm engaged exclusively in the practice of Social Security disability law. Because the Social Security Administration considers persons disabled only if their combined physical and mental impairments keep them from doing any work, regardless of whether it is their past work, the attorney/paralegal team must analyze each client's medical records and develop an argument that supports the person's entitlement to disability benefits. A paralegal in this type of practice will meet with clients to gather information about their past work, determine the physical requirements of that work, and discuss limitations the current illness or injury imposes on routine daily activities such as grocery shopping and performing housework. The paralegal requests names and addresses of all doctors who have treated a client and gathers information on all hospitalizations and treatment at facilities such as rehabilitation and pain-management clinics. The paralegal obtains clients' signatures of authorization to release medical and employment information and writes to doctors and hospitals requesting updated medical records.

Early in the preparation of a case, the paralegal may visit the Social Security Administration office to photocopy the client's file. Then the paralegal can help the attorney analyze the information in the file.

PARALEGAL PROFILE

NAME
Deborah Gardner
TITLE
Legal Assistant
Bandini and Sanchez
San Antonio, Texas

When I was in high school and college, I always intended to go to law school, but I became sidetracked and ended up working as a professional photographer.

I owned a small photography business. Recently I decided to renew my pursuit of a career in law, and a paralegal program seemed a quicker, more attainable way of doing that than going to law school. I wanted to have a marketable skill that I could put to use right away.

I earned my certificate about a year ago and got my first job, which was in the field of corporate law, a month before I graduated. I was very dissatisfied with the job because even though it had been advertised as a paralegal job, there were no paralegal duties whatsoever. The work was strictly secretarial, and I found I had no interest in the field of corporate law. After about eight weeks, I left.

It took me another month to find my current position. I work for a firm that does only personal injury—mainly auto accident cases, but some "slip and fall" and some product liability. There are four partners and two associates. I work for one of the partners, who has about 400 assigned files. Of those 400 files, 186 are assigned to me. Most are not yet litigated. I refer clients to doctors, gather records, interview new clients, verify loss of earnings, verify the special damages that will be claimed, and draft the demand letter that will be sent to the insurance company. The attorney reviews my draft, usually makes changes and additions, and sets the amount of the demand.

At this point, I am not involved with the settlement of the case. In our firm, only the attorneys actually negotiate with the adjusters as to what the case will settle for. Perhaps at some point I will be given that authority, but I've been at the firm only about seven months.

Once a case is litigated, I draft the complaint and initiate the various aspects of discovery—sending out interrogatories and requests for production, guiding our clients through the answering of the interrogatories that come in from the defense counsel, and summarizing depositions. I hated summarizing depositions in paralegal school, but it's very interesting to do in real life. I also send the statement of damages to the defense. I'm just now starting to draft some simple, basic motions; if it's complicated at all, then the attorney drafts it.

The thing I like most about my job is the client contact. I call clients all day long and chat with them: "How are you doing? Are you still being treated by the doctor? Is the doctor helping you at all?" We like to let the client know that we are still here. I try to get a feel for how much longer the client will be in treatment. In most cases, as long as the client is receiving treatment, we don't start the settlement phase.

I've been involved with only one trial. I put together a trial notebook, summarized all the depositions, and organized the exhibits. I did a lot of research, which I really like. I researched the doctrine of imminent peril and found some cases that were very similar—this was a motorcycle accident case, and I even found a motorcycle case. So the attorney was very pleased.

Differences Between Paralegals and Lawyers

Another way to answer the question "What is a paralegal?" is to state what a paralegal is not: A paralegal is *not* a lawyer. A lawyer must meet strict requirements and be licensed to practice law in a given state or other jurisdiction. A paralegal is not licensed—or eligible for a license—to practice law. Although exactly what constitutes practicing law is another gray area (as you will see when you study Chapter 11), a paralegal who gives legal advice to a client or represents a client in court is considered to be engaging in the unauthorized practice of law, which is prohibited in every state.

No Legal Definition

At the present time no laws provide a definition of the term paralegal. No state imposes minimum qualifications on the paralegal profession, nor does any state require licensing of paralegals.

One way that the word lawyer is commonly defined is in terms of the license that the lawyer holds: a lawyer is a person licensed to practice law. Perhaps someday the position paralegal will be defined similarly in terms of the license that the paralegal holds: a paralegal will be a person licensed to practice specified paralegal activities.

POINTER: Many consumer groups, bar associations, and paralegal associations are calling for the licensing of paralegals. Paralegal licensure will be discussed in Chapter 11.

DRAMATIC GROWTH OF THE PARALEGAL PROFESSION

In 1980, there were 36,000 paralegals employed in the United States. By 1988, the number had increased to approximately 83,000.[5] The U.S. Department of Labor estimates that the need for paralegals will increase by 75.3 percent between 1988 and 2000, making paralegal the nation's fastest-growing profession.[6] By the turn of the century, the number of paralegals is expected to increase to 145,000.[7] What is causing this dramatic growth?

Historical Development

The first paralegals were legal secretaries who, because of their work experience, developed the ability to perform many legal tasks. As lawyers became increasingly overworked, legal secretaries performed more and more tasks that traditionally had been performed only by lawyers.

The new paralegal profession was officially recognized in the late 1960s, when the American Bar Association formally approved and encouraged the use of paralegals. In a 1968 report the ABA concluded that the assistance provided by paralegals enables attorneys to render professional services to more people, thereby making legal services more fully available to the public. The ABA formed a special committee to consider "all appropriate methods for developing, encouraging, and increasing the training and utilization of nonlawyer assistants to better enable lawyers to discharge their professional responsibilities."[8]

The next important step in the development of the profession was the establishment of paralegal educational programs. The first paralegal schools opened in the early 1970s. Today, more than 600 educational institutions provide paralegal training.

Another significant milestone was the formation of two paralegal professional associations, the National Federation of Paralegal Associations (NFPA) in 1974 and the National Association of Legal Assistants (NALA) in 1975. Formed to promote and protect the interests of the profession, these associations have specific functions that are discussed later in this chapter.

Reasons for Growth

The growth of the paralegal profession is tied closely to the snowballing growth of the entire legal services industry, of course. In addition, the presence of paralegals in a law office offers attractive economic benefits to client and firm alike.

Growth of the Legal Services Industry. During the 1980s, the paralegal profession benefited from the astounding growth of the legal services industry. In 1980, $26 billion was spent on legal services in the United States; just eight years later, in 1988, the annual figure had increased to $76 billion.[9] Nationwide, more than 10 million lawsuits were pending in state and federal courts in 1988. This huge number of cases was handled by over 700,000 lawyers, who constituted more than two-thirds of all of the lawyers in the world. The incredible growth of the legal services industry partially explains why the number of paralegals has risen so dramatically.

Profitability to Law Firms. Lawyers in private practice have discovered that the efficient use of paralegals results in higher profits for law firms. The bottom line is that paralegals make money for law firms. Profitability is one of the most important reasons for the growth in the number of paralegals.

POINTER: You will often hear someone say that a lawyer is in "private practice." The law offices of lawyers in private practice, commonly known as private law firms, are designed to serve the general public. Individuals and businesses who need legal services, and are able to pay for such services, consult private law firms. Private law firms and other types of law firms are discussed in Chapter 2.

Figure 1-1 illustrates how paralegals enhance a law firm's profitability. Suppose a client desires to set up a simple inter vivos trust. Suppose the law firm charges a flat fee of $1,500 for this task, which takes a lawyer or a paralegal six hours to complete. As a general rule, law firms pay higher salaries to lawyers than to paralegals. Suppose a lawyer's salary and benefit package equals $70 per hour and a paralegal's equals $20 per hour. If a lawyer performs the entire task of setting up the inter vivos trust, the actual cost to the law firm is $420 (6 × $70). After paying the lawyer, the firm will net $1,080 ($1,500 − $420).

What happens if we factor a paralegal into the equation? Because a paralegal can do much of the work, suppose the paralegal devotes 4.5 hours to the task and the lawyer needs to spend only 1.5 hours on it. At $20 per hour for the paralegal, the actual cost to the law firm to have the task performed is $195 (4.5 × $20 + 1.5 × $70). After paying the paralegal and the lawyer, the firm nets $1,305 ($1,500 − $195). Employing a paralegal results in a net increase to the law firm of $225 ($1,305 − $1,080). Even if the flat fee charged to the client is reduced to $1,300, the law firm still nets $1,105 ($1,300 − $195). Using a paralegal has the net result of saving the client $200 ($1,500 − $1,300), increasing the net

FIGURE 1-1 THE PROFITABILITY OF USING PARALEGALS

TASK: SETTING UP A SIMPLE INTER VIVOS TRUST

1. LAWYER, NO PARALEGAL

Function	Lawyer Time*
1. Interviewing	1.0
2. Advising	1.0
3. Gathering information	1.0
4. Preparing papers	2.0
5. Executing and filing papers	1.0
*Assume lawyer hourly wage is $70.	6.0

Flat fee	$1,500
Actual cost (6.0 × $70)	$ 420
Net	$1,080

2. LAWYER AND PARALEGAL

Function	Lawyer Time	Paralegal Time*
1. Interviewing	0.0	1.0
2. Advising	1.0	0.0
3. Gathering information	0.0	1.0
4. Preparing papers	0.0	2.0
5. Executing and filing papers	0.5	0.5
*Assume paralegal hourly wage is $20.	1.5	4.5

Flat fee	$1,300
Actual cost (1.5 × $70 + 4.5 × $20)	$ 195
Net	$1,105

Net results
1. Savings to client of $200
2. Increased net to law firm of $25
3. Lawyer freed of 4.5 hours, resulting in increased income

to the law firm in the amount of $25 ($1,105 – $1,080), and freeing 4.5 hours (6.0 – 1.5) of the lawyer's time for other tasks that can generate income for the firm.

Affordability to Clients. Another reason for the growth in the number of paralegals is that paralegals are more affordable than lawyers. This was illustrated in the preceding example, where the use of a paralegal resulted not only in a lower cost to the client, but also a higher net for the law firm. Clients frequently call a law office and ask to speak to the paralegal because it is less expensive than speaking to the lawyer. Private law firms often bill clients on the basis of the amount of time spent by the firm's lawyers and paralegals on the client's matters. Some law firms routinely bill a minimum of three-tenths of an hour for any telephone conversation; if the law firm charges $200 per hour to talk to an attorney, a short telephone call will cost the client $60. In contrast, if the law firm charges $60 per hour to talk to a paralegal, the telephone call will cost the client only $18. Most clients appreciate the attorney delegating work to paralegals because it lowers the bill.

As the cost of obtaining legal services continues to rise (large law firms charge as much as $400 per hour for a senior partner's time, and the going rate for a lawyer in major metropolitan areas is $175 to $200 per hour), more and more people are being denied effective access to the legal system because they cannot afford to hire a lawyer. The presence of paralegals ameliorates this problem.

Cost-Effective Management of Law Firms. Between 1970 and 1988, the approximate number of lawyers in the United States doubled from 350,000 to 700,000. As the number of lawyers increased, the competition for business also increased. Private law firms were forced to develop more cost-effective methods to deliver legal services. One such method was employing paralegals. As we have seen, the use of paralegals is cost effective because it results in lower costs to the client and increased profits for the law firm. The key to efficient delivery of legal services is to have each task performed by the person capable of performing that task at the lowest cost.

The demand for cost effectiveness is here to stay. Successful law firms will continue to improve the way they do business, and one area of improvement will be the efficient use of paralegals.

PARALEGAL PROFILE

NAME
Linda Zwick
TITLE
Legal Assistant
Black, Kent & MacArthur
Santa Fe, New Mexico

I have always been a generalist, but here at Black, Kent I do primarily litigation and commercial work. I work for a litigation lawyer who does primarily civil rights defense and some general litigation. I also do creditor, bankruptcy, and collections work for a couple of lawyers in the commercial department.

My average day might consist of summarizing a deposition, organizing documents, and drafting answers to discovery requests such as interrogatories or requests for production. I often draft pleadings and correspondence in the collections and foreclosure cases we have. These drafts, of course, go on to the lawyer to be reviewed and sometimes revised. I also draft proposals for legal services that we submit to state agencies, such as the risk management division of the state—we try to get work representing the state in different kinds of cases.

I don't get an opportunity to do as much legal research as I would like. I do things like cite-checking more than actual research. Most of the research is just for my own benefit so that I'll understand the case better. But the lawyers don't ask me to research a particular issue in a case very often.

The thing I really like about my job is being self-directed. I have certain assignments that are given to me, but I have my own timetable and own system for organizing things—somebody doesn't stand over me saying, "Do this, and then this, and then that." I'm in charge of my own priority list and organize my own day, and I like that feeling of being in charge.

Paralegals need to be self-starters and need to be able to anticipate what the lawyer will want done. For example, when I'm working on a litigation case, I'll go ahead and draft the answers to some interrogatories that have come in even though the lawyer hasn't asked me to. Then, when the lawyer says, "We really need to get to work on these interrogatories," I say, "Here's a draft right here!" The lawyer gets kind of thrilled by that.

In this day and age, paralegals need to become familiar with computers and the types of software that are available. There are some amazing programs that we use that really make things easy—for instance, indexing tremendous numbers of documents. My collections system uses a "merge" feature so I can input information once and have the computer create a number of different documents from that one input. A lot of lawyers don't know what programs are available. If you can go in and introduce a system that will be faster and more economical, obviously a lawyer will be very happy with that.

PARALEGAL SKILLS

There exists no definitive list of skills and abilities that every paralegal should possess. Paralegals specializing in different areas of law perform different tasks and use different skills. However, certain skills, abilities, and personal characteristics enhance the effectiveness of all types of paralegals.

Communication Skills

Communication skills are extremely important for paralegals. Paralegals should be able to get ideas across both verbally and in writing.

Oral Communication Skills. Oral communication skills are important because paralegals are in constant contact with clients. Paralegals frequently participate in the initial client interview, talk with clients in order to obtain the information needed to draft various legal documents, and regularly communicate with clients regarding upcoming deadlines. In some cases, paralegals talk with the client more than the lawyer does.

POINTER: When communicating with a client, a paralegal is not permitted to give legal advice. After talking with a client, a paralegal should write the supervising attorney a memorandum summarizing the conversation and listing the client's questions. Then the attorney can either contact the client and give the necessary legal advice or authorize the paralegal to relay the information.

Paralegals also need good oral communication skills to conduct their frequent business with people other than clients. Some examples: Many paralegals perform investigative work, such as interviewing witnesses at an accident scene. A number of paralegals participate in settlement negotiations with insurance claims adjusters. And all paralegals must be able to communicate effectively with everyone who works in the law office: the office manager, law clerks, legal secretaries, word processors, telephone operators, receptionists, messengers, and private investigators.

Writing Skills. Writing skills are critically important to paralegals. Paralegals must be able to write clearly and concisely. When writing a letter to a client, for example, a paralegal should be able to explain detailed information in simple, understandable language.

POINTER: A paralegal's professional image depends largely on the quality of his or her writing. Always remember that your writing is a direct reflection of yourself; your own sense of personal and professional pride should keep you from writing documents that are sloppy or contain grammatical errors. Improving your writing skills should be one of the main goals of your paralegal education.

To envision how important writing skills are to a paralegal, consider the following documents that typically may be prepared by a litigation paralegal:

- Summaries of initial client interviews
- Complaints
- Answers
- Motions—motions to dismiss, motions to strike, motions for summary judgment, and so on
- Interrogatories and answers to interrogatories
- Requests for admissions and answers to requests for admissions
- Requests for production of documents
- Summaries of deposition transcripts
- Summaries of documents (such as the answers to interrogatories)
- Documents for a default judgment
- Legal research memoranda
- Briefs
- Settlement letters
- Settlement documents such as releases, settlement agreements, and stipulations to dismiss
- Subpoenas

Analytical Skills

Analytical skills are also important. Paralegals perform legal research, which is the process of searching for the rules of law that address the questions raised by the facts of a case. Performing legal research requires the ability to read, understand, analyze, and interpret the law. We will examine legal research in depth in Chapter 7.

A paralegal must be able to analyze a legal problem logically. Legal problems are analyzed by applying legal rules to the specific facts of the case. This process is known as legal analysis and is the subject of Chapter 8.

In addition, a paralegal needs good analytical skills when summarizing various legal documents. For example, summarizing a deposition transcript is a typical assignment performed by a litigation paralegal. A **deposition** is the questioning of a party or a witness under oath. At a deposition, the attorney's questions and the witness's answers are transcribed verbatim by a court reporter. The testimony is summarized and organized by the paralegal to provide the supervising attorney with easy access to selected topics. How to summarize a deposition is discussed in Chapter 9.

Figure 1-2 lists some tasks typically performed by paralegals. These tasks utilize writing skills, verbal skills, and analytical skills.

FIGURE 1-2 PARALEGAL SKILLS AND THEIR APPLICATION

WRITING SKILLS

- Legal Documents (contracts, wills)
- Complaints and Answers
- Interrogatories
- Deposition Summaries
- Intake Memos
- Legal Research Memoranda

VERBAL SKILLS

- Interviewing Clients
- Interviewing Witnesses
- Negotiating

ANALYTICAL SKILLS

- Reading Cases and Statutes
- Applying the Law to the Client's Case
- Summarizing Documents

Computer Skills

As an increasing number of law firms become automated, the computer is playing a larger role in the paralegal's daily activities. Computer applications used by paralegals include word processing, litigation support (including database management and case management), timekeeping and billing, and calendaring. These topics are discussed in Chapter 2. Paralegals also use computer skills when performing computer-assisted legal research, a topic that will be discussed in Chapters 6 and 7.

POINTER: Most employers consider the ability to use a computer a highly desirable, if not mandatory, skill. If you are not computer literate, then acquiring computer skills should be one of the main goals of your paralegal education.

Abilities and Personal Characteristics

When lawyers and paralegals themselves were asked what skills and personal qualities were important for a paralegal to possess, the majority indicated that the following characteristics were important:[10]

- Willingness to assume responsibility
- Maturity
- Ability to get along well with people
- Good verbal skills
- Good writing skills
- Analytical mind
- Willingness to accept direction from others
- Ability to function at a high level under stressful conditions
- Empathy
- Ability to understand legal terminology and procedures
- Interest in people
- Above-average intelligence
- Ambition

Interestingly, most respondents felt that the following factors, although useful, were not critical:

- Legal secretary experience
- Knowledge of bookkeeping
- Some law school courses
- Desire to eventually become an attorney

In this section we have looked at just some of the many skills and characteristics that are important for a paralegal to possess. Other, less universal, skills and characteristics are important in specific legal situations, which we will note as they arise.

WHAT DO ATTORNEYS LOOK FOR WHEN HIRING PARALEGALS?

NAME
Doug Barker
TITLE
Partner
Timms, Smith, Frisch & Johns
Houston, Texas

For four years, I was the partner who ran the paralegal program at Timms, Smith, Houston's largest law firm. Our paralegal program has approximately thirty paralegals, and they work across the various disciplines—litigation, trusts and estates, business, labor, and many other areas.

I think interpersonal skills are critical for a paralegal. Paralegals deal with clients, the opposing counsel, process servers and court reporters, and people who bring you substantive information such as investigators, third-party witnesses, and expert witnesses. If the paralegal is cold, demanding, or not diplomatic and tactful, then the people the paralegal deals with will be less accommodating.

A second critical skill is an ability to communicate in both written and oral form. Paralegals must communicate from our office to the outside world; much of that is on the telephone, and much of it is in writing.

A third important skill is a keen awareness of the importance of procedure and an actual working knowledge of procedure. Paralegals must have a sound appreciation of the procedural nuances in their area of specialization. Some lawyers are not good at keeping current with changes in procedure and the local rules, and the paralegal, as well as the secretary, must come to the rescue much of the time.

In terms of personal qualities and characteristics, I think "presence" is important, along with appearance and a sense of professionalism. The paralegal is an ambassador or representative of the firm, and the firm is evaluated by how the paralegal presents himself or herself.

When we hire a paralegal, we are looking for somebody who is going to take initiative and who is going to be a case manager. A shortcoming we see in many paralegals is that they don't take the initiative to move the case along. Instead, they feel that their job is project-oriented rather than big-picture, case-management-oriented. They sit and wait for the lawyer to give them a project such as, "Here's a deposition—please summarize it." They do it, and then they wait for the next project. We like to see paralegals who take the initiative and look for ways to advance the case. A paralegal should ask questions about the case and make suggestions and recommendations about what ought to be done. We can't have passive paralegals who sit at their desks with an assembly-line mentality—we want paralegals who are aggressive and determined to excel.

EDUCATION AND TRAINING

Because no state yet requires paralegals to be licensed, no formal educational requirements have been established for the profession. Nevertheless, most paralegals have received formal education. According to a recent NFPA survey, only 30 percent of paralegals had received formal training in 1982, while over 70 percent had received formal training by 1988.[11]

Employers differ in the amount of education they require; some require a bachelor's or associate's degree, others require a paralegal certificate, and still others require no formal training. However, there is a clear trend toward higher educational standards for the profession. According to a 1990 Legal Assistant Management Association (LAMA) survey designed to identify the educational criteria of medium-sized to large law firms and corporate legal departments, 72 percent of such employers required a four-year degree in 1990, whereas only 32 percent had required a four-year degree in 1980. And 49 percent of the employers surveyed required a paralegal certificate in 1990, whereas only 22 percent had required a certificate in 1980.[12] As the legal profession and the public become more knowledgeable about the paralegal profession, academic credentials are becoming increasingly important for paralegals.

Certificate Programs

The certificate program is the most prevalent type of paralegal education. Certificate programs are offered by proprietary and technical schools as well as by two-year and four-year colleges and universities. Many certificate programs do not require general education courses (although some four-year colleges admit only students who have completed their general education requirements). If general education courses are not required, students can complete the program and enter the workplace more quickly, sometimes in as little as three months. This makes certificate programs ideal for people who are making a career change and already have a degree and work experience. However, many educators do not recommend certificate programs for recent high school graduates or students who have not completed at least 30 semester units of college credit. These students may lack the broader educational background needed to function effectively as paralegals.

Associate's Degree Programs

Associate's degree programs are offered by two-year community colleges and four-year colleges and universities. Associate's degrees are two-year degrees requiring approximately 60 semester units. Associate's programs require general education courses in addition to general law courses and paralegal specialty courses. Although curricula vary, usually the student must complete general education courses plus certain required legal courses such as legal research, legal writing, and civil litigation. In addition, the student chooses from a list of paralegal specialty courses that might include such subjects as torts, contracts, real estate, probate and estate planning, family law, workers' compensation, bankruptcy, criminal law, corporate law, business law, law office management, immigration law, administrative law, international law and environmental law.

Bachelor's Degree Programs

Bachelor's degree programs in paralegal studies are offered by some colleges and universities. These four-year degree programs usually include general education courses, business courses, general law courses, and paralegal specialty courses.

ABA-Approved Programs

The American Bar Association approves institutions offering programs that meet certain ABA guidelines. ABA-approved schools must require students to complete both general education courses and paralegal specialty courses. The ABA reviews a school's curriculum, faculty, job placement service, and procedures and policies before granting approval.

Less than a quarter of all schools offering paralegal education are approved by the ABA. Many schools simply do not meet the stringent ABA guidelines.

Other schools have chosen not to pursue ABA approval, sometimes because they cannot afford the cost associated with gaining and maintaining approval or because they do not believe students should be required to take general education courses. Consequently, many schools that provide their students with a quality education are not ABA approved.

Opinions regarding ABA approval differ greatly from employer to employer. Some employers hire only graduates of ABA-approved programs. Other employers do not feel that graduation from an ABA-approved program is an important criterion for hiring paralegals. Figure 1-3[13] illustrates the importance of various criteria used by employers when hiring paralegals.

FIGURE 1-3 CRITERIA FOR HIRING PARALEGALS

	Graduation from ABA-Approved Program %	Graduation from Paralegal Program %	Bachelor's Degree %	Associate's Degree %	Experience in Any Law Office %	Experience in Own Law Office %
Mandatory	5	13	13	6	13	9
Major factor	12	16	18	9	32	25
Important	23	25	27	30	31	18
Minor factor	25	27	24	25	18	17
Not relevant	36	19	18	31	6	32

Source: From "Certification of Legal Assistants: A Report on an American Bar Association Survey" by Roger A. Larson, *Legal Assistants Update*, Vol. 5, Copyright 1986 American Bar Association. Reprinted by permission.

NALA-Recommended Educational Qualifications

The National Association of Legal Assistants has suggested certain minimum educational qualifications for a paralegal. According to NALA, a paralegal should meet one of the following criteria:

1. Successful completion of the Certified Legal Assistant (CLA) examination of the National Association of Legal Assistants, Inc.;
2. Graduation from an ABA-approved program of study for legal assistants;
3. Graduation from a course of study for legal assistants which is institutionally accredited but not ABA approved, and which requires not less than the equivalent of 60 semester hours of classroom study;
4. Graduation from a course of study for legal assistants, other than those set forth in (2) and (3) above, plus not less than six months of in-house training as a legal assistant;
5. A baccalaureate degree in any field, plus not less than six months of in-house training as a legal assistant;
6. A minimum of three years of law-related experience under the supervision of an attorney, including at least six months of in-house training as a legal assistant; or
7. Two years of in-house training as a legal assistant.[14]

"In-house training as a legal assistant" means on-the-job training in the duties and functions of a paralegal. This training is supervised by a lawyer.[15]

On-the-Job Training

Formal education in a paralegal program is only one step in becoming a competent professional. Paralegals, like lawyers, learn a great deal when they actually start working. On-the-job training broadens the knowledge gained through paralegal education. No matter how practical and realistic your school assignments are, you will still have much to learn once you begin working.

Many large law firms now have in-house training programs. These programs may provide newly hired paralegals with training in legal research (including computer-assisted research and a library orientation), the procedures used in drafting particular documents, and the firm's computer system (including training in the specific legal software used by the firm). According to the 1990 LAMA education survey, 44 percent of the law firms and corporations that employ paralegals offer formal in-house training programs.[16]

Certified Legal Assistant (CLA) Designation

The National Association of Legal Assistants sponsors a national certification program that designates qualified individuals Certified Legal Assistants. The CLA program is *voluntary*; a person does not have to be certified in order to be a practicing paralegal. In order to be certified, a candidate must apply for and successfully complete a comprehensive two-day examination. The candidate must then meet continuing education requirements in order to maintain the CLA designation.

NALA also offers specialty certification to paralegals who have already earned the CLA designation. The four-hour specialty exams are given in the areas of civil litigation, probate and estate planning, corporate and business law, criminal law and procedure, and real estate.

We reiterate that the CLA program is entirely voluntary; a person does *not* have to pass the CLA exam in order to be a practicing paralegal. According to NALA, the CLA designation "is a statement to the legal profession and the public that the legal assistant has met the high levels of knowledge and professionalism required by NALA's CLA program."[17]

PARALEGAL PROFILE

NAME
Mark McRill
TITLE
Family Law Paralegal
Christine Morris, a Law Corporation
Upland, California

As a family law paralegal, my primary responsibility is being in charge of discovery. In particular, I send interrogatories to the other side and check to see what has not been produced by the other side.

Marshaling assets, or finding out what the assets of the client are, is probably the single most important part of my job. I maintain the documentation of our client's assets. Asset research is very exacting and not a productive use of the attorney's time—that's why I do it.

Because we have so many cases, I review the files to make sure that nothing is falling between the cracks and that the case is moving along as it should. I'm also in charge of a sophisticated computerized calendaring program that we have.

I really like the flexibility of my job and being in charge of my own schedule, and I enjoy working with the attorneys. Another thing I like is helping the attorney solve the problems that invariably arise in a case. I'm the mechanic, and the attorney is the case specialist. But a lot of times I have ideas that the attorney hasn't thought of. It's fun when I suggest things that the attorney really likes, and it's fun when the attorney really begins to rely on me.

If you don't like numbers, and if you can't deal with people who like to talk about their problems, then family law is not for you. Sometimes I think family law paralegals need to know more about psychology than they do about the law.

TYPES OF EMPLOYMENT

Although most paralegals are employed by private law firms, the legal knowledge and skills typically possessed by a trained paralegal are valuable to many different types of employers. An extremely broad range of employment opportunity is available to paralegals.

Private Law Firms

Approximately 75 percent of paralegals work in private law firms.[18] The assignments, duties, and responsibilities of a paralegal may vary widely depending on the size of the firm and its area of specialization.

Paralegals working in large firms are more likely to specialize in one area. Large law firms are usually organized by specialty areas, such as the litigation department, the real estate department, the probate department, and so on. Paralegals are usually assigned to a particular department. In a small firm, paralegals may work in several different specialty areas.

Large firms are also characterized by a more distinct division of labor. Telephone operators answer the phones, receptionists greet clients, word processors generate documents, secretaries manage a variety of office details, and paralegals research and draft documents. In a small firm, a single person may function as operator, receptionist, word processor, secretary, and paralegal. In such a firm, the paralegal does whatever needs to be done.

Paralegals working in a large firm usually have access to more resources, such as an extensive law library, computers, and computer-assisted legal research systems. Large firms often have better in-house training programs and may be more willing to spend money on continuing education for paralegals.

Despite the many advantages of working in a large firm, many paralegals prefer the small-firm environment. Small firms often provide a paralegal with more varied experience, and some paralegals find small firms to be less stressful, less formal, more relaxed, and more personable.

In-House Legal Departments

Large businesses make up the second-largest employer of paralegals, employing almost 20 percent of the paralegals who responded to a 1991 survey.[19] Banks, insurance companies, and other large businesses often have their own legal departments, which are known as in-house legal departments.

Many in-house legal departments are too small to handle all the legal work of the business. For example, when the business is involved in litigation, it may need to retain a private law firm as outside counsel.

Mainly because of the high costs associated with retaining outside counsel, businesses are hiring more and more paralegals to assist their in-house attorneys. In-house paralegals are likely to be paid comparatively higher salaries and receive more benefits than paralegals working in law firms.[20]

Government

The government is the third-largest employer of paralegals. Federal, state, and local governments have established formal job classifications for different types of paralegal work. Paralegals work in many different federal agencies (e.g., the U.S. Department of Justice and the Securities and Exchange Commission) and state agencies (e.g., the state attorney general's office). On the local level, paralegals work for city attorneys, district attorneys, and public defenders.

Many federal employees do paralegal-type work but are not classified as paralegals. Examples include research analysts at the Federal Trade Commission, equal employment specialists at the Equal Employment Opportunity Commission, and procurement specialists at the Department of Defense.[21]

Other Types of Employment

Trailing private law firms, in-house legal departments, and the government are legal aid offices, which comprise the fourth-largest employer of paralegals. Legal aid offices provide legal services to those unable to afford private law firms and may receive funding from the government and private charities. Paralegals work in specialty areas such as consumer law, Social Security law, immigration law, landlord/tenant law, and family law.

Paralegals are also employed by various special-interest organizations such as lobbying groups, unions, consumer protection groups, environmental protection groups, and business associations.

Free-lance paralegals offer legal services to attorneys and work under the supervision of attorneys. Free-lancers essentially own their own paralegal businesses, selling legal services to attorneys and law firms. Most free-lancers are experienced paralegals with expertise in a legal specialty area such as probate or corporate law. Many free-lancers offer computerized litigation support services.

Paralegal service companies provide legal services to law firms. When a law firm needs temporary help, it contacts the paralegal service company, which provides the paralegals to do the work.

Many other types of employment are available to the individual with a paralegal background. Law office administration is a career path available to paralegals, since paralegals understand from first-hand experience how law offices are organized and managed. Teaching is another career option, although most teaching positions in paralegal programs are part-time. Writing is another possible career, since paralegals develop their research and writing skills. Technical writing, business writing, and article writing are examples of areas in which paralegals may work. Paralegal training could lead to employment as a law librarian. Finally, private investigation is a field in which paralegal work might provide some background.

PARALEGAL PROFILE

NAME
Mary Denty
TITLE
Probate Paralegal
Schmidt & Deaver
Milwaukee, Wisconsin

I began working as a legal secretary in 1955. As I learned more and more, I just naturally anticipated things that needed to be done on a case and started assuming more and more responsibilities. Eventually, I was basically handling the case. I guess you could say I just evolved into a paralegal—it was a natural progression from legal secretary to paralegal.

Over the years, I would take classes once in a while in areas such as probate procedures and federal estate tax. But there were no special classes that I took to become a paralegal—paralegals in my age group didn't have the educational opportunities that are available today.

I handle the probate from its inception. I meet with the client and interview the client. The attorney will usually meet with the client once, at the initial conference. Unless there is some peculiar problem that comes up, the attorney does not usually get involved from that point on. I prepare the papers and file them, and I inventory the estate assets and manage the assets, such as the bank accounts. I draft petitions and other documents. Basically, I handle all the work of the probate.

In probate work there is a lot of bookkeeping and record-keeping. I've always liked numbers and math and accounting, and I'm very detail-oriented, so probate is a natural field for me to be in. I also like the personal contact, the meeting with clients. There is a transition that occurs in a family during a probate, and you have to deal with the grief and the problems the family is going through.

PARALEGAL SPECIALTY AREAS

In addition to working in many different types of employment settings, paralegals also specialize in many different areas of the law. This section introduces you to some major paralegal specialty areas; you will learn more about these specialty areas throughout this book.

Because of the increasing complexity of the law, many lawyers have been forced to specialize in specific legal areas. There is simply too much law for any one individual to be familiar with it all. As lawyers become more specialized, the paralegals they employ also become more specialized. This trend toward greater specialization within the law will continue in the future.

Litigation

Litigation is the specialty area in which more than half of all paralegals work. Litigation paralegals are involved in all phases of a lawsuit. Because litigation occurs in many different areas of the law, litigation paralegals frequently specialize in a particular type of litigation, such as real estate litigation, personal injury litigation, or business litigation. Earlier in this chapter, we looked at the functions typically performed by litigation paralegals and the types of documents they draft. Chapter 9 examines the paralegal's role in the litigation process and contains samples of litigation documents frequently drafted by paralegals.

Business Transactional

A lawyer who specializes in activities other than litigation has what is called a **transactional practice**. Such a practice most often involves providing legal services in connection with individual transactions, such as the formation and dissolution of corporations and partnerships and corporate mergers and acquisitions. A paralegal who assists a lawyer in a business transactional practice might draft general partnership, joint venture, and limited partnership agreements; corporate charters, bylaws, minutes, shareholder agreements, and other documents related to the affairs of a corporation; and applications, statements, certificates, reports, and other documents related to the formation of business organizations. The paralegal might also arrange for the filing or recordation of documents that become public records. Chapter 5 examines business law concepts and how paralegals use them.

Real Estate Transactional

Real estate transactional paralegals draft leases, sales contracts, sales escrow instructions, deeds, promissory notes, mortgages, deeds of trust, installment sale contracts, and other documents evidencing rights with respect to real property. They supervise recordation of deeds, mortgages, deeds of trust, and various other documents. Real estate transactional paralegals prepare and analyze title reports, and investigate a party's rights with respect to the occupancy and use of a particular parcel of real property. Real property law concepts are discussed in Chapter 5.

Family Law

Family law paralegals are involved with divorce, child custody, child support, alimony, marital property settlement, and adoption. Family law paralegals draft property division and prenuptial agreements, as well as petitions, discovery requests, motions, and briefs in litigation involving marital dissolution and child custody matters. Family law concepts are discussed in Chapter 5.

Estate Planning and Probate

Estate planning and probate paralegals draft wills, trusts, and other estate planning documents and help determine how the assets of an estate are distributed. They supervise the administration of an estate, including the collection and maintenance of assets, the development of an inventory of assets, the filing of petitions with the probate court, and the preparation of accountings. Estate planning and probate paralegals also draft complaints, discovery requests, motions, and briefs in litigation involving will contests. Estate planning and probate concepts are discussed in Chapter 5.

Criminal Law

Criminal law paralegals must be familiar with the different types of crimes (infractions, misdemeanors, and felonies) as well as with procedural rules relating to search and seizure, arrest, bail, and probation. Criminal law paralegals draft complaints, discovery requests, motions, and briefs in criminal proceedings. Criminal law concepts are discussed in Chapter 4.

Administrative Law

Unique opportunities are available to paralegals specializing in administrative law because many administrative agencies permit paralegals or other nonlawyers to represent clients before them. This includes the right to represent clients at administrative hearings. Examples of federal administrative agencies that allow nonlawyer representation include the Internal Revenue Service, the Social Security Administration, and the United States Patent Office. Most states have a similar system authorizing nonlawyer representation. For example, some states allow nonlawyer representation at hearings before the Workers' Compensation Appeals Board. Administrative law is discussed in Chapter 3.

POINTER: This section has highlighted some of the larger and more traditional areas of law in which paralegals specialize. The many other specialty areas in which paralegals work include bankruptcy, immigration, labor, intellectual property (patents, copyrights, and trademarks), and environmental law. When trying to determine which specialty area is right for you, be sure to consider any special background or interests you have. For example, a nurse who is making a career change into the paralegal field might enjoy working in personal injury litigation, workers' compensation, or Social Security disability.

PARALEGAL SALARIES

How much do paralegals earn? The answer to this question depends on such factors as years of experience, education, type of employer, specialty area, and the geographic location in which the paralegal works.

Figures 1-4 through 1-7 are adapted from the 1991 *Legal Assistant Today* salary survey cited in note 18. Figure 1-4 shows the average salaries earned by paralegals (national averages) based on education, years of experience, type of employer, number of attorneys, and specialty area. Figure 1-5 is a profile of the "average

FIGURE 1-4 PARALEGAL SALARIES (NATIONAL AVERAGES)

	Average Salaries				
	Average	High	Low	%	# of Resp.
By Education:					
High School	26,307	44,000	6,000	7.0	41
AA Degree/College Credits	26,721	48,600	10,000	38.2	223
Bachelor's Degree	28,644	60,000	8,000	54.3	319
CLA	28,211	50,000	10,000	18.7	110
Certificate	27,294	50,000	10,000	24.2	142
By Years of Experience:					
0–2 Years	21,840	37,200	10,660	13.5	78
3–5 Years	24,499	44,000	10,000	22.7	134
6–10 Years	28,499	49,200	6,000	35.3	207
Over 10 Years	32,107	60,000	12,480	28.8	168
By Type of Employer:					
Private Firm	26,803	50,000	6,000	75.0	440
Corporation	31,273	50,000	14,400	19.1	112
Public Sector	25,495	44,752	10,660	4.9	29
By Number of Attorneys:					
0 Attorneys	31,684	60,000	16,000	2.6	16
1–5 Attorneys	25,466	50,000	6,000	37.8	222
6–19 Attorneys	27,832	48,600	13,500	29.1	171
20–50 Attorneys	28,573	45,600	13,000	17.9	105
Over 50 Attorneys	32,334	50,000	17,000	12.4	73
By Specialty (may be more than one answer):					
Litigation	27,929	49,200	6,000	36.3	213
Personal Injury	25,306	44,000	6,000	20.6	121
Corporate Law	31,001	50,000	13,000	16.0	95
Real Estate	27,386	48,000	8,000	15.3	90
Defense Litigation	27,429	44,000	13,520	9.2	54
Estate & Probate	25,200	45,000	10,000	9.0	52
Bankruptcy	25,587	50,000	10,000	8.7	54
Insurance	28,515	45,600	12,480	8.7	51
Workers' Compensation	24,897	44,000	10,800	7.7	45
Family Law	22,013	38,400	10,000	6.8	40
Consumer Law	31,165	47,000	13,760	6.5	37
Employment & Labor	30,902	47,500	19,500	4.6	28
Environmental	29,059	39,000	15,600	3.1	19

Source: *Legal Assistant Today* 1991 salary survey.

FIGURE 1-5 PROFILE OF THE AVERAGE PARALEGAL

Profile of Average Paralegal

% living in a metropolitan area with 100,000+ population:	52.1%
Average years of work experience:	7.78
Average gross salary, excluding bonuses:	$27,772
% not paid for overtime:	48.6%
% with company-sponsored retirement plan:	65.0%
% of employers contributing to retirement plan:	61.5%
% with health insurance:	84.3%
% with life insurance:	73.9%
% with disability insurance benefits:	62.7%
% with maternity benefits:	56.9%

Source: *Legal Assistant Today* 1991 salary survey.

paralegal.'' The information contained in this figure, such as the percentage of paralegals who are not paid for overtime, reflects the national average. Figure 1-6 is a regional breakdown of paralegal salaries, and Figure 1-7 lists the average annual salary for each of thirteen specialty areas.

PARALEGAL ASSOCIATIONS

During the 1970s, as the number of paralegals increased, paralegal associations were formed to promote and protect professional interests.

POINTER: Many paralegal associations encourage student membership. Joining an association is a good way to learn about the profession, keep abreast of recent developments in the field, and meet practicing paralegals. Networking with other paralegals may also provide employment opportunities.

The National Federation of Paralegal Associations (NFPA) and the National Association of Legal Assistants (NALA) are the two largest national paralegal associations. NFPA is comprised of over forty state and local paralegal associations representing over 16,000 paralegals throughout the United States. NFPA is currently examining the issue of limited licensure for paralegals through its Committee on the Delivery of Paralegal Services. NFPA participates on the ABA's Approval Commission, and its Education Task Force works with other paralegal organizations to bring about quality paralegal education throughout the country. NFPA also provides a legislative monitoring service. Through its Legislative Committee, NFPA files written testimony with state and federal legislatures on legislation affecting the paralegal profession. Finally, NFPA publishes a journal entitled the *National Paralegal Reporter* and a quarterly newsletter called the *Alert*.

FIGURE 1-6 PARALEGAL SALARIES BY REGION

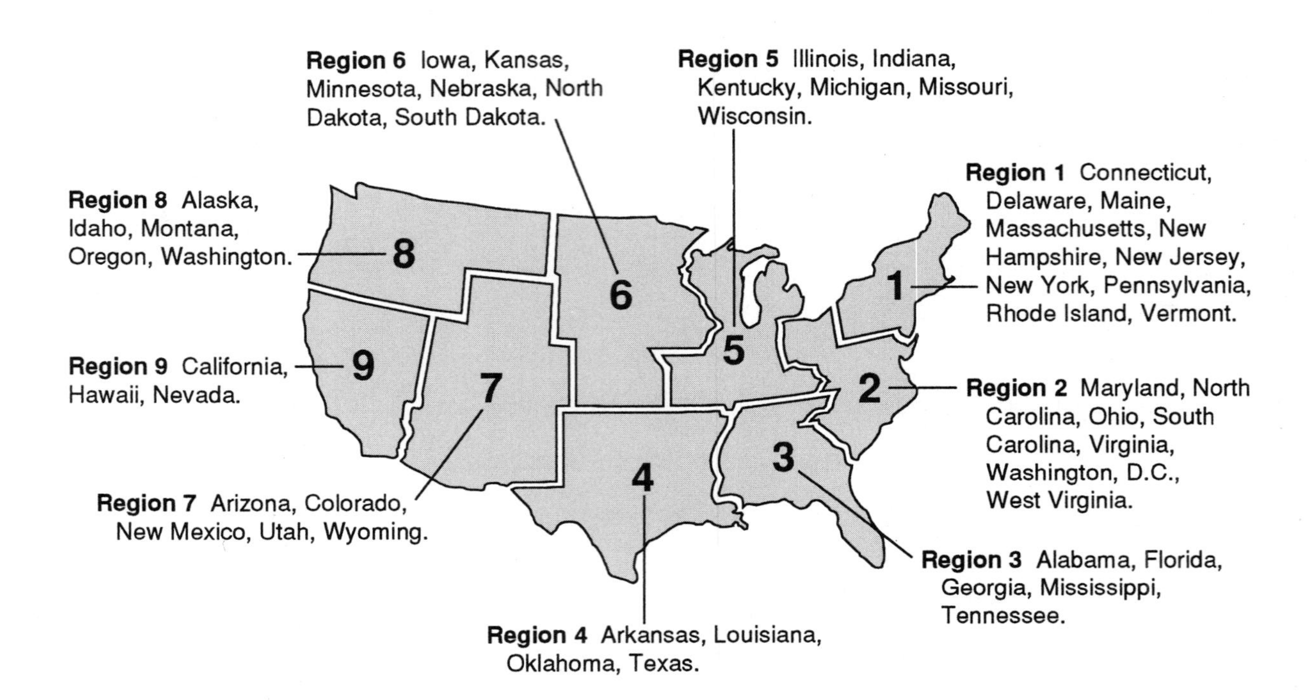

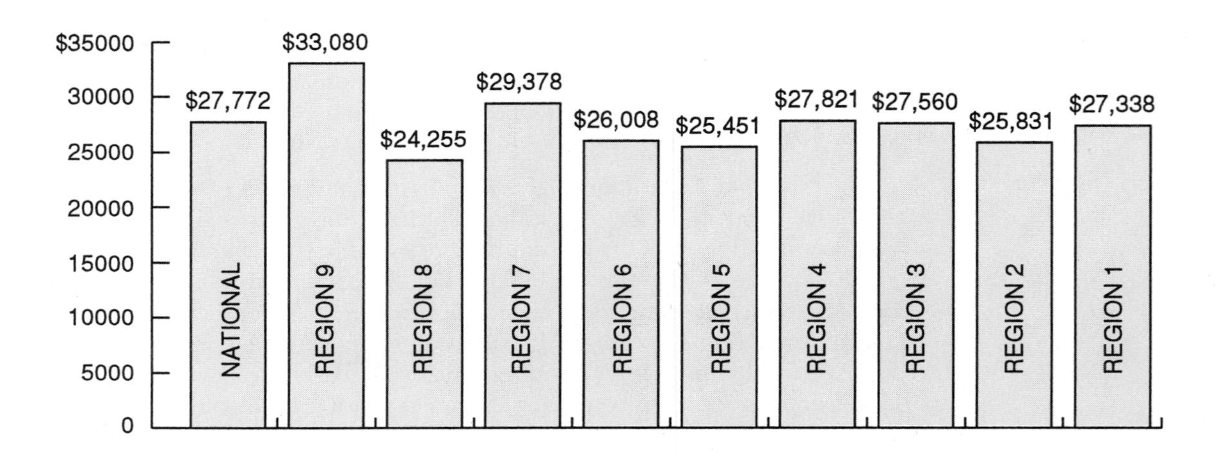

Source: *Legal Assistant Today* 1991 salary survey.

FIGURE 1-7 PARALEGAL SALARIES BY SPECIALTY AREA

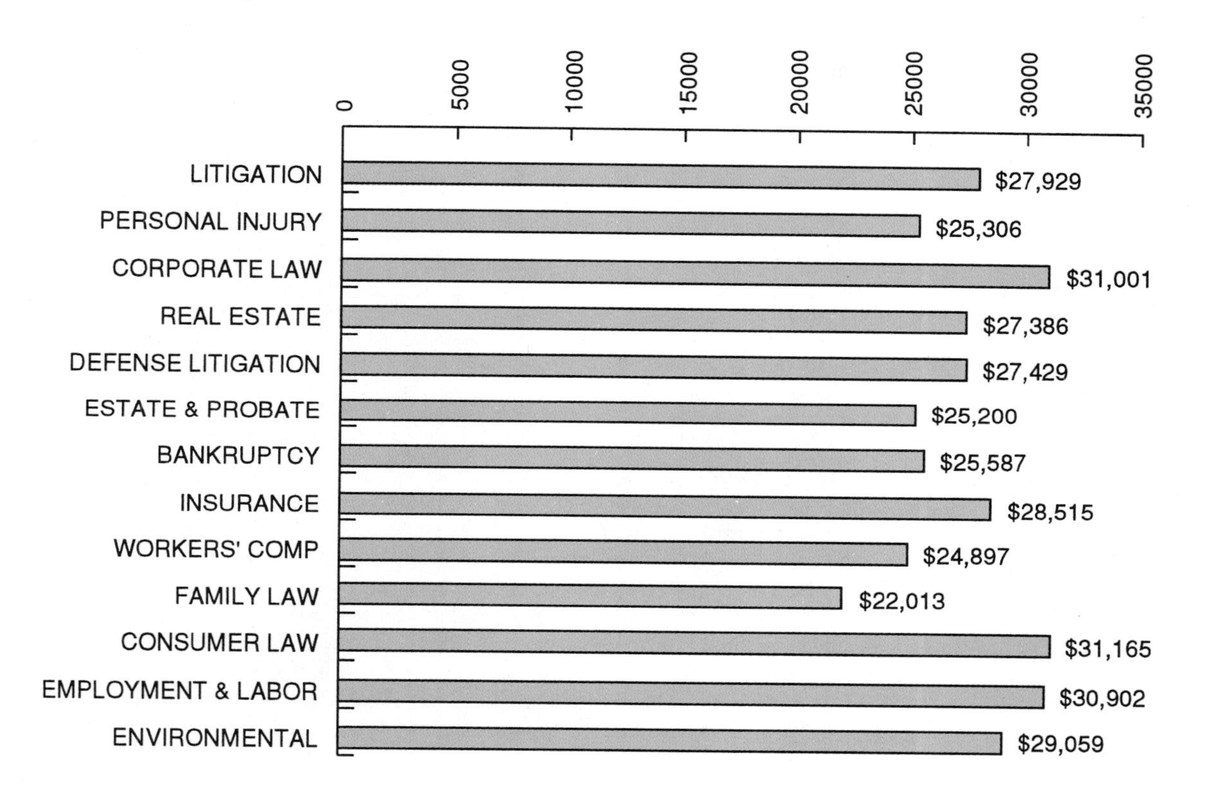

Source: *Legal Assistant Today* 1991 salary survey.

The National Association of Legal Assistants (NALA) represents over 9,000 paralegals nationwide. Its primary programs, which focus on the professional development and continuing education of paralegals, include the Certified Legal Assistant program, continuing education seminars and workshops, and three publications: a bimonthly magazine, *Facts and Findings*; an annual summary of developments within the profession, *Career Choice*; and a biannual report, *National Utilization and Compensation Survey Report*.

Other national associations include the Legal Assistant Management Association (LAMA), the Association of Legal Administrators (ALA), the National Paralegal Association (NPA), and the American Association for Paralegal Education (AAfPE). AAfPE hosts an annual national conference for paralegal educators and also publishes the *Journal of Paralegal Education*.

Augmenting the national associations are many state and local paralegal associations. Local associations often publish a newsletter, sponsor continuing education seminars, and do pro bono work (provide legal services free of charge).

Paralegals may also become associate members in the American Bar Association and in some state and local bar associations. The ABA publishes *Legal Assistants Update* and other publications for paralegals.

PARALEGAL PROFILE

NAME
Paul I. Everett
TITLE
Free-Lance Paralegal
President, Legal Management, Inc.
Providence, Rhode Island

I am President of Legal Management, Inc., which is a corporation specializing in consulting services to the legal field. Right now, my corporation consists of only myself—I am the president, chief financial officer, secretary, and worker in the field.

I contract my services to clients for a straight hourly wage. I can work for two or three clients at a time instead of working for just one law firm. I call myself a free-lance paralegal because I work only for corporations or law firms, whereas an independent paralegal does work directly for the public.

Currently, my main client is Triffin Motor Corporation. I'm working in its legal department as a corporate specialist. I'm writing corporate minutes, issuing stocks, and handling licensing matters throughout the United States. I also work on trademark licensing. I'm the only transactional paralegal—I support the transactional attorneys who are involved in sophisticated contract negotiations. I provide the attorneys with whatever they need, especially with reviewing contracts. I choose my own hours—Triffin gives me the work, and I get the work done in my own time frame. Because I'm a contractor, Triffin cannot tell me when to come in or how long to stay. But the job is pretty much full-time—I usually spend six or seven hours a day at Triffin.

At night, I work for some of my smaller clients. I am also working on a book, and I work on updates for the two books that I have already published. It seems like I'm always working. I also teach paralegal courses at night, although I'm not teaching this semester.

I like paralegal work because I don't sit and do one thing all day. I've got sixteen years of experience, so I can pretty much choose the types of assignments that I take. My assignments are usually very interesting and challenging. I started out as a litigation specialist, but now I find myself doing mostly corporate work. You can never maximize your education in the paralegal field—there's always another field or another area of law that you can go into.

I've found that as a self-employed free-lance paralegal, I'm much tougher on myself than any boss I could work for. I demand more of myself and work a lot harder than would be required if I were employed by a law firm.

I really enjoy being a free-lance paralegal because there is a lot of variety and a lot of opportunity. One thing I don't like is that I have to pay for my own health insurance. I'm also worrying about retirement, and I'm just now starting to set up a retirement plan. Another negative aspect of free-lancing is not knowing if you'll be working when your contract ends. But I've been free-lancing for twelve years and I've always had plenty of work.

My advice to paralegal students is don't be satisfied with anything less than exactly what you want. If you are employed by a law firm that doesn't meet your personal needs for growth, then leave. Pursue your dream.

ENDNOTES

1 U.S. Department of Labor, *Occupational Outlook Handbook* (1990–91 Edition), p. 11.

2 ABA Standing Committee on Legal Assistants, Position Paper on the Question of Legal Assistant Licensure or Certification (December 10, 1985). Approved February 1986.

3 National Association of Legal Assistants, *Model Standards and Guidelines for Utilization of Legal Assistants Annotated* (1984).

4 National Federation of Paralegal Associations, *What Is a Paralegal?* (1987).

5 U.S. Department of Labor Bureau of Labor Statistics, *Occupational Outlook Quarterly* (Spring 1990).

6 Ibid.

7 Ibid. However, this projection seems very low. In the January 1991 *Employment and Earnings*, the Bureau of Labor Statistics reported 229,000 people employed in the category "Technical, sales, and administrative support"; subcategory "Technicians, except health, engineering, and science"; sub-subcategory "legal assistants."

8 ABA Special Committee on Availability of Legal Services, Report Number 3 (1968).

9 U.S. Department of Commerce, *1991 U.S. Industrial Outlook*, pp. 52–54.

10 ABA, Special Committee on Legal Assistants, *The Training and Use of Legal Assistants: A Status Report*, Appendix C, D, E, and F (Preliminary Draft, 1973); William P. Statsky, *Introduction to Paralegalism*, 3d ed. (St. Paul: West, 1986), pp. 173–174.

11 Barbara Bernardo, *Paralegal* (Princeton: Peterson's Guides, 1990), p. 88.

12 1990 LAMA Education Survey, Question 2.

13 1984 ABA survey.

14 National Association of Legal Assistants, *Model Standards and Guidelines for Utilization of Legal Assistants Annotated*.

15 Ibid.

16 1990 LAMA Education Survey, Question 11.

17 National Association of Legal Assistants, *Model Standards and Guidelines for Utilization of Legal Assistants Annotated*.

18 Figure obtained from a 1991 salary survey conducted by *Legal Assistant Today*, Vol. 8, No. 5 (May/June 1991).

19 Of the 587 respondents to the survey cited in note 18, 19.1 percent were employed by corporations.

20 According to the 1991 *Legal Assistant Today* salary survey, the average annual salary of paralegals specializing in corporate law was $31,001, while the average annual salary of litigation paralegals was $27,929.

21 Christine L. Perko, ''Paralegals in the Federal Government,'' *Legal Assistants Update* 4 (1984), pp. 75, 77.

2 HOW LAW OFFICES ARE ORGANIZED AND MANAGED

Most paralegals work in law offices of one kind or another. As a paralegal who works in a law office, you are part of a professional team that provides legal services to one or more clients. To serve these clients well, you must understand how your law office is organized. You need a clear understanding of the role played by each member of the professional team. You need a good working knowledge of the day-to-day procedures that your office has adopted.

In this chapter, you will learn about several different kinds of law offices. You will learn how each type of office is structured and how office decisions are made. You will examine the role played by each person who is part of the professional team in the office. You will learn about the ways a law office manages money. Finally, you will be introduced to the types of operating procedures that most law offices use.

INTRODUCTION: THE WELL-MANAGED LAW OFFICE

From the start, it is important that you understand why a law office must be well organized and well managed: A well-organized, well-managed office provides legal services both effectively and efficiently.

The Effective Law Office

A law office provides services effectively when it provides the services that its clients need, when they need them. This seems simple enough. However, determining what services a client needs and then providing those services exactly when they are needed is no simple matter.

Identifying the Services a Client Needs. Frequently a client knows that legal services are needed to resolve a problem but does not know precisely what those services are. Before a lawyer performs legal services for a client, the lawyer must determine what the client hopes to accomplish by means of the legal services. Once the client's goals have been identified, the lawyer attempts to identify one or more possible courses of action that may be taken in an effort to accomplish the goals. The lawyer discusses the possible courses of action with the client. Often the client will ask the lawyer to recommend a course of action, based on the lawyer's experience with similar problems. However, even if the lawyer makes a recommendation, it is the client who makes the final decision on which course of action the lawyer will undertake on the client's behalf. Consider the following example.

> A client discovers that someone has been cutting and removing trees from land that he owns. The client realizes that legal services are needed and contacts a lawyer. They meet at the lawyer's office, where the lawyer interviews the client. Once the client has related the facts of the case, the lawyer must determine what the client wishes to accomplish by retaining her services and what possible courses of action are available. Among the possibilities are the following:
>
> 1. Suppose the client states that he is unconcerned about the value of the stolen timber, but simply wants the cutting and removal to stop. If this is the case, the lawyer may advise the client that a court order may be obtained prohibiting any further unauthorized activity on the land.
> 2. Suppose the client states that all of the trees on the land have already been removed and that he wants to recover the value of the stolen timber from the person who stole it. If this is so, the lawyer may advise the client that a lawsuit may be filed against the thief seeking compensation for the stolen timber.
> 3. Suppose the client wants to stop the unauthorized activity *and* recover the value of the stolen timber. In this case, the lawyer may advise the client that a court order may be obtained and that a lawsuit seeking compensation may be filed.
> 4. Suppose the client wants to see the thief put in jail. In that case, the lawyer may advise the client to press criminal charges and may refer the client to the local prosecuting attorney's office. The lawyer may then cooperate with that office in its investigation of the matter.

Paralegals often play an important role in assisting lawyers in determining what legal services a client needs. If a lawyer is unavailable to meet with a new client, a paralegal may handle the interview. In such a case, it will be up to the paralegal to determine, through the proper use of interviewing techniques, what the client hopes to accomplish by retaining the lawyer's services. The lawyer may also ask the paralegal to assist the lawyer in identifying possible courses of action designed to achieve the client's goals. The paralegal may do this by analyzing the facts of the case, conducting appropriate legal research, and then identifying possible courses of action for consideration by the lawyer and the client.

Providing Services that Meet Professional Standards of Quality. Once the services needed by a client have been identified and the client has requested that they be performed, the entire professional team must cooperate to provide the requested services. This cooperation is necessary to produce services of the quality that people expect from professionals.

POINTER: A **professional** is someone whose work requires specialized knowledge. In most cases, a professional acquires the basics of this knowledge through participation in a formal academic program and then continues to expand this knowledge through actual work experience. (That is why a professional is said to "practice" a profession, because the longer one works in a profession, the more proficient one becomes.) State and local governments have licensing requirements for many professions. In order to practice a licensed profession, one must obtain a license by meeting prescribed educational, testing, and work experience requirements. Unlicensed persons are prohibited from practicing licensed professions. The licensing of lawyers and paralegals is discussed in detail in Chapter 11.

Lawyers, like all licensed professionals, are legally obligated to provide services that are comparable in quality to those provided by similar professionals in the same community. As a part of the professional team, you will be helping the lawyers in your office provide services of this quality.

POINTER: In addition to complying with quality standards, lawyers are required to comply with ethical standards that govern both their professional and their personal activities. Ethical standards are specified in codes of professional conduct. Each jurisdiction that licenses lawyers has adopted such a code. A lawyer who violates this code may be disciplined. Technically, paralegals are not bound by the codes of professional conduct that apply to lawyers, nor are they subject to discipline for violating such codes. Paralegals are, nonetheless, ethically bound to honor these codes, as you will see in Chapter 10.

Providing Services on Time. Quality legal services are of little value unless they are provided on time. Because of this, law office personnel work constantly under deadlines. In a litigation practice there are deadlines for filing lawsuits, making motions, responding to discovery requests, preparing for trials, and filing appeals. In a transactional practice there are deadlines for finalizing agreements, filing reports with governmental agencies, and closing business deals.

POINTER: Some lawyers specialize in conducting lawsuits, while other lawyers specialize in activities that do not normally involve conducting lawsuits. A **litigator** is a lawyer who specializes in litigation—that is, the conduct of lawsuits and similar proceedings. Such a lawyer's practice is referred to as a **litigation practice**. A lawyer who specializes in other activities is said to have a transactional practice. Such a lawyer most often provides legal services in connection with individual transactions, such as the purchase and sale of a business, the development of a parcel of real estate, or the implementation of a plan to provide for the disposition of a person's property after death.

A lawyer's failure to meet a deadline can have disastrous consequences for a client. For example, if a client's lawsuit is not filed before the filing deadline set by law, the client may lose the right to bring the lawsuit. If the paperwork necessary to document the sale of an office building is not completed on time, the buyer may lose the loan needed to finance the purchase. To a great extent, then, providing legal services effectively depends on an ability to meet deadlines.

Malpractice. **Malpractice** occurs when a lawyer fails to provide the services that a client needs, fails to provide services that meet professional standards of quality, or fails to provide services to a client on time. Lawyer malpractice almost always causes harm to the client.

A client who is harmed by a lawyer's malpractice may sue the lawyer. If the client wins the lawsuit, the lawyer (or the lawyer's insurance company) must pay the client to compensate for the harm done. Most law offices are in business to make money. A law office that fails to provide services effectively not only fails to make money, it actually loses money!

The Efficient Law Office

A law office must provide services efficiently as well as effectively. A law office is efficient when each member of its professional team does the work for which she or he is best qualified. Again, this may seem simple enough. However, ensuring that the work in a law office is done by the person who is best qualified to do it requires careful planning.

Efficient Use of Expertise. Each person in a law office has a limited amount of time to do the work that needs to be done. And each law office has a limited number of lawyers, paralegals, and staff members. It does not make sense for the lawyers to do work that the paralegals have been trained to do. Lawyers should devote their available time to doing work that requires the training that only they have. Similarly, a paralegal should not normally be assigned work that a legal secretary has been trained to handle. Conversely, a legal secretary should not be assigned to perform a task that requires paralegal training, nor should a paralegal undertake work that requires a lawyer's particular expertise. Allowing people to perform tasks they are not qualified to do can have disastrous results and give rise to malpractice claims.

Just as the people who work in a given law office have different levels of expertise, they may have different areas of expertise as well. For example, one paralegal may have a great deal of knowledge and experience in cases involving the eviction of tenants who fail to pay their rent. If a landlord comes into the office seeking assistance in evicting a tenant, the case should be assigned to the paralegal who has expertise in that area. If, instead, the case is assigned to a paralegal who is expert at preparing wills, that paralegal will need to spend significant time studying eviction procedures before working on the new case.

Efficient Use of Office Systems. Because there is so much work to be done in a law office and only a limited amount of time in which to do it, an office must set up systems designed to ensure that specific tasks are accomplished promptly and efficiently by the team members best qualified to accomplish them. Most systems consist of a series of specified procedures performed by specified people in a specified order, resulting in the accomplishment of a task. Consider the following example.

> A judge agrees to issue a court order requested by a lawyer and asks the lawyer to prepare and submit the proposed language for the order. The lawyer verbally instructs a paralegal to draft a proposed order for submission to the judge. After reviewing the case and conducting the necessary research, the paralegal dictates the proposed order into a tape recorder and gives the tape to his secretary, who transcribes it and presents the typed document to the paralegal. The paralegal reviews the document, makes written changes, and returns it to his secretary, who retypes it and gives it to the lawyer. The lawyer reviews the document, makes written changes, and gives it to her own secretary, who retypes it and returns it to the lawyer. The lawyer proofreads the document, signs it, and returns it to her secretary, who then gives the original document to a messenger to deliver to the judge, files one copy of the document, and gives one copy to the paralegal.

The system described in our example involved four people in the law office. Its ultimate result was the submission of a proposed order to the judge. In the process of achieving this result, the system (1) allowed the paralegal to review and correct the paralegal's secretary's transcription; (2) allowed the paralegal to revise the paralegal's own work before submitting it to the lawyer; (3) allowed the lawyer to review and revise the paralegal's work; (4) allowed the lawyer to review and correct the lawyer's secretary's retyping of the document before its submission to the judge; and (5) allowed the paralegal to review the document submitted to the judge and to note any revisions to the paralegal's work made by the lawyer.

This is just one example of a system that permits a law office to function efficiently. Other commonly used systems will be discussed later in the chapter.

POINTER: Because people are a law office's most important resource, people who manage law offices usually devote a great deal of attention to efficient use of personnel. This is accomplished in part by taking full advantage of individual expertise and by establishing office systems. However, other office assets must be carefully managed as well. These assets include office space, equipment, and supplies. These assets are usually managed by using the same techniques other businesses use to contain overhead expenses, such as soliciting multiple bids for equipment purchases and ordering supplies on the basis of a system of inventory control.

Efficiency and Saving Money for the Client. No one wants to pay more for a service than they absolutely must. This is especially true when it comes to legal services, which are generally quite expensive. When legal services are provided efficiently as well as effectively, the client gets the needed legal services at the lowest possible cost.

As we noted in Chapter 1, the efficient placement of paralegals on the law office team can be very cost-effective. Law offices that charge their clients for services often base the fees they charge on the number of hours lawyers and paralegals spend performing services for each client. Law offices charge more for lawyer time than for paralegal time. Accordingly, using paralegals instead of lawyers to perform services permits a law office to charge its clients less money. This, of course, is very appealing to potential clients.

Professional Management

As the legal field has become more competitive, the importance of good organization and management in the law office setting has become more widely recognized. Management professionals who are experts in this field have become more numerous and more prominent.

Legal Consulting Firms. Many law offices now work with a legal consulting firm that reviews and analyzes the office's organization and procedures on a regular basis. Because these firms are knowledgeable about how things are done at a great many law offices, they can make suggestions for improvements based on what has—or has not—worked elsewhere. These firms specialize in the design of office systems for billing, timekeeping, document creation and management, calendar management, and communications. These systems are discussed under Financial Management in Private Law Firms and Law Office Procedures later in this chapter.

Professional Office Administrators. Most larger law offices now have a full- or part-time employee who serves as a professional office administrator. The important role of these administrators—and how they can assist you in doing your job as a paralegal—will be discussed under The Professional Team in a Law Office later in this chapter.

TYPES OF LAW OFFICES

Every law office is a unique reflection of the needs, goals, and personalities both of the people who work there and of the people who receive legal services there. But while each law office is unique in its legal practice, its organizational structure, and its decision-making process, law offices have enough similarities to enable us to group them into categories. The following discussion divides law offices into categories based on the clients that each is designed to serve.

Private Law Firms

You will often hear someone say that a lawyer is in **private practice**. Law offices whose lawyers are in private practice, commonly known as **private law firms**, are designed to serve the general public. Individuals and businesses who need legal services, and are able to pay for such services, consult private law firms.

General Practice and Specialized Practice. As you learned in Chapter 1, the law constitutes a vast, complex, and diversified body of knowledge. It is impossible for any one person to be an expert in every field of the law. This fact influences how private law firms are organized.

A client who needs legal services looks for a private law firm with lawyers and paralegals who have the knowledge and experience required to meet the client's needs. A client's needs can be simple or complex.

General Practice Law Firms. A **general practice law firm** is designed to meet the needs of clients who have relatively simple, routine legal problems. A general practice firm employs lawyers and paralegals who have a strong, broad knowledge of several fields of law and are therefore able to provide the basic legal services that these clients need. A general practice law firm may handle any combination of matters, including basic business contracts, relatively simple real estate transactions, personal or small-business bankruptcies, basic estate planning and probate, divorces, criminal matters, basic business litigation, and basic tort litigation.

Specialized Practice Law Firms. A **specialized practice law firm** is designed to meet the needs of clients who have complex, specialized legal problems. A specialized practice firm employs lawyers and paralegals who have concentrated training in a limited number of related fields of law. Because these legal professionals work only on matters in those fields, they tend to have extensive experience that can be very valuable to clients. A specialized practice law firm may specialize in an area such as securities litigation, antitrust litigation, labor law, immigration law, Social Security disability law, or the defense of so-called white-collar criminals.

The benefits of specialization become obvious when one considers, for example, a lawyer who specializes in immigration law. The law in this highly complex area can change frequently. A lawyer who practices in this field exclusively has a much better opportunity to become familiar with the complexities of immigration law and to keep track of changes in the law than does a lawyer who practices immigration law only occasionally. Moreover, an immigration law practice demands constant contact with the Immigration and Naturalization Service (INS), the federal agency that determines whether or not a person from another country will be granted a permanent or temporary visa to stay and to work in the United States. Local offices of the INS may have different internal procedures for such matters as filing documents and scheduling hearings. A lawyer who deals with a local INS office regularly will know what procedures to follow in any given situation. A lawyer who rarely deals with the office may need to spend a substantial amount of time reviewing regulations and talking to INS personnel in order to obtain the same knowledge.

Choosing a General Practice or a Specialized Practice Firm. Whether a client chooses a general practice law firm or a specialized practice law firm depends on the kind of legal services the client is seeking. A person who is selling a house, for example, might go to a general practice law firm, since such a transaction is relatively common and there are many general practice lawyers who have a good deal of experience with such transactions. On the other hand, a corporation that intends to sell a multi-million dollar shopping center might seek out a law firm with legal professionals who specialize in such transactions. Because such transactions are relatively rare, relatively few lawyers and paralegals have extensive—and valuable—experience handling them. Similarly, an individual with relatively few assets might go to a general practice law firm to have a simple will drawn. A very wealthy person, on the other hand, might seek out a firm with an estate planning specialist who has experience in structuring large estates in a manner that minimizes estate tax liability.

A client's choice of firm may also be based on considerations of cost. General practice law firms normally charge lower fees for legal services than specialized practice law firms do. Clients expect to pay more for the experience and specialized knowledge that a specialized practice law firm can offer.

Relationship Between Firm Size and Degree of Specialization. To some degree, a private firm's size is related to the nature of its practice.

General practice law firms tend to be relatively small in size. Because each lawyer and paralegal in the firm has the broad knowledge necessary to provide basic legal services, there is no need to hire a large number of individuals who specialize in different areas of law. The size of a general practice law firm depends to a large extent on the number of clients that the firm is able to attract.

Specialized practice law firms may be either large or small. One firm that specializes in immigration law may be able to serve the needs of most potential clients with a single lawyer, while another firm specializing in immigration law may deliver services at a more sophisticated level because each of its several lawyers is able to specialize in one area of immigration law. For example, one lawyer in the larger firm might specialize in obtaining visas for people who wish to establish a business in the United States, while another lawyer might specialize in obtaining visas for people who are seeking political asylum in the United States. Like a general practice law firm, a specialized practice law firm can be as large as needed to serve the clients it is able to attract.

The larger a private law firm is, of course, the more likely it is that the firm can afford to include professionals who specialize in different areas of law. Very large private law firms are frequently divided into departments according to legal specialty. A client may use one or several of a large law firm's departments. For example, a relatively small business client may use a small general practice law firm for routine legal matters such as reviewing contracts with suppliers or collecting delinquent accounts; but for help in designing a pension plan, it may rely on the employee benefits department of a large private law firm. A large corporation with many complex legal matters may make regular use of the large private law firm's many departments: business litigation, corporate, labor law, employee benefits law, and tax planning, to name a few.

Structure. Private law firms can be structured in any number of ways. Most firms are comprised of either (a) a sole practitioner, (b) an association of sole practitioners, (c) a group of lawyers who are partners, or (d) a group of lawyers who are shareholders in a corporation.

Sole Practitioner. A **sole practitioner** is a lawyer who practices law in a law office in which he or she is the only lawyer. Depending on the field of law in which the lawyer practices, a sole practitioner may have a few employees or many employees. A sole practitioner with a busy practice may rely heavily on paralegals for assistance.

Association of Sole Practitioners. Sometimes two or more sole practitioners will combine together to share overhead expenses. Such expenses may include rent for office space, the costs of computer equipment, law library expenses, and salaries for shared employees, like receptionists or word processing technicians. Although each sole practitioner has her or his own clients and cases, the lawyers may refer potential clients to one another or may cover court appearances for one another when scheduling conflicts occur. An association of sole practitioners may be as tightly or loosely structured as the lawyers' needs require.

Partnership. A private law firm may be comprised of a group of lawyers who form a partnership. These lawyers decide, as a group, which clients the partnership should serve and which cases it should accept. The lawyers then work together to serve the clients and handle the cases. The lawyers divide the profits and expenses of their partnership practice according to an agreed formula.

Corporation. A private law firm may also be comprised of a group of lawyers who form a corporation in which the lawyers are shareholders. The corporation owns all of the law firm's assets, receives all of the firm's income, and pays all of the firm's expenses. The corporation pays a salary to each shareholder, and excess profits may be paid out to shareholders in the form of dividends.

Hybrid Structures. These four basic structures can be combined in a variety of ways. For example, a single lawyer might form a corporation of which the lawyer is the sole shareholder. That corporation, in turn, might become a partner in a partnership that includes other corporations owned by one or more lawyers. Many similar combinations are possible. The combination chosen will depend on the needs and goals of the lawyers involved.

Decision Making. As you have already seen, the practice of law involves the making of many decisions on a daily basis. For example, decisions may need to be made about what course of action to recommend to a client, what steps to take to obtain a court order, or what arrangements to make to conclude the settlement of a lawsuit. These decisions that involve the practice of law are made by the lawyers responsible for handling the particular cases or transactions involved. But because a private law firm is a business, many decisions must also be made relating to how the firm is conducted as a business.

Decision Making by the Owners. Business decisions for a law firm are generally made by the lawyers who own the firm. In a private law firm structured as a partnership, for example, the partners make decisions, usually by majority vote. In a private law firm that has many owners, some decisions may be made by specially selected executive or management committees. Other decisions may be delegated to a single individual, such as the managing partner of a partnership or the chief executive officer of a corporation.

Decision Making by Committee. Some private law firms set up special committees that include not only the lawyers who own the firm, but also other lawyers, paralegals, and staff members. These committees are usually charged with making decisions or making recommendations relating to some specific area. Such committees make decisions on topics ranging from hiring new personnel to buying computer equipment to planning social events. This kind of shared decision making is becoming increasingly common and offers an opportunity for you as a paralegal to have a voice in how things are done at the law firm where you work.

The In-House Legal Department

Some businesses generate such a large amount of legal work that it is less expensive for them to hire lawyers and paralegals as employees than it is to obtain legal services from private law firms. The lawyers, paralegals, and support staff who are hired by a business to meet its legal services needs are usually organized as a separate department within the business. Such an **in-house legal department** is, in effect, a law office with a single client—the business. Many banks, insurance companies, investment companies, large manufacturing companies, and large retailing companies have in-house legal departments.

In-House Counsel and Outside Counsel. Many large businesses are served by both an in-house legal department and private law firms.

In-House Counsel. An in-house legal department usually handles routine, day-to-day legal work for the business client it serves. The lawyers and paralegals who work in the department are often specialists in one area of law. In a company that manages large shopping centers, for example, the in-house legal professionals will be specialists in shopping-center leases. In a company that sells fast-food restaurant franchises, the professionals will be experts in negotiating and drafting franchise agreements. A general manufacturing company will have professionals with a general business law background who can handle both transactional and litigation matters involving suppliers, labor unions, and customers.

Outside Counsel. Few businesses can afford to maintain an in-house legal department that is large enough or specialized enough to meet all of the business's legal needs. When needed services exceed the capacity of the in-house department, the business usually retains a private law firm as **outside counsel**. For example, when a company's in-house department has only general business expertise, it may hire a private law firm to handle occasional work in the highly specialized field of patents and trademarks. Similarly, when a business's in-house department consists of two transactional lawyers, it may hire outside counsel to represent the business in a complex products liability lawsuit.

Role of In-House Counsel as Liaison. An in-house legal department frequently acts as liaison between a business and its outside counsel. In-house lawyers may make recommendations to the business's management concerning the hiring of outside counsel. They may review the activities of outside counsel, coordinate the production of witnesses or documents needed by outside counsel, and review the bills received from outside counsel.

Structure. The in-house legal departments of most businesses are managed by a senior lawyer who is usually designated as the business's **general counsel**. If the business is organized as a corporation, the general counsel may hold an office in the corporation, such as vice-president for legal affairs.

The lawyers who work under the supervision of the general counsel are often identified as associate general counsel or assistant general counsel.

Decision Making. Major decisions regarding the operations of an in-house legal department are made by the same individuals who make decisions for the business as a whole. These individuals may be the owners of the business or, if the business is organized as a corporation, the business's officers or board of directors. Internal management decisions are usually made by the general counsel in consultation with other department personnel.

The Government Law Office

Some law offices have federal, state or local governments as their only clients. The best-known **government law offices** are those that participate in the criminal justice process. These offices are comprised of prosecutors or public defenders. Other government law offices, however, serve as in-house legal departments for a wide variety of governmental entities. These offices are comprised of legal professionals who work full-time for such government agencies as the Internal Revenue Service and the federal Food and Drug Administration.

Criminal Justice Law Offices. Two kinds of government law offices participate in the criminal justice system—offices comprised of prosecutors and offices comprised of public defenders.

Prosecutors. **Prosecutors** are lawyers who are employed by the government to represent the interests of the general public in criminal proceedings. (As you will learn in Chapter 4, a crime is viewed by the law as an offense against everyone, not just against the victim of the crime.) It is a prosecutor's job to investigate reported crimes, to file criminal charges against suspected perpetrators, and to obtain convictions at trial.

Public Defenders. Individuals who are charged with crimes but who cannot afford to hire a private law firm to represent them may qualify for representation by a public defenders' office. **Public defenders** are lawyers who are employed by the government, but whose clients are indigent criminal defendants. In areas where there are insufficient public defenders to represent all defendants who qualify for representation, courts may appoint lawyers in private practice to represent such defendants at government expense.

POINTER: The Sixth Amendment of the United States Constitution provides that "In criminal prosecutions, the accused shall enjoy the right . . . to have the Assistance of Counsel for his defence." The courts have interpreted this provision as requiring the government to provide professional representation for those criminal defendants who are unable to afford it.

Structure. Most prosecutors' and public defenders' offices are managed by a lawyer who is either elected by the general public or appointed by a public body or government official. The lawyer who heads a prosecutors' office in a local government jurisdiction is frequently known as the **prosecuting attorney** or the **district attorney**. The lawyer who heads a public defenders' office in a local government jurisdiction is usually known simply as the public defender. A public defenders' office for a county, for example, may be managed by a lawyer known as the county public defender, who is elected to that position by the county's voters or is appointed to that position by the county's governing board or by the chief judge in the county. The lawyer who heads a prosecutors' or public defenders' office may also handle some cases.

In addition to the prosecuting attorney or public defender, most criminal justice law offices employ other lawyers. Usually referred to as deputy or assistant prosecuting attorneys, district attorneys, or public defenders, these lawyers handle the vast majority of the cases in large criminal justice law offices.

Decision Making. Decisions regarding the internal management of prosecutors' and public defenders' law offices are generally made by the lawyer who heads the office in consultation with other lawyers in the office.

A prosecutors' law office is somewhat unusual in that it does not have a client who makes decisions authorizing the office to proceed with a particular course of action on the client's behalf. In a sense, the prosecutors themselves make the client decisions. They have authority to decide whether or not to file charges, to negotiate a plea bargain, or to take a case to trial. As a result, the decisions made by prosecutors are often subject to widespread scrutiny. The fact that the chief prosecutor is often a publicly elected official increases this degree of scrutiny. As a result, prosecutorial decisions may have extensive political repercussions and are carefully monitored by the media.

POINTER: As you will see in Chapter 10, lawyers are ethically obligated to take such action as may be necessary to ensure that the best interests of their clients are served. For prosecutors, this ethical obligation has a slightly different focus. Prosecutors are ethically obligated to take such action as may be necessary to ensure that the interests of justice are served.

Counsel for Governmental Entities. Governmental entities that make or enforce the laws have an obvious need for expert legal advice. Most legislative bodies and major government agencies have legal departments to advise them. These government law offices are similar in purpose to in-house legal departments, and can be found on all levels of government.

Cities. A city may have a **city attorney** who acts as a legal advisor to the city council and city officials. In a large city the city attorney's office may require a substantial staff of lawyers and paralegals. With the assistance of this staff, the city attorney provides advice to city agencies on matters ranging from zoning to tax collection and represents the city in litigation. In some cities, the city attorney serves as the prosecutor for violations of city ordinances.

Counties. The legal department of a county government functions much like a city attorney's office, but at the county level. Such a department is sometimes referred to as the office of the **county counsel** in order to distinguish it from the prosecutors' office or the public defenders' office for the county.

States. A state **attorney general's** office provides advice to the legislature, files suits involving violations of the state's regulatory laws, and represents the public interest in criminal appeals proceedings. An attorney general's office often has a large staff of lawyers and paralegals. Members of this staff are usually available to assist the general public in matters of statewide concern, such as consumer fraud.

Although in some states the attorney general's office provides advice to state agencies, many state agencies have their own legal departments. State agency legal departments are usually extremely specialized. For example, the state agency that oversees corporations usually has a legal staff qualified to provide the last word on complex questions regarding the state's corporations laws. Other agencies have legal staffs with equivalent levels of expertise.

Federal Government. The U.S. Department of Justice, headed by the Attorney General of the United States, serves as a legal department for the federal government as a whole. Most federal government agencies also have their own legal departments, usually consisting of a large staff of legal professionals at the agency's Washington, D.C. headquarters and smaller staffs at regional and local agency offices. Lawyers on staff at an agency's headquarters and its regional offices are usually involved in decisions concerning policy and operating procedures affecting the agency as a whole. Lawyers in an agency's local office advise staff members and administrative law judges on matters that are being processed in the local office.

Lawyers who work for federal agencies are involved in an extremely diverse range of activities. Some lawyers spend most of their time representing the government in court or at administrative hearings. For example, a staff attorney for the Equal Employment Opportunity Commission may represent the government in employment discrimination litigation, while a staff attorney for the Immigration and Naturalization Service may represent the government in deportation hearings. Other lawyers may never spend any time in court. A staff attorney for the Internal Revenue Service, for example, may research and write advisory opinions on tax law questions, while a staff attorney for the Securities and Exchange Commission may analyze public stock offerings to ensure compliance with federal regulatory laws.

Structure. Like an in-house legal department, the legal department of a governmental entity is usually managed by a senior lawyer, who may hold the title of **chief counsel**. Other lawyers in the office may be known as associate counsel, assistant counsel, or simply staff attorneys.

Decision Making. Internal management decisions in the legal department of a governmental entity are usually made by the chief counsel in consultation with the other lawyers in the department. The chief counsel is generally required to report to the head of the governmental entity that the department serves, whose approval may be required for major decisions.

Legal Aid and Public Interest Law Offices

Some law offices provide legal services for people who are unable to pay for them or for the benefit of the public at large. These law offices can be distinguished from private law firms and in-house legal departments because they are nonprofit. Like government law offices, they are designed to serve the public good. However, they often lack the resources available to government law offices and are not subject to as many restrictions.

Legal Aid Offices. Legal aid offices function much like private law firms do. The main difference is that legal aid clients are unable to pay the fees that private law firms charge. Legal aid offices often charge fees on a sliding scale tied to a client's income. Because the fees charged do not cover operational costs, these offices often solicit government funds or charitable contributions to make up the difference. Legal aid offices are usually organized to accommodate a large number of clients. These offices often specialize in fields of law that have the greatest practical application for people with low incomes—for example, landlord/tenant, consumer, and welfare benefits law.

Public Interest Law Offices. **Public interest law offices** are usually designed to benefit large segments of the general public rather than specific individuals. Most public interest law offices specialize in some field of public concern such as environmental law, civil rights law, or poverty law. Organizations that sponsor public interest law offices include the American Civil Liberties Union, the NAACP Legal Defense Fund, and the Sierra Club. Public interest law offices often file lawsuits that serve as test cases to establish or clarify legal rights. One office might, for example, sue a public official in connection with the administration of a welfare benefits program, seeking to improve some aspect of the program's administration. Another office might file a lawsuit to prevent oil drilling that threatens to harm a wilderness preserve or a lawsuit to halt logging operations that jeopardize the habitat of an endangered species.

Structure. The organization of legal aid and public interest law offices varies greatly. Most offices employ some lawyers on a full-time basis. These lawyers are usually referred to as **staff counsel**. Although staff counsel are paid, they usually make much less money than they would in a private law firm or an in-house legal department.

Staff counsel are often assisted by other lawyers on a part-time, volunteer basis. There is a strong volunteer tradition in the legal profession, and an increasing number of lawyers and paralegals regularly perform some legal services without pay on a **pro bono** basis. (This term comes from the Latin expression *pro bono publico*, which means "for the public good.") The interaction of paid and volunteer legal professionals often creates a sense of teamwork, which is one of the most rewarding aspects of working in this kind of law office.

Decision Making. The decision-making process for legal aid and public interest law offices varies as much as the organizational structure. Very often these law offices are organized as nonprofit corporations governed by a board of directors comprised of volunteers from the community. The directors usually have some expertise in the areas of public concern in which the office specializes. Often the board appoints an executive director, who is in charge of the day-to-day management of the office.

THE PROFESSIONAL TEAM IN A LAW OFFICE

As a paralegal who works in a law office, you will be part of a professional team. To understand your role on the team, you will need to understand the roles of its other members. Although the specific makeup of professional teams varies from office to office, certain roles must be filled everywhere. The following discussion will introduce you to the roles played by most of the individuals with whom you will be working in a law office.

Lawyers

A **lawyer** is a person who is licensed by a state or other jurisdiction to practice law. Exactly what constitutes "practicing law" is a frequent subject of debate, as you will see when you study Chapter 11. Broadly speaking, the **practice of law** includes representing clients in court, giving clients legal advice, and preparing documents of a legal nature for clients. A lawyer is sometimes referred to as an **attorney** or, less frequently, a **counselor**, a **barrister**, or a **solicitor**. These terms originated long ago in English courts to identify special roles played by lawyers in certain types of legal proceedings. These distinctions survive in Great Britain even today, where barristers present oral arguments to the courts, while solicitors advise clients and prepare written memoranda to assist barristers with their arguments. In the United States, however, these terms are now used interchangeably with the term lawyer.

Owners. Private law firms are owned by lawyers. As we explained earlier, the owners of a private law firm can structure their relationship in any of several ways. The lawyers who are the owners of a firm are usually called **partners**, even though technically the firm may not be structured as a partnership. The term **senior partner** is often used to identify the lawyers who are long-time owners of the firm, who have practiced law for a long period of time, or who are owners of a substantial percentage of the firm. Lawyers who have been owners or who have practiced law for a relatively short period of time, or who have relatively small ownership interests, are frequently known as **junior partners**.

Associates. In most larger private law firms, far more lawyers are employees of the firm than are owners. While the compensation of a firm's owners may increase or decrease depending on the firm's profitability, lawyer employees are paid either fixed salaries or hourly rates, commonly supplemented by periodic bonuses. Bonuses may either be based on a set formula or be awarded at the discretion of the owners.

Partnership Track. Lawyers employed by a private law firm are usually referred to as **associates**. At most firms, most associates are **on the partnership track**, which means that they are expected to become co-owners of the firm some day. During the time that an associate is on the partnership track, the firm's owners constantly review her or his lawyering skills, administrative skills, and ability to attract clients for the firm. After a period of time that can range from four to twelve years, an associate on the partnership track who has performed satisfactorily may be invited to become a co-owner of the firm.

Other Associates. Associates who are not on the partnership track are sometimes referred to as **permanent associates** or **contract attorneys**. These associates sometimes work on a part-time, hourly basis. The term **senior associate** sometimes refers to a permanent associate, although it is also used to refer to an associate on the partnership track who has worked for the firm for several years.

Of Counsel. Lawyers who are affiliated with a private law firm, but who are neither owners nor employees of the firm, are often identified as being **of counsel** to the firm. This term has no universal definition. Lawyers who are of counsel may, for example, share office and employee expenses with the firm, have a business referral relationship with the firm, or assist the firm on specific projects. The title is sometimes given to owners of a firm who have retired and to lawyers who practice law on a part-time basis or who teach full-time but maintain an affiliation with a firm.

Law Clerks. Because law students are not licensed lawyers, they are unable to practice law. However, law offices frequently hire law students as **law clerks**. Clerkship often serves as a form of trial employment; students who perform well may be offered permanent positions after they become licensed.

Law students frequently work part-time during the school year and full-time during the summer. Many private law firms have developed "summer associate" programs designed to attract top law students to the firm. These firms anticipate that students who have a positive experience during the summer will want to join the firm after graduation.

Law students who work in law offices often conduct detailed legal research in connection with court cases or complex transactions. They may prepare first drafts of briefs and other documents to be filed with a court, and they may draw up first drafts of contracts and other legal documents.

Paralegals

As you learned in Chapter 1, a paralegal's role in a law office is to assist the lawyers in providing legal services to clients. What form this assistance takes depends on a number of things, including the type of law office, the areas of law in which it specializes, the makeup of the professional team, and—perhaps most important—the skills and experience of the paralegal.

Throughout this book you will be examining the multifaceted role of the paralegal in a law office. In Chapters 4 and 5, you will study several areas of law and consider how paralegals use basic legal concepts in their work. In Chapter 6, you will learn how paralegals use fact investigation skills. In Chapters 7 and 8, you will learn how a paralegal's legal research, analysis, and writing skills are used in a law office. Finally, in Chapter 9, you will consider a paralegal's role in the litigation process.

Administrators

Many law offices now have full- or part-time office administrators. The size and complexity of an administrator's job depends on the size and complexity of the office itself. Many administrative duties fall into one of three categories: personnel, facilities and equipment, and finances.

Personnel. The administrator usually plays a major role in the selection, hiring, oversight, performance review, and termination of nonlawyer office personnel. Administrators are responsible for ensuring that work is assigned in such a way that the skills of all employees are being used to maximum advantage. An administrator studies, formulates, and implements standard operating procedures for the office and is usually the person who mediates employee conflicts. Finally, the administrator handles employee-benefit matters such as health insurance and tax deductible savings plans.

Facilities and Equipment. The administrator of a law office is usually responsible for determining its needs with respect to space, furniture, computer and word processing equipment, communications equipment, and library resources. The administrator issues recommendations to the decision makers and then handles the details of purchasing, leasing, and disposing of these items.

Finances. A private law firm's administrator is sometimes charged with overseeing the firm's day-to-day billing, collections, and other bookkeeping operations. The administrator is often the firm's chief liaison with its bankers and certified public accountants. An administrator in any type of law office may be required to prepare—or to supervise the preparation of—budgets, financial statements, and other accountings.

From this overview you can see that an office's administrator is often the professional team member who is most knowledgeable about how the office operates. By developing a good relationship with the administrator in your office, you will have ready access to this knowledge. This will make your job as a paralegal much easier.

Secretarial Staff

Every law office requires a qualified secretarial staff. You are probably already familiar with the typical job skills of an office secretary: preparing correspondence and other documents, handling telephone and other communications, calendaring dates, filing, and so on. While all law office secretaries must have these skills, many have highly specialized skills as well. A secretary with specialized skills in the field of litigation, for example, would be thoroughly familiar with the host of rules that govern the preparation, filing, and handling of litigation documents. Legal secretaries may have specialized skills in a wide range of areas including criminal law, business transactions, real estate transactions, family law, estate planning, and probate. Experienced, technically skilled legal secretaries are always in great demand.

Bookkeeping Staff

Most private law firms employ full- or part-time bookkeepers to handle billing, collections, payroll, expense disbursements, and the preparation of financial reports. Most private law firms also retain independent certified public accountants (CPAs) who regularly review the firm's accounting procedures and who assist in the preparation of financial statements, management reports, and tax returns.

Other Office Staff

Larger law offices are likely to employ a variety of individuals who perform specific services: Word processing personnel are charged with the technical preparation of lengthy, complex documents; law librarians oversee the office's research resources; recruiting administrators seek and woo highly qualified professionals to augment the staffs of private law firms; marketing directors enhance a firm's visibility and increase the size and quality of its client base. From receptionists to file clerks to messengers, other office personnel perform their individual tasks as well.

Outside Service Providers

Law offices contract with outside service providers for many services that are needed regularly but not often enough to justify hiring a full-time employee. Often an **attorney service** is retained to file documents at the courthouse and personally deliver summonses and other legal documents. Private investigators may be hired to locate missing persons or conduct asset searches. Court reporting firms provide stenographers to make records of depositions and other proceedings. Title companies provide information on ownership of real property and handle the recording of legal documents pertaining to title matters. These are just a few of the service providers who may work with a law office on a regular basis.

FINANCIAL MANAGEMENT IN PRIVATE LAW FIRMS

Private law firms, like other businesses, exist to make money for their owners. As you have already seen, a firm's profitability is directly tied to how well it is managed. This is especially true when it comes to the management of money.

Billing Methods

Private law firms bill clients for legal services rendered. The amount billed for a particular service depends on the billing method being used.

Hourly Fee. The most common billing method is the **hourly fee**. In law offices that use the hourly fee billing method, certain personnel keep track of the time they spend working on individual client projects. Members of this group are said to be **timekeepers**. Lawyers and paralegals are usually timekeepers. Each timekeeper is assigned an hourly billing rate. The rates for experienced timekeepers are higher than those for less-experienced timekeepers, and the rates for lawyers are higher than those for paralegals. At the end of each billing period—usually a calendar month—the total number of hours spent by a timekeeper on a given project is multiplied by that timekeeper's hourly billing rate. When the amounts so obtained for all of the timekeepers working on the project are added together, the total sum is billed to the client for that project for the period in question. Some firms may adjust the amount to be billed upward or downward depending on such factors as the outcome obtained for the client, the complexity of the project, or the efficiency or skill of the timekeepers involved.

Consider, for example, a project on which a partner spent 1.3 hours, an associate spent 6.7 hours, and a paralegal spent 3.4 hours during a given month. Assume that the partner's billing rate is $250 per hour, the associate's billing rate is $150 per hour, and the paralegal's billing rate is $80 per hour. The amount to be billed to the client for work performed on the project during that month would be calculated as follows:

Partner	1.3	×	$250	=	$ 325
Associate	6.7	×	150	=	1,005
Paralegal	3.4	×	80	=	272
Total fee					$1,602

The bill sent to the client for this fee might resemble the bill in Figure 2-1.

FIGURE 2-1 EXAMPLE OF CLIENT BILL BASED ON HOURLY FEE METHOD

February 1, 1993

For services rendered during January 1993:

1/4	Telephone conference with client
1/6	Telephone conference with opposing counsel; letter to opposing counsel
1/10	Conference with client
1/11	Preparation for deposition of Ms. Patt
1/12	Deposition of Ms. Patt; telephone conversation with client
1/14	Preparation of papers in opposition to motion to continue trial date
1/29	Attended hearing on motion to continue trial date; telephone conference with client; prepared order denying continuance of trial date

TOTAL: $1,602.00

The hourly fee method of billing is suitable for any type of legal service. It is commonly used in connection with business and family law litigation and matters involving the documentation of complex business transactions.

Flat Fee. Some firms charge a **flat fee** for specific services that are relatively simple or routine. Services subject to flat fees have been performed by the firm so often that the owners know what personnel and other costs will be incurred. Examples include the preparation of a simple will, a review of documents in connection with the sale of a family residence, or the setting up of a new corporation.

Contingency Fee. In some cases a firm will base its fee on a preset percentage of the amount that the firm is able to win for a client in a lawsuit. This is known as a **contingency fee**. The contingency fee billing method is attractive to the client because no payment is demanded up front or during the course of the lawsuit. If nothing is recovered, the client is not required to pay a fee.

The percentage that a firm agrees to charge as a contingency fee usually depends on the likelihood that the case will be won and the anticipated amount of the award. Often a firm will charge a smaller percentage of the amount recovered if the case settles before trial. For example, a firm may agree to accept 25 percent of the client's recovery if a case is settled before trial but will charge 33 percent of any amount awarded to the client after trial.

Accepting a case on contingency is always a risky proposition for a law firm. If nothing is recovered in the lawsuit, the firm must absorb all of the costs it incurs in pursuing the case. Often a large recovery in one case will allow a firm to offset the costs incurred in an unsuccessful case. As you might expect, lawyers are most likely to agree to a contingency fee arrangement if the case is a strong one and a large recovery is expected. Examples of cases in which contingency fee arrangements are frequently used include actions to recover damages for personal injury, debt collection actions, and actions contesting a decedent's will.

Prepaid Group Plans. In recent years there has been an increasing use of prepaid group legal services plans. In return for payment of a monthly or annual fee, a client is allowed limited or unlimited access to certain legal services. These plans vary greatly. A typical plan might include an unlimited number of half-hour telephone conversations with an attorney, review by an attorney of up to three simple legal documents per year, and access to legal do-it-yourself publications and forms covering a wide variety of topics. These prepaid legal services plans are widely marketed and are sometimes made available as part of employee benefits packages.

Timekeeping

Earlier we noted that the hourly fee is the most common billing method among law firms. Because paralegals are designated as timekeepers by most private firms, it is important that you understand how timekeeping works.

Timekeeping Systems. Timekeeping systems vary somewhat from law firm to law firm. The important thing to remember, no matter what the system, is that every timekeeper is responsible for keeping a complete, detailed, and accurate record of the time that she or he spends on each client project.

Most systems keep track of time in fractions of a hour. The most commonly used increments of time are six minutes (one-tenth of an hour) and fifteen minutes (a quarter hour).

In most cases a timekeeper will record the actual time spent on each project. For example, if a timekeeper begins work on an assignment at 10:30 A.M. and finishes at 11:23 A.M., the timekeeper has spent 53 minutes on the project. This translates into .9 hours on a six-minute system and 1.0 hours on a fifteen-minute system.

Some firms have adopted standard time allotments for certain activities. For example, a policy may be that any telephone call lasting twelve minutes or less is automatically billed at .2 hours or that every court appearance is automatically billed at no less than 4.0 hours. Many firms have a policy of billing for time spent traveling to or from a court appearance or a meeting in addition to billing for the time actually spent in court or at the meeting. You should be familiar with the policies adopted by your firm.

Billable Hours. Most law firm budgets begin with the assumption that each of the firm's timekeepers will work a specified number of billable hours each year. A **billable hour** is an hour of work that can be billed to a client at the timekeeper's assigned hourly billing rate. Most law firms set a specific billable-hours goal for each timekeeper, commonly somewhere between 1,600 and 2,100 per year. If a firm's timekeepers fail to meet the billable-hours goals set for them, the firm's projected income will fall short of projected expenses, and its owners may lose money.

You should keep in mind that almost all firms carefully review billable hours when evaluating a timekeeper's job performance. A timekeeper who consistently fails to meet billable-hours goals does not make money for the firm and will rarely receive a favorable job review. A timekeeper who meets or exceeds billable-hours goals, however, will often be viewed as a highly valued employee.

Because many firms draw a connection between the number of billable hours attributable to a timekeeper and that timekeeper's job performance, many timekeepers are tempted to report spending more time on projects than they actually spend. Giving in to this temptation is usually a mistake. A timekeeper who appears to be spending excessive time completing assignments may be viewed as inefficient or even incompetent. Moreover, a firm is usually reluctant to bill clients for time spent inefficiently. So, even though a timekeeper records a large number of hours, the firm's owners may conclude that only a portion of the time can be justifiably billed to the client. This, of course, reduces the number of true billable hours attributable to the timekeeper. As you can see, a timekeeper who inflates time records may develop a reputation for inefficiency while failing to increase true billable hours.

Timekeepers often spend time on activities that benefit the firm but cannot be billed to clients. For example, timekeepers may perform administrative tasks, attend educational seminars, or participate in professional or community activities that enhance the firm's reputation. Many firms expect timekeepers to keep a record of these **nonbillable hours**. This is especially important for paralegals, who may spend a substantial amount of time on nonbillable activities in some law offices.

Recording Time. A common method of recording time is to keep an informal running tally of how you spend your time as the day progresses. Whenever you begin or end work on a project, you note the time. Because frequent interruptions may be part of your day, you may begin and end work on the same project many times. At the end of the work day, you complete a time sheet on which you list each project, briefly describe the work accomplished, and note the total time spent. The format of a typical time sheet is illustrated in Figure 2-2. It is critical that you complete a time sheet each day, as you will soon discover it is surprisingly difficult to remember details about the work that you did only two or three days ago.

FIGURE 2-2 TIME SHEET

Name ______________________ Date ____________

Client	Adverse Party	Description	Time From	To	Total Time in Decimals

Many law firms now use computerized timekeeping systems. Data is entered from the time sheet by a secretary, or in some cases directly by the timekeeper. The computer performs the hourly fee calculation at the end of the billing period and prints an itemized bill for the client. Computers may also be used to generate client billing histories and timekeeper billable-hour summaries.

Some firms, however, still use a manual billing system in which each entry on a timekeeper's time sheet is typed on a label. These labels are then affixed to a ledger card for each project. At the end of the billing period, the time reflected on the timekeepers' labels is totaled and the hourly fee is calculated. A detailed bill is then prepared for the client.

Accounting and Reports

Like any other business, a private law firm has an accounting system that keeps track of all aspects of its income and expenditures. The firm's bookkeepers and independent CPAs are responsible for implementation of this accounting system on a day-to-day basis. Because specific costs incurred on behalf of individual clients are usually billed to the clients, the firm's accounting system must be sophisticated enough to identify such costs and allocate them so that clients are properly billed. These costs can include such in-house services as photocopying and word processing, as well as court filing fees and fees charged by messengers, investigators, and other outside service providers.

Most law firms now use computerized accounting systems to one extent or another. One of the chief benefits of such systems is their ability to generate management reports that help identify cash flow and other problems as they develop.

Billing and Collections

Clients whose fees are determined on an hourly basis are usually billed monthly. Often a firm will request that new clients pay a deposit, or **retainer**, which is placed in the firm's trust account to secure payment for future services rendered. Each month the client authorizes the firm to withdraw money from the trust account to pay that month's bill.

POINTER: Although the word retainer usually refers to a client deposit from which fees are paid as they are incurred, the term has other meanings. It is sometimes used to describe a client's payment to a lawyer in return for the lawyer's promise to be available to handle the client's prospective legal needs. Although the practice of paying such retainers was once fairly common, it rarely occurs today. Retainer is also sometimes used to describe a nonrefundable fee that a lawyer charges in exchange for agreeing to accept a particular case.

Flat fees may be collected in advance or billed after the service has been rendered, depending on the client's credit history with the firm.

Contingency fees are usually deducted from the amount collected at the end of the lawsuit. As a general rule, the amount collected is deposited in the firm's trust account, and the funds are then disbursed to the firm and to the client according to the contingency fee agreement.

Like other businesses, private law firms must sometimes take legal action to collect fees. Some states require that a client be given the opportunity to submit a fee dispute to arbitration before a firm is allowed to file a lawsuit to collect an unpaid bill.

LAW OFFICE PROCEDURES

Professionals who provide legal services handle large amounts of information that must be recorded and organized for immediate retrieval when needed. To ensure that this happens and that no important information is lost or ignored, law offices adopt systems for the handling of information.

It is critical that you, as a paralegal, understand the systems that have been set up in the law office where you work. In many cases you will be the person who obtains information from original sources or who is most familiar with particular information. For optimal job performance, you must make sure that all information you handle is properly recorded and organized.

The File System

Virtually all law offices organize information according to files. For example, a file is opened for every new client. When the office is handling a number of legal projects for a single client, separate files are opened for each project.

Individual files are usually identified by name and number. A file's name usually identifies the client (as in "Shannon Stevens: General Representation") or the client and the project (as in "Margaret Stuart: Acquisition of Acme, Inc."). File numbering systems can be designed so that by simply looking at the number one can determine when the file was opened, who the responsible lawyer and paralegal are, and what the general nature of the matter is.

General information about an office's active and inactive files is maintained for a number of purposes. For example, as you will learn in Chapter 10, a lawyer may not represent a client if such representation would create a conflict of interest. Suppose a potential new client who wishes to sue Frank Thomas comes into the office. Someone must determine whether or not the office already represents Frank Thomas, since an office cannot sue one of its own clients. A master index of the office's files can be reviewed to determine whether or not the office already represents Frank Thomas. Like other general information about an office's files, this general index can be computerized for easy access and use.

POINTER: A conflict of interest may arise under any circumstance that prevents a lawyer from fully representing a client's interests. For example, when two clients of a lawyer have adverse interests in a matter, the lawyer cannot fully represent the interests of both because the lawyer would be required to take inconsistent positions. Similarly, a conflict may arise when a lawyer represents a client in a matter in which the lawyer has an interest.

Creating Documents

Almost all information used in a law office is recorded in the form of a document such as a letter, a memorandum, a set of notes, an agreement, or a court pleading.

Most law offices have a **style manual** that provides guidelines for the format of various types of documents. Most style manuals contain standard forms for documents, such as the standard form for a letter illustrated in Figure 2-3. You should be fully familiar with your office's style manual. This is especially important when it comes to documents that are to be submitted to a court, as many format rules for court documents are established by court regulation.

Virtually all documents created in a law office fall into one of three categories: Some are wholly original, created by the author from scratch. Others are created by modifying an existing document, such as a standard form agreement, to meet the author's needs. Still other documents are created by completing preprinted forms that request specific information.

Original Documents. First drafts of original documents may be dictated onto tape or written in longhand, then typed by a secretary or entered into a word processing system and printed. Alternatively, the author may compose documents

FIGURE 2-3 STANDARD FORM OF LETTER FROM STYLE MANUAL

LAW OFFICES OF
JOHN DOE, ESQ.
123 Main Street
Presque Isle, ME 04769-2655

Mary Roe, Esq.
Suite 8-A
213 First Street
Portsmouth, NH 03801-5463

Re: Standard Correspondence Format

Dear Ms. Roe

I am presenting to you a sample of our standards for all correspondence leaving this office. If a letter is directed to an attorney, ''Esq.'' should appear after the attorney's name. If directed to another professional, that person's name should be followed by a comma and the person's title (M.D., D.D.S., C.P.A.).

The name of the individual to whom the letter is directed should appear on the first line of the inside address; the company name (or law firm) should appear on the second line, followed by the address. If there is a suite number or apartment number, that information should appear on the line above the street address. If you wish the correspondence delivered to a post office box, that number should appear on the line above the city and state in the address. In other words, the postal service delivers to the bottom line in the address first and works its way up to the street address, suite number, company name, and finally to the individual.

Yours very truly

John Doe
for the firm

at the typewriter or the word processor. Word processing is now used almost universally in law offices, as it allows documents to be revised with relatively little effort. It also permits automatic formatting of documents to conform with an office's style manual.

Modification of Standard Documents. Existing documents can be modified in several ways. You can mark up a photocopy of the document, and a secretary can then retype it as modified. Or, you can enter modifications into a word processing system where the document is already stored. If your office systems are fully automated, you can call up the text of the existing document on the computer screen and modify it via the keyboard. Today's computer programs simplify the use of complex standard form documents that contain numerous alternative provisions. The computer asks the author a series of questions about the document and inserts or deletes language according to the author's answers.

Preprinted Forms. Preprinted forms are frequently used in litigation and some other areas of law, such as real estate. Traditionally, the requested information has been typed into the appropriate blank spaces on the form. In a state-of-the-art office system, however, a computer program will display the form on the computer screen, allow information to be inserted via the keyboard, and then print the completed form.

Managing Documents

One of the greatest challenges in any law office is managing documents. Computer storage of documents generated by the office saves space and makes retrieval relatively easy, but many of the documents handled in a law office are generated by outside sources. This means that they must be entered into the computer before they can be stored there. Furthermore, a computer is not always accessible when information contained in documents is needed—for example, when one is in court. As a result, every office must have some system for managing printed documents.

Document Clips. A commonly used approach to managing printed documents involves setting up a number of folders known as document clips for each file. Documents are then stored in the clips by category. For example, a file may have a correspondence clip for letters, a pleadings clip for documents filed in court, a discovery clip for documents generated during discovery proceedings, and a research clip for legal research memoranda. Documents are usually arranged within each folder in chronological order and may be indexed and tabbed for easy access.

Access to Documents Through the Use of Databases. Whether documents are maintained in a computer or in printed form, computers can be of great assistance in gaining access to the information contained in them. A complex lawsuit, for example, may involve hundreds of documents that are to be used as evidence. A computer database that includes a brief standard description of each of these documents will make it easy to identify quickly, for example, all correspondence directed by a specific individual to another individual or all documents that mention a specific topic.

Managing the Calendar

We have already emphasized that deadlines play a major role in the activities of a law office. To ensure that deadlines are not missed, all law offices have calendaring systems for recording significant dates.

Identifying Significant Dates. The most important aspect of any calendaring system is identifying the significant dates that must be calendared. Different offices have different procedures for doing this. For example, one procedure may specify that the first person who reviews a document coming into the office is charged with noting any significant deadlines reflected in the document; another procedure may assign this responsibility to the last person who reviews a document before it goes out. Because not all deadlines appear in documents, it is critical that anyone who becomes aware of a deadline that might not otherwise be noted make a note of it.

Tickler Systems. Many offices use a tickler-card calendaring system. Significant dates are recorded on multipart cards called tickler cards. A typical tickler card is illustrated in Figure 2-4. Information from the cards is entered into a computer, which then generates a master calendar on a weekly basis. The cards themselves are stored in a file according to date, so that a few days before the indicated deadline a copy of the card may be given to interested persons as a reminder.

FIGURE 2-4 TICKLER CARD

Calendaring & Tickler Card

Client: ______________________ File No.: ____________

Matter: ______________________ Atty: ____________

Reason for Calendaring: ______________________ Date of Request: ____________

Appearance or Action Reminder — Calendar — Tickler

Date of Event: ____________ Time: ________

Place: ______________________ ( ) ( )

Preparation Reminder Date: ____________ ( ) ( )

Personal Calendar. As a paralegal, you should keep a personal calendar on which you record deadlines that apply to projects with which you are involved. Each week you should compare your personal calendar against the office's master calendar to ensure that both calendars are accurate and complete.

Computer Software. Some firms are now expanding their calendaring systems through the use of case-management computer software. This allows a lawyer or paralegal who is keeping track of a lawsuit or transaction to develop a standard computerized record of events occurring during the course of the lawsuit or transaction. By calling up this record on the computer screen, they can quickly identify information that might otherwise be found only through a lengthy review of document clips.

Communications

Law offices are among the chief beneficiaries of the ongoing revolution in communications technology. In the past, when someone you wished to speak with was unavailable, it was necessary to leave a brief message with a receptionist or a secretary. Today many law offices have voice mail systems that allow you to leave a recorded message of any length. Law offices once were heavily dependent on messengers to deliver multiple drafts of documents. Now documents can be transmitted almost instantaneously by facsimile (FAX) transmission over telephone lines. When you go to work at a law office, you will receive training in the communications systems used there. While these new systems have made communications faster and simpler, they have also stepped up the pace of activity in most offices.

3 AN OVERVIEW OF THE AMERICAN LEGAL SYSTEM

The American legal system is a fundamental institution in our society. It provides the means for both creating and enforcing the law. To be a successful paralegal, you must understand how the American legal system operates.

Chapter 3 provides an overview of the American legal system. It begins with a discussion of the nature and purpose of law and the relationship between law and ethics and goes on to examine the different sources of law in our system. The chapter concludes with a discussion of the court system.

NATURE AND PURPOSE OF LAW

Because humans are social beings who constantly interact with one another, it is not surprising that problems and conflicts sometimes arise. Over the course of history, organized societies have established certain rules, or laws, to govern the relationships among individuals. For laws to be effective, a government must have the power to enforce them. With this in mind, English jurist William Blackstone defined law as "a rule of civil conduct prescribed by the supreme power in a state, commanding what is right, and prohibiting what is wrong."[1]

Law has evolved slowly over time. As the needs of modern society change, law will continue to evolve. The law is not a list of universal truths etched in stone, but rather a constantly changing set of rules that attempt to address the problems faced by our society.

Law is an attempt to regulate human activity. Human beings engage in such diverse activities, however, that it is impossible to have a law governing every type of situation that might arise. Sometimes there is no specific law that addresses the problem raised in a particular situation. Other times the law is not clear, or it is not clear how the law should be applied to the situation. The answers to legal problems are seldom black and white; usually they are some shade of gray. This will become clear once you develop an understanding of how the law is created and applied in our legal system.

RELATIONSHIP BETWEEN LAW AND ETHICS

Law and ethics are intimately connected. In fact, most of our laws are the product of the ethical beliefs of our society. The law of contracts is a good example. A contract is an agreement between two or more parties by which each party undertakes to perform, or not to perform, one or more specific acts. The law enforces contracts because of the ethical belief that people are obligated to honor commitments; when you agree to do something, you should do it.

However, law and ethics are not the same thing. Just because an act is legal does not necessarily mean it is ethical. At one time, owning slaves in the United States was legal, yet that did not mean that it was ethical. Conversely, just because an act is illegal does not mean it is unethical. Aiding fugitive slaves was illegal, yet that did not mean it was unethical.

CLASSIFICATION OF LAW

Because the law is so diverse and complex, it is easier to study the law if we break it down into classifications. Two common and useful classifications are (1) substantive versus procedural law and (2) criminal versus civil law.

Substantive Versus Procedural Law

Substantive law is law that creates and defines duties, rights, and obligations. For example, laws that state when and how a contract is formed are part of the substantive law of contracts. Laws that state when a person must pay damages for negligently or intentionally injuring another are part of the substantive law of torts.[2] Figure 3-1 lists other areas of substantive law.

FIGURE 3-1 EXAMPLES OF SUBSTANTIVE AND PROCEDURAL LAWS

Substantive	Procedural
Administrative Law	Administrative Procedure
Constitutional Law	Appellate Procedure
Contract Law	Civil Procedure
Corporation Law	Criminal Procedure
Criminal Law	
Real Property Law	
Tort Law	

Procedural law is law that describes the manner in which the substantive law may be enforced. Issues of procedural law include which court should hear a particular lawsuit, how the suit should be filed, and how the suit should proceed.

While substantive law defines rights, procedural law specifies the steps that must be followed in enforcing those rights.[3]

Paralegals must be familiar with both substantive law and procedural law. Chapters 4 and 5 will address several major areas of substantive law, and procedural law will be discussed in Chapter 9.

Civil Versus Criminal Law

Civil law defines a person's individual rights that are enforceable in a civil case. A civil case is an action between private parties involving a question of private rights, or an action by the government other than a criminal action. For example, Linda might bring a civil action against Tom for breaching a contract, or the government might bring a civil action against a careless driver who damages a mail truck. In a civil action, the **plaintiff** is the party who brings the suit. The plaintiff has the **burden of proof** or the duty of proving the facts in dispute. The burden of proof requires proof by a **preponderance of the evidence** (greater weight of the evidence).

Criminal law defines offenses against society that are punishable by the government in a criminal action. Criminal law is concerned with offenses against society as a whole, while civil law is concerned with private wrongs. For example, if Mary sets a building on fire, the government might bring a criminal action against Mary for having committed the crime of arson. In a criminal action, the government, represented by the prosecutor, has the burden of proving criminal guilt **beyond a reasonable doubt**. That is, the defendant is presumed innocent unless guilt is so clearly established that no reasonable doubt remains as to the defendant's guilt.

Sometimes a single act may result in both a civil action and a criminal action. For example, if Ed punches Paul in the nose, Paul could sue Ed in a civil action for battery. Paul would seek to recover money damages for injuries suffered. The government might also prosecute Ed in a criminal action for committing the crime of battery.

SOURCES OF LAW

One of a paralegal's main responsibilities is researching the law concerning a given subject. This section looks at the four different sources of law that you will soon be researching.

Constitutional Law

A **constitution** is the fundamental law of a nation or state. The federal government and each state have their own constitutions. Constitutions serve two main functions: (1) They provide a blueprint for government, setting forth the general organization and powers of the government; (2) they guarantee certain basic rights and liberties.

The United States Constitution is the supreme law of the land. This means that *any* law in violation of the Constitution will be declared unconstitutional and will not be enforced. Similarly, each state's constitution is the supreme law of that state.

The United States Constitution establishes a system of government called **federalism**, wherein power is divided between the central government (the federal government) and state governments. Consequently we have federal laws that are made by the federal government and state laws that are made by each of the fifty state governments. Federal law applies throughout the United States, whereas state law applies only in the state that adopts it. The state governments delegate power to smaller governmental entities (such as cities) that also have the power to make law.

The Constitution allocates power between the federal government and the state governments. Article 1, Section 8 enumerates those powers expressly given to the federal government, including the power to tax, to regulate interstate commerce, and to provide for the general welfare. The federal government also has implied powers, which are not expressly stated in the Constitution. For example, the federal government has the implied power to do whatever is necessary and proper to carry out the enumerated powers. The Tenth Amendment provides that all powers not given to the federal government are reserved to the states or the people.

The Constitution creates three different branches of government—the legislative, the executive, and the judicial. The Constitution allocates power among the three branches, thereby establishing a system of so-called checks and balances. Article 1 gives the legislative branch the power to make the law; Article 2 gives the executive branch the power to enforce the law; and Article 3 gives the judicial branch the power to interpret the law and to determine whether or not it violates the Constitution.

Case Law

An important characteristic of United States law is its reliance on previously decided cases when new cases are being heard. This practice originated in the **common law**, a system of law that developed in England. After the Normans conquered England in 1066, William the Conqueror established the King's Court, a system of royal courts that operated throughout England. As the number of courts and cases increased, officials began to record the more important decisions. The recorded decisions were then used by judges when deciding their cases. These accumulated decisions became known as the common law because they were commonly applied to all people throughout the realm. When English colonists came to North America, they brought with them the common law system.[4]

The common law is based on judicial precedent rather than legislative enactments (statutes). A **precedent** is a previously decided case used as authority when deciding a later case that is similar in facts or legal principles. In other words, judges look for past similar cases (precedents) in order to determine what the law is in the particular case before them. Similarly, when doing legal research, a paralegal searches for previously decided cases that are similar to the case under consideration. Case law, then, consists of the rules of law that can be extracted from previously decided cases similar to the case under consideration.

Stare Decisis. According to the doctrine of ***stare decisis*** ("to stand by that which was decided"), the rule of law established in a case governs all future cases that involve substantially the same fact pattern. In other words, the doctrine states that courts are supposed to stand by earlier decisions. *Stare decisis* thus helps make the law more predictable and reliable. If a court has already established a rule of law on the basis of a specific set of facts, that legal rule will be applied the same way whenever the same set of facts is presented again. If a new case has the same facts as a previously decided case, the new case will be decided in the same way.

Mandatory Versus Persuasive Precedent. As we have just seen, the doctrine of *stare decisis* states that the rule of law established in a case governs all future cases involving substantially the same fact pattern. In practice, however, this doctrine has a limited application. Sometimes courts will be *bound* to follow the earlier decision, and other times courts will merely be *persuaded* to follow the earlier decision. A **mandatory precedent** is one that must be followed. For example, a U.S. Supreme Court decision is a mandatory precedent, binding on all courts. A **persuasive precedent** may offer guidance, but does not have to be followed. A decision of one state's highest court, for example, might be persuasive in courts in other states but would not be binding in those other states.

Because of our federalism, we have two parallel court systems in the United States—the federal court system and the state court system. Courts in each system are grouped in a hierarchy: appellate courts (higher courts) are above trial courts (lower courts). Every federal or state trial court is directly under a particular appellate court, which is where appeals are taken. As a case is appealed, it works its way *up* the hierarchy. Precedent, however, flows *down* the hierarchy; in general, courts are bound to follow the decision of any court directly above them in the hierarchy. We will return to our discussion of the federal and state courts—and a summary of how *stare decisis* is applied in the dual system—later in the chapter.

Conflicting Precedent. Problems often arise in applying the doctrine of *stare decisis*. One problem is when conflicting precedents exist. For example, suppose Betty's dog Bootsie runs away from home. Fred, who lives down the street, discovers Bootsie in his backyard. Fred knows how much Betty loves Bootsie. As a practical joke, Fred calls her on the phone and says, "Betty, I've got some bad news. Bootsie was just run over by a cement truck." Five minutes later, Fred takes Bootsie home and tells Betty it was only a joke—Bootsie is really alive and well. Betty sues Fred for intentional infliction of emotional distress. Fred's lawyer finds a case from state *A* that holds (rules) that purposefully telling someone her pet has died when it really is alive is *not* intentional infliction of emotional distress. The paralegal working for Betty's lawyer finds a case from state *B* that says this *is* intentional infliction of emotional distress. The case precedents are clearly in conflict. When this happens, a court will usually follow the precedent that it considers to be the better reasoned case.

Conflicting precedents arise because courts are not always bound to follow the decisions of other courts. For example, suppose the Eleventh Circuit Court of Appeals was the court that held that purposefully telling someone her pet has died when it really is alive is *not* intentional infliction of emotional distress. If the same fact pattern comes before the Ninth Circuit Court of Appeals, a co-equal court, the Ninth Circuit is not bound to follow the decision of the Eleventh Circuit. If the Ninth Circuit holds that this *is* intentional infliction of emotional distress, conflicting precedents then exist.

No Precedent. Another problem arises when no precedent exists. This may be the first time someone has sued for intentional infliction of emotional distress on these facts. A case that raises a question of law not previously decided is called a **case of first impression**. Sometimes the court attempts to find an analogy between the facts of the case under consideration and the facts of a case for which there is a precedent established.

Factual Distinctions. Another problem arises when the facts in the case being cited as precedent are different from the facts in the case under consideration. When major factual distinctions exist, the cases are said to be "distinguishable." Courts are not bound to follow a precedent that can be distinguished. For example, suppose Betty's lawyer cites a precedent in which the defendant pulled a practical joke on a woman by informing her that her husband had been killed in an automobile accident. (The defendant knew that the husband was still alive.) In this case cited as a precedent, the court held that the defendant was liable for intentional infliction of emotional distress. Fred's lawyer would distinguish the precedent by arguing that a key fact is different—Betty's precedent involved informing a woman that her *husband* had been killed, whereas in the present case Betty was informed that her *dog* had been killed. The judge in the present case would not be bound to follow the precedent if the judge determines that the precedent has been sufficiently distinguished. Of course, no two cases are factually identical; therefore any two cases can be distinguished to some degree. When a precedent goes against your client's interests, it is always worthwhile to distinguish the facts of the precedent case from the facts of your client's case.

Overruling Precedent. Sometimes a court refuses to follow precedent. Changes in technology, economic conditions, or society's attitudes may convince a court to depart from precedent. Probably the most famous example of a court overruling precedent is the U.S. Supreme Court case of *Brown v. Board of Education*.[5] In *Brown*, the court held that separate educational facilities for whites and blacks were inherently unequal. Decided in 1954, this case expressly overruled the court's previous decision in *Plessy v. Ferguson*[6] (1896), which had upheld the constitutionality of "separate but equal" facilities. *Brown* reflected a change in society's attitude toward racial segregation. As Judge Musmanno of the Pennsylvania Supreme Court once stated, "Where justice demands, reason dictates, equality enjoins, and fair play decrees a change in judge-made law, courts will not lack in determination to establish that change. . . ."[7] Nevertheless, the vast majority of cases are decided according to precedent because of the doctrine of stare decisis.

A Sample Opinion. Our discussion of case law would not be complete without looking at an example of a court's opinion in a case. It is very important for a paralegal to be able to read and understand opinions. To illustrate how to read an opinion, we have numerically annotated a 1978 opinion by the Fifth Circuit Court of Appeals. It appears as Figure 3-2. The numerical annotations are explained in the following section.

FIGURE 3-2 ANNOTATED OPINION IN *NIETO v. PENCE*

1 640 578 FEDERAL REPORTER, 2d SERIES

Jenny NIETO, a/k/a Jenny Nieto Soto, Plaintiff-Appellant,

2 v.

Bill PENCE, Individually and d/b/a Import Motor Co., Inc., Defendant-Appellee.

3 No. 76-3983.

4 United States Court of Appeals, Fifth Circuit.

5 Aug. 21, 1978.

6 Rehearing Denied Oct. 20, 1978.

7 The United States District Court for the Western District of Texas at El Paso, William S. Sessions, J., in an action brought by a buyer under the Motor Vehicle Information and Cost Savings Act, held that actual knowledge on the part of the defendant dealer that the odometer reading on the vehicle was less than the number of miles it actually had traveled was required for liability. The buyer appealed. The Court of Appeals, Godbold, Circuit Judge, held that constructive knowledge was sufficient.

8 Vacated in part, reversed in part and remanded.

9 **1. Trade Regulation 🔑861**

Under Motor Vehicle Information and Cost Savings Act, transferor who lacks actual knowledge that odometer reading is incorrect may still have duty to state that actual mileage is unknown, and seller had duty to disclose that actual mileage was unknown where, in exercise of reasonable care, he would have had reason to know that mileage was more than that which odometer had recorded or previous owner had certified. Motor Vehicle Information and Cost Savings Act, §§ 401–411, 15 U.S.C.A. §§ 1981–1991.

2. Trade Regulation 🔑861

Violation of Motor Vehicle Information and Cost Savings Act does not necessarily lead to civil liability. Motor Vehicle Information and Cost Savings Act, § 409, 15 U.S.C.A. § 1989.

3. Trade Regulation 🔑864

Absent explanation, automobile dealer's sole dominion of vehicle tends to show his responsibility for altered odometer, and his failure to disclose that odometer reading is incorrect is evidence of intent to defraud. Motor Vehicle Information and Cost Savings Act, § 409, 15 U.S.C.A. § 1989.

4. Trade Regulation 🔑864

Vehicle transferor who lacked actual knowledge of accuracy of odometer reading may still be found to have intended to defraud and thus may be civilly liable for failure to disclose that actual mileage is unknown; if transferor reasonably should have known that odometer reading was incorrect, although he did not know to certainty that transferee would be defrauded, court may infer that he understood risk of such occurrence. Motor Vehicle Information and Cost Savings Act, § 409, 15 U.S.C.A. § 1989. 9

5. Federal Courts 🔑937

Where it was unclear whether district court's finding that individual was properly doing business as corporation was intended to preclude buyer's attempting to enforce judgment, under Motor Vehicle Information and Cost Savings Act, against such individual as such, or whether it would have that effect, and where Court of Appeals was likewise uncertain whether evidence adequately supported conclusion that, under Texas Law, individual was properly doing business as corporation, finding was vacated for reconsideration by the district court. Motor Vehicle Information and Cost Savings Act, §§401–411, 408(a, b), 409, 410, 15 U.S.C.A. §§ 1981–1991, 1988(a, b), 1989, 1990.

Miguel Solis, El Paso, Tex., for plaintiff-appellant. 10

Bill Pence, pro se.

Appeal from the United States District Court for the Western District of Texas. 11

Before GODBOLD, SIMPSON and MORGAN, Circuit Judges. 12

Source: Reprinted with permission from 578 F.2d 640. Copyright © 1978 by West Publishing Co.

FIGURE 3-2 ANNOTATED OPINION IN *NIETO v. PENCE* (Cont.)

13 GODBOLD, Circuit Judge:

14 Plaintiff in this case seeks to invoke civil liability under the Motor Vehicle Information and Cost Savings Act, 15 U.S.C. §§ 1981–1991, against an automobile dealer who sold her a motor vehicle and did not have actual knowldge, but may have had constructive knowledge, that the odometer reading on the vehicle was less than the number of miles it actually had traveled, and who failed to disclose that the mileage was unknown. The district court held that actual knowledge was required for liability. We conclude that constructive knowledge is sufficient, and reverse.

15 In 1975 plaintiff purchased in Texas from defendant,[1] used car dealer or dealers, for $600, a 10-year-old pickup truck with an odometer reading of 14,736 miles. Pursuant to the Act, defendant furnished to plaintiff an odometer mileage statement disclosure form. The Act requires that, pursuant to rules promulgated by the Secretary of Transportation, any transferor must give the following written disclosure to the transferee in connection with the transfer of ownership of a motor vehicle:

(1) Disclosure of the cumulative mileage registered on the odometer.

(2) Disclosure that the actual mileage is unknown, if the odometer reading is known to the transferor to be different from the number of miles the vehicle has actually traveled.

15 U.S.C. § 1988(a). The Act also provides,

It shall be a violation of this section for any transferor to violate any rules under this section or to knowingly give a false statement to a transferee in making any disclosure required by such rules.

15 U.S.C. § 1988(b).

Defendant stated on the disclosure form that the odometer reading at the time of sale was 14,736 miles. Defendant did not check the box on the form that says: "I further state that the actual mileage differs from the odometer reading for reasons other than odometer calibration error and that the actual mileage is unknown." Defendant had purchased the truck from another used-car dealer who certified the odometer reading at the time of transfer as 14,290 miles and did not state that the actual mileage was unknown. That dealer had bought the truck from another dealer who had certified the odometer reading at the time of transfer at 14,290 miles and had not stated that the actual mileage was unknown.

16 Plaintiff sued under 15 U.S.C. § 1989 which provides that:

"Any person who, with intent to defraud, violates any requirement imposed under this chapter shall be liable . . ."

17 The district court found that defendant had no actual knowledge that the odometer reading differed from the actual mileage and also that defendant did not intend to defraud plaintiff. The court made no finding whether defendant had constructive knowledge that the odometer reading differed from the actual mileage. There was evidence tending to establish that defendant reasonably should have known that the odometer reading differed from the actual mileage. The odometer reading was very low for a ten-year-old truck, and defendant Pence admitted he would be suspicious of an odometer reading of 14,000 miles on a truck that old. Pence had been in the auto business approximately 12 years.

18 [1] The legislative history indicates that a transferor who lacks actual knowledge that the odometer reading is incorrect may still have a duty to state that the actual mileage is unknown. The Senate Report addressed the very situation this case presents:

> [Section 1988] makes it a violation of the title for any person "knowingly" to give a false statement to a transferee. This section originally allowed a person to rely completely on the representations of the previous owner. This original provision created a potential loophole, however. For example, a person could have purchased a vehicle knowing that the mileage was false but

1. We use the singular "defendant" and the pronoun "he" for simplicity.

FIGURE 3-2 ANNOTATED OPINION IN *NIETO v. PENCE* (Cont.)

> received a statement from the transferor verifying the odometer reading. Suppose an auto dealer bought a car with a 20,000 mile odometer verification but any mechanic employed by that auto dealer could ascertain that the vehicle had at least 60,000 miles on it. The bill as introduced would have permitted the dealer to resell the vehicle with a 20,000 mile verification. In order to eliminate this potential loophole the test of "knowingly" was incorporated so that the auto dealer with expertise now would have an affirmative duty to mark "true mileage unknown" if, in the exercise of reasonable care, he would have reason to know that the mileage was more than that which the odometer had recorded or which the previous owner had certified.

1972 U.S. Code Cong. & Admin. News pp. 3971–72. Thus defendant had a duty to disclose that the actual mileage was unknown if, in the exercise of reasonable care, he would have had reason to know that the mileage was more than that which the odometer had recorded or the previous owner had certified. [18]

[2] The legislative history makes clear that, if defendant had constructive knowledge that the odometer reading was incorrect, he violated § 1989. A separate question is whether defendant can be civilly liable for the violation. Because § 1989 requires intent to defraud, a violation does not automatically lead to civil liability.

[3] Several district courts have considered whether a transferor can be civilly liable for a failure to disclose that a vehicle's actual mileage is unknown when he lacked actual knowledge [19] that the odometer reading was incorrect. One district court has held that a transferor can be found to have had the requisite intent to defraud only if he had actual knowledge that the odometer reading was incorrect. *Mataya v. Behm Motors, Inc.*, 409 F.Supp. 65, 69–70 (E.D.Wis. 1976). Other district courts have held that a transferor may have intended to defraud even if he lacked actual knowledge that the odometer reading was incorrect. *Pepp v. Superior Pontiac GMC, Inc.*, 412 F.Supp. 1053, 1055–56 (E.D.La.1976) (intent to defraud may be inferred from gross negligence); *Jones v. Fenton Ford, Inc.*, 427 F.Supp. 1328, 1333–36 (D.Conn. 1977)(intent to defraud inferred from recklessness); *Kantorczyk v. New Stanton Auto Auction, Inc.*, 433 F.Supp. 889, 893 (W.D.Pa.1977) (intent to defraud found in reckless disregard); *see Stier v. Park Pontiac, Inc.*, 391 F.Supp. 397 (S.D.W.Va.1975) (court held that transferors with constructive knowledge may be liable without discussing intent to defraud); *Duval v. Midwest Auto City, Inc.*, 425 F.Supp. 1381, 1387 (D.Neb.1977) (court held transferor with constructive knowledge liable without discussing intent to defraud).[2] [20]

[4] We hold that a transferor who lacked actual knowledge may still be found to have intended to defraud and thus may be civilly liable for a failure to disclose that a vehicle's actual mileage is unknown. A transferor may not close his eyes to the truth. If a transferor reasonably should have known that a vehicle's odometer reading was incorrect, although he did not know to a certainty the transferee would be defrauded, a court may infer that he understood the risk of such an occurrence.[3] [21]

2. District courts have also inferred intent to defraud in cases where the defendant was charged with tampering with a vehicle's odometer yet claimed ignorance. *Delay v. Hearn Ford*, 373 F.Supp. 791 (D.S.C.1974); see *Klein v. Pincus*, 397 F.Supp. 847 (E.D.N.Y.1975). Absent an explanation, a defendant's sole dominion of a vehicle tends to show his responsibility for an altered odometer, and his failure to disclose that the odometer reading is incorrect is evidence of intent to defraud. In tampering cases, however, the inferences courts have drawn go to show that the defendant tampered with the odometer, and thus the inferences tend to show actual knowledge as well as intent to defraud.

3. Our conclusion is rooted in the facts of this case. The Senate Report suggests that auto dealers should adopt business practices reasonably calculated to uncover incorrect odometer readings. Plaintiff presented no evidence that defendant had not adopted such business practices, and defendant offered no evidence that he had. Thus we do not

FIGURE 3-2 ANNOTATED OPINION IN *NIETO v. PENCE* (Cont.)

22

Moreover, unless a violation of the Act can lead to civil liability the Act is toothless. The district court holding there could be no intent to defraud in the absence of actual knowledge countered this obvious argument by noting that the U.S. Attorney General can petition for injunctive relief even when the transferor lacks an intent to defraud. *Mataya, supra*, 409 F.Supp. at 69–70; *see* 15 U.S.C. § 1990. *But see Jones, supra*, 427 F.Supp. at 1333. But such relief, although theoretically available, is unlikely. Private prosecution is needed to make the Act effective.

23

[5] Plaintiff asserts that the court erred in finding that defendant Pence properly did business as Import Motor Co., Inc., and in failing to find that Pence is individually liable in this suit. Plaintiff signed a form titled "Retail Order for a Motor Vehicle" which describes the specific vehicle and gives the terms of and conditions of the so-called "order." The "order" is "accepted" by the seller, presumably by its being initialled. The "order" form was headed, in large type, "Pence Enterprises, Inc." and, on the next line, in smaller but clearly legible type, "Import Motor Co., Inc." The form bears initials described as those of the salesman, and opposite the word "manager's," the initials "B.P.," which we infer are the initials of Pence. In his pro se brief on appeal Pence says that he was employed by Import Motor Co., Inc., as its sales manager. Various correspondence from Pence to the district court is on a letterhead of Import Motor Co., Inc., and signed by Pence as "owner," and the original pleading filed in this case by Import is signed by Pence as "owner." In other instances he has referred to himself as president of Import. At trial Pence testified that he was president of Pence Enterprises, Inc., which did business as Import Motors, Inc., and was sales manager of Import Motors. However, it was not until January 1976, after this suit was filed, that Pence Enterprises, Inc., (or Pence individually, it is not clear which) filed a certificate of authority to do business under the assumed name of Import Motor Co., Inc., which the parties appear to presume is required by Texas law.

We are unclear whether the court's finding that Pence was properly doing business as Import Motor Co., Inc., was intended to preclude the plaintiff's attempting to enforce a judgment against Pence individually, or whether it would have that effect. Nor are we certain that the evidence adequately supports the conclusion that, under Texas law, Pence was properly doing business as Import Motors. We, therefore, vacate this finding in order that the court may reconsider it and enter new findings and conclusions.

23

24

VACATED in part, REVERSED in part and REMANDED.

need to decide whether a court might infer from the failure to adopt such practices that a dealer knew his practices would work to defraud some of the people with whom he would deal or conversely whether a court might infer from the adoption of such practices that a dealer lacked constructive knowledge or intent to defraud.

Explanation of Opinion

1. The opinion can be found in volume 578 of the *Federal Reporter, 2d Series*, beginning on page 640.
2. The name of the case is *Nieto v. Pence.* Nieto was the plaintiff in the trial court and the appellant (the party bringing the appeal) in the appellate court. Pence was the defendant in the trial court and the appellee (the party against whom an appeal is brought) in the appellate court.
3. Docket number or calendar number of the case
4. Name of the court writing the opinion
5. Date of the decision
6. Date on which a rehearing was denied
7. The one-paragraph summary of the opinion is written by the editors of the reporter, *not* by the court, and therefore is not officially "law." However, this summary can be an important aid when doing legal research because it quickly tells you what the case is about.
8. Explanation of what will happen procedurally as a result of the decision
9. Headnotes. Headnotes are one-paragraph summaries of each point of law addressed in the case. Again, because headnotes are written by the editors, not by the court, they are not official law. Headnotes are numbered consecutively (here, 1–5). Each headnote number corresponds to a bracketed number in the actual text of the opinion. If you wanted to read only that portion of the opinion dealing with headnote 3, then you would go to the section of the opinion beginning with [3].

   In reporters published by West Publishing Company, editors write the headnote paragraphs summarizing each point of law addressed in the opinion and then assign a topic and a key number to each headnote. Headnotes 1 and 2 have been assigned the topic Trade Regulation and the key number 861. (How to research case law using the West key number system will be explained further in Chapter 7.)
10. These are the attorneys representing the parties; note that here Pence is representing himself.
11. Name of the court from which the appeal is taken
12. Names of the judges deciding the case
13. This is the name of the judge writing the opinion of the court. Note that the opinion of the court actually begins here; everything preceding this point was written by the editors.
14. This introductory paragraph briefly summarizes the legal and factual basis of the plaintiff's claim, the holding of the trial court, and the appellate court's holding. The holding is the rule of law announced by the court in a case.
15. These paragraphs summarize the relevant *facts* of the case. When reading an opinion, pay close attention to the facts. Remember: the more similarities that exist between the facts of the case you are reading and the facts of your client's case, the more likely the law of the case will be applied to your client's case. If the two cases are factually dissimilar,

then it is much more doubtful that the law of the case you are reading will be applied to your client's case.

16. This paragraph states the rule, or law, that will be applied in this case. The rule here is a federal statute, 15 U.S.C. § 1989.
17. This paragraph provides additional facts. Such facts as ". . .defendant reasonably should have known that the odometer reading differed from the actual mileage" help form the basis of the court's holding in the case. Be aware that sometimes the facts of the case will be found scattered throughout the opinion instead of at the beginning.
18. After setting forth the facts, the court is now ready to address the first issue raised in the case. An **issue** is a point of law disputed by the parties. Sometimes the court will identify the issue for you by making a statement such as "The issue raised in this case is whether. . . ." Other times, such as here in our sample opinion, you must identify the issue yourself by reading the opinion carefully. The first issue raised in this case might be stated in this way: Does a seller of a motor vehicle who lacks actual knowledge that an odometer reading is incorrect still have a duty to state that the actual mileage is unknown? The rule the court must apply to answer this issue is 15 U.S.C. § 1988, which makes it a violation for any person "knowingly" to give a false statement concerning the odometer reading to a buyer. But what does it mean to "knowingly" give a false statement? If the seller lacks actual knowledge that the odometer reading is incorrect, is it possible to "knowingly" give a false statement? To answer that question, the court must determine what the legislature intended when it used the word "knowingly." Here the court reviews the legislative history in order to determine the legislative intent. The Senate report relating to the legislation in question clearly indicated that if, in the exercise of reasonable care, the seller would have reason to know that the mileage was more than the odometer indicated, the seller has the duty to state that the actual mileage is unknown.
19. The second issue raised in the case might be stated this way: May a seller of a motor vehicle who lacks actual knowledge that the odometer reading is incorrect nevertheless be found to have the required "intent to defraud" and thus be found liable for failure to disclose that the vehicle's mileage is unknown?
20. Here the court reviews the case law addressing the issue. One case, *Mataya v. Behm Motors*, is cited for the rule that the seller has the required "intent to defraud" only if the seller has *actual knowledge* that the odometer reading is incorrect. However, five cases are cited in support of the proposition that sellers may have the required "intent to defraud" even if they lack actual knowledge that an odometer reading is incorrect. These five cases support the court's decision in this case and serve as precedent. Are these cases binding or persuasive in character? Note that all the cases cited by the court are federal district court cases. District

courts are trial courts in the federal court system, whereas the court deciding the *Nieto* case is a federal appellate court. Appellate courts are not bound to follow the decisions of trial courts. Therefore the cases cited by the court are persuasive precedents.

21. The **holding** is the rule of law announced by the court in a case. The holding is the way in which the legal issue in the case is decided. Only the holding of a case is binding on courts in subsequent cases. Most of the time the court will state what the holding of the case is. Other times you will need to determine the holding on your own.
22. Rationale supporting the holding
23. Under [5], the court looks at an unrelated issue: Is the defendant, Pence, *individually* liable in this case? The trial court found that Pence was properly doing business as Import Motors. A **finding** is the decision of a court on a factual issue. However, the appellate court is not sure whether that finding was intended to preclude a judgment against Pence individually. Nor is the court sure that that finding was supported by the evidence. Therefore the court vacates, or sets aside, the finding.
24. The procedural consequences of the court's holding: The court vacates the trial court's finding that Pence was properly doing business as Import Motors. The court reverses the trial court's judgment in favor of Pence. A judgment is the final decision of a court determining the rights and responsibilities of the parties. The court remands (sends back) the case to the trial court for a new trial to be carried out in a manner consistent with the principles announced by the court in its opinion.

Statutory Law

So far we have discussed two sources of law, constitutional law and case law. Statutes are the third source of law we will consider.

Statutes are laws enacted by state and federal legislatures. The term statutory law also encompasses laws (such as municipal ordinances) passed by lesser governmental bodies.

Codification. Historically, cases were the chief source of law in our Anglo-American common law system. Since the middle of the nineteenth century, however, statutes have become our chief source of law. Much of the common law that was made in earlier centuries has been enacted into statute by legislatures, a process known as **codification**. Today, legislatures are better suited to respond to the issues facing our society than are courts. Courts deal with only those issues raised in actual cases, while legislatures are free to address whatever issues they choose. In addition, we have seen how courts look to the past for guidance and are hesitant to overturn established precedents. Legislatures, looking to the future, are free to make sweeping and comprehensive changes in the law.

Ranking Statutory Law and Case Law. Legal researchers who are looking for the law that applies to a particular situation frequently check statutes first. Statutory law ranks above case law in the law hierarchy. This means that if there exists a statute that addresses the legal issue and factual situation presented in a case, the case will be decided on the basis of what the statute says. However, because statutes tend to be written in broad language, it is the function of the courts to interpret a statute and apply it to specific factual situations. Therefore researchers must check also for any cases that apply the statute. Cases help the researcher understand what the statute really means. For example, in the sample case of *Nieto v. Pence*, the court had to determine whether the defendant had an "intent to defraud" as required by the statute in order for liability to exist. The court had to interpret the statute and apply it to the specific factual situation.

A Sample Statute. The following statute, 15 U.S.C. § 1989, is the one that was interpreted and applied in the sample case of *Nieto v. Pence.* The statute is published in Title 15 of the *United States Code*, Section 1989.

§ 1989. Civil actions to enforce liability for violations of odometer requirements; amount of damages; jurisdiction; period of limitation

(a) Any person who, with intent to defraud, violates any requirement imposed under this subchapter shall be liable in an amount equal to the sum of—

(1) three times the amount of actual damages sustained or $1,500, whichever is the greater; and

(2) in the case of any successful action to enforce the foregoing liability, the costs of the action together with reasonable attorney fees as determined by the court.

(b) An action to enforce any liability created under subsection (a) of this section, may be brought in a United States district court without regard to the amount in controversy, or in any other court of competent jurisdiction, within two years from the date on which the liability arises.

(Pub.L. 92-513, Title IV, § 409, Oct. 20, 1972, 86 Stat. 963.)

Administrative Law

Administrative law is the fourth source of law we will discuss. **Administrative law** consists of the rules, regulations, orders, and decisions made by administrative agencies. **Administrative agencies** are governmental bodies such as boards, bureaus, commissions, departments, divisions, and offices that have the power to make rules, enforce rules, and decide controversies arising under those rules.

Although the U.S. Constitution created only three branches of government—legislative, executive, and judicial—and did not mention administrative agencies, agencies are sometimes known as the fourth branch of government. Administrative agencies influence American life in such important areas as national defense, taxation, labor relations, occupational safety, environmental protection, education, and trade and commerce.

Federal Administrative Agencies. Federal administrative agencies can be classified as either **executive agencies** or **independent agencies**. Executive agencies are considered part of the executive branch of government, while independent agencies are separate from the executive branch.

Most administrative agencies are executive agencies. Executive agencies include each of the departments represented in the president's cabinet (U.S. Departments of Transportation, Agriculture, Commerce, etc.) as well as agencies within those departments. For example, the Occupational Safety and Health Administration (OSHA) functions within the Department of Labor. The term executive agency applies also to certain agencies that function outside the cabinet departments but are not considered independent; the Office of Management and Budget is an example.

Independent agencies are made up of either five-member or seven-member commissions appointed by the president. Examples of independent agencies include the Environmental Protection Agency (EPA), Federal Communications Commission (FCC), Securities and Exchange Commission (SEC), and National Labor Relations Board (NLRB).

Delegating Legislative Power to Agencies. Administrative agencies are created by acts of Congress called *enabling statutes.* A federal agency has only the power expressly stated by Congress in its enabling statute. Typically, enabling statutes delegate to administrative agencies three kinds of power: (1) rulemaking power, (2) enforcement power, and (3) the power to adjudicate controversies. Rulemaking power is legislative power; enforcement power is executive power; and the power to adjudicate controversies is judicial power. Administrative agencies therefore exercise the same types of power that have been given to the three separate branches of government by the Constitution.

The **Administrative Procedure Act (APA)** outlines the basic procedures to be followed in rulemaking and adjudication. Congress enacted the APA in 1946 to standardize agency procedures, curb the arbitrary exercise of power, and promote fairness in agency hearings.

Rulemaking. Rulemaking is the process by which an administrative agency creates rules and regulations. Rules made by an administrative agency have the force of law. The APA provides for two types of rulemaking, informal and formal.

Informal rulemaking, which is sometimes known as notice-and-comment rulemaking, follows three steps. First, notice of the proposed rule must be published in the *Federal Register*, which prints both proposed rules and adopted rules. Second, interested parties must be given the opportunity to submit written data, views, or arguments concerning the proposed rule. At the discretion of the agency, an informal hearing on the proposed rule may be held. Third, after evaluating public comments, the agency must publish the final rule in the *Federal Register.*

Formal rulemaking allows interested parties a more extensive opportunity to comment on a proposed rule. If the statute delegating rulemaking power to the agency requires that rules be made "on the record" after opportunity for an agency hearing, then the APA's formal rulemaking procedures must be followed.

Formal rulemaking begins with a public notice of the proposed rule, followed by a hearing to determine the relevant facts. The hearing is similar to a trial in that interested parties have a right to testify and cross-examine witnesses. After the hearing, the agency makes formal findings of fact, reaches conclusions of law, and adopts the final rule. The findings of fact, conclusions of law, final rule, and transcript of the proceedings together make up what is called the record.

Enforcement. Administrative agencies are empowered to enforce the rules they make. Agencies investigate suspected violations of rules and have the power to compel disclosure of information by such means as issuing subpoenas.

Adjudication. Administrative agencies have power that is judicial in nature. An agency determines the facts of a case and applies its rules to the facts in a manner similar to that of a court. The Administrative Procedure Act sets standards that agencies must meet when performing their judicial function, although the procedures used vary among agencies.

Most cases begin with an agency investigation of a possible violation. Often, when evidence of a violation exists, the case is settled through a consent order procedure: the offender consents to an order to cease and desist in the violation.

If the dispute is not settled through consent order, it reaches the hearing stage. Administrative agency rules and policies are litigated at hearings conducted by an **administrative law judge**. The administrative law judge makes an initial decision that may be appealed by any party; if no appeal is entered, the judge's decision becomes final. In an appeal, briefs are submitted and oral arguments may be heard by the agency. If the agency involved is the SEC (Securities and Exchange Commission), for example, the appeal is made to the commission. Following the appeal, the agency reaches a final decision.

Judicial Review. Nearly all administrative agency actions are subject to review by the courts. When a court reviews an agency's exercise of its rulemaking power, the court determines whether the agency has (1) acted within the scope of the authority granted to the agency by Congress or (2) violated any constitutional provision. When a court reviews an agency's exercise of its adjudicatory or judicial function, the court determines whether the agency has (1) violated any procedural requirements; (2) violated any constitutional provision; (3) exceeded its jurisdiction; (4) reached a decision that is arbitrary, capricious, or an abuse of the agency's discretion; or (5) reached a decision that is not supported by substantial evidence. Courts also have limited power to review the agency's interpretation of the applicable law.

THE COURT SYSTEM

A **court** is a tribunal established by a government to settle disputes. The federal government has its own court system, as does each of the fifty states and the District of Columbia.

The federal court system and most state court systems have a common basic structure. This structure is best described as a pyramid with the highest (supreme) court at the top, the intermediate appellate courts in the middle, and the trial courts at the bottom. Some less-populated states have two levels instead of three. Figure 3-3 is a simplified view of the federal and state court structures.

FIGURE 3-3 SIMPLIFIED VIEW OF FEDERAL AND STATE COURT STRUCTURES

FEDERAL COURT SYSTEM

U.S. Supreme Court

U.S. Courts of Appeals

U.S. District Courts

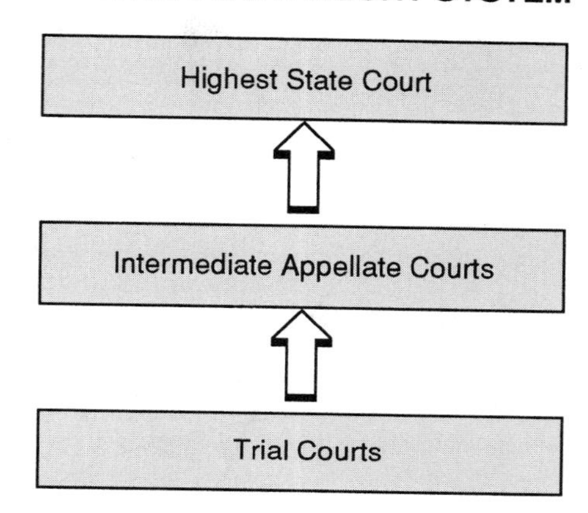

Trial Courts and Appellate Courts

Trial courts are courts of original jurisdiction, which means they are where the litigation (lawsuit) begins. **Jurisdiction** is a court's power to hear and determine a case. Some trial courts have **limited jurisdiction**. For example, a trial court might be limited to hearing cases in which the amount in controversy is less than $25,000. Other trial courts have **general jurisdiction** or **unlimited jurisdiction**.

Appellate courts are courts of appeals, which review the record of what took place at trial to determine if the trial court made an error. Appellate courts do not hear new evidence (no witnesses are called), and they do not challenge the trial court's findings of fact. Appellate courts review only questions of law and procedure.

An appellate court will overturn the decision of a trial court only if a reversible error was committed. A **reversible error** is an error that substantially affects the appellant's (appealing party's) legal rights and must be corrected in order to prevent a miscarriage of justice. A reversible error is also known as a **prejudicial error**. An appellate court will not overturn the decision of a trial court if only a harmless error was committed. As an example of a harmless error, suppose a trial judge allows a witness to testify about matters that are irrelevant to the lawsuit, but the irrelevant testimony does not affect the appellant's legal rights or prejudice the outcome of the case. The error will be declared harmless and the trial court's decision will not be overturned. As an example of a reversible or prejudicial error, suppose a trial judge incorrectly instructs the jury as to the applicable law in the case. Because this error may have affected the appellant's legal rights, the trial court's decision will be overturned.

Federal Courts

Article III of the U.S. Constitution provides that the "judicial power of the United States shall be vested in one Supreme Court, and in such inferior courts as the

Congress may from time to time ordain and establish.'' Congress has established a federal court system consisting of district courts, courts of appeal, the U.S. Supreme Court, and various special courts. Examples of special courts include the United States Claims Court, United States Tax Court, and the United States Military Courts.

District Courts. District courts are the trial courts in the federal court system. Ordinarily, a federal lawsuit begins in a district court. District courts have general jurisdiction, which means they have the power to hear and decide most cases.

Each federal judicial district is located entirely within a particular state. Sparsely populated states have one judicial district that covers the entire state; other states have two, three, or four districts.

U.S. Courts of Appeals. Appeals from the district courts are made to the courts of appeals. Congress has established twelve judicial circuits (eleven numbered circuits plus the D.C. Circuit), each with a circuit court of appeals that hears appeals from the district courts located within it. For example, appeals from the district courts located in Illinois, Indiana, and Wisconsin are made to the Seventh Circuit. There is also a thirteenth circuit, called the Federal Circuit, which has national jurisdiction over particular types of cases. Figure 3-4 shows the geographical boundaries of the U.S. courts of appeals.

POINTER: Court rules vary from circuit to circuit. Therefore it is important to consult the rules for the particular court that is hearing the appeal.

The U.S. Supreme Court. The United States Supreme Court is the highest court in the nation. It consists of nine justices, including the chief justice and eight associate justices. The Supreme Court is an appellate court, although it does have original (trial) jurisdiction in certain types of cases. Most of the cases it reviews come from the U.S. Courts of Appeals, although some come from the highest court in a state (for example, when a state law is challenged as being in violation of the U.S. Constitution) and other federal courts.

When appealing a case to the U.S. Supreme Court, a party must petition for a **writ of certiorari**, an order issued by the Supreme Court to a lower court commanding the lower court to send the record of a case to the Supreme Court for review. Whether the Court will issue a writ, and therefore consider an appeal, is entirely discretionary; there is no absolute right to appeal to the Supreme Court in most cases.

State Courts

Most state court systems have the same three-tiered model as the federal court system. The case begins in the trial court, may be appealed (as a matter of right) to an intermediate appellate court, and may then be appealed to the highest court in the state. However, the state supreme court may choose not to hear the appeal. If a federal constitutional issue is involved, a writ of certiorari may be filed with the U.S. Supreme Court. Again, the U.S. Supreme Court may choose not to hear the appeal.

FIGURE 3-4 THE FEDERAL COURTS OF APPEALS

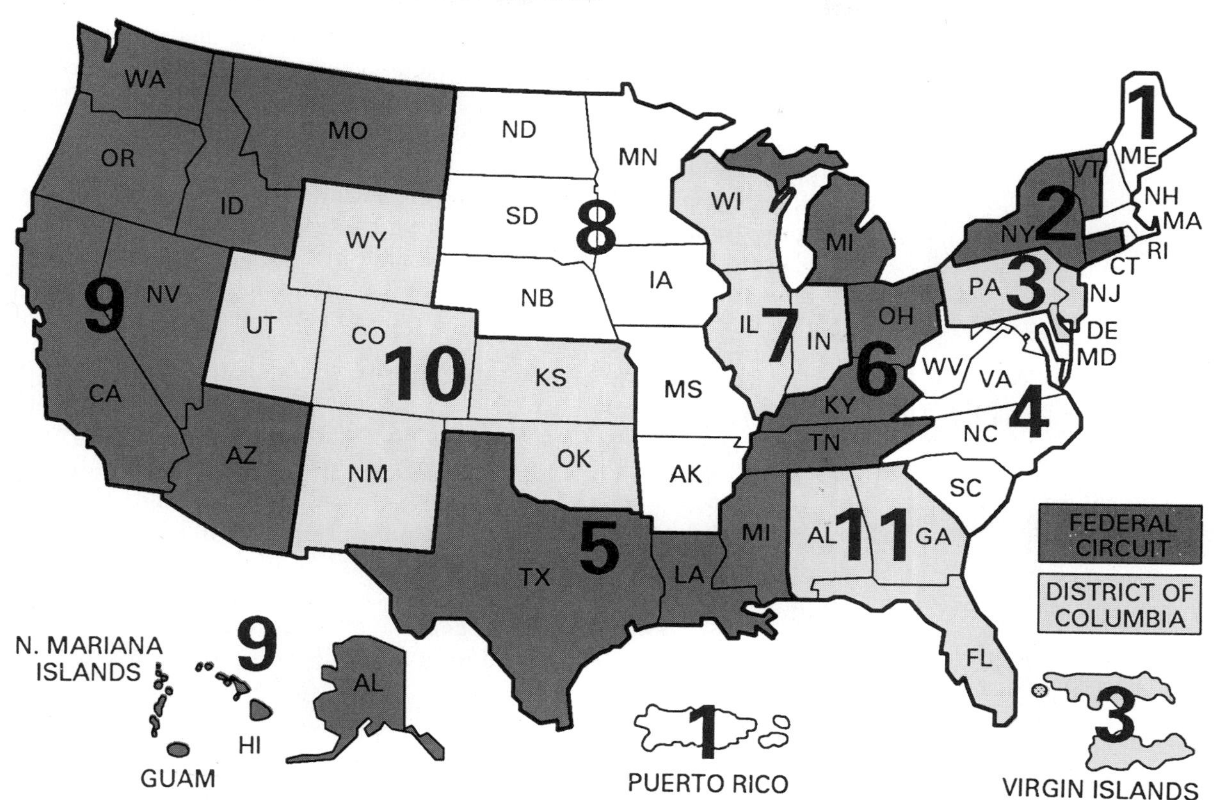

State trial courts are usually divided into two groups—courts of limited jurisdiction and courts of general (unlimited) jurisdiction. Courts of limited jurisdiction have titles such as municipal court, city court, or police court. Jurisdiction is limited to cases in which the amount in controversy is less than a particular amount (such as $10,000 or $25,000). Jurisdiction may also be limited by the subject matter of the case. For example, family law courts can hear only cases involving divorce and child custody matters, while probate courts can hear only cases involving the administration of a decedent's estate. Most states also have a small claims court in which the most a party may ask for ranges from $1,500 to $2,500.

In every state there is a court of general (or unlimited) jurisdiction for each county. These courts are known as superior courts, district courts, or circuit courts.

Every state has at least one appellate court, and most states have two. The intermediate court is frequently called the court of appeals, while the highest court in the state is usually called the supreme court. In New York, trial courts are called supreme courts while the highest court is called the court of appeals.

Applying *Stare Decisis* in the Court System

As we have just seen, the court system in the United States is a dual court system in which the state court systems parallel the federal court system. This dual court system creates certain problems in applying the doctrine of *stare decisis*. When, for example, is a state court bound to follow a federal court decision? Here is a summary of how *stare decisis* works:

1. U.S. Supreme Court decisions interpreting and applying federal law are binding (mandatory) on all federal and state courts.
2. The decisions of the highest court of a state are binding on all other courts in that state; they are persuasive in other states and in federal courts.
3. U.S. Court of Appeals decisions interpreting and applying federal law are binding on lower federal courts within the appellate court's jurisdictional boundaries and are persuasive in other federal courts and state courts. For example, the U.S. District Court for the Southern District of Texas is not bound by a decision of the Eleventh Circuit Court of Appeals, the decisions of which are binding only on those federal district courts located in Alabama, Florida, and Georgia. Figure 3-4 shows the jurisdictional boundaries of the U.S. Courts of Appeals. In addition, courts on the same level of the hierarchy are not bound to follow an opinion of a co-equal court. For example, the Court of Appeals for the Ninth Circuit is not bound to follow a decision of the Court of Appeals for the Fourth Circuit. See Figure 3-5 for a simplified view of *stare decisis* in the federal court system.
4. The decisions of a state's intermediate appellate court are binding on all lower state courts within its jurisdictional boundaries, may also be binding on lower courts in the state that are outside its jurisdictional boundaries, and are persuasive in other states and in federal courts.

JURISDICTION

Jurisdiction means the power of a court to hear and decide a case. In order for the decision of a court to be binding on the parties, a court must have two kinds of jurisdiction: (1) jurisdiction over the subject matter of the lawsuit, and (2) jurisdiction over the parties.

Subject Matter Jurisdiction

Subject matter jurisdiction refers to the court's power to hear and decide a particular *type* of case. For example, a particular state court might have subject matter jurisdiction only over divorce cases or cases in which the amount in controversy does not exceed $25,000. The subject matter jurisdiction of the federal courts is set forth in Article III, Section 2 of the U.S. Constitution:

> The judicial power shall extend to all cases, in law and equity, arising under this Constitution, the laws of the United States, and treaties made, or which shall be made, under their authority; to all cases affecting ambassadors, other public ministers and consuls; to all cases of admiralty and maritime

FIGURE 3-5 *STARE DECISIS* IN THE FEDERAL COURT SYSTEM

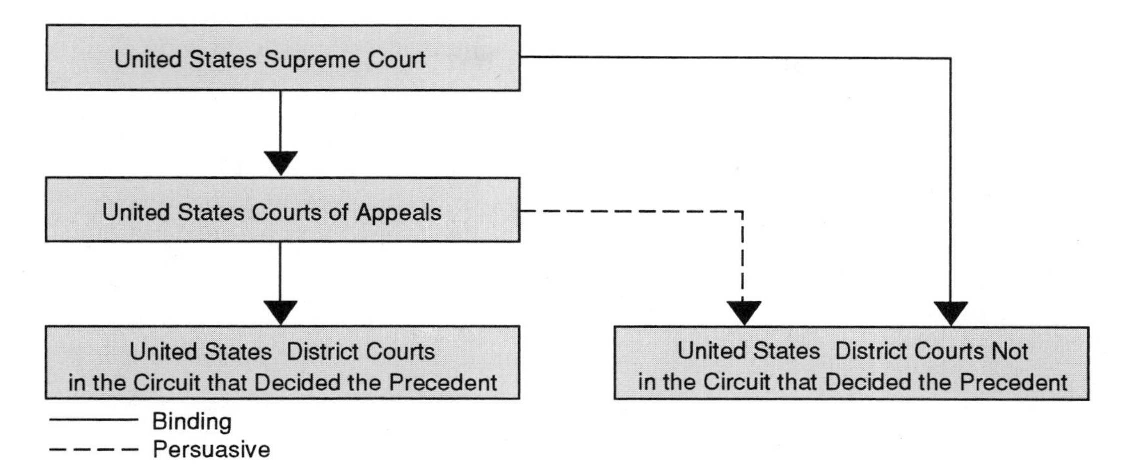

> jurisdiction; to controversies to which the United States shall be a party; to controversies between two or more States; between a State and citizens of another State; between citizens of different States; between citizens of the same State claiming lands under grants of different States, and between a State, or the citizens thereof, and foreign states, citizens or subjects.

Personal Jurisdiction

Once it is determined that a court has jurisdiction over the subject matter of a lawsuit, it must be determined whether the court has jurisdiction over the parties to the lawsuit. **Personal jurisdiction** is the power of the court to enter a personal judgment (impose personal liability) against a party to the action. A court has personal jurisdiction over a plaintiff because the plaintiff submits to the court's jurisdiction by filing the lawsuit in that court. The issue of personal jurisdiction, then, involves whether or not the court has the power to make the *defendant* come into that court. In other words, does the court have personal jurisdiction over the defendant?

In general, courts have jurisdiction over people and property located within the territorial boundaries of the states in which they are located. Jurisdiction is not a problem, therefore, when the defendant resides in the state in which the lawsuit is filed. The state in which the lawsuit is filed is known as the **forum state**.

The question of personal jurisdiction arises when the defendant is a nonresident of the forum state. The rules requiring personal jurisdiction over a defendant are designed to protect the defendant from having to defend in a state with which she or he has little connection. In order to ensure fairness to a defendant, and in order for personal jurisdiction to exist, a defendant must have "minimum contacts" with the state in which the lawsuit is filed.

Minimum Contacts. The minimum contacts test was established by the U.S. Supreme Court in the case of *International Shoe Co. v. State of Washington*, 326 U.S.

310 (1945). In that case, the Court stated that minimum contacts exist between a defendant and the state in which the lawsuit is filed if forcing the defendant to defend a lawsuit in that state does not offend traditional notions of fair play and substantial justice.

Minimum contacts is established if the cause of action arises out of the defendant's activity in the state. A **cause of action** is the legal claim on which the plaintiff is suing. Breach of contract, for example, is a cause of action. If a Texas defendant enters into a contract in Georgia, or commits a tort (civil wrong, such as a battery) in Georgia, then the Georgia courts have personal jurisdiction over the defendant. Minimum contacts is also established if the defendant conducts business within the state, and that business is the subject matter of the lawsuit. For example, a business based in New York that advertises in Florida and sells its products in Florida has minimum contacts with Florida, and the Florida courts have personal jurisdiction over the business.

Consider one more example. In *World-Wide Volkswagen Corp. v. Woodson*, 444 U.S. 286 (1980), one of the defendants was a New York automobile retailer who sold an automobile in New York to New York residents. The automobile was subsequently involved in an accident in Oklahoma, and suit was filed in Oklahoma. Because the defendant had no connection with Oklahoma other than the fact that the accident occurred there, the defendant did not have "minimum contacts" with Oklahoma. The Oklahoma court did not have personal jurisdiction over the defendant because it would not be fair to make the defendant defend the lawsuit in Oklahoma.

Long-Arm Statutes. A **long-arm statute** is a state law giving courts within the state jurisdiction over nonresident defendants. Some states have broad long-arm statutes that give the state courts jurisdiction over any nonresident defendant who has minimum contacts with the state. Other states have long-arm statutes that specify certain types of transactions or activities that would give the state courts jurisdiction over residents of a different state. For example, a state's long-arm statute might provide that if a nonresident motorist is involved in an accident within the state, the state courts may exercise personal jurisdiction over the nonresident motorist.

Notice. Considerations of fairness also require that defendants be notified of the lawsuit. This is accomplished through **service of process**, which is the delivery of the complaint and the summons in the lawsuit to the defendant. This topic will be discussed in Chapter 9.

In Rem Jurisdiction

***In rem* jurisdiction** is jurisdiction over property. Courts in a state have the power to decide claims regarding property located within the state. For example, if a resident of Nebraska and a resident of Rhode Island are involved in a lawsuit over the ownership of property located in New Mexico, then the New Mexico court has *in rem* jurisdiction to determine the rightful owner.

In rem jurisdiction is an alternative to personal jurisdiction. In order to hear and decide a case, a court must have either power over the person or power over the property involved in the action.

DIVISION OF JURISDICTION BETWEEN FEDERAL AND STATE COURTS

Because of the dual court system in the United States, some types of cases are tried in federal courts and others are tried in state courts. The first step in learning to determine whether federal or state is the proper court is recognizing that three types of cases exist: (1) cases that must be heard in federal court, (2) cases that may be heard in either federal court or state court, and (3) cases that must be heard in state court.

Exclusive Federal Jurisdiction

The federal courts have exclusive jurisdiction over certain types of cases. Cases involving antitrust laws, bankruptcy, trademarks, copyrights, patents, federal crimes, admiralty laws, suits against the United States, suits to review decisions of federal administrative agencies, and certain claims based on federal statutes must be brought in the federal courts.

Concurrent Federal and State Jurisdiction

Concurrent jurisdiction means that the case may be heard in either federal or state court. The two basic types of cases that may be heard in either federal or state court are federal question cases and diversity of citizenship cases.

Federal Question. **Federal question** cases arise whenever the plaintiff's claim is based on the U.S. Constitution, a treaty, or a federal statute. There is no minimum dollar amount requirement. For example, a plaintiff alleging that his or her constitutional rights have been violated may bring the action in federal or state court regardless of the dollar amount the plaintiff claims to have been damaged.

A plaintiff who sues in federal court on the basis of a federal question may join separate claims arising under state law when both claims are based on the same set of facts. This doctrine, known as **ancillary jurisdiction**, permits federal jurisdiction over nonfederal matters that are factually related to the federal question. For example, suppose a racial minority plaintiff is physically beaten by a group of police officers for no apparent reason. The plaintiff alleges a violation of rights under the equal protection clause and the Civil Rights Act. Both allegations are federal questions, therefore federal question jurisdiction exists in the federal court. The plaintiff also has a claim based on the tort of battery, which is a state law question. If all claims are heard in the same federal court, then the federal court has ancillary jurisdiction over the tort claim.

Diversity of Citizenship. **Diversity of citizenship** exists whenever the plaintiff and defendant are citizens of different states and the dollar amount in controversy exceeds $50,000. The citizenship of an individual is the state of domicile (residence), while the citizenship of a corporation is both the state of incorporation and the state where it has its principal place of business. (A corporation is a ''person'' in the eyes of the law, which means that a corporation can sue and be sued.) For example, suppose Juan is a resident of New Hampshire, and Widget Corporation is incorporated in Delaware and has its principal place of business in Alabama. If Juan sues Widget Corporation in federal court, diversity of citizenship jurisdiction exists provided that the amount in controversy exceeds $50,000.

POINTER: In a case involving multiple parties, diversity of citizenship exists only if each plaintiff has a different citizenship from each defendant. In other words, diversity is destroyed if one plaintiff is a citizen of the same state as one defendant. For example, if the plaintiffs are residents of Pennsylvania, New Jersey, and Iowa and the defendants are residents of Ohio and Iowa, diversity does not exist.

Whenever a case involves either a federal question or diversity of citizenship, the plaintiff may file the action in either federal or state court. However, if the plaintiff chooses to bring either a federal question case or a diversity of citizenship case in state court, the defendant usually has the right to remove (transfer) the case to federal court. This is known as **removal jurisdiction**.

Exclusive State Jurisdiction

State courts have exclusive jurisdiction over all other matters. For example, state courts have exclusive jurisdiction over cases involving divorce, probate, torts, contracts, and property if a federal ancillary claim or diversity of citizenship is not involved.

Figure 3-6 summarizes the division of jurisdiction between federal and state courts.

VENUE

Venue refers to the geographic location where a lawsuit *should* be brought. If the court has the power to hear this particular type of case (subject matter jurisdiction) and the power to bind the parties to its decision (personal jurisdiction), then the question of venue arises: Is this court in the geographic neighborhood where the case should be heard?

Venue rules reflect the policy that a case should be heard in the neighborhood where it is most convenient for the parties. State venue rules typically require that the case be heard in the county where the incident occurred or where one of the plaintiffs or defendants resides. If a particular court is not the proper venue, then the court will shift the case to a more convenient location.

POINTER: Venue rules vary from state to state. Consult your state's venue statute.

The federal venue statute is 28 U.S.C. § 1391. For cases based solely on diversity of citizenship, venue is proper in the district (1) where all plaintiffs reside, or (2) where all defendants reside, or (3) where the cause of action arose. For cases not based on diversity jurisdiction, venue is proper in the district (1) where all plaintiffs reside, or (2) where the cause of action arose.

FIGURE 3-6 FEDERAL AND STATE JURISDICTION

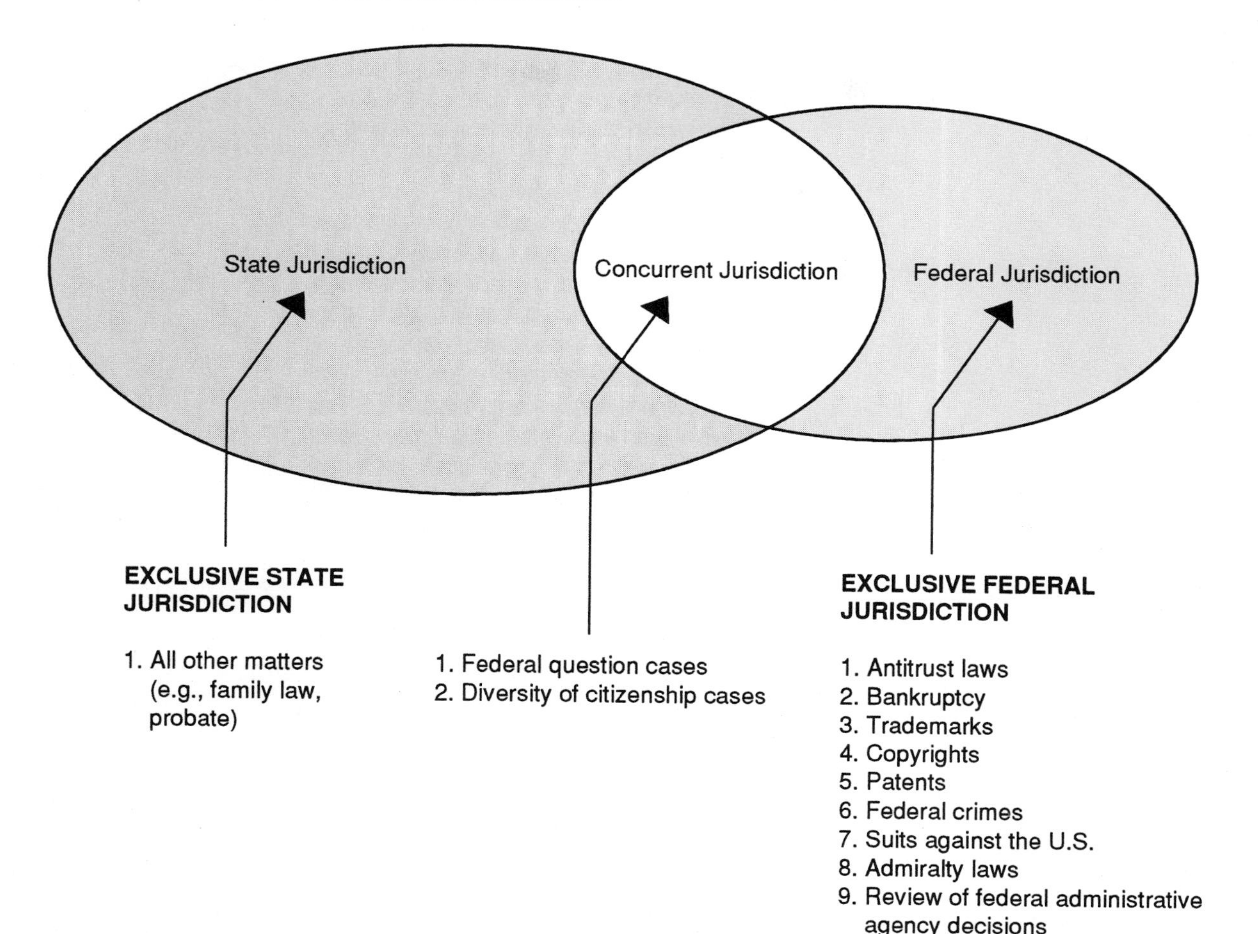

ENDNOTES

1 Kenneth W. Clarkson et al., *West's Business Law*, 4th ed. (St. Paul: West, 1989), p. 3.

2 Tort law is discussed in Chapter 5.

3 Ronald Anderson, Ivan Fox, and David Twomey, *Business Law and the Legal Environment* (Cincinnati: South-Western, 1990), p. 7.

4 J. David Reitzel et al., *Contemporary Business Law*, 4th ed. (New York: McGraw-Hill, 1990), pp. 11–12; Kenneth W. Clarkson et al., *West's Business Law*, 4th ed. (St. Paul: West, 1989), pp. 4–5.

5 *Brown v. Board of Education*, 347 U.S. 483 (1954).

6 *Plessy v. Ferguson*, 163 U.S. 537 (1896).

7 *Flagiello v. Pennsylvania Hospital*, 208 A.2d 193 (1965).

4 LEGAL TERMS AND CONCEPTS: CONTRACTS, TORTS, AND CRIMINAL LAW

INTRODUCTION: LEGAL LITERACY

Terminology plays a critically important role in the law. As you study to become a paralegal, you will learn the meanings of many legal terms. Once you begin working as a paralegal, however, you will discover that simply knowing standard definitions of various legal terms is not enough. This is true for several reasons.

First, most legal terms do not have a single precise definition. This is partly because many of them have been in use for hundreds of years, and with the passage of time their meanings have changed. Words that once had very precise meanings may have broader meanings now. The term heir, for example, traditionally referred only to those persons entitled to inherit the property of someone who died without leaving a will. Today the term is widely used by both judges and lawyers to refer to anyone who inherits property.

Second, many terms have more than one distinct meaning. For example, in law the term estate means both ''an interest in real property'' and ''the property owned by a person at his or her death.''

Third, the full definition of many legal terms requires reference to rules of law. For example, suppose someone asks you what a general partner is. You might begin by saying that a general partner is a member of a partnership. Then you would have to explain that a partnership is an association of individuals or legal entities who are the co-owners of a business and who share profits and losses generated by the business among themselves—or words to that effect. Next you might explain that a general partner is a partner who has particular legal rights and obligations with respect to the partnership; perhaps you would discuss what those particular rights and obligations are. You might conclude by comparing a general partner's rights and obligations with those of a limited partner. In short, you could not provide a fully accurate definition of general partner without referring to the legal rules that establish a general partner's rights and obligations.

This raises another problem. It is impossible to reduce the law on any given subject to a set of simple and precise rules. The law is often complex and sometimes uncertain. As a result, virtually every legal rule has exceptions. The more simply a rule is stated, the less accurate it may be. Legal scholars devote considerable time and energy to formulating legal rules. While everyone recognizes that these rules, often referred to as black-letter law or hornbook law, are useful, everyone acknowledges that these rules are by nature imprecise and incomplete. In order to ascertain what the law is on a particular subject, it is not enough to rely on the black-letter law. One must research the statutes and cases and then spend a fair amount of time analyzing them. This process will be examined in Chapters 7 and 8.

The purpose of Chapters 4 and 5 is to help you become familiar with several basic legal terms and concepts. In any legal dictionary most of the terms we introduce here will have multiple technical definitions. Those definitions should not concern you now. The definitions used in these chapters are intentionally neither technical nor comprehensive. They are designed to help you understand the basic meaning of terms. Similarly, the legal rules stated in these chapters are deliberate oversimplifications designed to give you a basic understanding of the law on various subjects.

In this chapter you will examine three areas of the law that form the foundation for every law student's study: the law of contracts, the law of torts, and criminal law. In the next chapter, you will study legal terms and concepts in the areas of real property law, business law, estate planning and probate, and family law.

As you begin your study of the law, keep in mind that the law is sometimes referred to as a "seamless web." You cannot unravel a web unless you locate a seam and find a thread to begin pulling. Similarly, you cannot understand the law unless you find the right place to begin your study of it. The problem is, there is no "right place" to begin a study of law. You cannot really understand the law as a whole until you understand all of its parts, and you cannot really understand any part unless you understand the law as a whole: thus the seamless-web analogy. But you must begin somewhere, and once you have begun, you will find that as you understand each part of the law, your understanding of the law as a whole will increase also.

CONTRACT LAW CONCEPTS

A **contract** is an agreement between two or more parties by which each party undertakes to perform, or not to perform, one or more specific acts.

Contracts form the basis of virtually all business relationships and many nonbusiness relationships as well. As you learned in Chapter 3, one of the basic purposes of law is the governing of relationships. With this objective in mind, the law provides that any contract that meets certain requirements imposes a legal obligation on each of the parties to the contract to perform in accordance with the contract. The parties to a contract may use the courts to enforce these legal obligations. For example, a party may ask a court to order a nonperforming party to perform in accordance with the contract, or to pay money to the other parties to compensate them for losses incurred as a result of the nonperformance. A contract that imposes on its parties legal obligations that are enforceable in court is said to be valid, binding, or enforceable.

In this brief overview of the law of contracts, you will learn how a contract is formed; the circumstances that excuse a party from performing in accordance with a contract; the grounds on which a party can prevent enforcement of a contract; and the remedies available to a party who has incurred loss due to another party's failure to perform under a contract.

Formation of a Contract

In order for a valid contract to be formed, each party to the contract must outwardly express an intention to be bound by its terms. Such an expression of intention need not be in any particular form. If the expression of intention consists of words, either spoken or written, the resulting contract is known as an **express contract**. The promissory note illustrated in Figure 4-1 is a simple example of an express contract. If the expression of intention consists of one or more actions, the resulting contract is known as an **implied contract**. Whatever form the outward expression of intention takes, the expression must be such that an average, reasonable person would interpret the words or actions involved to be an expression of an intention to be bound by the terms of a contract.

The parties' expressions of intention always arise in the context of one party's offer to be bound by the terms of a contract, and another party's acceptance of that offer.

Offer. All contracts begin with an offer. An **offer** is a proposal made by a party expressing the party's intention to enter into a contract. In order to constitute an offer, a proposal must meet three requirements: (1) it must consist of words or acts that an average, reasonable person would consider an expression of an intention to be bound by the terms of a contract; (2) all the essential terms of the proposal must be definite and certain; and (3) the proposal must be intentionally communicated to the party to whom it is being made.

In many situations, of course, the foregoing requirements will not be met. A proposal that is obviously made as a joke does not constitute an offer, since an average reasonable person would not consider a proposal made in jest the expression of an intention to be bound by a contract. An invitation to enter into negotiations to sell an item does not constitute a valid offer, because such an invitation is not an expression of an intention to be bound, and the terms of sale are unsettled. Similarly, a proposal to sell an item at a price to be agreed on later is not a valid offer, because an essential term of the sale is uncertain.

POINTER: Almost every United States jurisdiction has adopted a statute governing commercial purchase and sale contracts based on Article II of the Uniform Commercial Code (U.C.C.). The U.C.C. is somewhat liberal in its analysis of the existence

FIGURE 4-1 PROMISSORY NOTE

INSTALLMENT NOTE — INTEREST EXTRA

$ ________________ ________________, California ________________________________, 19____

In installments as herein stated, for value received, I/we jointly and severally promise to pay to

____

____

____

or order, at ____ the sum of

____ DOLLARS

with interest from ________________ on unpaid principal at the rate of ________________ per cent per annum, interest payable __________, beginning __________; principal payable in installments of

____ DOLLARS

or more on the ____________ day of each ____________ month, beginning on the ____________ day of ________________________, 19____, and continuing until ____________________

____

____

____

____

Should default be made in payment of any installment of principal or interest when due the whole sum of principal and interest shall at the option of the holder of this note become immediately due. Principal and interest payable in lawful money of the United States. If action be instituted on this note I/we promise to pay such sum as the Court may fix as attorney's fees.

______________________________ ______________________________

______________________________ ______________________________

of an offer—for example, taking the approach that a proposal may constitute an offer even if it is silent concerning one or more essential terms. Under such circumstances, a court may treat the silence as consent to terms that are reasonable on the basis of custom, prior dealings between the parties, and the intentions of the parties in entering into the contract. For example, if the parties to a contract for the sale of merchandise agree to establish a price for the merchandise at a future time, and then fail to do so, the parties will be deemed to have agreed to the payment of what would be a "reasonable" price for the merchandise at the time of delivery.

Acceptance. For a valid contract to be formed, an offer must be accepted by the party to whom the offer was made. To constitute an **acceptance**, a response to an offer must meet three requirements. First, the response must consist of words or acts that an average, reasonable person would consider an expression of an intention to be bound by *all* of the terms of the offer. If the response rejects any of the terms of the offer, or proposes additional conditions or terms, the response is considered a rejection of the offer. A response that itself meets the requirements of an offer is considered a **counter-offer** to the party who made the original offer. Second, the response must be intentionally communicated to the party making the offer. Third, the response must be communicated before the offer expires or is revoked by the party who made the offer.

POINTER: Again, the U.C.C. takes a somewhat liberal approach in its analysis of the acceptance of an offer. Under the U.C.C., a party responding to an offer may propose additional terms without being deemed to have rejected the offer. If the additional terms are consistent with the original offer, and the party making the original offer does not reject them, the additional terms become part of the contract. If the additional terms are inconsistent with the original offer, the original offer is deemed accepted without the additional terms, unless the party responding to the original offer expressly states that such party's acceptance is conditioned on approval of the inconsistent terms by the party making the original offer.

Consideration. Under some circumstances, an offer and an acceptance are not enough to form a valid contract. A contract in which any party promises to perform the terms of the contract at a future date is known as an **executory contract**. For an executory contract to be valid, at the time the contract is made each party must agree to incur an obligation in exchange for obtaining a right. This bargained-for exchange is known as **consideration**.

Suppose, for example, that on August 1 a seller offers to sell 500 units of merchandise to a buyer for $5,000, with delivery and payment to take place on September 1. The buyer accepts the offer on August 2. An executory contract has been formed, since the parties have promised one another to perform at a future date. Moreover, consideration is present. The seller has incurred an obligation to deliver the merchandise to the buyer and a right to require the buyer to pay $5,000. The buyer has incurred an obligation to pay the seller $5,000 and a right to require the seller to deliver the merchandise.

The requirement that consideration be present in executory contracts is related to the concept of fairness. If a party incurs an obligation in entering into a contract, it is only fair that the party be permitted to enforce its rights under that contract in court. On the other hand, if a party to a contract has not incurred any obligation under the contract, it does not seem fair for that party to use the courts to enforce its rights under the contract.

An example of an agreement that lacks consideration is an agreement to make a gift. The giver incurs an obligation to give the gift, but obtains no right to demand anything from the recipient. Similarly, the recipient obtains a right to demand the gift, but incurs no obligation to do anything for the giver. The law does not recognize such an agreement as a valid contract.

Performance and Breach

Once a contract has been formed, the parties are expected to perform in accordance with the terms of the contract. Under some circumstances a party's failure to perform as agreed is excused. Under other circumstances a party may establish a defense to enforcement of the contract that will justify nonperformance. Most often, however, a party's failure to perform is a violation or **breach** of the contract. If a party to a valid contract suffers a loss as a result of another party's breach of the contract, the nonbreaching party may sue the breaching party in court to enforce the contract. The facts that the nonbreaching party must prove in order to prevail in the lawsuit are suggested by the standard form of a complaint for breach of contract, which is illustrated in Figure 4-2.

Excuses for Nonperformance. Under some circumstances, a party to a valid contract is excused from performing as required by the contract. The most frequently encountered **excuses** for nonperformance are nonsatisfaction of a condition, impossibility, impracticability, and frustration of purpose.

Nonsatisfaction of a Condition. Many contracts include terms that specify how future events will affect a party's obligation to perform. An event that must occur before a party is required to perform is a **condition precedent**. An event that must occur at the same time a party is required to perform is a **condition concurrent**. An event that, if it occurs, will terminate a party's obligation to perform is a **condition subsequent**. The nonoccurrence of an event that constitutes a condition precedent or concurrent, or the occurrence of an event that constitutes a condition subsequent, excuses a party's nonperformance.

Suppose, for example, that a seller agrees to deliver 500 units of merchandise to a buyer for $5,000. If the contract provides that the buyer must pay before the seller must deliver, the buyer's payment is a condition precedent to the seller's performance. If the buyer fails to pay, the seller is excused from delivering the merchandise. Suppose, instead, that the contract provides that if the buyer pays in advance by check, the seller must deliver the merchandise within ten days of receipt of the check unless the check fails to clear through the bank within eight days of receipt. Failure of the check to clear within eight days is a condition subsequent to the seller's performance. Once the seller receives the buyer's check, the seller is obligated to deliver the merchandise within ten days. If, however, the check fails to clear within eight days, the seller is excused from delivering the merchandise.

POINTER: Note that in the last example the condition subsequent could also have been stated as a condition precedent. The contract might have provided that if the buyer pays in advance by check and the check clears within eight days of receipt of the check, then the seller must deliver the merchandise within ten days of receipt of the check. If the contract is stated this way, both the tender of the check and the clearing of the check are conditions precedent to the buyer's performance.

Impossibility, Impracticability, and Frustration of Purpose. Sometimes there occurs an event that none of the parties to a contract expected. In fact, the terms of the contract may have been based on an assumption that this event would not occur. The occurrence of such an event might make it impossible or impracticable (that is, unreasonably difficult) for one or more of the parties to perform. Alternatively, the occurrence of such an event might render the performance of one party valueless to another party, thereby frustrating that party's purpose for entering into the contract in the first place. A party for whom performance is

FIGURE 4-2 STANDARD FORM OF A COMPLAINT FOR BREACH OF CONTRACT

SHORT TITLE:	CASE NUMBER:

______________ (number) **CAUSE OF ACTION—Breach of Contract** **Page** _____

ATTACHMENT TO ☐ Complaint ☐ Cross-Complaint

(Use a separate cause of action form for each cause of action.)

BC-1. Plaintiff (*name*):

alleges that on or about (*date*):
a ☐ written ☐ oral ☐ other (*specify*):
agreement was made between (*name parties to agreement*):

☐ A copy of the agreement is attached as Exhibit A, or
☐ The essential terms of the agreement ☐ are stated in Attachment BC-1
☐ are as follows (*specify*):

BC-2. On or about (*dates*):
defendant breached the agreement by ☐ the acts specified in Attachment BC-2
☐ the following acts (*specify*):

BC-3. Plaintiff has performed all obligations to defendant except those obligations plaintiff was prevented or excused from performing.

BC-4. Plaintiff suffered damages legally (proximately) caused by defendant's breach of the agreement ☐ as stated in Attachment BC-4 ☐ as follows (*specify*):

BC-5. ☐ Plaintiff is entitled to attorney fees by an agreement or a statute
☐ of $
☐ according to proof.

BC-6. ☐ Other:

Form Approved by the
Judicial Council of California
Effective January 1, 1982
Rule 982.1(21)

CAUSE OF ACTION—Breach of Contract

CCP 425.12

made impossible or impracticable, or whose purpose in entering into the contract is frustrated, is usually excused from performing in accordance with the contract.

Suppose, for example, that a factory owner enters into a contract to manufacture and deliver a specified product to a buyer for an agreed price. A war breaks out unexpectedly, and all supplies of a certain raw material needed to manufacture the product are cut off. The factory owner's nonperformance will likely be excused on the grounds of impossibility. Suppose, instead, that the necessary raw material is still available, but because of the sudden war the price of the raw material needed to produce each unit of product increases to ten times the agreed price that the buyer is to pay for each unit. The factory owner's nonperformance would likely be excused on the grounds of impracticability or frustration of purpose. Performance, although possible, would be impracticable because the factory owner would be required to undertake unexpected, extraordinary, and unreasonable expense in order to perform. Moreover, the factory owner's purpose in entering into the contract—making a profit by selling the product at the agreed price—would be entirely frustrated: payment of the agreed price by the buyer would not cover even one-tenth of the factory owner's costs of production.

Defenses to Enforcement. Under certain circumstances, a court will refuse to enforce a contract even though there has been an offer, an acceptance, and consideration. The question of enforcement usually arises when one party fails to perform in accordance with the contract and the other party sues to enforce it. The nonperforming party may justify nonperformance by proving that there exist certain circumstances that provide a **defense** to enforcement of the contract. The law recognizes several defenses. Some defenses are based on circumstances indicating that a party's outward expression of an intention to be bound by the terms of the contract did not reflect an actual intention to be bound. Other defenses are based on public policies that certain kinds of contracts should not be enforced.

POINTER: The existence of either an excuse or a defense will provide grounds for a court's refusal to enforce a contract. Although the law designates some grounds for nonenforcement as excuses and others as defenses, there is no practical difference between the two designations.

A contract to which a defense exists is either a void contract or a voidable contract. A **void contract** imposes no legal obligations on the parties and may not be enforced in court by any party. A **voidable contract** does impose legal obligations on the parties, but the law gives one of the parties a right to ''avoid'' these legal obligations by canceling the contract. In other words, the parties to the contract may enforce the legal obligations imposed by the contract in court only if the party having the power to cancel the contract chooses to affirm the contract independently. You will see examples of these two kinds of contracts as our discussion progresses.

Void contracts—and voidable contracts that are cancelled—are not valid, binding, or enforceable. As a result, a party to such a contract who fails to perform does not suffer any consequences from the nonperformance.

Capacity. The law protects certain groups whose members may not be able to understand the significance of entering into a contract. Members of these groups are said to lack the legal capacity to enter into a contract. Any contract to which such a person is a party is voidable; that is, the party who lacks capacity has the power to either cancel or affirm the contract.

In almost all jurisdictions, **minors**—that is, persons who have not reached the so-called age of majority, which is 18 years—lack the legal capacity to enter into a contract. Persons who have mental disabilities that impede their understanding of the nature and consequences of a contract are also considered to lack capacity in almost all jurisdictions. In some jurisdictions, a person who enters into a contract while intoxicated or drugged may avoid the contract if the other party was aware of such person's condition at the time.

POINTER: In some jurisdictions and under some circumstances, a contract entered into by a person who lacks capacity is void, rather than merely voidable. In some jurisdictions, for example, a contract entered into by a person who has been declared of unsound mind by a court is void, while a contract entered into by a person of unsound mind who has not been so declared by a court is voidable.

Mistake and Ambiguity. As a general rule, a contract requires a meeting of the minds—that is, an agreement of the parties concerning the terms of the contract. When any or all of the parties to a contract misunderstand what the terms are, the validity of the contract may be affected.

When the words used to express the terms of a contract are clear and unambiguous, but all of the parties are mistaken in that the words used do not convey what they intended, the contract is void. When the words are clear and unambiguous, but only some of the parties are mistaken in that the words did not convey what they intended, the contract is binding if the nonmistaken parties have relied on the contract in good faith.

When the words used to express the terms of a contract are ambiguous, the parties disagree on what they mean, and all parties are equally responsible for the ambiguity, the contract is void. But if there is a disagreement over ambiguous terms and fewer than all of the parties are responsible for the ambiguity, the contract is binding if the nonresponsible parties have relied on the contract in good faith.

Fraud. When a party enters into a contract in reliance on fraudulent (that is, false) representations made by another party, the validity of the contract is affected. For example, when a party convinces another party to enter into a contract by misrepresenting the terms of the contract to that party, the contract is voidable by that party. When a party convinces another party to sign a written contract by representing to that party that she or he is signing something else, the contract is void.

Duress. When a party enters into an agreement under **duress**—that is, as a result of a threat or the use of force—the contract is voidable by that party.

Illegality. If parties enter into a contract in order to achieve an illegal purpose, the contract is void. For example, in jurisdictions where gambling is illegal, a gambling contract is void. A contract with a legal purpose is void if it requires a party to commit an illegal act. For example, a contract that requires an unlicensed party to provide professional services for which a license is legally required is void.

Unconscionability. Sometimes the terms of a contract may be so heavily weighted in favor of one of the parties that enforcement of the contract seems grossly unfair. Such contracts most frequently arise in situations where one party has substantially more bargaining power than the other one does, and so no real negotiation of the terms of the contract is possible. When confronted with such a situation, a court may elect not to enforce the contract or those terms of the contract it finds **unconscionable**—that is, so unreasonable, oppressive, or grossly unfair that the conscience of the court is shocked. Instances in which a court will refuse to enforce a contract on the basis of unconscionability are rare. In the vast majority of cases, a court will not interfere with the bargain struck by the parties, even if it means that one party's lack of sophistication or poor judgment in entering into the contract will result in a loss.

Statute of Frauds and Parol Evidence Rule. Every jurisdiction has laws that require certain types of contracts to be in writing if they are to be enforced by a court. These laws are designed to avoid the problems that can arise when parties attempt to prove the terms of an oral (that is, spoken) contract in court. Collectively, such laws are known as the **statute of frauds**. Most jurisdictions, for example, require that a contract to buy and sell land must be in writing, which means if two parties orally contract to buy and sell a parcel of land but fail to put the contract in writing, the contract will not be enforceable in court.

A related concept that governs written contracts is the **parol evidence rule**. With some exceptions, the parties to a written contract may not submit evidence in court concerning the terms of their contract if that evidence is inconsistent with the written contract itself. This rule is designed to ensure that written contracts record the terms of the contract completely and correctly.

Remedies

A party to a valid contract who suffers a loss as a result of another party's breach of the contract may elect one of several remedies as compensation for the injury. The remedy chosen depends on the nature of the loss and what the injured party desires to achieve.

POINTER: A party who is injured by the actions of another usually has a number of remedies from which to choose. Although the discussion that follows focuses on remedies available to a party who is injured as the result of a breach of contract, throughout this chapter and this book you will be introduced to additional remedies that are available in a number of other situations. Choosing an appropriate remedy requires careful consideration of the benefits and limitations of each remedy available while keeping in mind the goal that the injured party hopes to achieve.

Rescission. An injured party may rescind a contract. **Rescission** is termination of the contract and the return to each party of the consideration given by that party under the contract. The goal of rescission is to return each party to its position prior to entering into the contract. Sometimes the consideration cannot be returned—for example, when one party has performed services for another party. In such situations, the party enjoying the benefit of the nonreturnable consideration may be required to compensate the party who conferred the benefit for the fair market value of the benefit.

Rescission is also available to a party who has a defense to enforcement of a contract. Such a party may rescind the contract by giving notice to the other parties and offering to return any consideration given by them.

Damages. Under most circumstances, a party who suffers a loss as a result of another party's breach of a contract will ask a court to award **damages**, a sum of money that must be paid to an injured party by the party responsible for the loss. An award of damages may be designed to either (1) place the injured party in the same position it would have been in had the breaching party performed in accordance with the contract or (2) place the injured party in the same position it was in prior to entering into the contract.

To obtain damages that would confer the same benefits as performance, the injured party must prove that the loss suffered was consequential, foreseeable, unavoidable, and certain. A loss is **consequential** if it was in fact caused by the breaching party's breach. A loss is **foreseeable** if the parties could have anticipated at the time that they entered into the contract that such a loss would likely result from a breach. A loss is **unavoidable** if the party suffering the loss was unable to make reasonable arrangements in time to avoid the loss. A loss is **certain** if the loss can be calculated fairly accurately in monetary terms.

Suppose, for example, that a wholesaler enters into a contract with a retailer by which the wholesaler agrees to deliver 100 units of merchandise to the retailer on September 1 for $10 a unit. The wholesaler contacts a manufacturer, tells the manufacturer about the contract with the retailer, and then enters into a contract with the manufacturer, who agrees to manufacture the 100 units of merchandise for $9 a unit and to deliver the units to the wholesaler by August 31. The manufacturer then fails to deliver the units to the wholesaler as promised by August 31, the wholesaler is unable to deliver to the retailer on September 1, and the retailer is excused from paying the wholesaler because of the wholesaler's failure to perform. As a result of the manufacturer's failure to perform, the wholesaler loses the $100 profit that it would have earned had the entire transaction taken place as planned. Under these circumstances, the wholesaler can recover damages in the amount of $100 from the manufacturer. The wholesaler's loss is consequential in that it resulted from the manufacturer's failure to perform; it is foreseeable in that the parties could have anticipated that the loss would occur if the manufacturer failed to perform; it is unavoidable in that the wholesaler had insufficient time to obtain replacement merchandise elsewhere; and it is certain in that the wholesaler's loss can be precisely calculated by subtracting the price per unit to have been paid to the manufacturer from the price per unit to have been received by the wholesaler.

If a party's loss is not consequential, foreseeable, unavoidable, and certain, the party may nonetheless recover damages designed to restore it to the position it was in prior to entering into the contract. If the injured party conferred benefits on the breaching party, the court may award damages in the amount of the fair market value of those benefits. If the injured party incurred any costs in attempting to perform under the contract, it may be awarded damages sufficient to reimburse those costs.

Specific Performance. When rescission or damages are inadequate remedies for a breach, a court may order the breaching party to perform the terms of the contract. This remedy is known as **specific performance**. Specific performance is rarely granted, because damages are usually sufficient to compensate a party who suffers a loss as the result of a breach. Specific performance is appropriate when the subject of the contract is a unique, irreplaceable asset. For example, contracts to buy and sell land are frequently the subject of lawsuits that seek specific performance.

HOW PARALEGALS USE CONTRACT LAW CONCEPTS

- Drafting written contracts
- Investigating the merits of a claim for breach of contract
- Drafting complaints, discovery requests, motions, and briefs in litigation involving breach of contract

TORT LAW CONCEPTS

The law imposes a general duty on everyone to refrain from violating the rights of others. When a breach of this duty causes injury, the party causing the injury is held responsible and is required to compensate the injured party.

A **tort** is a breach of a duty imposed by law that results in injury to another. While in some ways similar to the law of contracts, the law of torts is fundamentally different. Under contract law, duties are imposed by agreement with the consent of the parties involved. Under tort law, duties are imposed by law without the consent of those on whom they are imposed.

In order to recover compensation from someone who commits a tort, an injured party must prove three things: breach of a duty, causation, and damages.

Duty

The general duty imposed on everyone to refrain from violating the rights of others actually consists of three specific duties: a duty to refrain from committing certain types of acts intentionally, a duty to exercise a reasonable degree of care at all times and under all circumstances, and a duty to ensure that certain activities are conducted safely.

Intentional Torts. An **intentional tort** is a breach of the legal duty to refrain from committing intentional acts that cause injury to others. The intent with which an act is committed may be either general or specific. General intent consists of knowledge that one's act will result in specific consequences. Specific intent consists of a deliberate intention to bring about specific consequences by one's act.

Injury to Physical Person. Some intentional torts involve injury to the physical person of another. These include battery (harmful or offensive physical contact), assault (inciting fear of harmful or offensive physical contact), false imprisonment (restraining free movement), and intentional infliction of emotional distress (outrageous conduct causing severe emotional distress).

Injury to Reputation. Some intentional torts involve injury to another's reputation. These include malicious prosecution (initiating legal proceedings, especially criminal proceedings, without probable cause), abuse of process (using legal process to bring about a result other than that for which the process is designed), defamation (actions harming the reputation of another), and invasion of privacy.

Injury to Property. Some intentional torts involve injury to another's property. These include trespass (physical invasion of land), nuisance (interference with another's reasonable use and enjoyment of land), and conversion (exercising control over another's property).

Interference with Business Relationships. Some intentional torts involve interference with business relationships. Inducing breach of contract is one such tort; another is interference with prospective economic advantage (taking business away from another using unfair methods).

Fraud. One of the most important intentional torts is **fraud**, sometimes referred to as intentional misrepresentation or deceit. Fraud usually consists of making a false representation about an important fact, with knowledge that the representation is false and with the intent to deceive someone into taking action in reliance on the false representation. A party seeking compensation for fraud must prove that the injury suffered resulted from reliance on the false representation, and that such reliance was reasonable under all of the circumstances. Under some circumstances, failure to disclose an important fact may give rise to fraud.

Negligence. **Negligence** is a breach of the legal duty to exercise reasonable care at all times and under all circumstances. Most lawsuits involving personal injury or property damage include an assertion that the party being sued has been negligent. A standard form of a complaint for negligence is illustrated in Figure 4-3. The possibility of negligence is investigated every time there is an automobile accident, a fire, or someone slips and falls in a supermarket.

Everyone is legally required to act with the degree of care that a reasonable person would be expected to use under the same circumstances. Although this is an objective standard, there is sometimes disagreement about what a reasonable person would be expected to do under particular circumstances. As a result, negligence is an area of law where the ability to research previous cases involving similar circumstances is critical.

In some situations a party is legally required to act with a higher degree of care than would be expected from the average, reasonable person. Higher

FIGURE 4-3 STANDARD FORM OF A COMPLAINT FOR NEGLIGENCE

SHORT TITLE:	CASE NUMBER:

_______________ (number) **CAUSE OF ACTION—General Negligence** **Page** _____

ATTACHMENT TO ☐ Complaint ☐ Cross-Complaint

(Use a separate cause of action form for each cause of action.)

GN-1. Plaintiff (*name*):

alleges that defendant (*name*):

☐ Does _______ to _______

was the legal (proximate) cause of damages to plaintiff. By the following acts or omissions to act, defendant negligently caused the damage to plaintiff
on (*date*):
at (*place*):

(*description of reasons for liability*):

Form Approved by the
Judicial Council of California
Effective January 1, 1982
Rule 962.1(3)

CAUSE OF ACTION—General Negligence

CCP 425.12

standards of care apply, for example, to members of certain professions and to companies that provide public transportation (airlines, railroads, bus companies). Statutes may establish a higher standard of care for specified parties under specified circumstances.

A party who fails to exercise the required degree of care is considered to be at fault and therefore responsible for any injury suffered by another as a result of the failure.

Strict Liability. Under certain circumstances the law imposes an absolute duty on a party to ensure that a specific activity is conducted safely. Because it is absolute, a party who breaches this duty must compensate anyone who suffers injury as a result of the activity, even though the injury was not brought about intentionally or as a result of negligence. This obligation to compensate others for injury regardless of one's intention or one's failure to exercise reasonable care is known as **strict liability**.

Strict liability applies to many activities that involve risk of serious harm to people or property. These activities are generally so risky that they cannot be rendered completely safe no matter how carefully they are conducted. Examples include use of explosives, fumigation with deadly poisons, crop dusting, and keeping dangerous wild animals. Strict liability shifts the economic cost of injuries resulting from these activities to those parties who engage in, and therefore benefit from, such activities.

Perhaps the area in which strict liability has its broadest application is the field of products liability. Commercial suppliers of defective products are strictly liable for injuries caused by the products. Strict liability applies to retailers and wholesalers as well as to manufacturers.

Suppose, for example, that a sleeping person is badly injured when an electric blanket catches fire. The cause of the fire is traced to a design defect in the blanket's wiring. Because strict liability applies to more than one party in products liability claims, the injured person has a claim for compensation against both the manufacturer of the blanket and the retailer who sold the blanket. The manufacturer is liable even though the manufacturer may have used reasonable care in designing the blanket, and the retailer is liable even though the retailer played no part in designing the blanket. At first glance this may appear to be unfair. However, both the manufacturer and the retailer profited from the sale of the blanket. They, rather than the consumer, should bear any loss resulting from a defect in the blanket. Allowing the consumer to assert a claim against both of them increases the likelihood that the consumer will be fully compensated, since at least one of them should be in a position to pay the claim.

Causation

A party who seeks compensation for an injury resulting from the breach of a legal duty must show that the breach was both the cause in fact and the proximate cause of the injury.

Cause in Fact. To be eligible for compensation, an injured party must show that another's breach of duty was the **cause in fact** of the injury. In other words, the party must show that the injury would not have occurred "but for" the breach of duty. If the injury would have occurred regardless of the breach of duty, the party who breached the duty has no obligation to compensate the injured party.

Proximate Cause. In certain situations, even though a party's breach of duty is the cause in fact of an injury, the law does not require that party to compensate the injured party. These are situations in which the injury would not have occurred but for an independent intervening act that was not reasonably foreseeable by the party breaching the duty. Because it would be unjust to hold the party breaching the duty responsible for the consequences of an act beyond the party's control, no obligation to compensate arises.

When a breach of duty is a cause in fact of an injury, and no unforeseeable intervening act arises, the breach of duty is said to be the **proximate cause**, as well as the cause in fact, of the injury.

Damages and Other Remedies

The remedy known as damages is available to any party who has been injured by a tort, unless the party committing the tort can establish a defense to liability. When damages are inadequate to compensate an injured party, the party may obtain a court order requiring the party committing the tort to cease doing so.

Damages. An injured party is entitled to be compensated in full for injuries suffered. Accordingly, a court will order a party who is at fault to pay an injured party a sum of money known as **compensatory damages**. A party who is physically injured, for example, can recover medical expenses, lost wages, and, in a case of permanent disability, compensation for loss of future earnings. Under some circumstances a party may recover damages for pain and suffering. When there is an injury to property, the owner may recover the expenses of repairing or replacing the property.

In cases involving intentional torts, a court may award a sum of money known as **punitive damages** (or **exemplary damages**) for the purpose of punishing a wrongdoer and making an example of the wrongdoer to others. Although the injured party receives the sum awarded, the amount of the award is not designed to compensate the injured party, but rather to deter others from similar conduct in the future. As a result, punitive damages can be substantially higher than the compensatory damages awarded to an injured party.

Defenses. Under certain circumstances, the obligation of someone who has committed a tort to compensate the injured party may be reduced or altogether avoided. The party committing the tort must prove that the facts give rise to a **defense** to liability.

Defenses to Intentional Torts. The most common defenses to liability for intentional torts include consent of the injured party to the conduct involved, self-defense, defense of others, necessity (that is, the conduct causing injury was necessary to avoid a greater injury), and privilege (that is, the party had a legal right to engage in the conduct causing injury).

Defenses to Negligence and Strict Liability. The most common defenses to liability for torts involving negligence or strict liability are contributory negligence, comparative negligence, and assumption of risk.

Contributory Negligence and Comparative Negligence. On some occasions, an injury is partially the result of negligence on the part of the injured party. Suppose, for example, that an automobile accident results when a car runs a stop sign and is hit by a speeding car. The driver of the car that ran the stop sign is injured. The accident could have been avoided if either of the drivers had been obeying the law. Clearly, both drivers were negligent, and each driver is partially responsible for the accident that resulted in the injury; suppose, however, that the driver of the car that ran the stop sign sues the driver of the speeding car for compensation. In some United States jurisdictions, the driver of the speeding car could assert the defense of **contributory negligence**. In these jurisdictions the injured driver would be precluded from recovering anything from the speeding driver because the injured driver's own negligence contributed to the injury. In other United States jurisdictions, the driver of the speeding car could assert the defense of **comparative negligence**. In these jurisdictions the injured driver's recovery would be reduced to the same extent that the injured driver's own negligence was responsible for the injury. For example, if a judge or jury determined that the injured driver was 25 percent responsible for the accident causing the injury and the speeding driver was 75 percent responsible, the injured driver could recover from the speeding driver only 75 percent of the amount necessary to compensate for the injury. In some comparative negligence jurisdictions, an injured party may receive a proportionate recovery regardless of the extent of his or her negligence; in other jurisdictions, an injured party may recover only if she or he is less than 51 percent responsible for the injury; and in still other jurisdictions, an injured party may recover only if he or she is less than 50 percent responsible for the injury.

Assumption of Risk. Another defense to actions involving negligence or strict liability is **assumption of risk**. This defense bars recovery by the injured party if the injured party knew of the risk involved in undertaking a particular activity and voluntarily proceeded in the face of such risk. The defense of assumption of risk is accorded only limited recognition in some United States jurisdictions.

Injunction. Under some circumstances, a court will order someone to cease conduct that constitutes a tort. An **injunction** is a court order requiring someone to perform, or to refrain from performing, certain acts. For an injunction to be issued, at least three requirements must be met. First, the injury must be such that monetary compensation is an inadequate remedy. This may be the case when, for example, the party committing the tort will continue to do so unless restrained by court order. Second, the injunction itself must be feasible to enforce. Third, the hardship that would be suffered by the injured party if the injunction were not issued must outweigh the hardship that the party bound by the injunction will suffer if it is issued. Cases in which injunctions are sometimes issued include those involving defamation, invasion of privacy, trespass, and interference with prospective economic advantage.

HOW PARALEGALS USE TORT LAW CONCEPTS

- Investigating the merits of a claim that arises from the commission of a tort
- Drafting complaints, discovery requests, motions, and briefs in litigation involving personal injury, property damage, harm to reputation, interference with business relationships, fraud, and products liability

CRIMINAL LAW CONCEPTS

As we have just seen, the law of torts provides a remedy to someone who is injured by the actions of another. But certain actions are considered so injurious to society as a whole that the law invests the government with the authority to punish those who engage in such actions. A **crime** is an act that is subject to punishment by the government acting on behalf of society as a whole. Some acts are both crimes and torts. A party who commits such an act is subject to both criminal liability and civil liability. **Criminal liability** is determined in a criminal proceeding brought by the government and is punishable by a fine or imprisonment or both. **Civil liability** is determined in a civil (that is, noncriminal) proceeding brought by an injured party and is punishable by an award of damages to the injured party.

Classification of Crimes

Crimes are classified as felonies, misdemeanors, and infractions. Classification of a particular crime depends on its seriousness and its consequences. The same crime may be a felony or a misdemeanor, depending on the circumstances.

Felonies. A **felony** is an extremely serious crime that is usually punishable by a term of imprisonment exceeding one year. Examples of felonies include murder, rape, robbery, burglary, and arson.

Misdemeanors. A **misdemeanor** is a less serious crime, usually punishable by a term of imprisonment of one year or less. Examples of misdemeanors include assault, battery, and false imprisonment. Crimes that may be felonies or misdemeanors, depending on the circumstances, include larceny, embezzlement, and receiving stolen property.

Infractions. An **infraction** is a minor crime, usually punishable by a fine. Most traffic violations are infractions.

Elements of a Crime

Every crime is defined in terms of two elements: a specific physical act and a specific mental state that accompanies the commission of the physical act. The commission of a specified physical act without the required mental state, or the presence of a specified mental state without the commission of the accompanying physical act, does not constitute a crime.

Actus Reus. An ***actus reus*** is the particular physical act that must be done in order to commit a particular crime. For example, the *actus reus* for arson is setting a building on fire.

The same physical act may serve as the *actus reus* for more than one crime. For example, **homicide**—that is, the act of one human being killing another—is the *actus reus* for the crimes of murder, voluntary manslaughter, and involuntary manslaughter.

Mens Rea. ***Mens rea*** is the particular mental state that must accompany a specified *actus reus* in order for the *actus reus* to constitute a crime. *Mens rea* is usually defined in terms of both a positive aspect and a negative aspect. The positive aspect of *mens rea* consists of those things that must be present in the actor's mind; the negative aspect of *mens rea* consists of those things that must be absent from the actor's mind.

The positive aspect of *mens rea* for a particular crime usually consists of one of several distinct mental states identified by terms such as ''actual intention,'' ''wantonness,'' and ''criminal negligence.'' Although the terms used to identify these distinct mental states are well established, they are not precisely defined. For example, ''actual intention'' implies a conscious intention or desire to commit the *actus reus.* ''Wantonness'' implies the knowing and intentional commission of an act that creates a very high probability that the *actus reus* will occur. ''Criminal negligence'' implies the commission of an act that the actor should have known would create a high probability that the *actus reus* would occur.

The negative aspect of *mens rea* for a particular crime usually consists of the absence of circumstances that would justify or excuse commission of the *actus reus.* Examples of circumstances that might justify an actor's conduct include self-defense, defense of others, and defense of property. Examples of circumstances that might excuse an actor's conduct include insanity, involuntary intoxication, and coercion.

Occasionally the *mens rea* for a crime may be defined in terms of a single word that implies both the positive and the negative aspects of the *mens rea* involved. For example, on the positive side the term **malice** implies the presence of either actual intention or wantonness; on the negative side it implies the absence of justification, excuse, or any factor that might mitigate, or reduce responsibility for, one's acts (such as sudden anger arising in response to adequate provocation).

As we have noted, crimes may have the same *actus reus* requirement but different *mens rea* requirements. For the crime of murder, for example, the *actus reus* is homicide and the *mens rea* is malice. For the crime of voluntary manslaughter, the *actus reus* is homicide and the *mens rea* consists of (1) the presence of actual intention or wantonness; (2) the absence of justification or excuse; and (3) the presence of some mitigating factor, such as sudden anger arising in response to adequate provocation by the person who is killed. For the crime of involuntary manslaughter, the *actus reus* is homicide and the *mens rea* is (1) the presence of criminal negligence or an intention to do nonserious bodily harm and (2) the absence of justification or excuse.

Criminal Procedure

Because of the serious consequences when someone is convicted of a crime, special procedural requirements have been developed to increase the certainty that only those actually guilty of crimes are convicted. Probably the best known of these is the requirement that the evidence presented by the government be so persuasive that the judge or jury is able to find the accused guilty ''beyond a reasonable doubt.'' Other safeguards include a criminal defendant's right to refuse to testify, and the right to be represented by a lawyer. A criminal defendant, once acquitted of a crime, may not be tried again for that same crime, and the government may not appeal the acquittal.

There is a well-developed body of law governing the rights of a criminal suspect with respect to arrest, search and seizure, confessions, and pretrial identification procedures. Evidence obtained in violation of a suspect's rights is subject to exclusion—that is, it may not be used against the suspect at trial.

POINTER: Many of the rules which govern criminal procedure and the rights of criminal suspects are based on provisions of the United States Constitution. For example, the Fourth Amendment provides, in part, that ''the right of the people to be secure in their persons, houses, papers, and effects, against unreasonable searches and seizures, shall not be violated.'' The Fifth Amendment includes provisions that no person shall ''be subject for the same offence to be twice put in jeopardy of life or limb,'' and that no person ''shall be compelled in any criminal case to be a witness against himself.'' The Sixth Amendment guarantees the accused the right ''to a speedy and public trial, by an impartial jury,'' the right ''to be confronted with the witnesses against him,'' and the right ''to have the Assistance of Counsel for his defence.''

HOW PARALEGALS USE CRIMINAL LAW CONCEPTS

- Helping to determine whether or not available evidence supports the filing of criminal charges
- Helping to determine whether or not available evidence is admissible in a criminal proceeding
- Drafting complaints, discovery requests, motions, and briefs in criminal proceedings

5 LEGAL TERMS AND CONCEPTS: REAL PROPERTY, BUSINESS, ESTATE PLANNING AND PROBATE, AND FAMILY LAW

In Chapter 4, you studied the law of contracts, which governs duties imposed by agreement; the law of torts, which governs duties imposed by law and enforceable by private persons; and criminal law, which governs duties imposed by law and enforceable by the government. In this chapter, you will study four additional areas of law: the law of real property, the law of business, estate planning and probate, and family law. As you study these areas of the law, you will recognize a number of terms and concepts from Chapter 4. You will see, for example, that much of the law of real estate and the law of business is based on the law of contracts. Contract law concepts also play a role in estate planning and probate, and in family law as well. This interplay of concepts illustrates the truth of the statement that the law is a ''seamless web.'' Having begun to unravel that web in Chapter 4, you will find that as you explore new areas of law in this chapter, your understanding of the terms and concepts introduced in the last chapter will be enhanced.

REAL PROPERTY LAW CONCEPTS

From the beginnings of civilization to the present, land has been viewed as a resource of incomparable value. It is an enduring asset, and its availability is limited. Because of its enduring qualities, land, along with the structures and other improvements constructed upon it, is referred to as **real property**. Due to the high economic and social value of real property, an extensive and complex body of law governs its ownership and use.

Ownership

It is often useful to think of the ownership of land as a "bundle of rights." Rarely does a single party have complete and exclusive control over the possession and use of a parcel of land. In most cases, many parties have rights with respect to a given parcel. A party's rights with respect to a parcel of land are known as an **estate in real property**. Early English law developed an elaborate system of classifying the various types of estates that were recognized by the law at that time. Although the greater part of this system of classification has relatively little application now, much of the legal terminology in use today is derived from it.

Fee Simple. The most comprehensive estate in real property is known as fee simple absolute, or, more commonly, **fee simple**. An owner of a parcel in fee simple has a largely unrestricted right to determine who may possess or occupy the property and how the property will be used. The rights of a fee-simple owner are subject to the government's power to restrict the use and improvement of property and to acquire property for the common good. The rights of a fee-simple owner are also limited by any rights that the owner, or one of the owner's predecessors, may have granted to others.

Limited Estates in Real Property. The owner of a parcel in fee simple has a virtually unrestricted right to sell, donate, or otherwise transfer that property. In contrast to fee simple, other types of estates recognized by the English system of classification incorporate various restrictions on transfer. These restrictions determine, for example, who can inherit the property in the future, or who will take title to the property on the happening of a specified event. By granting one or more of these limited estates to others, a fee-simple owner can sometimes control the ownership or use of property long after the owner's death. In order to prevent this practice from unduly restricting the ownership and use of property by future generations, an elaborate series of rules has been developed for determining the validity of these grants. These limited estates and the rules that regulate them are rarely used today and are beyond the scope of this discussion. However, lawyers and paralegals who specialize in real estate law are occasionally called on to deal with these limited estates, so they must have at least a general familiarity with them.

Limited Rights with Respect to Real Property. Often an owner of a parcel in fee simple will grant others limited rights with respect to that parcel. An **easement** is a right to use a parcel for a particular purpose. For example, most owners give utility companies easements to enter onto their property to maintain poles, wires, pipes, and other equipment in return for the right to use the companies' services. A **profit** is a right to remove some natural resource such as timber or minerals from a parcel. A **covenant** is a promise regarding the use of a parcel, such as a promise to maintain a parcel in its natural state in order to accommodate rainwater drainage. An **equitable servitude** is a promise not to perform specified acts on a parcel, such as a promise not to conduct manufacturing operations there.

Tenancy in Common. An estate in real property may be owned by one or several people. There are several methods by which two or more people can own an estate in real property. **Tenancy in common** is a method by which two or more people, known as **co-tenants**, own a single estate in real property. This arrangement is most often used when a parcel is owned in fee simple.

Each co-tenant is said to have an undivided ownership interest in the real property involved. This means that each co-tenant has rights with respect to the entire parcel, including the right to occupy the entire parcel and the right to use the entire parcel. Exercise of these rights by all of the co-tenants is often impractical, so frequently the co-tenants will have a contract among themselves governing use, compensation for use, and division of income and expenses.

Co-tenants need not have equal undivided ownership interests. For example, one co-tenant may have an undivided two-thirds interest, while the other co-tenant has an undivided one-third interest. The fact that the co-tenants' undivided interests are unequal does not in itself affect the right of each co-tenant to occupy and use the entire parcel. It does, however, affect each co-tenant's share of the parcel if it is physically divided up, and each co-tenant's share of the proceeds if it is sold as whole.

Without a contract to the contrary, any co-tenant may ask a court to order **partition**—that is, physical division or sale of the parcel—at any time. Unless an agreement among the co-tenants provides otherwise, a co-tenant is free to transfer the co-tenant's undivided interest by selling it, by pledging it to creditors, or by making a gift of it during life or at death.

Joint Tenancy. **Joint tenancy** is a method by which two or more people, known as **joint tenants**, own a single estate in real property. Joint tenancy is similar to tenancy in common in many ways, although it differs in two important respects. First, joint tenants have a right of survivorship, which means that when a joint tenant dies, the remaining joint tenants automatically inherit the deceased joint tenant's ownership interest. Second, joint tenants always have equal undivided ownership interests.

Any joint tenant may terminate, or sever, the joint tenancy at any time by transferring the joint tenant's ownership interest to a third party. When such a termination occurs, the joint tenancy automatically becomes a tenancy in common.

Tenancy by the Entirety and Community Property. **Tenancy by the entirety** and **community property** are methods by which a husband and a wife own a single estate in real property. Under both methods of ownership, the husband and the wife have equal undivided ownership interests. Both methods of ownership terminate on the dissolution of the marriage or the death of either spouse. When a tenancy by the entirety terminates on the death of a spouse, the surviving spouse automatically inherits the deceased spouse's ownership interest. Community property does not include such a right of survivorship.

Leaseholds

A **leasehold** is an estate in real property by which the owner of a parcel of land, known as the **landlord** or **lessor**, grants a right to occupy and use the property to another party, known as the **tenant** or **lessee**. On termination of the leasehold, the right to occupy and use the property reverts back to the landlord.

Types of Leaseholds. Leaseholds can be classified into categories based on the duration of the tenant's right to occupy and use the property.

Tenancy for Years. A **tenancy for years** is a leasehold that is scheduled to terminate on a fixed date. A tenancy for years may be of any duration that the parties choose. It terminates automatically on expiration of the agreed term without the giving of notice by any party.

Periodic Tenancy. A **periodic tenancy** is a leasehold that continues in effect for successive periods of time until either party gives notice that the leasehold will terminate at the end of a specified period. The most common types of periodic tenancies are week-to-week, month-to-month, and year-to-year tenancies, although the parties may agree on any base period they desire.

Tenancy at Will. A **tenancy at will** is a leasehold that continues in effect until notice of termination is given by either party. It differs from a periodic tenancy in that it is established without reference to a base period.

Tenancy at Sufferance. A **tenancy at sufferance** is a leasehold that automatically arises when a tenant wrongfully refuses to relinquish possession of property on termination of a tenancy for years, periodic tenancy, or tenancy at will. It continues until such time as the landlord takes action to remove the tenant from possession.

Tenant's Duties and Landlord's Remedies. The rights and duties of a landlord and a tenant are usually determined by agreement of the parties. A **lease** is a written contract that documents this agreement. In the absence of an agreement between the parties, the law governs the general rights and duties of the parties to a leasehold.

The duties of a tenant normally include a duty to pay rent, a duty to avoid using the property for illegal or other objectionable purposes, and a duty to avoid damaging the property. The parties may agree that the tenant is obligated, among other things, to keep the property in good repair, to provide insurance for the property, and to pay taxes on the property.

If the tenant breaches any of the tenant's obligations, the landlord may sue to recover damages resulting from the breach. In the event of a serious breach, the landlord may declare the leasehold terminated and may take legal action to have the tenant evicted from the property. **Eviction** is the physical removal of a tenant from the leasehold premises. This may be accomplished through an **unlawful detainer proceeding**, which is a special court proceeding in which the only issue is the tenant's right to possession.

Landlord's Duties and Tenant's Remedies. The duties of a landlord normally include a duty to deliver possession of the property to the tenant, a duty to allow the tenant to enjoy use of the property without interference, and, in the case of residential properties in some jurisdictions, a duty to keep the property in a condition that is fit for human habitation.

If a landlord breaches any of the landlord's obligations, the tenant may sue to recover damages resulting from the breach. Under some circumstances, the tenant may elect to terminate the leasehold or may withhold rent owed to the landlord and use it to fulfill the landlord's obligations.

POINTER: The respective rights and duties of landlords and tenants are covered by statutory law in many jurisdictions. Some statutory provisions may apply only in the absence of an agreement between a landlord and a tenant to the contrary; other statutory provisions may apply despite the existence of an agreement between a landlord and a tenant to the contrary. When investigating the rights or duties of a landlord or a tenant in a particular situation, it is always advisable to research applicable statutory law in addition to reviewing the lease between the parties.

Subleases. Unless prohibited from doing so by the landlord, a tenant may enter into a leasehold arrangement for the parcel with another party. This arrangement is known as a **sublease**. The tenant who has now assumed the role of landlord is known as the **sublessor**, and the party who has assumed the role of tenant is known as the **sublessee**. The rights, duties, and remedies of a sublessor and a sublessee usually parallel those of a landlord and tenant.

Transfers of Ownership

In many respects a transfer of fee-simple ownership of real property is similar to any other transaction involving the transfer of an asset. However, some special requirements and procedures do apply in real property transactions.

Sales Contracts. In most jurisdictions the statute of frauds requires that contracts for the sale or other transfer of real property must be in writing in order to be enforceable.

Real property sales contracts usually include representations from the seller concerning the property. The most important of these representations concern the status of title to the property. Because determining the ownership of real property can be a complex matter, few buyers are willing to rely on the seller's representations alone. In almost all cases, a title insurance company or lawyer is commissioned to conduct a search of the public records to confirm that the status of title is as represented. Most buyers obtain insurance that provides for reimbursement of the buyer in the event that someone successfully challenges the buyer's title to the property after the sale closes.

Because real property sales transactions are often complex, most sales contracts provide that someone other than the buyer or seller will handle the collection and disbursement of the money and documents involved. In some jurisdictions a professional escrow holder performs this function. In other jurisdictions these matters are handled by a lawyer.

Because real property is considered to be a unique asset, the remedy of specific performance is available if a seller breaches a sales contract. A buyer may obtain a court order requiring the seller to perform the contract.

Deeds. A **deed** is a document that evidences a transfer of title to real property. A deed must adequately identify the parties to the transaction and the real property involved. It must be signed, or **executed**, by the party who is transferring title. A standard form of a simple grant deed is illustrated in Figure 5-1.

A number of different types of deeds are in use. They differ with respect to the extent to which the party executing the deed guarantees the condition of title. A **general warranty deed**, for example, contains extensive representations as to the executing party's authority and the status of title. A **quitclaim deed**, in contrast, simply releases whatever ownership interest in the property the executing party possesses.

Recording Deeds. In order to minimize confusion concerning title to real property, all jurisdictions have established systems for recording deeds. By recording a deed, the parties to the deed give notice to the world that title to the real property involved has been transferred. Because recorded deeds are public records that are generally available for inspection, everyone is considered to have knowledge of the contents of such deeds, regardless of whether they do in fact inspect them.

Recording deeds helps eliminate fraudulent real property transfers and the disputes that accompany them. Suppose a property owner sells property to a buyer, who then records the deed. The former owner then attempts to sell the property to a second buyer. If the second buyer searches the public records, the second buyer will discover that the property has already been sold, and will refuse to go through with the sale. Even if the second buyer fails to search the public records and goes through with the sale, the second buyer is prevented from challenging the first buyer's title because the second buyer is considered to have had notice of the first buyer's deed. The first buyer, by recording the deed, has obtained protection from claims raised by subsequent buyers.

Virtually any document affecting the ownership of real property may be recorded. To guard against the recordation of fraudulent documents, most jurisdictions require that recorded documents be **notarized**—that is, executed or acknowledged in the presence of a public official known as a **notary**.

Real Property Financing

Many buyers borrow money in order to purchase real property. To secure repayment of money borrowed, lenders frequently require that buyers give them liens on the real property. Generally speaking, a **lien** or **encumbrance** is an interest in property that allows its holder to order the sale of the property in order to raise money to pay off a debt owed by the property owner to the lienholder. Liens may be given on any type of property. Property subject to a lien is known as **collateral**. In addition to securing repayment of loans to purchase real property, liens on real property can be used to secure repayment of other types of loans and payment of other types of debts (such as judgments).

FIGURE 5-1 STANDARD FORM OF A GRANT DEED

RECORDING REQUESTED BY:

AND WHEN RECORDED MAIL THIS DEED AND, UNLESS OTHERWISE SHOWN BELOW, MAIL TAX STATEMENTS TO:

NAME

ADDRESS

CITY &
STATE
ZIP

Title Order No. Escrow No.

SPACE ABOVE THIS LINE FOR RECORDER'S USE

GRANT DEED

DOCUMENTARY TRANSFER TAX $ ______________
☐ computed on full value of property conveyed, or
☐ computed on full value less liens and encumbrances remaining at time of sale.

Signature of Declarant or Agent Determining Tax Firm Name

FOR VALUABLE CONSIDERATION, receipt of which is acknowledged, I (We), ______________
(name of grantor(s))
______________,
grant to ______________
(name of grantee(s))
all that real property situated in the City of ______________
(or in an unincorporated area of) ______________ County, California,
(name of County)
described as follows (insert legal description):

Assessor's parcel No. ______________
Executed on ______________, 19______, at ______________
(City and State)

STATE OF CALIFORNIA
} SS
COUNTY OF ______________

On this ____ day of ________, in the year 19____, before me, the undersigned, a Notary Public in and for said State, personally appeared ______________
______________, personally known to me (or proved to me on the basis of satisfactory evidence) to be the person ____ whose name ____ ________ subscribed to the within instrument, and acknowledged to me that ____ he ____ executed it.

WITNESS my hand and official seal.

____
Notary Public in and for said State.

(This area for official notarial seal)

MAIL TAX
STATEMENTS TO ______________
NAME ADDRESS ZIP

Mortgages. The most common type of lien on real property is documented by a contract known as a **mortgage**, which contains all of the terms governing a lender's right to sell real property collateral that secures repayment of a loan. When a buyer borrows money secured by real property, the loan is usually documented with a mortgage and a promissory note. A **promissory note** is a contract which contains all of the terms for repayment of a loan.

Promissory notes often provide for repayment of a loan by means of a series of regular periodic payments. When one or more of these payments is missed, the borrower is considered to be in **default**—that is, in breach of a contractual obligation to repay the money. Most promissory notes allow the borrower a "grace period" to **cure** the default—that is, to make up the missed payments. If the default remains uncured, the promissory note may give the lender the right to **accelerate** the maturity date of the loan, which means that the lender may suspend the agreed-on repayment schedule and declare the full loan immediately due and payable.

If the borrower defaults and fails to cure within the grace period, the lender may initiate a legal proceeding to enforce the terms of the mortgage. This legal proceeding is known as **foreclosure**. At the conclusion of the foreclosure proceeding, the court issues a judgment ordering the sale of the real property collateral at auction.

If the proceeds of the sale of the collateral are insufficient to pay off the loan secured by the mortgage, the lender may seek a judgment against the borrower for the balance. This is known as a **deficiency judgment**. Many jurisdictions limit the circumstances under which a lender may obtain a deficiency judgment. For example, in some jurisdictions a lender who takes a mortgage to secure a loan used to purchase an owner-occupied residence may not obtain a deficiency judgment. This reduces the borrower's risk in buying the residence, since the most that the borrower can lose in the event of a foreclosure is the amount that the borrower has actually invested in the residence.

In many jurisdictions the law gives a borrower who is in default a right to prevent sale of the mortgaged property by paying the loan in part or in full. In some jurisdictions a borrower even has the right to buy back the property within a limited period of time after the sale is completed. A borrower's right to prevent or cancel a sale by paying off the loan is known as a **right of redemption**.

Deeds of Trust. A second type of lien on real property is documented by a contract known as a **deed of trust**. Under a deed of trust, the borrower (known as the trustor) conditionally conveys title to the real property collateral to a third person (known as the trustee) for the benefit of the lender (known as the beneficiary). The trustee is typically given a **power of sale** that enables the trustee to sell the real property collateral at auction if the borrower defaults on the loan. This avoids the need for a formal foreclosure proceeding, although the lender may elect to use such a proceeding instead of authorizing the trustee to exercise the power of sale. In some jurisdictions, different rules regarding deficiency judgments and the right of redemption apply to deeds of trust and to mortgages. Once the loan has been repaid, the trustee reconveys title to the real property collateral to the borrower.

Lien Priorities. In many situations, a parcel of real property may be subject to more than one lien. As a general rule, priority among liens is determined on the basis of the order in which the documents evidencing the liens were recorded.

When a borrower defaults and real property collateral is sold pursuant to a lien, the property remains subject to all liens that have a higher priority than the lien under which the sale occurs. All liens that have a lower priority than the lien under which the sale occurs automatically terminate. In most jurisdictions a lienholder has a right to cure any default on a loan that is secured by a lien with a higher priority. This preserves the lienholder's ability to enforce the lienholder's own lien.

Installment Sale Contracts. Another method for financing the purchase of real property is an **installment sale contract**, under which a seller agrees to convey title to real property to a buyer on the buyer's completion of a series of payments that constitute the purchase price. A buyer who misses a payment loses the right to obtain title, and the seller is entitled to keep the portion of the purchase price that has already been paid.

Because the enforcement of an installment sale contract can have very harsh results, some jurisdictions have adopted rules that in effect modify these contracts for the benefit of the buyer. Such rules may impose a grace period for payment, may require the seller to refund a portion of the purchase price, or may require a sale of the real property pursuant to a foreclosure proceeding.

HOW PARALEGALS USE REAL PROPERTY LAW CONCEPTS

- Investigating the rights a party has with respect to the occupancy and use of a particular parcel of real property
- Drafting leases, sales contracts, sales escrow instructions, deeds, promissory notes, mortgages, deeds of trust, installment sale contracts, and other documents evidencing rights with respect to real property
- Supervising recordation of deeds, mortgages, deeds of trust, and other documents
- Preparing and analyzing title reports
- Drafting complaints, discovery requests, motions, and briefs in litigation involving real property, including actions for breach of a sales contract, breach of a lease, partition of property owned by co-tenants, foreclosure of a mortgage, and recovery of possession of leased property

BUSINESS LAW CONCEPTS

The law plays a role in virtually every aspect of running a business. Accordingly, every business person needs a basic understanding of the legal concepts that govern business relationships. You have already studied the law of contracts, which underlies all business relationships. Now you will study some other areas of law that affect the running of a business.

Organizational Structures

An individual or a group of individuals who decide to go into business must choose a structure for organizing the business. To some degree, the choice of an organizational structure is a matter of economics and business judgment. But because the choice of structure determines the legal rights and obligations of the business's owners to one another and to third parties, the legal implications of the choice must be considered as well.

Sole Proprietorship. The simplest form of business organization is the **sole proprietorship**. A business organized as a sole proprietorship is owned by one individual. (In some jurisdictions, a husband and wife may be treated as a single owner.) Because the business has a single owner, there is no need for agreements or legal rules that govern the relationship of a business's owners to one another.

With respect to third parties, the law makes no distinction between a business operated as a sole proprietorship and its owner. The owner is personally liable for all of the business's debts. All of the owner's assets, including those that have nothing to do with the business, can be used to satisfy a judgment related to some activity of the business.

The establishment of a sole proprietorship involves few formalities. Usually the owner must obtain a business license from a local government agency. If the owner is doing business under any name other than his or her own, the owner must comply with local requirements for registering the name. The owner must also meet all federal, state, and local requirements for the handling of payroll taxes and mandatory insurance. The termination of a sole proprietorship generally does not involve any action beyond that usually associated with the winding up of a business.

Virtually any type of business can be organized as a sole proprietorship. Small retail businesses and businesses offering professional services are often operated as sole proprietorships.

General Partnership. A **partnership** is an association of individuals or legal entities known as **partners**, who are the co-owners of a business and who share among themselves the profits and losses generated by the business. A partnership is, in essence, based on a contract among the partners. In most cases this is an express contract that may be written or oral. In some situations, however, the law will treat individuals as partners in the absence of an express contract if all of the circumstances establish that the individuals are conducting themselves as partners would.

In a **general partnership** there is one class of partners, who are known as **general partners**. A general partnership is ordinarily formed for the purpose of engaging in an ongoing business.

Relationship of General Partners to One Another. The relationship of general partners to one another is governed by the terms of their partnership agreement. When the partners' written or oral agreement fails to cover all the aspects of their relationship, the areas not covered are governed by statutory law. In almost all states this statutory law is based on the Uniform Partnership Act.

A partnership agreement usually covers such subjects as the contribution that each of the partners will make to the partnership; how the partnership's business will be run; how the partnership's property will be managed; how profits and losses generated by the partnership business will be divided among the partners; how partnership decisions will be made; what happens when one of the partners dies, becomes disabled, retires, or otherwise decides to withdraw from the partnership; and how and when the partnership will be terminated.

General partners are held to a very high standard of honesty and accountability in their dealings with one another. Each partner must account to the partnership and hold for its benefit any profits which the partner receives from any transaction involving the partnership's business, or from any use of its property. A partner may not compete with the partnership's business, or appropriate for the partner's own benefit any business opportunity from which the partnership as a whole might benefit.

Relationship of General Partners to Third Parties. Special rules protect third parties when they deal with partnerships. Which rules apply depend upon whether the partnership is a general partnership, a joint venture, or a limited partnership. The broadest rules apply in the case of a general partnership.

Any contract that a general partner enters into on behalf of a general partnership is binding on the partnership, unless the other party to the contract knows that such partner was not authorized by the other partners to enter into the contract.

All of the partners of a general partnership have **joint and several liability** with respect to the partnership's debts. This means that anyone who is owed money by the partnership may collect the entire debt from any one of the partners. It is then up to the partners to obtain reimbursement from one another. This rule applies when the partnership breaches a contract resulting in damages to a third party, as well as when a partner, acting within the scope of the partnership's business, commits a tort that injures a third party. All of a partner's assets, including those that have nothing to do with the partnership's business, can be used to satisfy a judgment against the partnership.

Formation and Termination. A general partnership is formed when the partners enter into a contract, preferably written, that governs the terms of their partnership. Some jurisdictions require the filing or publication of a statement designating the name of the partnership and identifying its partners. Of course, any legal requirements that generally govern the commencement of a business apply to a business conducted by a partnership.

A general partnership is terminated in two steps. The first step is called **dissolution**. Dissolution may be caused by any number of events, including a decision by all of the partners to dissolve the partnership, the bankruptcy of the partnership, or any event that makes it illegal to continue the partnership's business. Dissolution also results when an existing partner dies or withdraws from the partnership or when a new partner is admitted to the partnership, unless the partnership agreement provides otherwise. Any partner may unilaterally decide to dissolve the partnership, but if such decision violates the partnership agreement, such partner may be liable to the other partners for damages. Under some circumstances a partner may ask that a court issue an order dissolving the partnership.

Under some circumstances the partnership agreement or statutory law may give those partners who wish to continue the partnership business the right to do so if they buy out any partner who is departing from the partnership. If that right is not given, or if the remaining partners choose not to continue the business, the partners proceed with the second step in terminating the partnership, known as **winding up**. The partners wind up the partnership by selling its property, paying its debts, and distributing any excess assets among the partners as provided in the partnership agreement or by statutory law.

Use. A general partnership is a suitable organizational structure for most types of businesses. General partnerships are most commonly used when a business has relatively few co-owners, all of whom are actively engaged in conducting the partnership's business. Very large general partnerships are rare and are usually found only in professional service businesses such as law and accounting.

Joint Venture. A **joint venture** is a partnership formed for a single business transaction or limited series of transactions. In this respect it differs from a general partnership, which is ordinarily formed for the purpose of engaging in an ongoing business.

The relationship of joint venturers to one another is governed by the same rules that apply to general partnerships. Similarly, the rules that govern the relationship between a general partnership and third parties apply to the relationship between a joint venture and third parties.

Like general partnerships, joint ventures are created by contract. A joint venture terminates on completion of the transaction for which it was formed.

Types of business transactions that are sometimes organized as joint ventures include acquisition, development, and sale of a specific parcel of real property and development, manufacture, and sale of a single specialized product.

Limited Partnership. A **limited partnership** is a partnership in which there are two classes of partners: the general partners, who have all the rights and obligations of partners in a general partnership, and the **limited partners**, who have both limited rights and limited obligations.

The relationship among the partners of a limited partnership is governed by the terms of their partnership agreement, which is virtually always in writing, and by statutory law. In almost all states the statutory law is based on some form of the Uniform Limited Partnership Act.

Most of the differences between a general partnership and a limited partnership concern the role of the limited partners. Limited partners are prohibited from actively participating in the partnership's business and have only limited voting rights with respect to decisions concerning how business is conducted. A limited partner is entitled to a share of the partnership's profits in accordance with the partnership agreement but is not personally liable for any of the partnership's debts—although any money or property that the limited partner has contributed to the partnership may be applied to satisfy those debts. A limited partnership, then, allows an individual or legal entity to invest in a business and share in its profits, yet limits potential losses to the amount originally invested. This is not possible in a general partnership, in which all of the partners have potentially unlimited liability for the partnership's debts.

A limited partnership is formed when the partners enter into a written agreement and meet a jurisdiction's requirements for filing a certificate of limited partnership. Once the partnership is formed, limited partners may sell or otherwise transfer their ownership interest in the partnership unless the partnership agreement provides otherwise.

Like a general partnership, a limited partnership is terminated through a two-step process of dissolution and winding up. A limited partnership may be dissolved on the occurrence of an event specified in the partnership agreement, on the vote of all general partners and a majority of the limited partners, or when a court order requires dissolution. A limited partnership is also dissolved when it no longer has any general partners, as they are the partners who conduct the partnership's business. Following dissolution, a limited partnership is wound up much like a general partnership.

The limited partnership organizational structure is especially suitable for businesses that require a large amount of start-up capital, such as businesses that develop real property.

Corporations. A **corporation** is a legal entity regarded by the law as having a completely separate existence from the individuals or entities who own it. It is, for most intents and purposes, a "person" with the same legal rights and obligations an individual has. It can enter into contracts, sue and be sued, own property, conduct a business, incur tax liability, commit torts, and commit crimes.

A corporation is organized, or **incorporated**, under the laws of a state or other jurisdiction. Its existence and actions are governed by those laws, by its basic organizational document, known as a **charter** or **articles of incorporation**, and by its rules and regulations, known as **bylaws**. A standard form of articles of incorporation is illustrated in Figure 5-2.

Shareholders. A corporation is owned by its **shareholders**, also known as **stockholders**. Shareholders are individuals or entities who have purchased an ownership interest in the corporation in the form of shares of stock. A corporation need only have one shareholder.

Shareholders have the right to vote on certain matters affecting the corporation's business and to elect or remove the individuals who oversee the corporation's activities. They have a right to share in the corporation's profits in the form of payments known as **dividends**. As a general rule, they are not personally liable for the corporation's debts. However, when the circumstances are

FIGURE 5-2 STANDARD FORM OF ARTICLES OF INCORPORATION

ARTICLES OF INCORPORATION

I

The name of this corporation is ______________________________

II

The purpose of the corporation is to engage in any lawful act or activity for which a corporation may be organized under the General Corporation Law of California other than the banking business, the trust company business or the practice of a profession permitted to be incorporated by the California Corporations Code.

III

The name and address in the State of California of this corporation's initial agent for service of process is:

Name ______________________________

Address ______________________________

City ____________________ State __________ ZIP __________

IV

This corporation is authorized to issue only one class of shares of stock; and the total number of shares which this corporation is authorized to issue is ______________________________

(Signature of Incorporator)
____
(Typed Name of Incorporator)

such that the shareholders have failed to treat the corporation as a separate entity and it would be unjust to allow the shareholders to escape personal liability, a court may disregard the corporate entity and hold the shareholders personally liable. This action is known as **piercing the corporate veil**.

Directors. The activities of a corporation are directed by a group of individuals known as a **board of directors** or **board of trustees**. The individual directors are elected—and may be removed—by the shareholders. The powers and duties of directors are governed by statutory law and by a corporation's charter and bylaws. In directing the corporation's activities, a director must exercise the same degree of care that an ordinarily prudent person would exercise with respect to that person's own affairs. A director may not enter into any transaction with the corporation by which the director might secretly profit. A director may not appropriate a business opportunity that might be of value to the corporation.

Officers. The board of directors of a corporation hires individuals known as **officers** to manage the day-to-day affairs of the corporation. The officers of a corporation usually include a president or chief executive officer, a vice-president, a secretary, and a treasurer or chief financial officer. The powers and duties of the officers are governed by statutory law, by the corporation's charter and bylaws, and by directives issued by the board of directors.

Formation and Termination. Formation of a corporation involves several steps, including the filing of articles of incorporation, the issuance of shares, the election of a board of directors, and the selection of officers. Because the sale of corporate shares offers many opportunities for fraud, both federal and state laws extensively regulate both the initial issuance of shares by a corporation and the subsequent resale of those shares by shareholders. Shareholders may enter into agreements among themselves governing the transfer of shares in order to preserve control of the corporation.

Unless its charter limits its existence to a specific term, a corporation may, theoretically, exist forever. As a practical matter, a corporation is terminated by a vote of its board of directors and its shareholders. On termination, a corporation liquidates its assets, pays its debts, and then distributes any remaining cash or assets to its shareholders.

Use. Virtually any type of business may be organized as a corporation. It is the preferred form of organization for large business enterprises.

Agency

An **agent** is a person who represents someone else, known as a **principal**, with respect to the principal's dealings with third parties. This form of representation is known as **agency**. It plays a large role in business transactions. Examples of principal and agent relationships include an employer and an employee, a partnership and its partners, and a corporation and its officers.

The rights and obligations of principals and agents are governed by a series of legal rules. Before considering these rules, we must emphasize the important distinction between an employee and an independent contractor. An **employee** is hired to perform services under the direct control and supervision of an employer, who determines not only the result to be accomplished, but also the method to be used to achieve that result. An **independent contractor**, by contrast, is hired by an employer to achieve a specified result only. Unlike employees, independent contractors are free to use whatever means they choose to achieve a result. An employee is always an agent of an employer, while an independent contractor may or may not be an agent of an employer.

POINTER: A person may perform virtually any service as either an employee or an independent contractor. Suppose, for example, that a mason is hired to build a brick wall. If the employer supervises the task by telling the mason exactly what to do and how and when to do it, the mason will be considered an employee. If, instead, the employer simply asks the mason to build the wall in whichever manner the mason deems best, and then allows the mason to do so, the mason will be considered an independent contractor.

Obligations of Principal and Agent to One Another. The obligations of a principal to an agent depend to some extent on the specific relationship between them. As a general rule, a principal is obligated to compensate an agent for the agent's services. A principal is also required to compensate an agent for any expense or loss the agent may incur in the course of performing the agent's authorized duties.

An agent is a **fiduciary** of the principal, which means that the agent has a duty to provide diligent and faithful service, placing the principal's interests above the agent's own interests. Agents are obligated to use reasonable care, diligence, and skill in performing their authorized duties. An agent may not compete with the principal, nor may an agent take personal advantage of an opportunity that might be of benefit to the principal. An agent must account to the principal with respect to all activities handled on the principal's behalf. An agent must compensate the principal for any injury suffered as a result of the agent's acts or omissions.

Liability of Principal to Third Parties. An agent may create legal obligations that are binding on the principal if authorized to do so by the principal or by law. Under some circumstances a principal may be bound by the actions of an agent even if the agent did not have authority. This occurs when a third party reasonably believes that an agent has the authority to bind the principal and the principal has failed to take reasonable action to prevent such a belief from arising.

An agent is obligated to inform the principal about matters related to the agent's representation of the principal. Because third parties are entitled to rely on this obligation, the law considers a principal to be informed of matters communicated to an agent, even if the agent has in fact failed to communicate such matters to the principal.

When an agent commits a tort at the direction of the principal, the principal is, of course, liable for any injury to the injured third party. But when a tort results from an agent's own intentional or negligent act, the principal may also be liable. If the tort is committed by an agent who is an employee acting in the course of employment, the principal is liable. This rule of liability is known as ***respondeat superior*** and is justified on the ground that any damages resulting from a tort that occurs in the course of employment should be treated as a cost of doing business and therefore absorbed by the business owner. Notwithstanding this justification, a principal is generally not held liable for torts committed by an independent contractor.

Liability of Agent to Third Parties. When an agent makes a representation that the agent has authority to act on behalf of a principal when in fact the agent does not have such authority, the agent is liable for any injury suffered by a third party who relies on that representation. As a general rule, an agent is not personally liable for any obligation that the agent incurs on behalf of the principal with authorization. However, an agent is always liable for the agent's own torts, even if committed at the principal's direction.

Uniform Commercial Code

The **Uniform Commercial Code** (**U.C.C.**) is a model code that covers several areas of business law. It has been adopted in one form or another by almost all United States jurisdictions. It contains detailed legal rules covering such subjects as the purchase and sale of goods, banking transactions, the sale of the assets of a business, the handling of documents that serve as evidence of debt or of ownership of goods, and the creation and enforcement of liens on property other than real property.

Sales. Article II of the Uniform Commercial Code provides a comprehensive set of rules governing all aspects of contracts that involve the purchase and sale of goods. The U.C.C. rules cover the formation, form, and interpretation of such contracts; the kinds of obligations they impose; what constitutes performance and breach under them; and the remedies available to a party who has suffered damages due to their breach.

Liens on Personal Property. Article IX of the Uniform Commercial Code provides a comprehensive system for the creation and enforcement of liens in collateral consisting of **personal property**—that is, property other than land and the improvements thereon known collectively as real property. In brief, the system requires that each lien be the subject of a written agreement. Depending on the type of collateral involved, the lienholder may be required to take some action that puts third parties on notice of the lien's existence. In most cases, this action involves the filing of a notice of lien, which becomes a public record. If the borrower defaults and fails to cure within the time allowed, depending on the type of collateral, the lender may take possession of the collateral or cause it to be sold at a public or private sale. When there are two or more liens on the same collateral, the rights of the lienholders are determined in accordance with a system of priorities established by the U.C.C.

Bankruptcy

When a business is in financial trouble and unable to pay its debts, it may seek protection from its creditors under the law of **bankruptcy**. The rights and obligations of a debtor in bankruptcy and its creditors are determined by federal statutory law. The law of bankruptcy is a highly specialized field, which we can discuss only briefly here.

Bankruptcy proceedings are handled by special federal bankruptcy courts. A bankruptcy proceeding commences with the filing of a petition by the debtor or the debtor's creditors. The proceeding usually ends in either **liquidation** or **reorganization** of the debtor. In a case of liquidation, the debtor's assets are sold and the proceeds, if any, are divided up among the creditors in accordance with a system of priorities. In a case of reorganization, the debtor remains in business while paying its creditors off, in whole or in part, in accordance with a plan approved by the court.

Individuals, as well as businesses, can take advantage of the law of bankruptcy, although somewhat different rules apply for each.

HOW PARALEGALS USE BUSINESS LAW CONCEPTS

- Drafting general partnership, joint venture, and limited partnership agreements
- Drafting corporate charters, bylaws, minutes, and shareholder agreements
- Drafting applications, statements, certificates, reports, and other documents related to the formation of business organizations
- Drafting security agreements and financing statements related to liens on personal property
- Arranging for filing or recordation of documents that become public records
- Drafting petitions, discovery requests, motions and briefs in bankruptcy litigation

ESTATE PLANNING AND PROBATE LAW CONCEPTS

A special body of law governs how an individual's property is disposed of after death. The property an individual owns at death is referred to as an **estate**. **Estate planning** is the process by which a legal professional works with an individual to plan for the disposition of an estate. After an individual dies, the estate is usually distributed by means of a court proceeding known as **probate**.

Estate Planning

Through the use of statutory law, wills, trusts, and other techniques, an individual can plan for the disposition of her or his estate after death.

Intestacy. When a person dies without having made any legally valid arrangements for the disposition of that person's estate, such individual is said to have died **intestate**. An intestate individual's property is distributed in accordance with the **intestacy statute** of the jurisdiction of the individual's principal residence. An intestacy statute identifies the deceased person's **heirs**, who are the individuals entitled to inherit the property. The statute ranks these heirs in order of priority. For example, an intestacy statute may provide that a deceased person's property be distributed to the person's spouse, or to his or her children if he or she had no living spouse, or to his or her parents if he or she had no living spouse or children, and so on. Intestacy statutes generally provide that the property of a person who dies without any living relatives belongs to the government. This is known as **escheat**.

An intestacy statute functions as an automatic estate plan for individuals who do not make any other estate-planning arrangements, or whose arrangements fail to meet legal requirements for validity.

Wills. A **will** is a document in which an individual declares how she or he wishes her or his estate to be disposed of after death. A will is considered valid and may be enforced by a court if it meets certain requirements.

Testamentary Intent. In order for a document to constitute a valid will, the individual executing the document must intend at the time of execution that the document serve as the the individual's will. This required intent is known as **testamentary intent**.

A will may be challenged as invalid on the grounds that the individual who made the will, known as the **testator**, lacked testamentary intent. Testamentary intent may be missing if a testator lacks the capacity to form the intent or the freedom necessary to express true intent.

Capacity. A person who lacks the mental ability to understand the nature of a will, the nature and extent of his or her property, and the identities of the persons who would normally be expected to inherit that property, is considered to be incapable of testamentary intent. Persons who have such mental ability, but who suffer from delusions that prevent them from making rational decisions about the disposition of their property, are also considered to be incapable of testamentary intent. In most jurisdictions, persons under a certain age are considered to lack the capacity to form testamentary intent.

Freedom. A person who has the capacity to form testamentary intent may nonetheless be prevented by outside factors from executing a will that truly reflects that intent. For example, a will is invalid if a person executes it in reliance on misrepresentations as to its purpose or contents, or in reliance on factual misrepresentations that play a role in the persons' decision to execute the will. A will is similarly invalid if executed by mistake. A will that is executed by a person as a result of the **undue influence** of another is also invalid. The concept of undue influence is broad enough to include any kind of mental or physical coercion that has the effect of displacing the will of the testator with the will of the person responsible for the coercion.

Revocation. A will is invalid if, prior to the testator's death, the testator expresses an intention that the will be revoked. This intention is usually expressed by executing a later will which supersedes the earlier will, or by physically destroying the will.

Formalities. In some jurisdictions a **holographic will**—that is, a signed will that is entirely in the testator's own handwriting—is valid. With the exception of holographic wills in those jurisdictions that recognize their validity, all wills must meet certain formal requirements imposed by a statute in each jurisdiction known as the **statute of wills**. These formal requirements usually include execution of the will by the testator in the presence of disinterested witnesses, a verbal acknowledgement by the testator to the witnesses that the executed document is in fact the testator's will, and execution of the will by the witnesses. Some jurisdictions have approved form wills that comply with the jurisdiction's statute of wills. An example of such a form will appears in Figure 5-3.

FIGURE 5-3 A TYPICAL FORM WILL

INSTRUCTIONS

1. *READ THE WILL.* Read the whole Will first. If you do not understand something, ask a lawyer to explain it to you.

2. *FILL IN THE BLANKS.* Fill in the blanks. Follow the instructions in the form carefully. Do not add any words to the Will (except for filling in the blanks) or cross out any words.

3. *DATE AND SIGN THE WILL AND HAVE TWO WITNESSES SIGN IT.* Date and sign the Will and have two witnesses sign it. You and the witnesses should read and follow the Notice to Witnesses found at the end of this Will.

CALIFORNIA STATUTORY WILL OF

Print Your Full Name

1. Will. This is my Will. I revoke all prior Wills and codicils.

2. Specific Gift of Personal Residence (Optional—use only if you want to give your personal residence to a different person or persons than you give the balance of your assets to under paragraph 5 below). I give my interest in my principal personal residence at the time of my death (subject to mortgages and liens) as follows: (Select one choice only and sign in the box after your choice.)

a. Choice One: All to my spouse, if my spouse survives me; otherwise to my descendants (my children and the descendants of my children) who survive me.

b. Choice Two: Nothing to my spouse; all to my descendants (my children and the descendants of my children) who survive me.

c. Choice Three: All to the following person if he or she survives me: (Insert the name of the person):

____

d. Choice Four: Equally among the following persons who survive me: (Insert the names of two or more persons):

____
____
____
____

3. Specific Gift of Automobiles, Household and Personal Effects (Optional—use only if you want to give automobiles and household and personal effects to a different person or persons than you give the balance of your assets to under paragraph 5 below). I give all of my automobiles (subject to loans), furniture, furnishings, household items, clothing, jewelry, and other tangible articles of a personal nature at the time of my death as follows: (Select one choice only and sign in the box after your choice.)

a. Choice One: All to my spouse, if my spouse survives me; otherwise to my descendants (my children and the descendants of my children) who survive me.

FIGURE 5-3 A TYPICAL FORM WILL (Cont.)

b. Choice Two: Nothing to my spouse; all to my descendants (my children and the descendants of my children) who survive me.

c. Choice Three: All to the following person if he or she survives me: (Insert the name of the person):

____

d. Choice Four: Equally among the following persons who survive me: (Insert the names of two or more persons):

____

____

____

____

4. Specific Gifts of Cash. (Optional) I make the following cash gifts to the persons named below who survive me, or to the named charity, and I sign my name in the box after each gift. If I don't sign in the box, I do not make a gift. (Sign in the box after each gift you make).

Name of Person or Charity to receive gift (name one only—please print)	Amount of Cash Gift
	Sign your name in this box to make this gift
Name of Person or Charity to receive gift (name one only—please print)	Amount of Cash Gift
	Sign your name in this box to make this gift
Name of Person or Charity to receive gift (name one only—please print)	Amount of Cash Gift
	Sign your name in this box to make this gift
Name of Person or Charity to receive gift (name one only—please print)	Amount of Cash Gift
	Sign your name in this box to make this gift
Name of Person or Charity to receive gift (name one only—please print)	Amount of Cash Gift
	Sign your name in this box to make this gift

FIGURE 5-3 A TYPICAL FORM WILL (Cont.)

5. Balance of My Assets. Except for the specific gifts made in paragraphs 2, 3 and 4 above, I give the balance of my assets as follows:
(Select one choice only and sign in the box after your choice. If I sign in more than one box or if I don't sign in any box, the court will distribute my assets as if I did not make a Will.)

a. Choice One: All to my spouse, if my spouse survives me; otherwise to my descendants (my children and the descendants of my children) who survive me.

b. Choice Two: Nothing to my spouse; all to my descendants (my children and the descendants of my children) who survive me.

c. Choice Three: All to the following person if he or she survives me: (Insert the name of the person):

____

d. Choice Four: Equally among the following persons who survive me: (Insert the names of two or more persons):

____

____

____

____

6. Guardian of the Child's Person. If I have a child under age 18 and the child does not have a living parent at my death, I nominate the individual named below as First Choice as guardian of the person of such child (to raise the child). If the First Choice does not serve, then I nominate the Second Choice, and then the Third Choice, to serve. Only an individual (not a bank or trust company) may serve.

Name of First Choice for Guardian of the Person

Name of Second Choice for Guardian of the Person

Name of Third Choice for Guardian of the Person

7. Special Provision for Property of Persons Under Age 25. (Optional—Unless you use this paragraph, assets that go to a child or other person who is under age 18 may be given to the parent of the person, or to the Guardian named in paragraph 6 above as guardian of the person until age 18, and the court will require a bond; and assets that go to a child or other person who is age 18 or older will be given outright to the person. By using this paragraph you may provide that a custodian will hold the assets for the person until the person reaches any age between 18 and 25 which you choose.) If a beneficiary of this Will is between age 18 and 25, I nominate the individual or bank or trust company named below as First Choice as custodian of the property. If the First Choice does not serve, then I nominate the Second Choice, and then the Third Choice, to serve.

Name of First Choice for Custodian of Assets

Name of Second Choice for Custodian of Assets

FIGURE 5-3 A TYPICAL FORM WILL (Cont.)

Name of Third Choice for Custodian of Assets

Insert any age between 18 and 25 as the age for the person to receive the property:
(If you do not choose an age, age 18 will apply.)

8. I nominate the individual or bank or trust company named below as First Choice as executor. If the First Choice does not serve, then I nominate the Second Choice, and then the Third Choice, to serve.

Name of First Choice for Executor

Name of Second Choice for Executor

Name of Third Choice for Executor

9. Bond. My signature in this box means a bond is not required for any person named as executor. A bond may be required if I do not sign in this box:

No bond shall be required.

(Notice: You must sign this Will in the presence of two (2) adult witnesses. The witnesses must sign their names in your presence and in each other's presence. You must first read to them the following two sentences.)

This is my Will. I ask the persons who sign below to be my witnesses.

Signed on ________________ at ________________, California.
(date) (city)

Signature of Maker of Will

(Notice to Witnesses: Two (2) adults must sign as witnesses. Each witness must read the following clause before signing. The witnesses should not receive assets under this Will.)

Each of us declares under penalty of perjury under the laws of the State of California that the following is true and correct:

a. On the date written below the maker of this Will declared to us that this instrument was the maker's Will and requested us to act as witnesses to it;
b. We understand this is the maker's Will;
c. The maker signed this Will in our presence, all of us being present at the same time;
d. We now, at the maker's request, and in the maker's and each other's presence, sign below as witnesses;
e. We believe the maker is of sound mind and memory;
f. We believe that this Will was not procured by duress, menace, fraud or undue influence;
g. The maker is age 18 or older; and
h. Each of us is now age 18 or older, is a competent witness, and resides at the address set forth after his or her name.

Dated: ________________, ________

Signature of witness

Print name here:

____

Residence Address:

____

____

Signature of witness

Print name here:

____

Residence Address:

____

____

AT LEAST TWO WITNESSES MUST SIGN
NOTARIZATION ALONE IS NOT SUFFICIENT

Trusts. A **trust** is a relationship with respect to the ownership and management of specific property. Title to the property is held by a **trustee**, who is required to hold and use the property for the benefit of someone else, known as a **beneficiary**. Trusts are frequently used when a person who desires to give property to someone lacks confidence in the intended recipient's ability to manage or make use of the property responsibly. By creating a trust, the gift giver can ensure that the property is properly managed by a competent trustee, while the beneficiary enjoys the benefits of ownership.

Estate planning involves the use of **express trusts**, created by means of a written or oral expression of an intention to create the trust.

In order for a trust to arise, the person creating the trust, known as the **trustor** or **settlor**, must have an intention to create the trust for a legal purpose. The trustor must designate as the subject of the trust specific property that must then be transferred to a designated trustee who has specific duties with respect to the property. The trustor must also designate a beneficiary who accepts the benefits of the trust.

A trust created under the terms of a will to become effective on the trustor's death is known as a **testamentary trust**. A document that creates a testamentary trust must meet the same formal requirements as a will.

A trust created by a trustor to become effective during the trustor's lifetime is known as an **inter vivos trust** or a **living trust**. Such trusts are usually created by a document known as a **declaration of trust**. In some jurisdictions a written document is not required to create an inter vivos trust with respect to personal property. A major advantage of an inter vivos trust is that it is already in place and operating at the testator's death, so there is no need to obtain court approval of a will creating the trust.

Other Methods of Disposition. In addition to wills and trusts, there are a few other methods of disposition available to estate planners. When title to property is held in joint tenancy, a deceased joint tenant's interest is automatically transferred to the joint tenants who survive her or him. In some jurisdictions, a deceased spouse's interest in community property is automatically transferred to the surviving spouse in the absence of other arrangements. Life insurance policy benefits and pension plan benefits can be conferred automatically at death by designating the intended recipient as the policy or plan beneficiary. By setting up a savings account in trust for a designated beneficiary, the account's owner can ensure that the account will pass automatically to the beneficiary on the owner's death.

Probate

Probate is the court proceeding by which a deceased person's estate is transferred to the persons entitled to it. When a person dies **testate** (having left a will), the probate proceeding is concerned with establishing the validity of the will and ensuring that the decedent's property is distributed in accordance with it. When a person dies intestate, the probate proceeding is concerned with identifying the decedent's heirs as established by the intestacy statute and then arranging for distribution of the decedent's property to those heirs.

Because probate proceedings can be time-consuming and expensive, it is sometimes desirable to formulate an estate plan that avoids the need for probate. Through the use of inter vivos trusts, joint tenancy, life insurance, and other estate planning techniques, probate can be avoided in some cases. Some jurisdictions provide simple procedural alternatives to probate for estates that do not exceed a specified value.

Will Contests. One of the chief purposes of probate is to establish the validity of a decedent's will. In most cases this is not an issue. However, anyone who would directly benefit from a declaration that a will is invalid (such as someone who would inherit under the intestacy statute) may challenge, or **contest**, the will. The usual grounds for contests include lack of capacity, fraud, mistake, and undue influence. Will contests usually involve a full-scale trial, resulting in a judgment that either confirms or rejects the validity of the will.

Estate Administration. Following a decedent's death and during the course of probate, the decedent's affairs must be put in order. This is usually handled by a **personal representative** appointed for the estate by the court. A personal representative who is named in a will is known as an **executor**. A personal representative for the estate of someone who dies intestate is known as an **administrator**. The personal representative is responsible for identifying and taking charge of the decedent's assets, paying the decedent's debts, and arranging for distribution of the estate's assets to the persons entitled to them. The personal representative must file accountings and reports with the court during the course of probate. When the estate's assets are ready for distribution, the court issues an order that officially transfers title to the decedent's assets to the appropriate persons and directs the personal representative to distribute such assets accordingly.

HOW PARALEGALS USE ESTATE PLANNING AND PROBATE CONCEPTS

- Helping to determine how the assets of an estate are to be distributed
- Drafting wills, trusts, and other estate planning documents
- Supervising the administration of an estate, including collection and maintenance of assets, the development of an inventory of assets, the filing of petitions with the probate court, and the preparation of accountings
- Drafting complaints, discovery requests, motions, and briefs in litigation involving will contests

FAMILY LAW CONCEPTS

In keeping with the importance of the family unit in society, domestic relationships form the subject of an extensive body of law. This diversified area of the law embraces such subjects as marriage, divorce, paternity, adoptions, guardianships, emancipation of minors, and conservatorships. The only one of these subjects that we will discuss here is **marital dissolution**, more commonly known as divorce.

The dissolution of a marriage raises many emotionally charged and intellectually challenging issues, many of which are suggested by the standard form of petition for dissolution of a marriage, illustrated in Figure 5-4. Among the most important of these issues are property division, support obligations, and child custody.

Property Division

There are few areas of law in which the rules differ from jurisdiction to jurisdiction as much as they do in family law. This is especially true of the rules that govern the disposition of a married couple's property on divorce. In the United States there are two basic systems for determining the property rights of a wife and husband: the common law system and the community property system. These systems are quite different from one another, and there are marked differences even among those jurisdictions that have adopted the same system. For this reason, only the most basic principles of the two systems can be discussed here.

Common Law System. The common law system is based on English law. In one form or another this is the system used in about four-fifths of the jurisdictions in the United States.

In common law jurisdictions the earnings of each spouse during marriage, as well as property acquired with those earnings, are considered to belong to that spouse. The logical consequence of this rule is that on dissolution of the marriage, each spouse is entitled to that spouse's property. This can create an unfair result when one spouse has taken primary responsibility for child care and household matters during the marriage, giving the other spouse the opportunity to pursue employment and consequently acquire wealth. For this reason, virtually all common law jurisdictions have adopted a variety of rules designed to achieve an equitable distribution of the couple's property by taking into account each spouse's contribution to the family's welfare. The application of these rules constitutes a substantial part of the divorce proceeding.

Community Property System. The community property system is based on Spanish and French law and is the system used in one form or another in about one-fifth of the jurisdictions in the United States, including Arizona, California, Idaho, Louisiana, Nevada, New Mexico, Puerto Rico, Texas, and Washington.

In community property jurisdictions, all property acquired by a spouse prior to marriage, and all property acquired by gift or inheritance during marriage, is that spouse's **separate property**. All property acquired by either spouse during marriage (with the exception of property acquired by gift or inheritance) is **community property**. On dissolution of the marriage, each spouse is entitled to that spouse's separate property and one-half of the community property. In community property states, divorce proceedings frequently focus on the classification of specific property as separate or community and alternative methods for achieving an equal division of community property.

Property Division by Agreement. The rules we have discussed do not prevent a couple from entering into a contract governing the division of their property.

FIGURE 5-4 STANDARD FORM OF PETITION FOR DISSOLUTION OF MARRIAGE

ATTORNEY OR PARTY WITHOUT ATTORNEY (*Name and Address*): TELEPHONE NO.: *FOR COURT USE ONLY*

ATTORNEY FOR (Name):

SUPERIOR COURT OF CALIFORNIA, COUNTY OF
STREET ADDRESS:
MAILING ADDRESS:
CITY AND ZIP CODE:
BRANCH NAME:

MARRIAGE OF
PETITIONER:
RESPONDENT:

PETITION FOR
☐ Dissolution of Marriage
☐ Legal Separation
☐ Nullity of Marriage
☐ And Declaration Under Uniform Child Custody Jurisdiction Act

CASE NUMBER:

1. RESIDENCE (Dissolution only) ☐ Petitioner ☐ Respondent has been a resident of this state for at least six months and of this county for at least three months immediately preceding the filing of this Petition for Dissolution of Marriage.

2. STATISTICAL FACTS
   a. Date of marriage:
   b. Date of separation:
   c. Period between marriage and separation
      Years: Months:
   d. Petitioner's Social Security No.:
   e. Respondent's Social Security No.:

3. DECLARATION REGARDING MINOR CHILDREN OF THIS MARRIAGE
   a. ☐ There are no minor children.
   b. ☐ The minor children are:

Child's name	Birthdate	Age	Sex

   c. IF THERE ARE MINOR CHILDREN, COMPLETE EITHER (1) or (2)
   (1) ☐ Each child named in 3b is presently living with ☐ petitioner ☐ respondent at (*address*):

   and during the last five years has lived in no state other than California and with no person other than petitioner or respondent or both. Petitioner has not participated in any capacity in any litigation or proceeding in any state concerning custody of any minor child of this marriage. Petitioner has no information of any pending custody proceeding or of any person not a party to this proceeding who has physical custody or claims to have custody or visitation rights concerning any minor child of this marriage.
   (2) ☐ A completed Declaration Under Uniform Child Custody Jurisdiction Act is attached.

4. ☐ Petitioner requests confirmation as separate assets and obligations the items listed ☐ in Attachment 4 ☐ below:

Item	Confirm to

(Continued on reverse)

Form Adopted by Rule 1281
Judicial Council of California
1281 (Rev. July 1, 1991)

PETITION
(Family Law)

Civil Code, § 4503
Cal. Rules of Court, rule 1215

FIGURE 5-4 STANDARD FORM OF PETITION FOR DISSOLUTION OF MARRIAGE (Cont.)

MARRIAGE OF (*last name, first name of parties*):	CASE NUMBER:

5. DECLARATION REGARDING COMMUNITY AND QUASI-COMMUNITY ASSETS AND OBLIGATIONS AS PRESENTLY KNOWN
   a. ☐ There are no such assets or obligations subject to disposition by the court in this proceeding.
   b. ☐ All such assets and obligations have been disposed of by written agreement.
   c. ☐ All such assets and obligations are listed ☐ in Attachment 5 ☐ below (*specify*):

6. Petitioner requests
   a. ☐ Dissolution of the marriage based on
      (1) ☐ irreconcilable differences. CC 4506(1)
      (2) ☐ incurable insanity. CC 4506(2)
   b. ☐ Legal separation of the parties based on
      (1) ☐ irreconcilable differences. CC 4506(1)
      (2) ☐ incurable insanity. CC 4506(2)
   c. ☐ Nullity of void marriage based on
      (1) ☐ incestuous marriage. CC 4400
      (2) ☐ bigamous marriage. CC 4401
   d. ☐ Nullity of voidable marriage based on
      (1) ☐ petitioner's age at time of marriage. CC 4425(a)
      (2) ☐ prior existing marriage. CC 4425(b)
      (3) ☐ unsound mind. CC 4425(c)
      (4) ☐ fraud. CC 4425(d)
      (5) ☐ force. CC 4425(e)
      (6) ☐ physical incapacity. CC 4425(f)

7. Petitioner requests the court grant the above relief and make injunctive (including restraining) and other orders as follows:

	Petitioner	Respondent	Joint	Other
a. Legal custody of children to	☐	☐	☐	☐
b. Physical custody of children to	☐	☐	☐	☐
c. Child visitation be granted to	☐	☐	☐	☐
☐ supervised as to (*specify*):				
d. Spousal support payable by (wage assignment will be issued)	☐	☐		
e. Attorney fees and costs payable by	☐	☐		

   f. ☐ Terminate the court's jurisdiction (ability) to award spousal support to respondent.
   g. ☐ Property rights be determined.
   h. ☐ Wife's former name be restored (*specify*):
   i. ☐ Other (*specify*):

8. If there are minor children of this marriage, the court may order you, *without further notice*, to pay child support in accord with the California Child Support Guideline. A wage assignment will be issued.

9. **I have read the restraining orders on the back of the Summons, and I understand that they apply to me when this petition is filed.**

   I declare under penalty of perjury under the laws of the State of California that the foregoing is true and correct.

Date:

▶ ______________________________
(SIGNATURE OF PETITIONER)

....
(TYPE OR PRINT NAME OF ATTORNEY)

▶ ______________________________
(SIGNATURE OF ATTORNEY FOR PETITIONER)

1281 (Rev. July 1, 1991)

PETITION
(Family Law)

Page two

This frequently occurs in the course of dissolution proceedings. Sometimes couples enter into a property division agreement before getting married, in which case the contract is known as a **prenuptial agreement** or **antenuptial agreement**. These agreements can cover everything from one future spouse's ownership interest in the other's business partnership to which future spouse will obtain custody of the family pet in the event of a dissolution.

Support Obligations

While married, spouses have a legal obligation to financially support one another and the children of their marriage. Under many circumstances this obligation continues after a marriage is dissolved.

The rules that define an individual's obligations to a former spouse and to children of a former marriage vary from jurisdiction to jurisdiction. The discretion of the judge often plays a large role in the awarding of spousal support, while child support is usually determined on the basis of fairly specific mandatory guidelines. In most jurisdictions a spouse who was employed outside the home during the marriage is required to contribute to the support of a spouse who worked in the home during the marriage until such spouse becomes self-supporting by obtaining appropriate education or training and a job. As a general rule, both spouses are required to contribute to the financial support of their minor children after the marriage ends, regardless of which spouse has custody of the children.

All jurisdictions have procedures to ensure that awards of spousal and child support can be enforced against a spouse required to provide support. Depending on the jurisdiction, a court may order that support be deducted from the wages of a provider spouse, that assets of a provider spouse be deposited with a trustee to secure future payment, that assets of a provider spouse be sold to pay support, or that a provider spouse be jailed until support obligations have been brought current.

Child Custody

The rules that govern the custody of children by divorced spouses vary from jurisdiction to jurisdiction. Judges commonly have broad discretion to design custody orders that best accommodate the needs and interests of the children and the parents. Such orders may provide for sole custody by one parent, joint custody by both parents, or custody by a non-parent. The best interests of the child are usually given paramount consideration in making custody decisions. Maintaining the stability and continuity of the child's environment is also an important factor. Emotional factors are usually given greater weight than purely economic ones.

In cases involving sole custody, parental visitation rights are generally guaranteed, even if visitation must be supervised or otherwise restricted. In extreme circumstances, such as those involving child abuse, visitation may be denied.

HOW PARALEGALS USE FAMILY LAW CONCEPTS

- Drafting property division and prenuptial agreements
- Drafting petitions, discovery requests, motions, and briefs in litigation involving marital dissolution and child custody matters

6 FACT INVESTIGATION: GETTING THE WHOLE STORY

MEMORANDUM

DATE: December 3, 1992

TO: Kim Starbard

FROM: Myrna Jackson, Esq.

SUBJECT: New Client Interview: John and Mary Smith

Earlier this week I spoke by telephone with John Smith. About two months ago John and his wife, Mary, purchased a used 1991 Allied Motors CS10 automobile from Lemon Motors. At the time of purchase, the car's odometer reading indicated that it had been driven only 1,956 miles, which is extremely low for a year-old car. (The car had been acquired by Lemon Motors as a trade-in from its former owner.) The Smiths' purchase price for the car included a premium for the low mileage.

Last week the car stalled in traffic and had to be towed to a garage. The mechanic contacted the manufacturer to inquire about the car's warranty and was told that the manufacturer's records indicated the car had been in for service three months ago, at which time the odometer read over 30,000 miles. The mechanic told the Smiths that, based on inspection of the engine, the car could very well have over 30,000 miles on it.

As you can imagine, the Smiths were astonished by this news. Mr. Smith returned to Lemon Motors and demanded an explanation, but the people he spoke with were very noncommittal. The Smiths want to know whether or not they have a legal claim against Lemon Motors, and they have retained us to advise them in that regard.

Please contact the Smiths and set up an appointment to interview them next week. Find out everything you can that might assist us in determining whether or not the Smiths are entitled to be compensated by Lemon Motors.

INTRODUCTION: GETTING THE WHOLE STORY

Paralegals spend lots of time and energy gathering factual information. In this chapter you will study the information-gathering skills that every paralegal needs. You will learn how to tailor a search for information. You will be introduced to the basic skills involved in interviewing people, and you will learn how to organize and record the information you obtain from your interviews. Finally, you will be introduced to three important sources of information frequently used by paralegals: government records, computer databases, and physical evidence.

Developing Information-Gathering Skills

Because paralegals must gather and organize information on a daily basis, paralegals with well-developed information-gathering skills will be highly valued members of any professional team.

Basic Skills That Every Paralegal Needs. Every paralegal must develop basic information-gathering skills in at least four areas: interviewing, searching government records, researching computer databases, and handling physical evidence. Outlined in Figure 6-1, these skills will be examined in detail throughout this chapter.

How Paralegals Use Information-Gathering Skills. Because it is impossible to catalog here all the ways paralegals use information-gathering skills, let's take a brief look at the responsibilities of three specialists—one in litigation, one in real estate transactions, and one in family law—and see how these paralegals put their information-gathering skills to work.

Litigation Specialist. A paralegal who specializes in litigation must gather information that will enable a law office to prosecute or defend a lawsuit successfully. Because virtually all lawsuits arise out of one or more events, litigation paralegals spend a great deal of time gathering information to reconstruct events. This involves determining exactly what happened, how it happened, and why it happened.

Suppose a client who was injured in an automobile accident wants to file a lawsuit to recover compensation for the injuries suffered. Before the lawsuit can be filed, an investigation must be undertaken to identify all the parties who may have had some responsibility for causing the accident. A paralegal participating in this investigation would attempt to locate and interview the drivers of the automobiles involved, any passengers in those automobiles, and any bystanders who might have witnessed the accident. The paralegal might research government records to determine if other accidents have occurred at the same location, a fact that would signal a possibly dangerous condition for which the municipality might be responsible. In an effort to determine whether or not a manufacturer's design defect could have contributed to the accident, the paralegal might use a computer database to ascertain the safety records of the automobile models involved. The paralegal might visit the accident site to collect debris, take photographs of the location and any physical evidence such as skid marks, and prepare a diagram illustrating what occurred based on witnesses' accounts of

FIGURE 6-1 BASIC SKILLS THAT EVERY PARALEGAL NEEDS

Interviewing

- Identify and locate individuals who have information that may be useful
- Formulate questions for an interview
- Conduct interviews in a manner that assists people and encourages them to provide a maximum amount of useful information
- Record accurately the information obtained in interviews
- Organize and communicate the information obtained

Searching Government Records

- Identify which government records may contain information that would be useful in a particular situation
- Determine the location of those records
- Obtain the records from the government agency that maintains them

Researching Computer Databases

- Be familiar with databases that contain information relevant to the field of law in which you work
- Master the basic computer skills necessary to access those databases

Handling Physical Evidence

- Make significant observations when visiting the site of an event
- Record information about a site through the use of photography and diagrams
- Identify physical objects that may be important sources of information
- Locate and communicate with people who are experts in analyzing physical objects

the accident. The paralegal might contact and coordinate the activities of experts who can determine the causes of accidents by examining the damaged automobiles, other evidence such as road debris and skid marks, and the actual physical injuries suffered by the individuals involved.

Real Estate Transactions Specialist. A paralegal who specializes in real estate transactions must gather information that will enable a law office to document a real estate transaction fully and accurately.

Suppose a client desires to purchase a large residential apartment building. A paralegal involved in the transaction would likely interview the buyer about the terms of the purchase and the building's manager or tenants about possible problems with the building. The paralegal might search government records for a variety of information: to confirm who holds title to the property, to determine whether the building was constructed in accordance with required permits, and to ascertain whether the current owner has been cited for any building code violations. The paralegal might use a computer database to locate information about recent selling prices for similar buildings. The paralegal might visit the building to confirm information about its condition. The paralegal might contact and coordinate the activities of experts qualified to evaluate the structural condition of the building or detect the presence of any hazardous materials on the site.

Family Law Specialist. A paralegal who specializes in family law must gather information that will enable a law office to represent the interests of its clients properly in any number of family law proceedings.

Suppose, for example, that a wife, seeking a divorce, is uncertain about the extent or value of the couple's assets because her husband has managed all their financial affairs. Information about these matters must be obtained so that the wife may request appropriate orders for spousal support and division of the couple's property. A paralegal working on the case would, of course, begin by interviewing the wife and might also interview the couple's accountant, banker, and stock broker. The paralegal might interview the husband's employer. The paralegal might search government records to ascertain the existence of any property held in the names of the husband, the wife, or both. The paralegal might use a computer database to obtain information about the husband's business or the market value of the couple's investments. The paralegal might contact and coordinate the activities of experts capable of locating hidden assets or determining the value of assets such as real property, pension plans, jewelry, or privately held businesses.

Practice Makes Perfect. Although you will learn quite a bit about paralegal information-gathering skills by studying this chapter, this will not change the fact that the only way you can acquire these skills is by practicing them. This book can provide you with general guidelines and specific tips about how to practice a skill, but your real learning can come only through trial and error. For this reason, each time you practice an information-gathering skill you should take some time afterward to think about what was accomplished and how you accomplished it. Think about what you did that worked, what you did that did not work, and what you would do differently if you had the chance to do it again. By taking time to evaluate each experience, you will increase your mastery of each skill.

Tailoring a Search for Information

Before you use your information-gathering skills, you need to identify the precise information you are trying to gather. You can tailor your search for information by following three steps: (1) identifying the events or transactions about which you need information; (2) identifying your purpose in gathering that information; and (3) identifying areas of inquiry that are relevant to your purpose.

For example, in the memorandum that appears at the beginning of this chapter, a supervising attorney has asked Kim, a paralegal, to gather information about a specific transaction: the Smiths' purchase of an automobile that allegedly had substantially more mileage than was indicated on the car's odometer. The purpose in gathering this information is suggested by the memorandum itself: the Smiths want to know if they are entitled to compensation from Lemon Motors because of the mileage discrepancy.

Suppose you were the paralegal who received this memorandum from your employer. By focusing on your purpose in gathering information from the Smiths, you should be able to identify areas of inquiry that are relevant to your purpose. For example, when interviewing the Smiths, you will want to ask them about the circumstances under which they learned that their car's odometer reading was incorrect. You will not, however, want to ask them how long they owned their previous car or why they decided to buy a domestically produced car instead of an import. Such information would be irrelevant to your purpose in interviewing them. By focusing on your purpose in gathering information, then, you can eliminate possible areas of inquiry about which you need not be concerned. This will permit you to concentrate your time and energy on finding out what you need to know.

POINTER: As you learn more about an event or transaction and about the law that governs your client's interests or rights, you will identify additional areas of inquiry. As you will discover in Chapter 8, when rules of law are considered in connection with the facts of a case, disagreements often arise over how a particular rule of law applies to a particular set of facts. These disagreements constitute "legal issues" that must be resolved in the course of resolving the case. As the legal issues involved in a case become clear, the need arises to gather additional information relevant to those issues. You will see how this occurs as you follow the development of the *Smith v. Lemon Motors* case in subsequent chapters of this book.

Focusing on your purpose in gathering information enables you to tailor your search in another important way. It helps you to determine how selective you should be about the information you are gathering. For example, during your initial interview of the Smiths, you will want to learn as much as possible about the purchase transaction. You will attempt to gather as much information as possible without overly concerning yourself about its source, its reliability, or its admissibility as evidence in court. (As you will learn in the next section, evidence is admissible if it meets certain requirements laid down in the rules of evidence.)

Whenever you are gathering information it is wise to stop frequently and recall your purpose in gathering the information. This will help you to avoid much wasted time and energy.

Dealing with the Rules of Evidence

In almost every dispute, each party has a different version of the underlying facts. At trial, a judge or jury is required to determine, as best it can, which version of the facts is correct. The judge or jury—known as the **trier of fact**—makes its determination on the basis of the evidence each party presents in an attempt to prove its version of the facts. Most evidence consists of witness testimony, documents, and physical objects.

The outcome of a lawsuit depends on which version of the facts is accepted by the judge or jury. For this reason, it is imperative that the trier of fact consider only evidence that is both relevant and reliable. In order to ensure that this is the case, only evidence that meets certain requirements may be submitted to the trier of fact for consideration. These requirements are known as **rules of evidence**. Evidence that meets the requirements of the rules of evidence is known as **admissible evidence**.

An examination of the rules of evidence is beyond the scope of this chapter. You will have an opportunity to study the rules in depth when you take advanced courses in civil litigation and criminal procedure. For now, simply keep in mind that only some of the information you gather will be admissible in court.

INTERVIEWING CLIENTS AND WITNESSES

One of the chief ways in which paralegals assist lawyers is by interviewing people. In a busy law office, lawyers rarely have time to interview everyone who may have useful information about an event or a transaction. Paralegals are often asked to locate individuals who may have useful information and to determine what information they actually have. If the information appears to be valuable, a paralegal may be directed to obtain that information by means of a thorough and systematic interview and to record and organize the information for a lawyer's use.

Clients are the people most frequently interviewed by paralegals. Paralegals interview potential or new clients to obtain a narrative of the events that have led the client to seek the services of a lawyer. In a litigation practice, paralegals often interview clients in order to prepare responses to requests for information from other parties to the litigation. Litigation paralegals may also interview clients in the course of drafting sworn statements to be submitted to the court or preparing outlines of oral testimony to be presented at trial. In a transactional practice, paralegals may interview clients to obtain the detailed information necessary to draft contracts and other legal documents such as wills.

Paralegals often interview people who are not clients. In a litigation practice, these individuals are frequently potential witnesses. Such witnesses may be either percipient witnesses or expert witnesses. A **percipient witness** is someone who has first-hand knowledge of some fact related to an event or transaction, knowledge usually based on sensory observation. An individual who has seen two automobiles collide, for example, is a percipient witness to that event. An **expert witness** is someone who does not necessarily have first-hand knowledge of a particular event or transaction, but has an expert knowledge of events or transactions of the type that are in question. For example, an expert witness may be someone who has extensively examined automobiles that have been involved in many different kinds of collisions. This expert may not have observed a particular collision, but by examining the automobiles involved, the expert may be able to explain how the collision occurred.

In a transactional practice, paralegals interview individuals who are not necessarily potential witnesses, but who have useful information nonetheless. A real estate paralegal, for example, may interview a real estate broker about the terms negotiated in a particular lease transaction; an estate planning paralegal may interview a client's financial advisor about the nature and extent of the client's assets.

Determining Who Knows What

The first step in gathering any information you need is determining who has that information. This is an especially important step when gathering information through interviews.

Identifying Potentially Knowledgeable Individuals. When beginning a search for information about a particular event or transaction, it is useful to draw up a list of people who may have knowledge you need. Drawing up such a list requires you to think both logically and creatively: you must think about the event or transaction in question and then about all the people who may have played a role in that event or transaction.

Suppose, for example, you want to draw up a list of people who might be knowledgeable about the transaction described in the memorandum at the beginning of this chapter. Assume that your purpose in talking to these people is the same as your purpose in interviewing the Smiths—namely, to gather information that would be useful in determining whether or not the Smiths are entitled to compensation from Lemon Motors. The central fact that underlies the Smiths' potential claim is the discrepancy between the car's odometer reading and its actual mileage. This will be a key area of inquiry in any interview you conduct. Accordingly, you decide to draw up a list of people who might have knowledge about the car's odometer reading, its actual mileage, or both.

POINTER: Note that you have just tailored your search for information using the three steps discussed earlier in this chapter. You have identified the transaction you are interested in, identified your purpose in gathering information, and identified a key area of inquiry that is relevant to that purpose.

In drawing up a list, it is often useful to take a chronological approach. Choose a significant point in time, and then ask yourself: Who might have had knowledge at this point in time? Who might have had knowledge before this point in time? Who might have had knowledge after this point in time?

Returning to our example, suppose the point in time you select is the day the Smiths purchased their car from Lemon Motors. Who knew about the car's odometer reading at this point in time? The Smiths, of course, and the sales representative who sold them the car. Who might have known about the car's odometer reading before this point in time? Thinking in reverse chronological order, you might come up with the following people: the mechanic at Lemon Motors who checked over the car before it was put on the lot; the sales representative who inspected the car before accepting it as a trade-in; the former owner of the car; anyone who repaired the car while it was in the former owner's possession; anyone who borrowed the car while it was in the former owner's possession; the sales representative who sold the car to the former owner; the person at the dealership who inspected the car when it was delivered from the manufacturer; and the manufacturer. Having exhausted these possibilities, you then ask yourself who might have known about the car's odometer reading *after* its purchase by the Smiths. The list here is shorter: the Smiths; anyone who repaired the car while it was in the Smiths' possession; and anyone who borrowed the car while it was in the Smiths' possession.

The same process can be used to compile a list of people who may be knowledgeable about the car's actual mileage. Such a list is shown in Figure 6-2. Note that the list has been arranged in chronological order.

FIGURE 6-2 INDIVIDUALS WHO MAY HAVE KNOWLEDGE ABOUT THE CAR'S ACTUAL MILEAGE

1. Manufacturer
2. Personnel at auto dealership that sold car to former owner
   a. Person responsible for inspecting new merchandise
   b. Mechanic
   c. Sales representative
3. Former owner
4. Mechanics who serviced the car while it was owned by former owner
5. People knowledgeable about the former owner's driving habits
   a. Family
   b. Friends
   c. Co-workers
   d. Employer
6. Lemon Motors sales representative who inspected the car before accepting it as a trade-in
7. Lemon Motors mechanic who checked over the car before it was put on the lot
8. Sales representative who sold the car to the Smiths
9. Anyone whose expertise would enable them to make an estimate of the car's mileage based on its physical condition

Locating Potentially Knowledgeable Individuals. Thus far you have compiled a list of people whose roles in an event or transaction make them possible sources of useful information. Your next step is to locate specific individuals who actually fill the roles you have identified.

Your initial source of information is the client. Returning to our example, the Smiths should be able to give you the name and business address or telephone number of the sales representative who sold them the car, any other personnel at Lemon Motors with whom they have had any contact, and the mechanic who repaired the car after it broke down.

Building on the information you receive from the client, you can contact the identified individuals to obtain information about other individuals. For example, the Lemon Motors sales representative who sold the Smiths their car, if cooperative, should be able to provide both the name of the fellow sales representative who inspected the car before Lemon Motors accepted it as a trade-in and the name of the Lemon Motors mechanic who checked the car before it was put on the lot. The mechanic who repaired the car for the Smiths after it broke down should be able to provide, from the information obtained from the manufacturer at the time of the repairs, the name of the auto dealership that sold the car to the former owner and the name of the former owner.

While the foregoing series of inquiries will enable you to gather the information necessary to locate percipient witnesses, a different procedure is followed to locate expert witnesses. Suppose, for example, you want to locate someone who has the expertise necessary to inspect the Smiths' car and provide you with a reliable estimate of its actual mileage based on that inspection.

One of the best ways to locate expert witnesses is by talking to lawyers and paralegals who have been involved in cases or transactions similar to the one in which you are involved. These lawyers and paralegals can give you the names of experts with whom they have worked and provide you with an idea of various experts' strengths and weaknesses. Sometimes an opponent's expert makes such an impressive showing in court that a lawyer or paralegal will recommend that expert instead of one they have used themselves.

When it is not possible to locate an expert by means of professional referral, you may find it useful to consult the directories of expert witnesses that appear in law-oriented publications. Many expert witnesses advertise in national and local legal newspapers and magazines. Some bar associations maintain expert witness lists that are available for the asking. Many professional associations also maintain lists of their members who are available to act as expert witnesses.

Determining Whether an Interview Is Worth Pursuing. Once you have located the individuals on your list, your next step is to contact them to find out whether they actually have information that you need. Keep in mind that your list consists of *potentially* knowledgeable individuals. It is likely that some people on your list may have played a role in the event or transaction you are concerned about but do not have useful information. A telephone call to each individual will usually reveal whether that person has sufficient information to warrant an extended, face-to-face interview.

When contacting an individual for the first time, you should identify yourself, the lawyer you work for, and your client. Explain briefly the nature of the inquiry you are conducting, and then ask a few questions to determine the extent of the individual's knowledge about the event or transaction that concerns you. By focusing your questions on the individual's role in the event or transaction, you will often get a good idea about what the individual knows.

Suppose you learn that the former owner of the Smiths' car had it serviced at a small auto repair shop owned by Julio Valenzuela. A possible approach to your initial conversation with Mr. Valenzuela is illustrated in Figure 6-3.

The conversation illustrated in Figure 6-3 demonstrates how a few simple questions can help you identify an individual who may have useful information. But not everyone on your list will be a good candidate for a face-to-face interview. Suppose you learn that the former owner of the Smiths' car also had it serviced at the Oil Exchange, a repair shop owned by Arthur Chen. A possible approach to your initial conversation with Mr. Chen is illustrated in Figure 6-4.

FIGURE 6-3 INITIAL CONVERSATION WITH POTENTIAL WITNESS JULIO VALENZUELA

Paralegal: Good morning, Mr. Valenzuela. My name is Kim Starbard. I am a paralegal who works for Myrna Jackson, an attorney here in town. Mrs. Jackson represents Mary and John Smith, who purchased a used 1991 Allied Motors CS10 from Lemon Motors a few months ago. I have been told that the former owner of the car had it serviced at your garage. If you have a moment, may I ask you a few questions?

Mr. Valenzuela: Sure, but I only have a minute.

Paralegal: The former owner of the car was Tim Duncan. Does that name ring a bell?

Mr. Valenzuela: It certainly does. I remember him well. He was one of the fussiest customers I have ever had to deal with.

Paralegal: Do you recall what kind of work you did for Mr. Duncan?

Mr. Valenzuela: Routine maintenance stuff. Oil changes. Tune-ups. Duncan was very particular about maintaining his car.

Paralegal: A question has come up about the car's mileage. Would you happen to have any records that might indicate the car's mileage on the occasions you worked on it?

Mr. Valenzuela: Sure do. Funny you should mention that. I remember the first time he brought that car in I was amazed that a car with such high mileage was in such good shape. But then, Duncan seemed obsessed with keeping that car in A-1 mint condition.

Paralegal: Mr. Valenzuela, your information is very helpful. Could I drop by your garage tomorrow to discuss it with you in a bit more depth? I promise it won't take up much of your time.

Based on the conversation illustrated in Figure 6-4, you would probably determine that a face-to-face interview with Mr. Chen would not be worthwhile.

Formulating Questions and Conducting the Interview

Once you have identified an individual who has useful information, you should schedule a face-to-face interview with that person. A face-to-face interview has several advantages. It allows you to establish a personal rapport that cannot be established by telephone or letter. It gives you an opportunity to assess the interviewee's **demeanor**—that is, the person's overall impression of credibility. Most important, it allows you to implement a number of interviewing techniques that will help you obtain a maximum amount of information.

The Interview Environment. When planning an interview, you must consider a number of practical matters: selecting a convenient and comfortable location, maximizing privacy, eliminating distractions, and allocating sufficient time.

FIGURE 6-4 INITIAL CONVERSATION WITH POTENTIAL WITNESS ARTHUR CHEN

Paralegal:	Good morning, Mr. Chen. My name is Kim Starbard. I am a paralegal who works for Myrna Jackson, an attorney here in town. Mrs. Jackson represents Mary and John Smith, who purchased a used 1991 Allied Motors CS10 from Lemon Motors a few months ago. I have been told that the former owner of the car had it serviced at your garage. If you have a moment, may I ask you a few questions?
Mr. Chen:	Sure, if they're quick questions.
Paralegal:	The former owner of the car was Tim Duncan. Does that name ring a bell?
Mr. Chen:	No. This is a high-volume operation. We must have five hundred cars in here each month.
Paralegal:	What kind of work do you do?
Mr. Chen:	We do twenty-minute "while you wait" oil changes. All makes, all models.
Paralegal:	Would you happen to have any records that might indicate whether or not you worked on Mr. Duncan's car?
Mr. Chen:	Not unless he was in here within the last four weeks. We keep work orders on file for only a month.
Paralegal:	Well, I think that's all I need to know. Thank you for your time.

Selecting a Convenient and Comfortable Location. The location you select for an interview should be both convenient and comfortable for the interviewee.

Under most circumstances, the interviewee will be cooperating with your investigation on a voluntary basis, so your effort to make everything as convenient as possible will encourage cooperation. Moreover, interviewees view your willingness to accommodate them as an expression of your appreciation of their voluntary efforts.

An interviewee who is uneasy with the interview surroundings will not concentrate fully and may withhold information simply to get through the interview as quickly as possible. One who is comfortable with the surroundings, however, will be able to focus on the business at hand and be ready to cooperate with you.

In many respects the most logical place to hold an interview is the law office in which you work. The location is convenient for you. You are able to ensure privacy and minimize distractions, and the surroundings impart a sense of seriousness and professionalism that will make a positive impression on many interviewees. But unfortunately there may be negatives. Your office location may be inconvenient for some interviewees, and some may be intimidated by the very seriousness and professionalism that make it a fine setting for others. Therefore you should make a real effort to determine the interviewee's preference when you set up an interview. Be willing to meet with the interviewee at her or his place of business or residence or at some neutral location such as a restaurant, if that is what the person prefers.

Maximizing Privacy and Eliminating Distractions. Ideally, every interview should be conducted in complete privacy, free from all distractions. As a practical matter, however, this is not always possible. Given the available setting, then, your goal should be to maximize privacy and eliminate distractions to the greatest extent possible.

Privacy is of paramount importance when interviewing a client. As you will learn when you study Chapter 10, confidential communications between a lawyer and a client are privileged. In other words, neither the lawyer nor the client can be legally required to disclose the content of these communications. However, the privilege applies only if the circumstances of the communication indicate an intention that the communication be confidential. Obviously, whether or not a communication is made in a private setting is a critical factor in determining whether or not it is intended to be confidential. The attorney-client privilege extends to confidential communications between a client and a lawyer's employees, but to preserve the privileged nature of your communications with clients, you must ensure that they occur in private.

Privacy is important even when the interviewee is not a client. An interviewee who is speaking with you alone is better able to concentrate on your questions and may have a tendency to be more open with you. When others are present, the interviewee may be distracted by their reactions or may be less frank than in a one-on-one interview.

Interruptions and outside distractions make it difficult to adhere to a preplanned interview format, and disrupt an interviewee's focus and train of thought. Because an interview is most effective when it is carefully structured, every effort should be made before the interview to minimize the possibility of interruptions and to eliminate outside distractions.

Allocating Sufficient Time. If either you or the interviewee feels rushed, the interview will suffer. You need time to ask all the questions you prepared prior to the interview, as well as questions suggested by the interviewee's answers as the interview progresses. The interviewee needs time to think about your questions and respond to them in an unhurried manner.

Ideally, the time set aside for an interview should be open-ended so that both you and the interviewee can take all the time you need to complete the interview. Of course, this is not always possible. Once you have conducted a number of interviews, you should develop an ability to estimate in advance how long a particular interview may take. You should then be certain that enough time is set aside to accommodate this estimate. When you are uncertain, it is better to set aside too much time than not enough. It is always preferable to conduct an interview in a single meeting, rather than stop the interview at midpoint and then have to make arrangements to continue it at some later time.

Formulating Questions. To obtain a maximum amount of information during an interview, you must prepare ahead of time. Because you will already have identified the information you are seeking, you will be able to formulate some questions in advance. Other questions will occur to you as the interview progresses and you receive answers to your prepared questions. You will need a systematic approach to questioning that will enable you to ask both the questions you have formulated ahead of time and those that suggest themselves to you as the interview moves along.

Taking a Chronological Approach. One of the most effective ways to structure an interview is chronologically. This approach has two distinct advantages. First, it enables you to do a thorough job of questioning the interviewee. Second, it helps the interviewee recall information that might otherwise be passed over or "forgotten."

Most interviews are attempts to obtain information about a series of events. Events unfold one at a time, over time. Thus the best way to examine a series of events is one at a time, in chronological order. When taking a chronological approach to questioning, you must focus on three goals: First, identify each individual event that has occurred. Second, identify the order in which these events occurred. Third, go back and examine the events one at a time.

Identifying Events in Chronological Order. Suppose, for example, that you are interviewing the Smiths for the first time. Your first goal is to identify each event that occurred, and your second goal is to place these events in chronological order. Both goals can be achieved through a single, simple line of questioning.

Your first question should attempt to identify the first relevant event about which the Smiths have any knowledge. Keeping in mind that the car is the one object that links all of the events that you are interested in, you might ask the Smiths, "When did you first learn of the car's existence?" Suppose Mr. Smith answers, "When I read about it in a classified ad in the newspaper." You now have the first event in the time line of events around which you will structure the interview.

To identify the second event in the time line, simply ask, "What happened next?" Suppose Mr. Smith says, "I called the dealer to make an appointment to see the car." Again, you ask, "What happened next?" Mr. Smith says, "We went to the dealer, where a sales representative showed us the car." Continue to ask the Smiths what happened next until they have identified each event that occurred from the time they first heard about the car until the present. At the conclusion of the questioning, you will have written down a time line like the one shown in Figure 6-5.

When establishing a time line, it is important to avoid becoming sidetracked by asking detailed questions about individual events before you have completed the time line. It is also important that you not suggest answers by asking questions such as, "You went to see the sales representative next, right?" The way to avoid these pitfalls is to focus on asking one and only one question until the time line is completed: "What happened next?"

Examining Events One at a Time. Once you have completed the time line, you can go back and ask a series of questions about the first event. In formulating

FIGURE 6-5 SMITH INTERVIEW TIME LINE

Read about car in ad
Called dealer for appointment
Sales representative showed them car
Talked it over
Called sales representative to say they would take car
Went to dealer to sign papers and pick up car
Drove car for two months with no problems
Car broke down in traffic
Went to repair shop
Learned that warranty records showed high mileage
Had car repaired
Called dealership to complain
Visited dealership
Called lawyer and made appointment for this interview

your questions, keep in mind the what-when-where-who-why-how of the event. After you have finished questioning about the first event, move on to the second event, and so on, until you have covered all of the events that have been identified.

Returning to our example, you might ask the following questions about the first event identified by Mr. Smith:

- When did you see the classified ad?
- What newspaper was it in?
- Why were you looking at the classified ads?
- What did the ad say?
- Did you save a copy of the ad?

By the time you have finished asking about each event that an interviewee has identified, you should have most of the information that the interviewee is able to give you.

Asking Open-Ended Questions. When formulating questions, avoid wording them so narrowly that the interviewee has no choice but to answer in a particular way. It is equally important that your questions not suggest the answer that the interviewee is expected to give. In either case, you may be denying the interviewee an opportunity to tell you what the interviewee knows, and you may be missing out on important information. To encourage the interviewee to tell you everything she or he knows, practice asking questions in the broadest, most open-ended way possible.

Suppose, for example, you are interviewing Iris Ramos, the Lemon Motors sales representative who inspected the car at the time the dealership purchased it from its former owner. You want to know whether or not there was anything about the appearance of the car that might have caused Miss Ramos to question whether it actually had only 1,956 miles on it. You might start by asking a very broad question and follow with a series of increasingly more specific ones:

- Did you notice anything unusual about the appearance of the car?
- Was there anything about the car's appearance that seemed inconsistent with the car's odometer reading of 1,956 miles?
- Can you describe the condition of the car's paint?
- Were there any chips or scratches in the paint?

By beginning with broader questions, you can obtain information that might otherwise be missed. Suppose, for example, that Miss Ramos had noticed some oxidation of the car's paint when she examined the car. If the only question you ask her about the paint is a very specific one (''Were there any chips or scratches in the paint?''), she won't have a chance to tell you about the oxidation. Similarly, if you ask Miss Ramos a leading question (''Was the car's paint in generally good condition?''), she will probably answer, ''Yes.'' Your question will have suggested that this is the answer you are looking for. If, instead, you ask Miss Ramos a fairly broad, nonsuggestive question (''Can you describe the condition of the car's paint?''), she may think about it and then tell you, ''I seem to recall noticing some oxidation.''

When you are searching for specific information, it is often difficult to remember to ask broader questions before asking more specific ones.

For example, when asking the Smiths about the classified ad they saw for the car, you will no doubt want to know whether or not the ad specified the car's mileage. But you are better off asking, ''What did the ad say?'' before asking, ''Did the ad specify the car's mileage?'' In response to the broader question, the Smiths might tell you that the ad mentioned an 'almost new' car with less than 2,000 miles on it; in response to the narrower question, they would simply tell you that the ad stated that the car had less than 2,000 miles on it. By failing to ask the broader question, you will have missed the important fact that the dealership claimed that the car was ''almost new.''

Filling in the Gaps. When interviewing a witness, it is important to help the witness search her or his memory in a systematic way. One memory will often trigger another memory that might otherwise have been forgotten.

Suppose, for example, that you are asking the Smiths about their contacts with Lemon Motors' personnel after the Smiths found out that warranty records indicated the car actually had over 30,000 miles on it. Mr. Smith has told you that he went to the dealership and talked to several people, but he can't recall all of them. You might help Mr. Smith jog his memory by questioning him as demonstrated in Figure 6-6.

By asking Mr. Smith questions that required him to fill in the gaps before, after, and between the two events he initially recalled, you helped him to recall three people he talked to on the same day he talked to Andy and the manager. Your questions ''guided'' Mr. Smith through his visit to the dealership, with one memory triggering another. Once again, by using a chronological approach, you obtained information that might otherwise have been passed over or forgotten.

FIGURE 6-6 MEMORY JOGGING BY FILLING IN THE GAPS

Paralegal:	Mr. Smith, who did you talk to at the dealership?
Mr. Smith:	Andy, our sales representative, who I had an appointment with, and the manager.
Paralegal:	Did you see anyone before you saw Andy?
Mr. Smith:	Now that I think about it, I talked to David in the service department, because I couldn't find Andy when I first arrived.
Paralegal:	Did you see anyone before you saw David?
Mr. Smith:	No.
Paralegal:	Did you see anyone after you saw David, but before you saw Andy?
Mr. Smith:	Yes, I talked to the receptionist who helped me find Andy.
Paralegal:	Did you see anyone after you saw David, but before you saw the receptionist?
Mr. Smith:	No.
Paralegal:	Did you see anyone after you saw the receptionist, but before you saw Andy?
Mr. Smith:	No.
Paralegal:	After you saw Andy, did you see anyone else?
Mr. Smith:	The manager.
Paralegal:	Did you see anyone after you saw Andy, but before you saw the manager?
Mr. Smith:	No.
Paralegal:	Did you see anyone after you saw the manager?
Mr. Smith:	Yes, the manager took me over to see Sarah, in customer relations.
Paralegal:	Did you see anyone after you saw Sarah?
Mr. Smith:	No, I went home.

Uncovering Corroborative Information. When interviewing, you should be on the lookout for sources of information that might corroborate—that is, verify or confirm—information you obtain from the interviewee. When the facts of a matter are disputed, it is critical that you have many reliable sources of information that will either confirm your client's version of the facts or disprove your opponent's version.

Suppose, for example, a dispute has arisen concerning the mileage on the Smiths' car at the time it was sold to Lemon Motors by its former owner. The former owner contends that the mileage was 1,956; Lemon Motors and the Smiths contend that the mileage must have been at least 30,000. You have been asked to draft a list of mileage-related questions that will be asked of the former owner when his deposition is taken. Recall from Chapter 1 that a deposition is the questioning of a party or a witness under oath. (Depositions and other discovery techniques will be discussed in detail in Chapter 9.)

When drafting the questions, be sure to identify sources of information that will either confirm or disprove the former owner's testimony and, by extension, the former owner's version of the facts. Using your own knowledge about how people treat the cars they own, draw up a list of possible sources of information, including people, documents, and physical objects. You can ask yourself the following questions:

1. Based on my own knowledge about the kind of people who may know a car's mileage at any given point in time, who may have known what this car's mileage was before it was sold to Lemon Motors?
2. Based on my own knowledge about the kinds of records that are kept concerning a car's mileage, what records may exist concerning this car's mileage?
3. Based on my own knowledge about objects that might indicate a car's mileage, what objects may exist that indicate this car's mileage?

Your list of possible sources of information might be similar to that illustrated in Figure 6-7.

FIGURE 6-7 POSSIBLE SOURCES OF CORROBORATIVE INFORMATION ABOUT THE CAR'S MILEAGE AT THE TIME OF ITS SALE TO LEMON MOTORS

People

1. Former owner
2. Mechanics who serviced the car while it was owned by former owner
3. People knowledgeable about the former owner's driving habits:
   a. Family
   b. Friends
   c. Co-workers
   d. Employer
4. Lemon Motors personnel who inspected the car before accepting it from the former owner as a trade-in

Documents

1. Car maintenance notebook maintained by former owner
2. Car mileage log maintained by former owner for employer reimbursement or for tax purposes
3. Auto expense reimbursement requests submitted by former owner to employer
4. Service orders prepared by mechanics who serviced the car

Objects

1. Car

You will notice that the first question you asked yourself is similar to the one you asked when attempting to identify individuals who might be worth interviewing. You will also notice that the second question was relatively easy to answer once you focused on each individual you identified in response to the first question, and then asked, "What records might this individual have kept?" Finally, you will notice that you were not able to come up with much in response to the third question. While that may have been the case here, there are many kinds of cases in which physical objects are important sources of information.

Figure 6-8 illustrates some deposition questions you might come up with based on your list of possible sources of corroborative information.

FIGURE 6-8 DEPOSITION QUESTIONS FOR FORMER OWNER

1. While you owned the car, did you ever have it serviced by a professional mechanic?
2. If so, who?
3. If so, when?
4. If so, what was done?
5. If so, do you still have any of the service orders?
6. Did you maintain a notebook in which you kept track of the occasions on which the car was serviced?
7. If so, where is it now?
8. While you owned the car, did you ever give rides to anyone on a regular basis?
9. If so, who?
10. Did you ever lend your car to anyone?
11. If so, who?
12. Who, besides yourself, was familiar with your driving habits?
13. Did you ever use the car for business purposes?
14. If so, did you maintain a mileage log for tax purposes?
15. If so, where is it now?
16. Did your employer reimburse you for mileage?
17. If so, did you maintain a mileage log for reimbursement purposes?
18. If so, where is it now?
19. Were you required to submit auto expense reimbursement requests to your employer?
20. If so, do you still have copies of any of those requests?

Although our example has focused on obtaining sources of corroborative information from an adverse party, these same techniques can and should be used to uncover sources of corroborative information when interviewing your employer's clients and their witnesses.

Encouragement and Feedback. Obtaining the information you need from an interviewee requires more than just asking the right questions. You need to establish a rapport that will encourage the interviewee to answer your questions fully and frankly.

Putting Interviewees at Ease. Interviewees are sometimes nervous, especially at first. If you sense that an interviewee is nervous, don't hesitate to begin the interview with some small talk.

The interviewee will no doubt want to know who he or she is dealing with. Introduce yourself and tell the interviewee a bit about your education, how long you have been a paralegal, and the areas of law in which you work. Tell the interviewee about the law office itself—the number of lawyers, the areas of practice, and how you came to be affiliated with the firm.

Be sure to say how much you appreciate the interviewee's willingness to be interviewed. Ask the interviewee if she or he had any trouble finding the interview location, and whether or not the time scheduled for the interview turned out to be convenient.

Ask the interviewee if he or she has any questions before the interview starts. Answer those questions as fully as you can.

Letting Interviewees Know You Understand What They Are Telling You. A simple way to encourage interviewees to answer your questions fully is to reassure them constantly that you are listening to, and understand, what they are saying. If you appear disinterested, an interviewee will cut answers short. Unless you let the interviewee know that you are "following" a complicated narrative or explanation, the interviewee may become frustrated and give up.

The easiest way to signal your interest and understanding is to maintain regular eye contact with the interviewee (not always easy if you are taking notes), and nod your head. It is also a good idea to use expressions like "I see" and "I understand" at appropriate points in the interviewee's narrative. When dealing with an unusually complex matter, it is sometimes useful to say something like, "Let me make sure I understand this," and then summarize what the interviewee has told you.

If you do not understand what an interviewee is telling you, by all means request clarification. You should not, however, preface your request by suggesting that the interviewee didn't explain something clearly. A remark such as "that was a very confusing explanation" will discourage the interviewee and may put the interviewee on the defensive. Instead, assign yourself the blame for failing to understand; say something like "I'm sorry, I missed that—would you mind repeating it?" or "I'm having some difficulty keeping all this straight. Can you help me out?" This approach invites the interviewee to sympathize with you, and helps to minimize the chance that the interviewee will become impatient.

Letting Interviewees Know They Are Doing Well. Some interviewees may lack confidence in their abilities to answer your questions clearly or completely. This can lead to a growing sense of frustration as the interview progresses, causing the interviewee to simply stop cooperating.

It is easy to prevent this from happening if you make an effort to let the interviewee know that he or she is doing a good job. A few well-timed comments should provide the necessary reassurance: "That's very helpful information." "You have a good memory!" "You explained that well."

Expressing Your Appreciation for Interviewee's Efforts. At appropriate times during the course of an interview, you should let the interviewee know how much you and your client appreciate the interviewee's efforts. Telling an interviewee, for example, "I appreciate the fact that you took the time to explain that to me so thoroughly" or "I can tell that you are really giving this your best shot, and I appreciate it" will encourage the interviewee to continue to cooperate.

At the conclusion of the interview you should, of course, thank the interviewee for her or his time and effort, and let the interviewee know that you found the interview to be valuable.

Dealing with Emotional Interviewees. At times you will be required to question people about topics that have strong emotional associations for them. For example, you may need to interview a client who is involved in a marital dissolution proceeding about events surrounding the breakup of the marriage. Or you may be required to interview a close relative of someone who recently died in connection with an action to contest a will. Or you may be required to interview someone who is engaged in a bitter dispute with a former business partner.

Under these and similar circumstances, you should anticipate that the interviewee's emotional associations will affect the interview. As an interviewer, of course, you would prefer that an interviewee provide you with the information you are seeking in a calm, rational, and dispassionate manner. While most interviewees will appreciate this and will attempt to hold their emotions in check, the expression of emotion is inevitable. Such expression can range from a sudden emotional outburst to quiet tears to foul language to subtle sarcasm. While the nature and intensity of emotional expression cannot be predicted in advance, you should at least prepare yourself mentally for the fact that you may have to deal with it in the course of an interview.

The greatest problem you will face in dealing with emotional expression is that it tends to get the interviewee off track. For example, a client going through a divorce may prefer to expound on the undesirable qualities of a spouse rather than to answer your questions about the couple's earnings and assets. A client involved in a business dispute may want to talk about the lying and cheating ways of a former business partner instead of telling you about the business.

An effort to get an interviewee back on track by simply continuing to ask questions is usually unsuccessful. Allowing the interviewee to continue on, while the level of emotion continues to rise, does not help either. In most cases, the best thing to do is to acknowledge the interviewee's emotional expression, express empathy, and gently remind the interviewee why it would be a good idea to get on with the interview. For example, you might deal with the distraught interviewee going through a divorce by saying, "It sounds like you've had to put up with a lot. I'm sure it must have been difficult for you. I hope the information you can give me will enable our office to help you get this whole thing resolved." Or you might tell the interviewee who is expressing anger toward a former business partner, "Behavior like that would make anyone angry. A dishonest partner is every business person's worst nightmare. If you can provide me with some more information about the business itself, maybe our office will be able to help you recover at least some of the money you've lost."

Dealing with emotional interviewees, then, is largely a matter of drawing on your own powers of empathy and common sense. It is important to remember, however, that your job is not to provide personal counseling or to assume the role of an emotional support person, even though some clients may seem to expect this. If it is apparent to you that a client or other individual you are dealing with is having emotional difficulties, you should speak with the lawyer handling the case about referring the individual to a mental health care professional.

Recording and Organizing Information

Once you have completed the face-to-face portion of an interview, your work is only half finished. You still face the task of recording the information you have obtained, organizing it, and then communicating it to the people who have a need for it.

Making a Record of the Interview. Most interviewers take notes during interviews. Notes need not be extensive, but they must be detailed enough to remind you of what the interviewee said. If you wrote down your questions before the interview, you may want to note the interviewee's response to each question on the same paper. After the interview is over, you may want to review your notes and expand them to include information that is still fresh in your memory but which did not get written down during the interview.

Some interviewers like to tape record or even videotape interviews. This may make some interviewees uncomfortable. Since an interview is usually most successful when the interviewee is at ease, an interviewer should find out whether or not taping the interview may pose a problem. One obvious advantage of taping is that it provides a comprehensive and accurate record of the interview. One not-so-obvious disadvantage of taping is that it is more difficult to prepare a memorandum summarizing the interview when dealing with a tape than it is when dealing with a set of notes that record only the most important points in the interview.

Organizing and Communicating Information Obtained in the Interview. The information you obtain in an interview will be of little use unless it is organized and communicated in a format that is appropriate for your law office's needs. Four commonly used formats are the narrative memorandum, the client-intake memorandum, the witness statement, and the declaration or affidavit.

The Narrative Memorandum. In a narrative memorandum, the information obtained at an interview is presented in the form of a third-party narrative.

The information is usually arranged chronologically, or by subject matter. An excerpt from a chronological narrative memorandum that might have been prepared after an initial interview with the Smiths is illustrated in Figure 6-9.

The Client-Intake Memorandum. In many law offices, after a paralegal has interviewed a new client for the first time, the paralegal prepares what is known as a client-intake memorandum. The content of such a memorandum varies from office to office, but it usually contains basic information about the client, a third-party narrative, and interviewer comments. An excerpt from a "client intake" memorandum that might have been prepared after an initial interview with the Smiths is illustrated in Figure 6-10.

FIGURE 6-9 EXCERPT FROM NARRATIVE MEMORANDUM

DATE: December 12, 1992

TO: Myrna Jackson, Esq.

FROM: Kim Starbard

SUBJECT: Initial Interview with John and Mary Smith

On December 10, 1992, I met with and interviewed Mary and John Smith.

In late August 1992, the Smiths were in the market for a car for Mary. They were looking at newer used cars. On Sunday, August 23, John saw an ad in the Daily News classifieds advertising an "almost new" 1991 Allied Motors CS10. The car was being offered for sale by Lemon Motors. The ad stated that the car had had only one owner and had been driven less than 2,000 miles. John telephoned Lemon Motors that evening and made an appointment to see the car on Monday morning.

The next morning, Mary and John met with Andy Lipinski, a sales representative for Lemon Motors. Mr. Lipinski showed them the car, which appeared to be in mint condition. John recalls having looked at the odometer reading, which was 1,956. He asked Mr. Lipinski how old the car was. Mr. Lipinski told him the car's registration papers indicated that it had been purchased new in June 1991. John asked Mr. Lipinski why the mileage was so low. Mr. Lipinski stated that he wasn't exactly sure, but that the car had been acquired as a trade-in from its former owner, and that Lemon Motors' service department had "checked everything out, and everything's fine."

FIGURE 6-10 EXCERPT FROM CLIENT-INTAKE MEMORANDUM

DATE: December 12, 1992
TO: Myrna Jackson, Esq.
FROM: Kim Starbard
RE: Intake Interview: Smith v. Lemon Motors

CLIENT: John and Mary Smith
246 Las Palmas Drive
Playa del Mar, CA 90276-2655
(310) 357-9135

NATURE OF CASE: Possible claim for damages based on purchase of car with incorrect odometer reading.

DATE OF INTERVIEW: December 10, 1992

FACTS:

In late August 1992, the Smiths were in the market for a car for Mary. They were looking at newer used cars. On Sunday, August 23, John saw an ad in the Daily News classifieds advertising an "almost new" 1991 Allied Motors CS10. The car was being offered for sale by Lemon Motors. The ad stated that the car had had only one owner and had been driven less than 2,000 miles. John telephoned Lemon Motors that evening and made an appointment to see the car on Monday morning.

The next morning, Mary and John met with Andy Lipinski, a sales representative for Lemon Motors. Mr. Lipinski showed them the car, which appeared to be in mint condition. John recalls having looked at the odometer reading, which was 1,956. He asked Mr. Lipinski how old the car was. Mr. Lipinski told him the car's registration papers indicated that it had been purchased new in June 1991. John asked Mr. Lipinski why the mileage was so low. Mr. Lipinski stated that he wasn't exactly sure, but that the car had been acquired as a trade-in from its former owner, and that Lemon Motors' service department had "checked everything out, and everything's fine."

COMMENTS:

The Smiths would make excellent witnesses at trial. They come across as intelligent and sincere individuals. They are articulate and make a good appearance.

FUTURE ACTION:

I told the Smiths that we would review their case, conduct some legal research, and contact them next week to discuss their options.

The Witness Statement. A witness statement is a first-person narrative signed by the person providing the information contained in the statement. Although such statements are not necessarily admissible in court as evidence, they are frequently used by law enforcement agencies, private investigators, and others to pin down an interviewee's version of the facts. An excerpt from a witness statement that might have been prepared after an initial interview with the Smiths is illustrated in Figure 6-11.

FIGURE 6-11 EXCERPT FROM WITNESS STATEMENT

I, John Smith, state:

1. In late August 1992, my wife, Mary, and I were in the market for a used car for my wife. On Sunday, August 23, I saw an advertisement in the Daily News classified section. The advertisement stated that Lemon Motors was offering a 1991 Allied Motors CS10 for sale. The advertisement further stated that the car was "almost new," had had only one owner, and had less than 2,000 miles on it. That evening I telephoned Lemon Motors and made an appointment for the following morning to see the car.

2. On Monday morning, August 24, my wife and I visited the Lemon Motors showroom. We met Andy Lipinski, a sales representative for Lemon Motors. Mr. Lipinski showed us the car, which appeared to be in excellent condition. I observed the car's odometer reading to be 1,956. I asked Mr. Lipinski how old the car was. He told me that the car's registration records indicated that it had been purchased new in June 1991. I asked Mr. Lipinski why the car had such low mileage. He told me that he did not know, but that the car had been acquired from its former owner as a trade-in, and that Lemon Motors' service department had "checked everything out, and everything's fine."

. . . .

____

JOHN SMITH

The Affidavit or Declaration. An **affidavit** is a written statement of facts signed by someone who has sworn under oath before a person authorized to administer oaths that the facts contained in the statement are true. A **declaration under penalty of perjury** is like an affidavit except that the person signing the statement does not take an oath but instead declares in the statement "under penalty of perjury" that the facts contained in the statement are true. Affidavits and declarations are almost always prepared for use as evidence in court, and therefore should contain only information that is admissible in accordance with the rules of evidence. An excerpt from a declaration under penalty of perjury that might have been prepared after an initial interview with the Smiths is illustrated in Figure 6-12.

FIGURE 6-12 EXCERPT FROM DECLARATION UNDER PENALTY OF PERJURY

I, JOHN SMITH, declare:

1. I am a party to this action. The facts set forth in this declaration are personally known to me and I have first-hand knowledge of them. If called as a witness to testify, I could and would testify competently to the same.

2. In late August 1992, my wife, Mary, and I were in the market for a used car for my wife. On Sunday, August 23, I saw an advertisement in the Daily News classified section. The advertisement stated that Lemon Motors was offering a 1991 Allied Motors CS10 for sale. The advertisement further stated that the car was "almost new," had had only one owner, and had less than 2,000 miles on it. That evening I telephoned Lemon Motors and made an appointment for the following morning to see the car.

3. On Monday morning, August 24, my wife and I visited the Lemon Motors showroom. We met Andy Lipinski, a sales representative for Lemon Motors. Mr. Lipinski showed us the car, which appeared to be in excellent condition. I observed the car's odometer reading to be 1,956. I asked Mr. Lipinski how old the car was. He told me that the car's registration records indicated that it had been purchased new in June 1991. I asked Mr. Lipinski why the car had such low mileage. He told me that he did not know, but that the car had been acquired from its former owner as a trade-in, and that Lemon Motors service department had "checked everything out, and it was fine."

. . . .

I declare under penalty of perjury under the laws of the State of California that the foregoing is true and correct. Executed this 10th day of December, 1992, at Playa del Mar, California.

____

JOHN SMITH

OBTAINING INFORMATION FROM OTHER SOURCES

Although much of the information that a paralegal gathers is obtained from individuals, there are many other sources of information that a paralegal should know how to utilize. Three of the most commonly used sources of information—government records, computer databases, and physical evidence—are discussed here. You should be aware, however, that there are many other available sources of information, some of which you may deal with only if you work in a particular field of law. For example, paralegals who work in the field of personal injury law frequently deal with medical records.

In many situations much of the information you need will not be publicly available. Often the only source of such information will be an adverse party in a lawsuit or some other person who will not cooperate with your investigation. In such cases, the only way you will be able to obtain the information you need will be by using certain legal procedures that require an adverse party or other person to reveal information to the parties to a lawsuit. These procedures, collectively known as *discovery*, will be discussed in detail in Chapter 9.

Searching Government Records

An amazing amount of information is contained in records maintained by governmental agencies. Most of these records are available for inspection by the general public.

Does a Useful Government Record Exist? Government records exist on all levels of government and contain information on a vast array of subjects. When you need information of any type, it is always worthwhile to consider whether there exists a government record that may contain that information.

Because there are no comprehensive directories of government records, determining whether or not a useful record exists is somewhat challenging.

As a general rule, government records do exist for every type of activity that is regulated by the government. When you are dealing with such an activity, review the statutes and regulations that govern it to determine if there are requirements for filing reports or other information with a regulatory agency. Contact the agency to find out what kinds of information may be available from its files.

If you choose to specialize in a particular field of law, you will soon become familiar with the government records available in that field.

You should also keep in mind that the government maintains basic records that apply to everyone. These include birth, marriage, and death records; driver's license records; professional licensing records; and records relating to court proceedings.

Locating the Agency That Has the Records You Need. Even when you are certain that records exist, determining which government agency has the records you need is not always an easy task. If you are dealing with a regulated activity and you review the applicable statutes or regulations, they should indicate which agency is responsible for accepting and maintaining required reports. Otherwise, you should consult government and telephone directories for names, addresses, and telephone numbers of government agencies; then make direct inquiries to those agencies that seem most promising.

Obtaining the Records You Need. Government agencies have a variety of procedures for making records available to the public. Some agencies will copy records and forward them for a fee. Other agencies permit inspection and copying only at the agency's office. Some records may be available through an agency-maintained computer database, while others may be available in commercial databases. In almost every case you will need to contact the agency to inquire about its particular procedures.

Researching Computer Databases

As you might expect, a paralegal should have the basic library research skills necessary to locate information contained in newspapers, periodicals, and books maintained in a public or university research library. Increasingly, however, paralegals are being called on to access this same information in another form: the commercial computer database. Thanks to continuing advances in computer technology, information that might otherwise be accessible only through time-consuming research in several libraries is now immediately available on the computer screen.

Paralegals working in diversified fields of law now have access to a wide array of sophisticated and specialized databases. In personal injury and medical malpractice litigation, for example, paralegals make use of Medis, a database comprised of medical journals, newsletters, and textbooks. Paralegals who work in the business litigation and business transactional areas may use Exchange, which includes corporate and industry reports, investment and research reports, Securities Exchange Commission filings, and information on the domestic and international economies, and NAARS, which includes annual reports and proxy statements for publicly traded companies. Paralegals in many fields make use of Nexis, which consists of general news, business, and financial publications as well as sources of information in such specialized areas as patents.

A full explanation of the use of computer databases is beyond the scope of this book. As you continue your training as a paralegal, however, you should take advantage of every opportunity available to develop and increase your proficiency as a computer database researcher.

Handling Physical Evidence

Paralegals are sometimes called on to assist in the collection, analysis, and preservation of physical evidence. This is most frequently the case for paralegals who specialize in litigation.

Evidence Related to the Setting of an Event. Often the physical setting of an event can yield important clues about how, why, and even whether something happened. Information about the scene of a crime, or the scene of an event resulting in personal injury or property damage, can be critically important in court.

As a paralegal, you may be asked to visit the scene of an event, either alone or with a witness to the event. When visiting the scene alone, you can make detailed observations about what you find. When visiting the scene with a witness, you can question the witness while having the witness "walk you through" what happened in relation to the physical layout of the site.

In either event, you will need to make a record of the information you obtain. You should make a written record of your findings in the form of a memorandum. You should also make diagrams of the site, taking care to depict the relationship of various features of the site to one another accurately. You should take photographs of visual evidence such as skid marks and property damage as well as of any site features that can be more easily explained or understood with the aid of a photograph.

As you gain experience in visiting sites, your powers of observation will steadily improve, as will your ability to record and communicate your observations accurately.

Physical Objects as Evidence. Physical objects are often a valuable source of information and can be especially useful as visual aids at a trial. You can usually draw up a list of physical objects that may have value as evidence by using the techniques discussed earlier in this chapter in the section headed Uncovering Corroborative Information.

As a paralegal, you may be asked to inspect and record your observations about a physical object. In the Smiths' case, for example, you might be asked to inspect their car with an eye to making a detailed record of its visual appearance.

Obtaining the maximum amount of information from the inspection of a physical object often requires a level of expertise beyond that of a paralegal or a lawyer. For example, in the Smiths' case, only a person thoroughly familiar with external and internal automobile mechanics would be capable of making a physical inspection of the car for the purpose of ascertaining its actual mileage. In such a situation, you may be called on to help locate and to coordinate the activities of a qualified expert.

7 LEGAL RESEARCH: FINDING THE LAW

MEMORANDUM

DATE: December 12, 1992

TO: Leslie Schermerhorn

FROM: Mark Samuel, Esq.

SUBJECT: Smith v. Lemon Motors

I just received a call from Tom Travers at Lemon Motors. He is anxious to find out the potential liability of the dealership for selling that car with a false odometer reading. I need you to do some initial research on this case. Are there any statutes or cases addressing this situation? I told Tom that I would call him before 4:00 p.m., so please get back to me before then.

This chapter introduces you to the legal research process. The goal is to help you develop basic research skills and get you into the library researching the law as quickly as possible. This chapter is merely an introduction to legal research and is not intended to be a comprehensive guide. It basically discusses only one research method, the descriptive or key word method. The focus is on researching cases and statutes rather than Constitutional law, administrative law, or any other source of law.

INTRODUCTION

This chapter explains the steps you would follow in researching our sample case of *Smith v. Lemon Motors.* The *Smith* case provides a relatively simple and straightforward research situation. Many research situations are much more difficult and complex.

Figure 7-1, a blank Find-the-Law Worksheet, lists six steps in the legal research process that will be discussed in this chapter. By the end of this chapter, you should be able to complete a Find-the-Law Worksheet when given a research assignment.

FIGURE 7-1 BLANK FIND-THE-LAW WORKSHEET

FIND-THE-LAW WORKSHEET

1. ANALYZING THE FACTS

- Parties or Persons:
- Places, Objects, or Things:
- Legal Theories:
- Relief Sought:

2. IDENTIFYING THE ISSUE

Issue:

3. SECONDARY SOURCES

Encyclopedias:
Other:

4. STATUTORY LAW

Title and Section Number of Codes:
Statutory Law in the Codes:
Case Citations from Notes of Decisions:

5. CASE LAW

Topics and Key Numbers in Digests:
Case Citations from Digests:
Summaries of Cases:

6. SHEPARDIZE

Current Status of Statutes and Cases:

HAVE I CHECKED ALL POCKET SUPPLEMENTS?

Legal research is the process of searching for the rules of law that address the questions raised by the facts of your client's case. Legal researchers search for legal authorities, such as cases and statutes, that will be cited to a court in support of the contentions being made.

Legal authorities are classified as either **primary authority** or **secondary authority**. Primary authorities are what the law *is*, such as cases, statutes, and administrative regulations. Secondary authorities, such as legal encyclopedias and treatises, comment on, interpret, or criticize primary authorities. Primary authorities are the law itself, while secondary authorities do not have the force and effect of law.

You may remember from Chapter 3 that legal authorities are also classified as being either mandatory or persuasive. Mandatory precedents are those that must be followed, while persuasive precedents do not have to be followed. For example, the Oregon Supreme Court might consider a decision of the California Supreme Court persuasive, but the Oregon court would not be legally bound to follow the California court's decision.

When you research the law, your ultimate goal is to find **mandatory primary authority**, or law that courts in your jurisdiction must follow. If you are researching a state law issue, for example, then you hope to find a recent case decided by the state's highest court involving a fact situation the same as your own. If you can locate no mandatory primary authority, then you will search for persuasive primary authority that is relevant. Finally, if you can locate no primary authority of either kind, you will be forced to rely on secondary authority.[1]

STEP ONE: ANALYZING THE FACTS

Before actually beginning your legal research, you need to analyze the facts of the case carefully. Cases are won or lost on the facts. When attempting to identify the relevant facts of the case, it is helpful to think in terms of the following categories:

1. *Parties or persons* involved in the case
2. *Places, objects, or things* involved in the case
3. *Legal theories* (causes of action or defenses) involved in the case
4. *Relief sought* (e.g., money damages or injunction) in the case

These categories will help you identify descriptive words or key words that can be used in your research. As you will see later in the chapter, identifying descriptive/key words is an important step in your research because these are the words you will look for in various indexes; the indexes then cite you to the applicable law. The key words are also used in computer-assisted searches.

When identifying key words, try to think of as many words as possible for each of the four categories. For each word that you come up with, think of its synonyms, antonyms, closely related words, more generalized or broader words, and more specific or narrower words. Brainstorming each key word helps you generate a research vocabulary. Figure 7-2 illustrates how to brainstorm the key word "odometer."[2]

FIGURE 7-2 BRAINSTORMING KEY WORDS

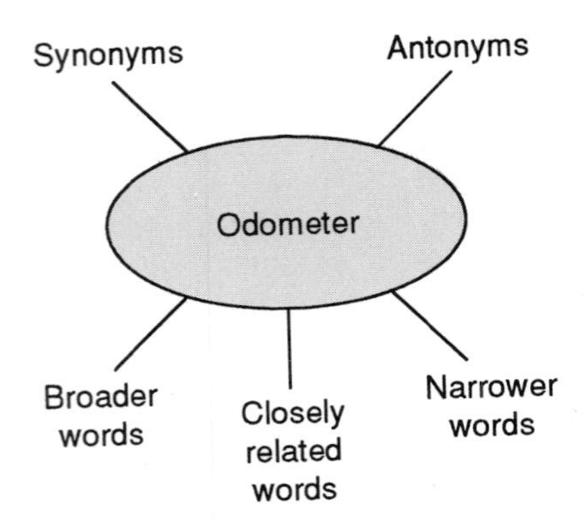

Refer back to the memorandum summarizing the facts of the *Smith v. Lemon Motors* case at the beginning of Chapter 6. An analysis of the facts involved in the *Smith* case, followed by brainstorming each key word you generate, might result in identification of the following key words:

1. *Parties or persons*—automobile dealership, buyer, seller
2. *Places, objects, or things*—motor vehicle, automobile, car, used car, CS10 automobile, odometer, speedometer, odometer tampering, speedometer tampering, miles, mileage

Notice how brainstorming a key word such as "motor vehicle" helps you come up with other words: automobile and car (synonyms) and used car and CS10 (narrower words).

3. *Legal theories*—breach of contract, fraud, misrepresentation, breach of warranty, indemnification
4. *Relief sought*—damages, money damages, treble damages, rescission, restitution

Most of the time, unique words yield better results than common words. The problem with using a common word such as "automobile" is that when you look up a common word in an index, it cites you to *too much* law. Usually a more specific or a unique word—in this case, "odometer"—will lead you to the law more quickly. However, if the key word is *too* specific, then the index may not contain a heading for that word and will not cite you to any law at all. That is why it is a good idea to brainstorm each key word that you come up with in an attempt to build a research vocabulary. The more key words you have to look up in the indexes, the better your chances of finding the applicable law.

Because you are just beginning your paralegal education, you may not yet know what key words to identify under the *Legal theories* and *Relief sought* categories. Concentrate on identifying key words describing the parties, persons, places, objects, and things involved in the case. These key words should lead you to the applicable law.

STEP TWO: IDENTIFYING THE ISSUES

Careful fact analysis and identification of descriptive/key words should suggest legal issues that need to be researched. A legal issue is raised when it is not certain how the law will be applied to the facts of the case. Early in the case, when your knowledge of the law and the facts may be sketchy, the issues will be stated in broad, tentative terms. For example, in *Smith v. Lemon Motors*, the initial statement of the issue might be: What is the potential liability of an automobile dealership for selling a car with a false odometer reading? As your research locates the applicable law, the legal issues tend to become narrower and more focused. Redefining the legal issues is continuous and ongoing throughout the research process.

STEP THREE: RESEARCHING SECONDARY SOURCES

When a researcher is unfamiliar with the area of law being researched, it is sometimes helpful to obtain background information by reading about the topic in a secondary source, such as a legal encyclopedia. Remember that statements in secondary sources are not the law and are not binding on a court. However, secondary sources will frequently lead you to primary sources such as cases and statutes. Ultimately, your goal is to locate mandatory primary authority.

Examples of secondary authority include dictionaries, thesauri, legal periodicals, treatises, encyclopedias, and *American Law Reports* (A.L.R.) annotations. Dictionaries and thesauri are sometimes a good place to begin your research because they define terms and help you build a research vocabulary. **Legal periodicals**, such as the *Stanford Law Review*, contain articles written by legal scholars analyzing a particular area of the law. **Treatises**, such as Prosser's *The Law of Torts*,[3] are also commentaries written by legal scholars covering a particular area of law. Treatises may be single- or multiple-volume works and frequently cover a broad area of law such as torts or contracts.

In this section, we will examine how to locate information in a legal encyclopedia and how to research in A.L.R.

Legal Encyclopedias

Legal encyclopedias summarize the entire body of American law and consequently provide a good starting point for your research. The two major national legal encyclopedias are *American Jurisprudence, Second Edition* (Am. Jur. 2d) and *Corpus Juris Secundum* (C.J.S.).[4] Each is organized alphabetically by topic and is written in narrative form. The encyclopedias provide extensive citations of court decisions supporting the particular rules of law stated.

One way to enter an encyclopedia is through the descriptive/key-word approach. Earlier we identified key words in our sample case of *Smith v. Lemon Motors*. When you look up these words in the general index to the encyclopedia, the index cites you to the relevant sections in the encyclopedia. For example, when you look up the key word ''odometer'' in the general index to Am. Jur. 2d, you find the following:[5]

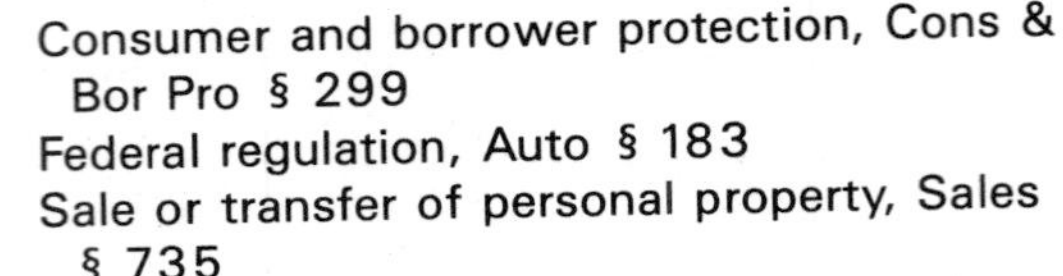
ODOMETERS
Consumer and borrower protection, Cons & Bor Pro § 299
Federal regulation, Auto § 183
Sale or transfer of personal property, Sales § 735

The second entry indicates that a federal regulation concerning odometers is discussed in the article "Auto" at Section 183. The articles in the index are written in abbreviated form; a Table of Abbreviations is found at the beginning of each volume. When you look up "Auto" in the Table of Abbreviations, you discover that "Auto" is an abbreviation for the article "Automobiles and Highway Traffic."

The next step is to enter the encyclopedia by locating the volume containing the article "Automobiles and Highway Traffic," Section 183. The articles are arranged alphabetically. Excerpts from this section follow in Figure 7-3.[6]

Figure 7-3 illustrates why it is sometimes helpful to begin your research in an encyclopedia. First, encyclopedias provide educational background information on a particular topic. Second, encyclopedias lead you to primary sources such as statutes (15 U.S.C. §§ 1983–1989) and cases (*Nieto v. Pence*, 578 F.2d 640).

American Law Reports Annotated

The *American Law Reports* (A.L.R.) reprints selected cases that deal with legal issues of widespread interest. The reprinted case is followed by an annotation that collects, organizes, and evaluates all of the case law relevant to the legal issue or fact situation raised in the reprinted case. In other words, an annotation is a comprehensive statement of all the law on a given legal point. If an A.L.R. annotation exists for the legal issue or fact situation being researched, then a tremendous amount of research has already been done for you. However, the range of topics covered by an A.L.R. annotation is narrow, and not all areas of the law are discussed in A.L.R.

A.L.R. consists of five series: A.L.R.1st (1919–1948); A.L.R.2d (1948–1965); A.L.R.3d (1965–1980); A.L.R.4th (1980 to date); and A.L.R. Fed. (1969 to date).

POINTER: A.L.R.1st, A.L.R.2d, and A.L.R.3d (until 1969) cover both state and federal topics. Since 1969, federal topics are covered in A.L.R. Fed., while A.L.R.3d and A.L.R.4th cover only state topics. Because much of the information covered in A.L.R.1st and A.L.R.2d is now outdated, your research should begin with the more recent series.[7]

The easiest way to enter A.L.R. is through the Index to Annotations. When you look up the key word "Odometer" in the Index to Annotations, you find the entry reprinted here as Figure 7-4.[8]

The index lists three A.L.R. annotations relating to the term "odometer." Let us assume we are interested in researching federal law. The second of the three annotations deals with the Motor Vehicle Information and Cost Savings

FIGURE 7-3 SAMPLE AM. JUR. 2d PAGE

§ 183. Odometers.

Federal legislation provides that it is unlawful for any person to advertise for sale, to sell, to use, or to install or to have installed, any device which causes an odometer to register any mileage other than the true mileage driven.[65] It is also provided by federal law that it is unlawful for any person or his agent to disconnect, reset, or alter the odometer of any motor vehicle with the intent to change the number of miles indicated thereon.[66] Another statute provides that it is unlawful for any person with intent to defraud to operate a motor vehicle on any street or highway knowing that the odometer of such vehicle is disconnected or nonfunctional.[67] Conspiracy with any other person to violate the above provisions is proscribed.[68]

* * *

The Secretary of Transportation is required to prescribe rules requiring any transferer of a motor vehicle to give the following written disclosure to the transferee in connection with the transfer of ownership of the motor vehicle: (1) disclosure of the accumulative mileage registered by the odometer; or (2) disclosure that the actual mileage is unknown, if the odometer reading is known to the transferor to be different from the number of miles the vehicle has actually traveled. Violation of such rules, or knowingly giving a false statement to a transferee in making a disclosure required by such rules, is proscribed.[70]

Any person, who with intent to defraud, violates any requirement imposed under the above statutes shall be liable in an amount equal to the sum of (1) three times the amount of actual damages sustained or $1,500, whichever is the greater; and (2) in the case of any successful action to enforce the foregoing liability, the cost of the action together with reasonable attorney fees as determined by the court.[71]

70. 15 USCS § 1988.

In action by buyer of used automobile against seller involving alleged violation of Motor Vehicle Information and Cost Savings Act (15 USCS §§ 1988, 1989), fact that seller gave buyer the odometer mileage statement representing the mileage as 4,121 miles was insufficient to support the finding that seller failed to disclose the fact that the actual mileage was unknown, where, although previous possessors of the automobile observed the odometer reading of 14,000 miles and an insurance claims representative noted mileage of 4,180 miles, there was no evidence that the seller knew or had reason to know that the disclosure statement received by it from the financial corporation which repossessed the automobile was in fact false; under Texas common law fraud theory, proof of damage was lacking, where, although trial court found that the difference between the price of a new car and the automobile purchased was $500, the proper measure of damages was the difference between the price buyer paid and the fair market value of the automobile actually received. Yates v Tindall & Son Pontiac (CA5 Tex) 531 F2d 293.

Transferor has duty, under 15 USCS § 1988, to state that actual mileage is unknown even if he lacks actual knowledge that the odometer reading is incorrect where, if transferror, in exercise of reasonable care, would have had reason to know that mileage was more than that which odometer had recorded or previous owner had certified. Nieto v Pence (CA5 Tex) 578 F2d 640.

71. Although used vehicle was misrepresented as to model and body type, this misrepresentation did not violate 15 USCS § 1988; even though regulations issued thereunder require disclosure of, among other things, model and body type, because § 1988 directs only that rules be enacted to require disclosure of odometer mileage, and entire Vehicle Information and Cost Savings Act of 1972 (15 USCS § 1981 et seq.) evinced no intention by Congress to extend civil liability into any other area. Purser v Bill Campbell Porsche Audi, Inc. (DC Fla) 431 F Supp 1235.

15 USCS § 1989.

Turning back the odometer 30,000 miles justified verdict of $300 actual and $3300 exemplary damages against used car dealer. Shulz v. Dreiling (Colo App) 526 P2d 1341.

Evidence supported jury verdict that dealer engaged in fraudulent representation concerning odometer reading, and $7,000 punitive damages award was not excessive. Cates v Darland (Okla) 537 P2d 336.

FIGURE 7-4 SAMPLE A.L.R. INDEX TO ANNOTATIONS ENTRY

ODOMETERS

Consumer protection, practices forbidden by state deceptive trade practice and consumer protection acts, 89 ALR3d 449. §§ 4, 5, 10[a], 21, 27

Motor Vehicle Information and Cost Savings Act (15 USCS §§ 1981–1991), validity, construction, and application of odometer requirement provisions, 28 ALR Fed 584

Tampering, construction and application of state statute making it unlawful to tamper with motor vehicle odometer, 76 ALR3d 981

Act, 15 U.S.C. §§ 1981–1991, which is federal statutory law. The annotation is found in volume 28 of A.L.R. Federal at page 584. The first page of this annotation is reprinted as Figure 7-5.[9]

The reprinted case that is the subject of this annotation is *Delay v. Hearn Ford*, 373 F. Supp. 791. The first page of this case as it is found in A.L.R. is reprinted here as Figure 7-6.[10]

The cases found in A.L.R. annotations are updated by pocket supplements. A **pocket supplement** or **pocket part** is a paperback supplement to a hardbound book, inserted in the book through a slit in its back cover, containing relevant cases decided *after* the hardbound book was printed. Many legal reference books use pocket supplements to update material. Pocket supplements must *always* be checked to ensure that your research is up to date. Selected case summaries from the A.L.R. Federal pocket supplement are found in Figure 7-7.[11]

STEP FOUR: RESEARCHING STATUTORY LAW

After educating yourself about the topic by reading secondary sources, the next step is to locate any relevant statutory law.

Statutory Codes

Both federal and state statutes are compiled and published in **statutory codes**. Federal statutes are published in the *United States Code* (U.S.C.), *United States Code Annotated* (U.S.C.A.), and *United States Code Service* (U.S.C.S.). U.S.C. is the **official code**, meaning it is published by the government and contains only the actual text of the statutes. U.S.C.A. and U.S.C.S. are **unofficial codes** published by private publishers. Both U.S.C.A. and U.S.C.S. are also **annotated codes**, which means they contain the statutory text plus valuable information about the statute, such as summaries of cases that have interpreted and applied the statute. Unless you are interested in reading only the statutory text, use an annotated code when you research statutes.

State statutes are published in individual state codes.[12] Although we will use a federal statute as our example of how to research statutory law, the same process would be used when researching state statutes.

FIGURE 7-5 SAMPLE A.L.R. ANNOTATION PAGE

ANNOTATION

VALIDITY, CONSTRUCTION, AND APPLICATION OF ODOMETER REQUIREMENT PROVISIONS OF MOTOR VEHICLE INFORMATION AND COST SAVINGS ACT (15 USCS §§ 1981–1991)

by

Barney J. Finberg, J.D.

§ 1. Introduction:
 [a] Scope
 [b] Related matters
 [c] Text of statutory provisions and regulations
§ 2. Summary and comment:
 [a] Generally

TOTAL CLIENT-SERVICE LIBRARY® REFERENCES

7 Am Jur 2d, Automobiles and Highway Traffic §§ 149, 309, 310, 313, 324, 654–657; 37 Am Jur 2d, Fraud and Deceit §§ 185 et seq.
3 Am Jur Pl & Pr Forms (Rev Ed), Automobiles and Highway Traffic, Forms 11 et seq.
3 Am Jur Legal Forms 2d, Automobiles and Highway Traffic § 33:16
1 Am Jur Proof of Facts 2d 677, Fraudulent Alteration of Odometer
13 Am Jur Trials 253, Misrepresentation in Automobile Sales
15 USCS §§ 1981–1991
US L Ed Digest, Motor Vehicles
ALR Digests, Automobiles and Highway Traffic §§ 36, 218
L Ed Index to Anno, Motor Vehicles
ALR Quick Index, Automobile Dealers; Automobiles and Highway Traffic; Fraud and Deceit
Federal Quick Index, Automobiles and Highway Traffic; Fraud and Deceit; Odometer

584 Consult POCKET PART in this volume for later cases and statutory changes

Researching in Statutory Codes

Statutory research begins by looking up descriptive or key words in the index to the appropriate code. For example, when you look up the descriptive/key word "odometer" in the Descriptive Word Index to *United States Code Annotated*, you find the following:[13]

ODOMETER
Motor Vehicles, generally, this index

FIGURE 7-6 SAMPLE A.L.R. SUBJECT OF ANNOTATION PAGE

Frank DELAY, Plaintiff,

v

HEARN FORD, Defendant

United States District Court, D. South Carolina, Rock Hill Division

March 19, 1974

373 F Supp 791, 28 ALR Fed 576

SUMMARY OF DECISION

The United States District Court for the District of South Carolina, Hemphill, District Judge, denied the defendant-dealer's motion for summary judgment in an action under the Motor Vehicle Information and Cost Savings Act, holding that there were potential and contested issues of fact as to whether the defendant had violated 15 USCS § 1984 by altering the odometer of an automobile, whether the defendant had violated 15 USCS § 1988(a)(2) and (b) by failing to disclose to the purchaser that the odometer reading did not actually reflect the actual miles the vehicle had traveled, and whether the plaintiff was entitled to statutory damages of $1,500 under 15 USCS § 1989(a)(1).

HEADNOTES

Classified to ALR Digests

Automobiles § 36 — public regulations and violations thereof — regulations protecting against fraud, misuse, or theft

1. Summary judgment should be denied the defendant in an action under the Motor Vehicle Information and Cost Savings Act where the plaintiff's affidavits established that at the time the plaintiff's car was traded

SUBJECT OF ANNOTATION

Beginning on page 584

VALIDITY, CONSTRUCTION, AND APPLICATION OF ODOMETER REQUIREMENT PROVISIONS OF MOTOR VEHICLE INFORMATION AND COST SAVINGS ACT (15 USCS §§ 1981–1991).

576

FIGURE 7-7 SAMPLE A.L.R. POCKET SUPPLEMENT PAGE

For latest cases, call the toll-free number appearing on the cover of this supplement.

§ 8. Private civil action

[a] Requirement of defendant's "intent to defraud"

Where auto dealer made several false and misleading representations to plaintiff—both through oral statements of its salesman and through preparation of odometer statement which did not alert plaintiffs to odometer defects—these representations were sufficiently reckless to meet "intent to defraud" requirement of 15 USCS § 1989(a) and to impose liability; court would reject dealer's "clerical error" defense, particularly since absence of odometer statement in dealer's file relating to automobile should have operated as "red flag" alerting dealer's personnel to possibility of odometer irregularity. Jones v Fenton Ford, Inc. (DC Conn) 427 F Supp 1328.

"Actual knowledge" standard is in no way compelled by "intent to defraud" requirement of 15 USCS § 1989(a). Jones v Fenton Ford, Inc. (DC Conn) 427 F Supp 1328.

Constructive knowledge, recklessness, or even gross negligence in determining and disclosing actual mileage traveled by vehicle may be sufficient to support finding of intent to defraud under Motor Vehicle Information and Cost Savings Act, 15 USCS §§ 1981 et seq. Auto Sport Motors, Inc. v Bruno Auto Dealers, Inc. (1989, SD NY) 721 F Supp 63.

Jury was correct in finding fraudulent intent on part of auto auction dealer, under 15 USCS § 1989, because evidence strongly showed that employee who prepared odometer statement never saw odometer statement from previous owner, which statement showed that automobile actually had 100,000 more miles on it than shown on odometer; practice of preparing odometer statements simply on basis of odometer reading and then failing to disclose that actual mileage is unknown demonstrates reckless disregard for basic purpose of statute; in light of dealer's duty under statute, such recklessness rises to level of fraudulent intent. Kantorczyk v New Stanton Auto Auction, Inc. (DC Pa) 433 F Supp 889.

* * *

Finding of violation of Motor Vehicle Information and Cost Savings Act (15 USCS §§ 1901 et seq.) was clearly erroneous where evidence indicated that defendant automobile dealer had been given false odometer report by party from which it bought automobile, and there was no evidence that dealer knew of actual mileage of automobile. Yates v Tindall & Son Pontiac (CA5 Tex) 531 F2d 293.

Although defendant with constructive knowledge that odometer reading was incorrect may have violated 15 USCS § 1988, he is not necessarily civilly liable for violation, since 15 USCS § 1989 requires intent to defraud; transferror who lacked actual knowledge that odometer reading was incorrect may still be found to have intended to defraud and be civilly liable under 15 USCS § 1989 for failure to disclose that vehicle's actual mileage is unknown in violation of 15 USCS § 1988(a)(2) if he reasonably should have known that vehicle's odometer reading was incorrect since, although he may not know to certainty that transferee would be defrauded, court may infer that he understood risk of such occurrence. Nieto v Pence (CA5 Tex) 578 F2d 640.

* * *

When you look up the heading "Motor Vehicles" and the subheading "Odometer" in the Descriptive Word Index, you find this:[14]

MOTOR VEHICLES—Cont'd
Notice—Cont'd
National Traffic and Motor Vehicle Safety, ante, this heading
Odometer laws and regulations, offenses, sentencing guidelines and statutory index, 18 Ap 4
Odometer requirements. Information and cost savings, ante, this heading

When you look up the heading "Motor Vehicles," subheading "Information and cost savings," sub-subheading "Odometer requirements," you find three pages of information, including the information reprinted here as Figure 7-8.[15]

FIGURE 7-8 SAMPLE U.S.C.A. GENERAL INDEX PAGE

MOTOR VEHICLES—Cont'd
Information and cost savings—Cont'd
Odometer requirements,
Acceptance of incomplete written disclosure by transferees acquiring ownership for resale prohibited, 15 § 1988
Access to and copying of documentary evidence, 15 § 1990d
Compliance with requirements, 15 § 1990f
Adjustment of mileage, 15 § 1987
Administrative proceedings, 15 § 1990d
Administrative warrants, entry, impoundment and inspection, necessity, 15 § 1990e
Advertising for sale, selling, etc., device causing odometer to register mileage other than true mileage driven, prohibition, 15 § 1983
Affidavits, administrative warrants, issuance on, entry, impoundment or inspection, 15 § 1990e
Alternate mileage disclosure requirements, approval by Secretary, 15 § 1988
Appropriations, authorization, 15 § 1990g
Attorney General,
Action to restrain violations, 15 § 1990
Collection, civil penalty, action by, 15 § 1990b
Referral to of information obtained indicating noncompliance with rules, etc., for investigative consideration, 15 § 1990d
Auction company, disclosure requirements, 15 § 1988
Defined, 15 § 1982

* * *

As you can see, the index entries refer you to specific statutes dealing with the descriptive word. The next step is to read the statutes to see if they are relevant. (You may want to review the sample federal statute, 15 U.S.C. § 1989, on page 70.)

For each relevant statute, read the annotations following the statute. The annotations include historical notes about the statute, library references, and, most important, Notes of Decisions, summaries of case decisions interpreting the statute. The cases are grouped under topic headings, which are indexed alphabetically at the beginning of Notes of Decisions. "Intent to defraud, elements of cause of action" is an example of a topic heading. An important part of statutory research is locating cases that interpret a statute. Figure 7-9 is a page from the Notes of Decisions following 15 U.S.C.A. § 1989.[16]

When a case summary in Notes of Decisions appears relevant, retrieve the actual case and read it. The process of retrieving a case is explained in the following section.

STEP-BY-STEP SUMMARY: RESEARCHING STATUTORY LAW

1. Look up descriptive words in descriptive word index.
2. Read the statutory sections to which the index entries refer you.
3. For each relevant statute, read the annotations, particularly the summaries found under Notes of Decisions, which highlight case decisions interpreting the statute.
4. For each relevant case summary, retrieve and read the case.

STEP FIVE: RESEARCHING CASE LAW

As a paralegal, one of your most important functions will be researching the case law that applies to a client's situation. This section introduces you to the case reporter and case citation systems used in finding case law and examines some actual research techniques for locating cases.

Case Reporters

Court decisions are published in volumes called **case reporters**. The decisions are compiled chronologically by date of issue.

State Courts. The decisions of state trial courts are not usually published.[17] This is because the weight of the precedent set by a state trial court decision is not sufficient to warrant publication in a reporter. Trial court opinions are filed with the clerk of the court and are a public record available for inspection.

State appellate court decisions are published in the state case reporter. Some states have separate reporters for their highest court and intermediate appellate courts. For example, California Supreme Court decisions are published in *California Reports*, while intermediate appellate court decisions are published in *California Appellate Reports*. Many state court decisions are also published in a regional reporter. Regional reporters publish court decisions from a particular geographic region

FIGURE 7-9 SAMPLE U.S.C.A. NOTES OF DECISIONS PAGE

Library References

Trade Regulation ⚿ 864.
C.J.S. Trade-Marks, Trade-Names, and Unfair Competition § 237.

Notes of Decisions

---

1. Purpose

Purpose of this section authorizing civil actions to enforce liability for violations of odometer requirements is to punish odometer tamperers by imposing civil penalties upon them and to reward buyer who discovers such tampering and brings it to attention of federal court. Delay v. Hearn Ford, D.C.S.C.1974, 373 F.Supp. 791. See, also, Shipe v. Mason, D.C.Tenn.1978, 500 F.Supp. 243, affirmed 633 F.2d 218; Stier v. Park Pontiac, Inc., D.C.W.Va.1975, 391 F.Supp. 397. ←

2. Retroactive effect

Whether or not odometer on used car in possession of dealer was rolled back prior to effective date of this subchapter, where the car was sold after that date, a civil action to enforce liability for violations of the odometer requirements could be maintained. Delay v. Hearn Ford, D.C.S.C.1974, 373 F.Supp. 791.

3. Elements of cause of action—Generally

As regards this chapter, all that is required of a purchaser before recovery will be allowed is that a change in the odometer reading has occurred and that the seller has failed to disclose the change; an intent to defraud arises from proof of the foregoing in the absence of an explanation of the odometer change. Bryant v. Thomas, D.C.Neb.1978, 461 F.Supp. 613.

All that is required of buyer of automobile before recovery will be allowed under this subchapter is proof of change in odometer reading and seller's failure to disclose change. Delay v. Hearn Ford, D.C.S.C.1974, 373 F.Supp. 791. ←

of the country. Some states no longer have a state reporter; court decisions from their jurisdiction are published only in the regional reporter. For example, Florida published the *Florida Reports* until 1948. Since that time, the decisions of the Florida Supreme Court have been published in *West's Southern Reporter*.[18] The seven regional reporters and the states they cover are shown in Figure 7-10.

FIGURE 7-10 REGIONAL CASE REPORTERS

Reporter	States Included
Pacific	Alaska, Arizona, California, Colorado, Hawaii, Idaho, Kansas, Montana, Nevada, New Mexico, Oklahoma, Oregon, Utah, Washington, Wyoming
North Western	Iowa, Michigan, Minnesota, Nebraska, North Dakota, South Dakota, Wisconsin
South Western	Arkansas, Kentucky, Missouri, Tennessee, Texas
North Eastern	Illinois, Indiana, Massachusetts, New York, Ohio
South Eastern	Georgia, North Carolina, South Carolina, Virginia, West Virginia
Southern	Alabama, Florida, Louisiana, Mississippi
Atlantic	Connecticut, Delaware, District of Columbia, Maine, Maryland, New Hampshire, New Jersey, Pennsylvania, Rhode Island, Vermont

Federal Courts. Federal trial court decisions are published in a reporter known as the *Federal Supplement*. United States Courts of Appeals decisions are published in the *Federal Reporter*. United States Supreme Court decisions are published in three different reporters: the *United States Reports*, which is the official (government-published) reporter; the *Supreme Court Reporter*, an unofficial reporter published by West Publishing Company; and the *United States Supreme Court Reports, Lawyers' Edition*, an unofficial reporter published by Lawyers Co-Operative Publishing Company. The unofficial reporters, which publish a case exactly as it appears in the official reporter, include editorial enhancements that aid legal research. Because of these research aids, the unofficial reporters are commonly used by paralegals, lawyers, and judges.

Case Citations

A **citation** is a method of legal shorthand used to identify authority, such as a case or statute. To find a case, you must be able to understand the case citation.

A case citation normally includes the following information: (1) the name of the case; (2) the volume, name, and page number of the reporter(s) in which the case is found; and (3) the year the decision was issued. Consider the following citation: *Tameny v. Atlantic Richfield Company*, 27 Cal. 3d 167, 610 P.2d 1330, 164 Cal. Rptr. 839 (1980). This citation tells us that the case may be found in volume 27 of the *California Reports, 3d Series* on page 167; in volume 610 of the *Pacific Reporter, 2d Series* on page 1330; and in volume 164 of the *California Reporter* on page 839.

Note that the *Tameny* case is published in three reporters. When two or more citations are given for the same case, these citations are known as **parallel citations**. Parallel citations are verbatim reprints of the same decision.

Published by The Harvard Law Review Association and now in its fifteenth edition, *A Uniform System of Citation*, commonly known as the Blue Book, is the standard reference on proper citation form. The Blue Book should be consulted whenever a question arises about citation form. For example, the Blue Book lists the standard abbreviations for every case reporter and tells you when a parallel citation should be included as part of a standard citation. Proper citation form should always be used when a document is being submitted to a court.

Case Digests

As we have seen, cases are published chronologically (by date of decision) in reporters, which makes it impossible to research a legal topic using only the reporters. Therefore, to research particular legal topics, case digests are used. A **digest** contains a series of one-paragraph summaries of court opinions (known as digests, blurbs, or squibs) organized by *topic*.

The digest system produced by West Publishing Company is the one most commonly used. West employs a key number system, assigning every point of case law a topic (from among more than 400) and a key number, which is actually a subtopic. A given topic may contain hundreds of key numbers. When a court sends its opinion in a case to West for publication, editors write headnote paragraphs summarizing each point of law involved in the case. Each headnote is then assigned the proper topic and key number and arranged in the appropriate digest with headnotes from earlier and later cases that have been assigned the same topic and key number. This means that once you discover the topic and key number of the legal point being researched, you can look up that topic and key number in the digest and find one-paragraph summaries of each case addressing that point of law. A key number is universal, which means that the same key numbers are used throughout all West publications and apply to both state and federal jurisdictions.

The various West digests encompass both state and federal court decisions. The most frequently used digests include *United States Supreme Court Digest*, which contains summaries of U.S. Supreme Court opinions; West's *Federal Practice Digest 3d*, which contains summaries of all federal court decisions from 1975 through 1987; West's *Federal Practice Digest 4th*, which contains summaries of all federal court decisions from 1988 to the present; and separate digests for almost every state. West also publishes regional digests for four of its regional reporters. The West digest system is summarized in Figure 7-11.[19]

Descriptive Word Method. The first step in locating case law through the digests is to look up your descriptive/key words in the index to the appropriate digest. If you are researching state court opinions, then use your state digest. If you are researching recent federal court decisions, then use *Federal Practice Digest 3d*

FIGURE 7-11 THE WEST DIGEST SYSTEM (NOT COMPREHENSIVE)

COURT	DIGEST
Federal	
U.S. Supreme Court	*U.S. Supreme Court Digest*
Federal courts, 1754–1938	*Federal Digest*
Federal courts, 1939–1961	*Modern Federal Practice Digest*
Federal courts, 1961–1975	*Federal Practice Digest 2d*
Federal courts, 1975–1987	*Federal Practice Digest 3d*
Federal courts, 1988–date	*Federal Practice Digest 4th*
State	
State courts	State digests
State court opinions in regional reporters	Regional digests[1]

[1]West currently publishes digests for only four of its regional reporters: Atlantic, South Eastern, North Western, and Pacific.

and *Federal Practice Digest 4th.* For example, when you look up the descriptive word "odometer" in the descriptive word index to West's *Federal Practice Digest 3d*, you find the page reprinted here as Figure 7-12.[20]

Under the heading "Odometers," the first index entry refers you to the digest topic Trade Regulation and the key number 861. ("Trade Reg" is an abbreviation for Trade Regulation; see the Table of Abbreviations at the beginning of each index volume.) When you look up Trade Regulation 861 in the digest, you find approximately three pages of case summaries (digests, blurbs, or squibs), including the page reprinted here as Figure 7-13.[21]

Skim the case summaries, looking for cases that are factually similar to your own case. For each case summary that appears relevant, retrieve the actual case and read it. Here, you would probably want to read *Nieto v. Pence*, *Delay v. Hearn Ford*, and possibly *Augusta v. Marshall Motor Co.* (Remember that the case citation tells you where the case is published. The *Delay* case is found in volume 373 of the *Federal Supplement* reporter at page 791.) Figure 7-14 explains a case digest summary.[22]

Known-Case Method. Sometimes you already know the citation of a relevant case when you begin your research. For example, when you did your background reading in Am. Jur. 2d, one of the cases you discovered was *Nieto v. Pence*, 578 F.2d 640 (1978). If you have the citation of a relevant known case, then follow this procedure:

1. Retrieve the case.

FIGURE 7-12 SAMPLE DIGEST INDEX PAGE

OCCUPATIONAL 111 F P D 3d—574

References are to Digest Topics and Key Numbers

FIGURE 7-13 SAMPLE PAGE FROM WEST'S *FEDERAL PRACTICE DIGEST 3d*

🔑849 TRADE REGULATION 102 F P D 3d—338

For later cases see same Topic and Key Number in Pocket Part

* * *

🔑 **861. In general.**

Library references

C.J.S. Trade-Marks, Trade-Names & Unfair Competition § 237.

C.A.Tex. 1978. Under Motor Vehicle Information and Cost Savings Act, transferor who lacks actual knowledge that odometer reading is incorrect may still have duty to state that actual mileage is unknown, and seller had duty to disclose that actual mileage was unknown where, in exercise of reasonable care, he would have had reason to know that mileage was more than that which odometer had recorded or previous owner had certified. Motor Vehicle Information and Cost Savings Act, §§ 401–411, 15 U.S.C.A. §§ 1981–1991.

Nieto v. Pence, 578 F.2d 640.

D.Mass. 1986. Amendment [M.G.L.A. c. 93A, § 3(1)] to Massachusetts statute [M.G.L.A. c. 93A, § 11] creating private cause of action based on unfair or deceptive acts or practices in trade or commerce, repealing the provision that the act did not apply to trade or commerce of person whose gross revenue was at least 20% derived from interstate commerce, did not apply to publication containing reproduction of copyrighted art works where the magazine issue in question was off the newsstands well before the effective date of the amendment.

Haberman v. Hustler Magazine, Inc., 626 F.Supp. 201.

D.C.Mass. 1984. Where transactions complained of did not occur primarily and substantially within Commonwealth of Massachusetts, New Jersey corporation was exempt from liability under Massachusetts statute governing unfair or deceptive acts or practices in conduct of trade or commerce. M.G.L.A. c. 93A, § 1 et seq.

Robyn Lee Yacht Charters, Inc. v. General Motors Corp., 584 F.Supp. 8.

D.C.Ohio 1977. Failure of odometer mileage statement to disclose last plate number of vehicle, as required by regulation promulgated pursuant to Motor Vehicle Information and Cost Savings Act, was not violation of that Act, absent any intent by dealer to defraud buyer with respect to mileage reading disclosed at time of purchase. Motor Vehicle Information and Cost Savings Act, § 409, 15 U.S.C.A. § 1989.

Augusta v. Marshall Motor Co., 453 F.Supp. 912, affirmed 614 F.2d 1085.

D.C.S.C. 1974. Fact that buyer of used car from dealer was prior owner of the car was not sufficient to excuse dealer from disclosing that odometer had been changed while in possession of dealer. Motor Vehicle Information and Cost Savings Act, § 409(a)(1), 15 U.S.C.A. § 1989(a)(1).

Delay v. Hearn Ford, 373 F.Supp. 791.

After January 18, 1973, seller of automobile must disclose actual mileage and disclose any prior tampering with odometer on car sold or be responsible for failure to so state under the provisions of the Motor Vehicle Information and Cost Savings Act. Motor Vehicle Information and Cost Savings Act, §§ 404, 408, 15 U.S.C.A. §§ 1984, 1988.

Delay v. Hearn Ford, 373 F.Supp. 791.

FIGURE 7-14 EXPLANATION OF A CASE DIGEST SUMMARY

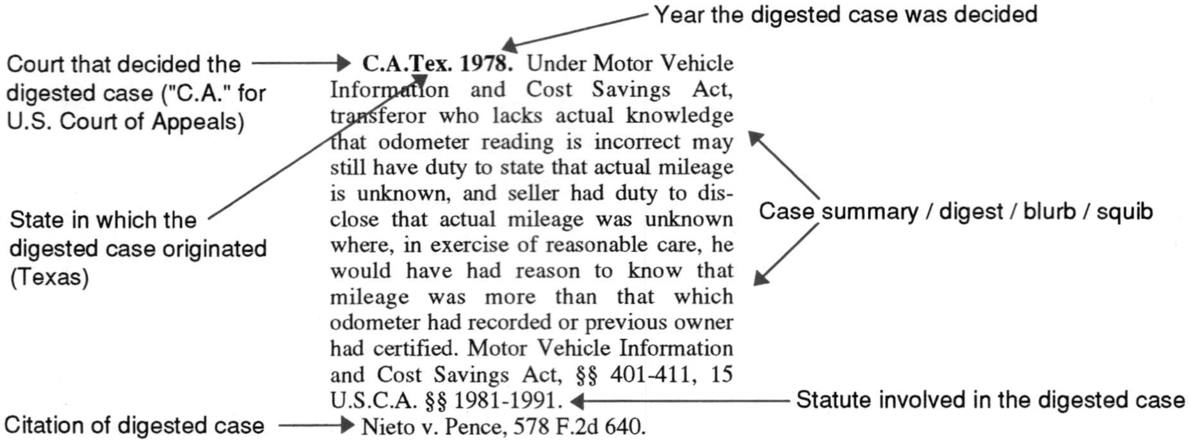
Year the digested case was decided
Court that decided the digested case ("C.A." for U.S. Court of Appeals)
State in which the digested case originated (Texas)
Case summary / digest / blurb / squib
Statute involved in the digested case
Citation of digested case
C.A.Tex. 1978. Under Motor Vehicle Information and Cost Savings Act, transferor who lacks actual knowledge that odometer reading is incorrect may still have duty to state that actual mileage is unknown, and seller had duty to disclose that actual mileage was unknown where, in exercise of reasonable care, he would have had reason to know that mileage was more than that which odometer had recorded or previous owner had certified. Motor Vehicle Information and Cost Savings Act, §§ 401-411, 15 U.S.C.A. §§ 1981-1991.
Nieto v. Pence, 578 F.2d 640.

Nieto v. Pence is reprinted at page 63.

2. Read the headnotes (one-paragraph summaries of each point of law addressed in the case).

Note that there are five headnotes in the *Nieto* case.

3. For each relevant headnote, retrieve the digest containing that topic and key number.

Here, headnotes 1–4 appear relevant because all are concerned with intent to defraud and liability under the statute, two questions being researched in the *Smith v. Lemon Motors* case. Headnotes 1 and 2 are Trade Regulation 861, and headnotes 3 and 4 are Trade Regulation 864. Therefore you would retrieve the digest containing Trade Regulation 861 and Trade Regulation 864. Headnote 5 appears irrelevant because it is concerned with a federal court procedural issue not being researched in *Smith*.

4. Skim the one-paragraph summaries found in the digest under your topic and key number.

Go back and examine Figure 7-13, which contains the one-paragraph summaries under Trade Regulation 861. Notice that the summaries in the digest are taken directly from the headnotes preceding the case; in other words, headnotes 1 and 2 preceding the text of the opinion in *Nieto* are entered directly into the digest under their assigned topic and key number (Trade Regulation 861). The digest is a compilation of headnotes.

5. For each one-paragraph summary that appears relevant (the facts are similar to your own case), retrieve the case and read it.

RESEARCHING CASE LAW, A SUMMARY

- Look up descriptive words in the descriptive word index to the appropriate digest.
- Retrieve those digests that contain the topics and key numbers to which the index entries refer you.
- Skim the one-paragraph summaries found under each topic and key number, looking for cases that are factually similar to your own case.
- For each relevant case summary, retrieve the actual case and read it.

STEP SIX: UPDATING THE LAW

Because the law is constantly changing, your legal research is never complete until you determine that the law you have discovered is still good law. *Shepard's Citations* is the most frequently used method of updating the law.

Shepard's Citations

Shepard's Citations is used to find out the subsequent treatment of cases, statutes, and other legal authorities. For example, in researching the sample case of *Smith v. Lemon Motors*, you discovered that *Delay v. Hearn Ford*, 373 F. Supp. 791 (1974) was a relevant case. But the *Delay* case was decided in 1974. What has happened since then? Is the *Delay* case still good law? Have any other cases cited the *Delay* case to support their reasoning? Has another case overruled the *Delay* case? (A case is overruled when the same court, or a higher court in the same system, rules directly opposite the earlier decision; an overruled case no longer has authority as a precedent.) To answer these questions, you need to use *Shepard's Citations* and do what is commonly referred to in law circles as **shepardize** your case.

Shepard's Citations is also used to locate additional cases "on point" (cases factually and legally similar to your own case). Once your research has located at least one relevant case, *Shepard's Citations* may lead you to other important cases.

How to Use *Shepard's Citations*. Figure 7-15 reprints the *Shepard's* citation for *Delay v. Hearn Ford*, 373 F. Supp. 791 (1974).[23] Under the entry for the *Delay* case (that is, under **—791—**) is a list of citations to cases that cited or referred to *Delay v. Hearn Ford*. *Delay v. Hearn Ford* is called the "cited case." Cases listed under the cited case are called "citing cases." Each time the cited case is referred to by a citing case, the citing case is listed under the cited case. In other words, if you look up and read one of the citing cases, you will find that it refers to *Delay v. Hearn Ford*. Every case that refers to or cites *Delay v. Hearn Ford* is listed under the *Delay* entry (that is, under **—791—**). The following is a sequential approach to locating and reading a *Shepard's* citation:

***1. Locate the Proper Set of* Shepard's Citations.** *Shepard's* publishes many different sets of **citators**, or sets that provide the subsequent history and treatment

FIGURE 7-15 SAMPLE PAGE FROM *SHEPARD'S CITATIONS*

FEDERAL SUPPLEMENT **Vol. 373**

-641-
18ALRF640s

-644-
US cert den
in423US841
a511F2d985
Mass
cc275NE[2]33

-649-
US cert den
in417US926
a494F2d855
Vt
cc129Vt564
cc283A2d863
cc303A2d803
cc303A2d804
Cir. 2
571F2d[5]746
465FS[4]190
Pa
251PaS34
379A2d318
Vt
134Vt66
349A2d225

-654-
Cir. 2
536F2d[2]519
602FS[5]852
681FS[4]1077
Cir. 3
457FS[3]349

-659-
s515F2d230

-661-
Cir. DC
c433FS[2]573
622FS[1]24

-665-
228CCL480
228CCL530
Cir. DC
393FS[1]1381
Cir. 2
394FS[2]223
394FS[4]223
394FS[6]223
Cir. 3
430FS[7]278
430FS[9]278
430FS[8]279
Cir. 4
398FS673
615FS622
Cir. 5
512F2d[2]160
512F2d[6]160
526F2d[1]1297
526F2d[1]1305
663F2d1334
715F2d[5]902
715F2d[6]902
715F2d[7]915
d389FS[10]1383
426FS[5]234
f473FS532
489FS1337
489FS[2]1338
489FS[5]1338
f511FS[9]286
541FS1033
Cir. 7
609F2d[19]1210
609F2d[3]1211
619F2d[6]627
752F2d[5]1239
490FS[1]1284
Cir. 8
580FS[6]1039
618FS[5]450
Cir. 9
511F2d[4]965
578F2d[9]750
578F2d[4]755
672FS[10]1285
Cir. 10
599F2d[6]375
Cir. 11
545FS726
CtCl
657F2d1186
657F2d1211
58FPC2708
EP§ 4.02
32AL[3]215s
52ALRF791n
52ALRF891n

-678-
a511F2d1404
77AL[2]641s

-683-
a425US748
a48LE[2]346
a96SC1817
s420US971
s423US815
s43LE[2]650
s46LE[2]33
s95SC1389
s96SC27
Cir. 2
414FS[1]139
Cir. 3
j535F2d815
Cir. 4
427FS508
Cir. 7
404FS[1]1407
Cir. 9
e395FS[1]98
402FS[1]1257
f407FS[1]1080
58FCC705
Calif
73CA3d379
140CaR759
NY
38NY[2]369
38NY[2]375
342NE[2]586
342NE[2]590
379NYS2d
[819
379NYS2d
[825
61ABA588
62ABA861
89AL[2]901s

-687-
US cert den
in417US936
in429US1026
r491F2d285
s392FS601
cc441F2d1266
cc535F2d966
97AL[2]549s

-699-
US cert den
in423US998
r509F2d820
j60LE[2]692
j99SC2117
Cir. 5
594F2d1006
Miss
544So2d815

-705-
Cir. 1
411FS[4]1293

-711-
Cir. 2
49BRW[1]176
94AL[2]647s

-716-
a488F2d529
Cir. 4
545FS710
Ore
61OrA202
656P2d351

-722-
Cir. 8
459FS173
77AL[2]641s

-727-
r509F2d1242
s339FS119

-734-
a514F2d30
s527F2d592
Cir. 2
431FS743
Cir. 4
398FS[1]467
398FS[5]467
3541CC869
Nebr
230Neb835
434NW21

-740-
Cir. 1
386FS[10]746
Cir. 6
376FS293
377FS[10]312
Ind
169InA111
346NE[2]652
47ALRF27n

-748-
US cert den
in422US1027
a510F2d971
Cir. 2
484FS[1]178
Cir. 3
620FS[1]1461
Cir. 5
616FS[6]447
Cir. 6
420FS378
420FS[7]379
Cir. 8
d545F2d[7]612
410FS[1]308
84FRD[9]142
NC
313NC716
332SE[2]457
28ALRF433n
28ALRF444n

-757-
Mass
369Mas704
341NE[2]904
NY
79NYM560
360NYS2d
[823

-762-
Cir. 4
e456FS[5]1102
550FS[5]707
Cir. 5
f633FS[5]431
Cir. 9
416FS[6]703
q509FS[5]85
29ALRF333n
29ALRF373n
72ALRF225n

-766-
Cir. 4
d406FS[2]1189
e479FS447
Cir. 5
600FS[1]1546

-771-
Cir. 10
514FS[2]364
Ark
9AkA89
654SW[2]602
Idaho
107Ida972
695P2d357
Tex
629SW[2]174
629SW[2]175

-774-
Ohio
600A90
395NE[2]909
14AL[3]330s
29ALRF909n
11ALRF815s

-778-
a510F2d969
Cir. 1
417FS197
d417FS[3]198
Cir. 3
605F2d[5]718
j648F2d878
460FS[3]648
d526FS[7]316
Cir. 5
517F2d[1]680
Cir. 6
752F2d[3]260
Cir. 7
536F2d[4]168
Cir. 9
514F2d[3]163

-791-
(28ALRF576)
Cir. 2
397FS[2]851
397FS[3]851
397FS[4]851
397FS[7]851
397FS[8]851
397FS[9]851
427FS[9]1333
Cir. 3
433FS[9]894
703FS[7]1160
Cir. 4
592F2d[6]761
f391FS[9]401
656FS[3]978
717FS[7]1099
Cir. 5
567F2d[4]1366
578F2d[3]642
578F2d[4]642
d412FS1055
459FS[9]187
Cir. 6
d404FS[1]629
d404FS[2]629
d410FS[7]769
d410FS[8]769
453FS[7]920
485FS[9]531
499FS[7]690
f499FS[10]692
499FS[11]692
500FS[9]45
Cir. 7
f404FS[9]1075
488FS[9]278
666FS1259
Cir. 8
849F2d[9]1109
425FS[3]1386
f461FS[7]616
f461FS[8]616
f498FS[7]703
Cir. 10
701FS[6]204
Colo
37CoA14
541P2d117
Ga
150GaA480
153GaA129
162GaA115
258SE[2]233
264SE[2]582
290SE[2]319
Ill
105IIA172
434NE[2]6
Mass
11MaA803
420NE[2]12
Mo
741SW86
NC
51NCA132
275SE[2]208
Ohio
41OA364
535NE[2]1382
Tex
536SW[2]95
561SW[2]890
Wis
87Wis2d126
273NW[2]778
1COA617§ 4
76AL[3]989n

-797-
Cir. 3
d418FS[2]695
e457FS[2]909
463FS[2]801
Cir. 4
d529F2d[2]603
Cir. 7
e495FS[1]83
e495FS[2]83
821D537
831D417
Pa
101PaC11
515A2d363
FRE§ 26.04

-800-
a487F2d138
Cir. 5
e520FS[3]175
Cir. 7
490FS[3]1290
NY
48NY[2]270
43NYAD[2]687
67NYAD[2]217
71NYAD[2]599
397NE[2]1311
353NYS2d
[385
414NYS2d
[694
422NYS2d
[643

-802-
(182PQ363)
Cir. 2
401FS[2]1213
402FS[3]844
416FS[2]531
465FS[4]1282
489FS[1]121
566FS[2]1347
Cir. 3
519FS[2]366
Cir. 4
723FS[1]1159
Cir. 5
399FS[1]1256
Cir. 7
d444FS[4]1213
Cir. 8
393FS[2]621

-809-
Okla
cc489P2d520
561P2d1373

-811-
Cir. 10
579F2d[7]568
Okla
742P2d1096
40AL[4]153n

-817-
Cir. 5
e534F2d1110
j534F2d1112
NY
102NYAD[2]72
102NYAD[2]75
100NYM[2]794
420NYS2d85
476NYS2d
[328
476NYS2d
[330
Continued

293

of cases and statutes. For example, a state *Shepard's* covers both cases and statutes in a given state, a regional *Shepard's* covers cases from each of the seven regional West reporters, and *Shepard's United States Citations* covers U.S. Supreme Court cases. The actual *Shepard's* volumes are dark red with titles printed in gold on the front cover and the binding. Make sure that the title of the volume covers the material you are shepardizing. For example, the *Shepard's* citation for *Delay v. Hearn Ford*, 373 F. Supp. 791 (1974), is found in *Shepard's Federal Citations, Federal Supplement*, 323 FS through 418 FS. A common mistake is to use the Statutes edition when shepardizing a case, and vice versa. *Carefully read the set's title printed in gold to make sure you are using the proper set.*

2. Locate the* Shepard's *Citation for the Cited Case (*Delay v. Hearn Ford*, 373 F. Supp. 791). As you can see in Figure 7-15, the ***Shepard's*** citation begins with the page number of the cited case printed in bold surrounded by dashes (**—791—**). The volume number is printed at the top of the page (Vol. 373).

3. Review the Citations for the Citing Cases. Under the *Shepard's* entry for 373 F. Supp. 791 (*Delay*) is a list of citations abbreviated in a style unique to *Shepard's*. The cases listed are those that have referred to or cited *Delay v. Hearn Ford*. These citing cases provide valuable information about the cited case. Using the list of citations under *Delay* for examples, here is the type of information you can learn about the cited case.

Parallel Citations. Any parallel citations of a case are found in parentheses directly below the entry of the case being shepardized:

—791—
(28ALRF576)

A parallel citation is the same case reported in a different place. Frequently a case appears in more than one reporter, perhaps a state reporter and a regional reporter. Here, *Delay v. Hearn Ford* is reported in the *Federal Supplement* and also in volume 28, A.L.R. Federal, page 576. (As we have already seen, *Delay* was the subject case of an A.L.R. annotation.) The fact that the abbreviation stands for A.L.R. Federal can be determined by referring to the Abbreviations–Reports table found at the beginning of each volume.

Treatment of the Cited Case. *Shepard's* will sometimes indicate how the citing case "treated" the cited case:

f391FS[9]401
d412FS1055

Here, the first citing case, 391 F. Supp. at 401, *followed* the *Delay* case, as indicated by the abbreviation "f." This means that the citing case cited *Delay v. Hearn Ford* as controlling precedent. The second citing case, 412 F. Supp. at 1055, *distinguished* the cited case, as indicated by the abbreviation "d." This means that the citing case is different either in law or in fact from *Delay v. Hearn Ford*. The different categories of case treatments, the abbreviations used, and an explanation of what each treatment means is found in a table at the beginning of each *Shepard's* volume. This table is reprinted in Figure 7-16.[24]

FIGURE 7-16 SAMPLE *SHEPARD'S CITATIONS* ABBREVIATIONS–ANALYSIS PAGE

ABBREVIATIONS–ANALYSIS

History of Case

a	(affirmed)	Same case affirmed on appeal.
cc	(connected case)	Different case from case cited but arising out of same subject matter or intimately connected therewith.
D	(dismissed)	Appeal from same case dismissed.
m	(modified)	Same case modified on appeal.
r	(reversed)	Same case reversed on appeal.
s	(same case)	Same case as case cited.
S	(superseded)	Substitution for former opinion.
v	(vacated)	Same case vacated.
US	cert den	Certiorari denied by U.S. Supreme Court.
US	cert dis	Certiorari dismissed by U.S. Supreme Court.
US	reh den	Rehearing denied by U.S. Supreme Court.
US	reh dis	Rehearing dismissed by U.S. Supreme Court.

Treatment of Case

c	(criticised)	Soundness of decision or reasoning in cited case criticised for reasons given.
d	(distinguished)	Case at bar different either in law or fact from case cited for reasons given.
e	(explained)	Statement of import of decision in cited case. Not merely a restatement of the facts.
f	(followed)	Cited as controlling.
h	(harmonized)	Apparent inconsistency explained and shown not to exist.
j	(dissenting opinion)	Citation in dissenting opinion.
L	(limited)	Refusal to extend decision of cited case beyond precise issues involved.
o	(overruled)	Ruling in cited case expressly overruled.
p	(parallel)	Citing case substantially alike or on all fours with cited case in its laws or facts.
q	(questioned)	Soundness of decision or reasoning in cited case questioned.

History of the Cited Case. In addition to the treatment afforded the cited case, *Shepard's* also provides information as to the subsequent history of the case, telling you, for example, whether the cited case was appealed and the result of any appeal. The abbreviation "a" means that the cited case was affirmed on appeal. The abbreviation "v" means that the cited case was vacated on appeal. When an appellate court reverses a lower court's decision, the appellate court usually vacates the lower court's opinion. This means that the opinion has no legal force and should not be considered as law. Again, if you do not know what a *Shepard's* abbreviation stands for, check the appropriate abbreviations table at the beginning of the volume (Figure 7-16).

Researching Particular Headnotes. The citations of the citing cases sometimes refer specifically to the headnotes of the cited case. As you learned earlier, a headnote is a one-paragraph summary of each point of law discussed in a case. Headnotes are found at the beginning of a case before the actual text of the opinion and are numbered consecutively. Some cases contain only one headnote; others contain over one hundred. For an example, see the five headnotes in *Nieto v. Pence* on page 63.

| 397FS²851 |
| 592F2d⁶761 |

In the first entry here, the superscript "2," which is found between the name of the reporter (F. Supp.) and the page number (851), refers to headnote 2 in the cited case of *Delay v. Hearn Ford.* This means that when the citing case cited *Delay v. Hearn Ford* at page 851 of the opinion, *Delay* was being cited for the principle of law stated in headnote 2 of *Delay.* In the second entry, the superscript "6" indicates that when the citing case cited *Delay* at page 761 of the opinion, *Delay* was being cited for the principle of law stated in headnote 6 of *Delay.*

Cases usually address more than one point of law, and therefore usually contain more than one headnote. However, sometimes only one point of law raised in a case (and therefore only one headnote) is relevant to the issue you are researching. By providing headnote numbers, *Shepard's* allows you to examine only those cases that address the specific point of law being researched, thereby saving time. For example, suppose your research led you to the case of *Delay v. Hearn Motors.* After reading the case, you learned that only a small portion of the case was relevant to the issue being researched, specifically the point of law addressed in headnote 2. You could then shepardize the *Delay* case, reading only those cases dealing with headnote 2 (397FS²851), eliminating those cases dealing with other headnotes (592F2d⁶761), and perhaps quickly checking those citing cases not listing a headnote number (d412FS1055).

Figure 7-17 is an explanation of a *Shepard's* citation.

How to Use the Supplements to *Shepard's*. *Shepard's* issues paper pamphlets to update the information contained in hardbound volumes. Before you begin shepardizing, make sure that you have gathered the hardbound volumes and paper pamphlets covering all time periods from the date of the decision to the present. In order to determine which hardbound volumes and paper pamphlets you need, *look at the front cover of the most recent paper pamphlet.* This pamphlet lists all of the hardbound volumes and paper pamphlets needed to ensure that your research is complete.

Pocket Supplements

As we have just seen, *Shepard's Citations* is one method of updating the law and making sure the law is current. Another method of updating the law is through the use of pocket supplements.

FIGURE 7-17 EXPLANATION OF A *SHEPARD'S* CITATION

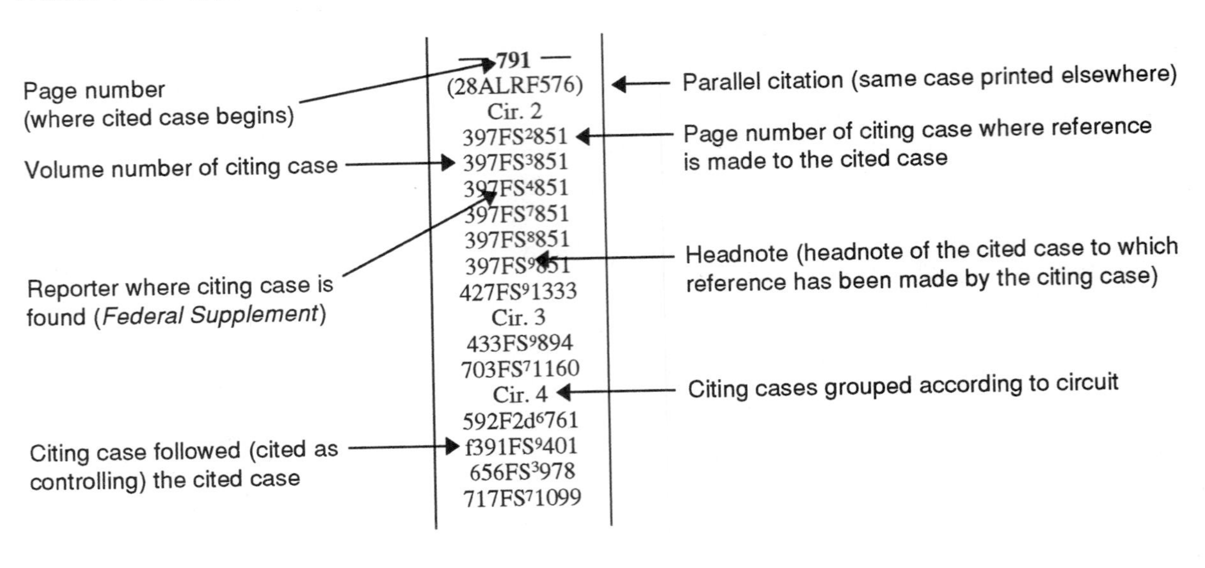

Legal material printed in hardbound volumes is frequently updated by pocket supplements. These pocket parts, as they are called, are inserted into a book's back cover. Pocket parts contain recent information updating the material in the hardbound volume.

In addition to pocket parts, many publications are updated by advance pamphlets. These softcover pamphlets periodically update the pocket parts. You must always check the pocket parts, advance pamphlets, and any other supplemental material to ensure that your research is current.

Figure 7-18 is a completed Find-the-Law Worksheet summarizing the steps we followed in this research assignment and the legal authority our research discovered.

COMPUTER-ASSISTED LEGAL RESEARCH

The two leading computer-assisted legal research systems are Lexis, a service of Mead Data Central, and Westlaw, a service of West Publishing Company. Each of these systems is an on-line system, which means that its information is stored in a distant database. Information from the database is retrieved through a telecommunication system and displayed on the computer terminal at your site.

Each system's databases contain the full text of cases, statutes, and a variety of other legal materials. Both systems are continually adding new databases and increasing the available information. In addition, each service provides instruction manuals, training disks, and training sessions conducted by live instructors. Teaching you how to actually perform computer-assisted legal research is beyond the scope of this book; our purpose here is merely to introduce you to how computer research works.

FIGURE 7-18 COMPLETED FIND-THE-LAW WORKSHEET

FIND-THE-LAW WORKSHEET

1. ANALYZING THE FACTS

- Parties or Persons: automobile dealership, buyer-seller
- Places, Objects, or Things: motor vehicle, automobile, car, used car, CS10, odometer, speedometer, odometer tampering, speedometer tampering, miles, mileage
- Legal Theories: breach of contract, fraud, misrepresentation, breach of warranty, indemnification
- Relief Sought: damages, money damages, treble damages, rescission, restitution

2. IDENTIFYING THE ISSUE

Issue: What is the potential liability of an automobile dealership for selling a car with a false odometer reading?

3. SECONDARY SOURCES

Encyclopedias: Am. Jur. 2d, Automobiles and Highway Traffic, Section 183
Other: 28 A.L.R. Fed. 584

4. STATUTORY LAW

Title and Section Number of Codes: 15 U.S.C. § 1981–1991
Statutory Law in the Codes: 15 U.S.C. §§ 1988, 1989
Case Citations from Notes of Decisions: *Delay v. Hearn Ford*, 373 F. Supp. 791; *Shipe v. Mason*, 500 F. Supp. 243, affirmed 633 F.2d 218; *Bryant v. Thomas*, 461 F. Supp. 613.

5. CASE LAW

Topics and Key Numbers in Digests: West's *Federal Practice Digest 3d*, Trade Regulation 861, 864.
Case Citations from Digests: *Nieto v. Pence*, 578 F.2d 640; *Augusta v. Marshall Motor Co.*, 453 F. Supp. 912, affirmed 614 F.2d 1085; *Delay v. Hearn Ford*, 373 F. Supp. 791.
Summaries of Cases: *Nieto v. Pence*: Under Motor Vehicles Information and Cost Savings Act, transferor who lacks actual knowledge that odometer reading is incorrect may still have duty to state that actual mileage is unknown, . . .

6. SHEPARDIZE

Current Status of Statutes and Cases: All current.

HAVE I CHECKED ALL POCKET SUPPLEMENTS?

You begin computer-assisted legal research just as you begin noncomputerized research—by identifying the descriptive/key words that you will use to search. After clearly defining the issues, you determine the appropriate legal authority. Where am I going to look? Am I looking for federal law or state law, for cases or statutes? Based on the legal authority you are searching for, you select the appropriate database, which is a group of related documents that are stored together. Lexis, for example, calls these units libraries and files, and its General Federal Library contains all federal cases and statutes. If the legal authority you are searching for is federal cases and statutes, and you are using Lexis, then you will select the General Federal Library. If the legal authority you are searching for is Florida cases, then you will select the database containing only Florida cases.

After selecting the appropriate database, your next step will be to develop a search request or query. The most common search technique is the descriptive word search. For example, you could search for a single word such as "odometer." After you type "odometer" on the keyboard, the computer will search all the information in the database and retrieve documents in which the word "odometer" is found.

You can also search for different variations of a term. The root expander (!) is used to retrieve different endings of a root term. For example, the search request/query "employ!" retrieves employ, employs, employed, employer, employee, and employment. An asterisk (*) is used to take the place of a single character. For example, the query "wom*n" retrieves woman and women.

Most computer searches involve more than one search term. The relationship between search terms is specified by using connectors. For example, the query "odometer or speedometer" retrieves documents containing either term or both terms. The query "odometer and speedometer" retrieves documents where both terms appear. You can also require that terms appear within a specified number of words of each other. For example, the query "odometer or speedometer w/5 tamper!" retrieves documents in which either the word odometer or the word speedometer appears within five words of the root term tamper or various endings of tamper.

Because the computer performs a literal word search, computer research works best when searching for unique words such as odometer. The computer is less effective when researching issues that can be expressed only in common terms—automobile, for example.

Although computers are a very powerful research tool, effective computer research requires a thorough understanding of the research process. And while computers may be able to retrieve legal authority quickly, you, the researcher, must be able to read the documents, analyze the information, and use the information in your legal writing.

ENDNOTES

1 Christopher G. Wren and Jill Robinson Wren, *The Legal Research Manual*, 2d ed. (Madison, WI: Adams and Ambrose, 1986), p. 41.

2 William P. Statsky, *Introduction to Paralegalism*, 3d ed. (St. Paul: West, 1986), p. 592.

3 William L. Prosser, *The Law of Torts*, 4th ed. (St. Paul: West, 1971). This so-called hornbook explains the basic principles of tort law and is designed primarily for law students.

4 State encyclopedias summarize state law and sometimes provide a good starting place for researching state law issues. However, not all states have a state encyclopedia.

5 *American Jurisprudence 2d* General Index, 1991 Edition, Index J–P, p. 922, "Odometers" entry. Reprinted with permission of Lawyers Cooperative Publishing Company, a division of Thomson Legal Publishing, Inc.

6 7A Am. Jur. 2d, Automobiles and Highway Traffic, Section 183, pp. 356, 357. Reprinted with permission of Lawyers Cooperative Publishing Company, a division of Thomson Legal Publishing, Inc.

7 Christina L. Kunz et al., *The Process of Legal Research*, 2d ed. (Boston: Little, Brown, 1989), p. 56.

8 A.L.R. Index to Annotations, Index M–R, p. 310, "Odometers" entry. Reprinted with permission of Lawyers Cooperative Publishing Company, a division of Thomson Legal Publishing, Inc.

9 28 A.L.R. Fed. 584. Reprinted with permission of Lawyers Cooperative Publishing Company, a division of Thomson Legal Publishing, Inc.

10 28 A.L.R. Fed. 576. Reprinted with permission of Lawyers Cooperative Publishing Company, a division of Thomson Legal Publishing, Inc.

11 28 A.L.R. Fed. Supplement (1990): Selected case summaries from the cases appearing under Section 8, Private Civil Actions, pp. 61–63. Reprinted with permission of Lawyers Cooperative Publishing Company, a division of Thomson Legal Publishing, Inc.

12 States also have annotated codes.

13 U.S.C.A. 1990 General Index M to O, p. 816, Odometer entry. Reprinted with permission of West Publishing Co.

14 U.S.C.A. 1990 General Index M to O, p. 368. Reprinted with permission of West Publishing Co.

15 U.S.C.A. 1990 General Index M to O, pp. 357–359. Reprinted with permission of West Publishing Co.

16 15 U.S.C.A. § 1989, pp. 147 and 148. Reprinted with permission of West Publishing Co.

17 Some states, such as New York, do publish selected trial court decisions.

18 Kunz et al., op. cit., p. 79.

19 For a comprehensive listing, see Kunz et al., op. cit., p. 85.

20 111 West's *Federal Practice Digest 3d*, p. 574. Reprinted with permission of West Publishing Co.

21 102 West's *Federal Practice Digest 3d*, pp. 338–340 (selected entries under key number 861). Reprinted with permission of West Publishing Co.

22 Christopher G. Wren and Jill Robinson Wren, op. cit., p. 14.

23 Reprinted from *Shepard's Federal Citations, Federal Supplement*, 323 FS–418 FS, Volume 4, 1990, p. 293, copyright © 1990 by McGraw-Hill, Inc. Reprinted by permission of Shepard's/McGraw-Hill, Inc. Further reproduction is strictly prohibited.

24 Reprinted from *Shepard's Federal Citations, Federal Supplement*, 323 FS–418 FS, Volume 4, 1990, p. xviii, copyright © 1990 by McGraw-Hill, Inc. Reprinted by permission of Shepard's/McGraw-Hill, Inc. Further reproduction is strictly prohibited.

8 LEGAL ANALYSIS AND WRITING: APPLYING THE LAW

MEMORANDUM

DATE: December 16, 1992

TO: Leslie Schermerhorn

FROM: Mark Samuel, Esq.

SUBJECT: Lemon Motors

Please prepare an office memorandum addressing the issue of whether or not Lemon Motors is liable for odometer tampering under 15 U.S.C. Sections 1988-1989.

After finding the law by performing legal research, the next step is applying the law that you found to the facts of your case. This process forms the basis for most legal writing. The purpose of this chapter is to improve your ability to (1) analyze a legal problem in a logical manner, and (2) write legal memoranda and briefs that are clear, concise, and organized.

INTRODUCTION

Good legal writing is characterized by the same qualities that characterize good writing in general. All good writing is clear, concise, and logically organized. Many people mistakenly believe that legal writing must contain archaic words and Latin phrases and must be unintelligible to a person not trained in the law. Nothing could be further from the truth.[1]

Legal writing differs from other types of writing in that it involves the application of rules of law to the facts of a particular case. The process of applying legal rules to specific facts in order to find a logical solution to a legal problem is called **legal analysis**.

The first part of this chapter introduces you to what is known as the IRAC method of legal analysis. IRAC is a mnemonic for Issue, Rule, Application, and Conclusion. IRAC is not only an approach to legal writing but also a method of legal problem solving. The IRAC method can be used whenever rules of law are applied to specific facts in order to solve a legal problem.

The second part of this chapter looks at two types of legal documents that follow the basic IRAC format, namely the office memorandum and the brief.

The chapter concludes with an explanation of how to write a case brief.

THE IRAC METHOD OF LEGAL ANALYSIS

When you use the IRAC method, you solve a legal problem by (1) identifying the issues, (2) stating the rules, (3) applying the rules to the facts, and (4) reaching a conclusion. Figure 8-1 is a simplified chart showing how the IRAC method could be applied to the legal problem raised in *Smith v. Lemon Motors*.

FIGURE 8-1 IRAC CHART

ISSUE	RULE	APPLICATION	CONCLUSION
When Lemon Motors sold the CS10 to the Smiths, did Lemon Motors have an intent to defraud?	Any person who, with intent to defraud, gives a false statement as to the actual mileage of a motor vehicle upon transfer, shall be liable for three times the amount of actual damages sustained or $1,500, whichever is greater.	The odometer on the CS10 was turned back before Tim Duncan traded in the car to Lemon Motors. Lemon Motors believed that the mileage reflected on the odometer was correct.	Lemon Motors lacked an intent to defraud.

Identifying the Issues

A **legal issue** is a problem that must be resolved in order to determine the outcome of a legal dispute. When the law is applied to the facts, certain problem areas arise. These problem areas are the legal issues that need to be analyzed.

In our sample case, *Smith v. Lemon Motors*, the applicable rule of law states that "Any person who, with intent to defraud, gives a false statement as to the actual mileage of a motor vehicle upon transfer, shall be liable for three times the amount of actual damages sustained or $1,500, whichever is greater." Let us assume the facts are that Tim Duncan traded in the car to Lemon Motors after its odometer had been turned back, and that Lemon Motors believed the mileage on the odometer was correct. When we begin to apply the law to the facts, we see that a question arises: Did Lemon Motors have an intent to defraud when it sold the car to the Smiths? We have now identified the problem area or legal issue that must be analyzed.

Narrowing the Issues. When a legal dispute first arises, the parties usually have incomplete knowledge of the facts and are not certain about the applicable law. Therefore the issues are not clearly defined. As the facts are discovered and the applicable law is researched, the issues become more focused.

For example, when the Smiths first learned that the mileage reflected on the odometer was inaccurate, they probably were unaware that the odometer had been turned back before Tim Duncan traded in the car to Lemon Motors. It is also likely they did not know that federal law provided for treble damages in odometer tampering cases. At this initial stage of the dispute, the issues would have been identified in very broad terms: Is Lemon Motors liable for what happened? If so, are the Smiths entitled to compensation from Lemon Motors? If so, how much?

As the law and facts were discovered, these issues would become narrower. Discovery of the federal statute, for example, led to this refinement of the issues: Does the statute apply in this case? Was there an intent to defraud? What does it mean to have an intent to defraud? Would a reasonably prudent automobile dealership have known that the car could not have been driven merely 1,956 miles? If so, would Lemon Motors be deemed to have an intent to defraud?

What Should Be Eliminated from Discussion? A legal issue exists when there can be disagreement over how a rule should be applied to particular facts. The measure of a true issue is that good arguments can be made on both sides. If there is no disagreement over how a rule should be applied, then the question of the rule's applicability is a nonissue and need not be discussed.

For example, look at the rule in our sample case. When we break the rule down into its component parts, we see that in order for the rule to apply, a person must "give a false statement as to the actual mileage of a motor vehicle upon transfer." There can be no disagreement as to how this section of the rule should be applied to the facts. It is a given that Lemon Motors gave a false statement as to the mileage. Lemon Motors can make no argument on this point. Therefore the question of the applicability of this section of the rule to the facts is a nonissue and need not be discussed.

Other matters that need not be discussed are irrelevant or immaterial matters and matters outside the scope of the problem being examined. A matter is irrelevant and immaterial if it does not affect the outcome of the case. For example, the parties may dispute the color of the 1991 CS10, but the color is irrelevant and immaterial to solving any legal problem here. A matter is outside the scope of the problem if addressing the matter is not necessary in order to solve the legal problem you are examining. For example, suppose your supervising attorney represents the Smiths in *Smith v. Lemon Motors* and asks you to write a memorandum analyzing all potential causes of action against Lemon Motors. (Recall from Chapter 3 that a cause of action is a legal theory on which the plaintiff's claim is based.) Your analysis of the law and the facts may suggest to you that causes of action exist against Tim Duncan. This topic, however, is beyond the scope of the problem being examined because you were asked only to analyze causes of action against Lemon Motors.

Another common difficulty in legal writing is determining how much space to devote to discussing a particular issue. When does an issue merit only brief discussion, and when should an issue be analyzed in depth? In general, the less certain the solution to a problem is, the more that issue needs to be discussed.

Stating the Rules

The second step in the IRAC process consists of stating the rules.

The rules of law used in legal analysis may be enacted laws (such as statutes) and/or case law. In some cases there is no dispute over which laws apply and what those laws mean. The only issue involves how the law will be applied to the specific facts of the case. For example, in *Smith v. Lemon Motors*, it is clear that 15 U.S.C. Sections 1988 and 1989 apply to the case and that these statutes provide for treble damages if a false statement is given with the intent to defraud. The only issue is whether Lemon Motors had an intent to defraud.

However, stating the rules is not always so easy. Sometimes the parties will disagree as to whether or not a particular rule applies. Other times they will disagree as to what a particular rule means. In these situations you must analyze the rules thoroughly before applying them to the facts.

Statutory Analysis. The first step in analyzing statutes is to break the statute down into its component parts, or elements. Our sample statutory rule is extracted from 15 U.S.C. §§ 1988–1989:

> Any person who, with intent to defraud, gives a false statement as to the actual mileage of a motor vehicle upon transfer, shall be liable for three times the amount of actual damages sustained or $1,500, whichever is greater.

This rule can be broken down into the following elements:

1. Person
2. Intent to defraud
3. Gives a false statement as to the actual mileage of a motor vehicle
4. Upon transfer
5. Shall be liable for
    a. three times the amount of actual damages sustained *or*
    b. $1,500, whichever is greater.

This statute consists of five separate elements. It imposes liability on a person only if all of the first four elements are present. To see if all four elements are present, we need to apply each element to the facts of the case.

1. Person

The statute applies to false statements made by any person. Is Lemon Motors, a corporation, a "person"?

2. **Intent to defraud**
   Did Lemon Motors act with an intent to defraud? What does it mean to have an "intent to defraud"?
3. **Gives a false statement as to the actual mileage of a motor vehicle**
   This is a given. The parties agree that Lemon Motors made a false statement.
4. **Upon transfer**
   This is another given. The false statement was made at the time of transfer.
5. **Shall be liable for three times the amount of actual damages sustained *or* $1,500, whichever is greater.**
   If the first four elements are present, then the person is liable under the statute.

When we break the rule down into its elements, we are able to identify the issues that need to be analyzed. The issues are those elements where disagreement exists. The most disagreement surrounds element 2, Intent to defraud. Therefore most of our time should be spent addressing this issue. There may be some disagreement as to element 1. Does the statute apply to a corporation? It seems fairly certain that it does. Because little disagreement exists on this issue, it merits only brief discussion. Elements 3 and 4 are givens and can be eliminated from any detailed discussion. These nonissues might be mentioned briefly only because each element must be shown to exist in order for the statute to apply.

Here is another example of how to break a statutory rule down into its elements.

> Rule 3-110. A lawyer shall not intentionally, or with reckless disregard, or repeatedly fail to perform legal services competently or fail to supervise the work of subordinate attorney and nonattorney employees or agents.

Rule 3-110 might be broken down into the following elements:

1. A lawyer
2. shall not
   a. intentionally, *or*
   b. with reckless disregard, *or*
   c. repeatedly

   fail to perform legal services competently, *or*
3. shall not
   a. intentionally, *or*
   b. with reckless disregard, *or*
   c. repeatedly

   fail to supervise the work of
   a. subordinate attorney *and* nonattorney employees *or*
   b. agents.

Statutory Interpretation. Frequently, the difficulty in understanding a statute is figuring out what the words of the statute mean. For example, in *Nieto v. Pence*, the sample case that we examined in Chapter 3, the court attempted to interpret the meaning of 15 U.S.C. Section 1988(b):

> It shall be a violation of this section for any transferor to violate any rules under this section or to knowingly give a false statement to a transferee in making any disclosure required by such rules.[2]

To understand this statute, you must determine what it means to "knowingly" give a false statement. In order to determine what the word "knowingly" means, you must determine what the legislature *intended* the word to mean. But how do you determine the legislative intent behind the statute?

As you learned in Chapter 7, one way to determine what a statute means is to locate cases that interpret it. Annotated codes contain not only notes of decisions that interpret statutes but also summaries of the changes made to statutes, which may enhance your understanding of legislative intent.

In addition, the words of a statute should be interpreted according to their *plain meaning*. You should presume that the legislature intended the words of a statute to be given their common, everyday meaning.

The *context* of the statute may also provide clues to the legislative intent. Read the surrounding statutory sections and consider the broader context in which the statute is found. If, for example, you attempt to determine the legislative intent behind 15 U.S.C. Section 1988(b) by reading the other subparagraphs of Section 1988, you will see that in its broader context this statute is part of the Odometer Requirements subchapter of the Motor Vehicle Information and Cost Savings Act. If you were unaware of this broader context, you might not realize that the word "transferor" refers to the transferor of a motor vehicle.

Finally, the *legislative history* is sometimes crucial in determining legislative intent. When attempting to determine the meaning of the statute, courts refer to speeches made on the floor of the legislature, committee reports, and prior drafts of the legislation. In *Nieto v. Pence*, the court determined the legislative intent behind the word "knowingly" by examining the Senate report on the legislation, which was found in the *U.S. Code Congressional and Administrative News*. Several other sources that contain legislative history include the *Congressional Record* and the *Congressional Index*.

Case Law Analysis. Case law is the body of legal rules and principles that comes to us through judicial decisions. Case law is judge-made law rather than legislative law. As you learned in Chapter 3, when judges decide the particular legal disputes that are before them, those decisions become law in the sense that they serve as precedents that will guide other judges in deciding similar disputes.

When analyzing a reported case to determine whether it is applicable to the case you are working on, you must ask yourself two questions: (1) How is the case similar to the case I am working on? (2) How is the case different from the case I am working on? The more similarities that exist, the more likely it is that the reported case will serve as a precedent and the conclusions of the reported case will be followed in your case. The more distinguishable (different) the cases are, the less likely it is that the reported case will be followed.

Let us quickly review the process we followed in researching the law applicable to our sample case of *Smith v. Lemon Motors*. We first discovered that a federal statute (15 U.S.C. Sections 1988 and 1989) provides for treble damages in odometer tampering cases. We then researched the case law interpreting this statute. We found several cases with facts substantially similar to *Smith v. Lemon Motors*.

After finding these cases, our next step is to carefully compare these reported cases with our case. How are the reported cases similar to our case? How are they different? For example, one case our research discovered was *Kantorcyzk v. New Stanton Auto Auction*, 433 F. Supp. 889 (W.D. Pa. 1977). In *Kantorcyzk*, an automobile buyer brought suit against the dealer and against the auctioneer from whom the dealer had obtained the automobile, alleging violations of the Motor Vehicle Information and Cost Savings Act. When the dealer purchased the vehicle at the auto auction, he was told that the mileage was 50,006, when in actuality it was 150,006. He had no way of knowing that the figure was different from what was represented to him. Given the condition of the car, it was reasonable for the dealer to believe the lower figure was accurate. The court held that the dealer did not intend to defraud the buyer. Since the dealer lacked actual knowledge of the tampering, the court found the dealer lacked the necessary intent to defraud. The auctioneer, however, was found to have fraudulent intent. Thus the plaintiff was able to recover from the auctioneer.

What are the similarities and differences between the *Kantorcyzk* case and the *Smith* case?

SIMILARITIES

1. In both cases, the defendant is an automobile dealership selling a used car it had purchased from a third party.
2. In both cases, the dealer sold the vehicle to a customer without knowing the mileage was greater than that indicated on the odometer.
3. In both cases, the odometer was turned back before the dealer acquired the car.
4. In both cases, it was reasonable for the dealer to believe the lower mileage figure was accurate.
5. In both cases, suit is brought against both the dealer and the person who sold the car to the dealer.

DIFFERENCES

1. In *Smith*, the party who sold the car to the dealer was a private individual. In *Kantorcyzk*, the party who sold the car to the dealer was an auctioneer.
2. In *Smith*, the represented mileage was approximately 2,000 while the actual mileage was approximately 30,000, a difference of 28,000 miles. In *Kantorcyzk*, the represented mileage was 50,006 while the actual figure was 150,006, a difference of 100,000 miles.

After carefully analyzing the similarities and differences, you are ready to use the reported case in your legal writing. If the holding of the reported case is favorable to your client and you want the case to be followed, then you will emphasize the factual similarities. You will de-emphasize the factual differences and show why these differences *are* not significant. However, if the holding of the reported case is unfavorable to your client and you do *not* want the case to be followed, then you will distinguish the case by emphasizing the factual differences.

For example, *Kantorcyzk v. New Stanton Auto Auction* is obviously a very good case for Lemon Motors, since it holds that the dealer did not have an intent to defraud. Lemon Motors would want this case to be followed and would therefore emphasize the factual similarities between the two cases. Lemon Motors would argue that the factual differences are insignificant. The Smiths, on the other hand, would argue that the factual differences *are* important, that the case *can* be distinguished, and that therefore it should not be followed.

Applying the Rules to the Facts

After stating the legal rule applicable to an issue, your next step is to apply the rule to the facts and determine whether the rule is satisfied. You must critically analyze the facts to determine which facts support application of the rule, which facts defeat application of the rule, and which facts might be interpreted in different ways to support both positions. The application section of your document is the most important section because this is where your argument is made. The reader must be convinced that the argument is sound and the conclusion is logical.

When you are developing arguments, it is very important to develop them for *both* sides. This is especially true when you are writing an office memorandum. As we will discuss later in this chapter, the purpose of an office memorandum is to summarize the applicable law and help your supervising attorney predict how the law will be applied to the client's case. The goal is to be objective in your analysis and to evaluate the client's case honestly. Your supervising attorney must not be misled concerning the relative strengths and weaknesses of each party's position. Therefore your fact analysis should examine the arguments that can be made by both sides.

Even when writing a brief, of which the goal is *not* objectivity but rather the strongest argument possible in favor of your client, you should analyze the opponent's factual arguments as an aid to developing your own arguments and anticipating counterarguments.

For an example of how to apply the rules to the facts of a case and how to develop arguments for both sides of an issue, consider the case of *Schmuck v. United States*, 489 U.S. 705 (1989):

> Schmuck purchased used cars, rolled back their odometers, and then sold the cars to retail dealers at artificially high prices. The retail dealers then sold the cars to unsuspecting customers. In order to transfer title to these customers, the Wisconsin Department of Transportation required that the dealers submit a title registration form for each sale, which the dealers

mailed in to the department. Schmuck was indicted for mail fraud, which was defined as mailing a writing for the purpose of executing a scheme to defraud.

Suppose your supervising attorney asks you to write an office memorandum analyzing whether or not Schmuck is guilty of mail fraud. The application section of your memorandum might look something like this:

> Schmuck would argue that mail fraud can be based only on a mailing that assists the perpetrator in carrying out the fraudulent scheme. The "mailing" element of the offense cannot be based on a mailing that is routine and innocent in and of itself, such as the mailing that took place here. This mailing occurred after the fraud had already been completed, did not further the execution of the fraud, was only tangentially related to the fraud, and was performed by the retail dealers rather than Schmuck himself. In fact, this mailing was counterproductive in that it created a paper trail from which the fraud could be discovered.
>
> On the other hand, the title registration mailings were part of the execution of the fraudulent scheme. This scheme was not really completed until the dealers resold the cars and title transferred to the buyers. If the dealers had not been able to resell the cars obtained from Schmuck, Schmuck's scheme would have failed. Although the mailings may not have directly contributed to the duping of the retail dealers or the customers, they were incident to an essential part of the scheme.

Reaching a Conclusion

The final step in the IRAC process is to draw a conclusion about how each issue you are analyzing will be resolved. Although you might be hesitant to take a position when analyzing a legal issue, most supervising attorneys will appreciate having the benefit of your thinking. A conclusion should be reached on each issue that you analyze. If you are not sure of the conclusion, then you might qualify your conclusion by using phrases such as "It is likely that . . ." or "It is probable that. . . ." If the facts have not yet been established, then you might phrase your conclusion based on an assumption that certain facts are true:

> Assuming that the odometer on the car was turned back before Tim Duncan traded in the car to Lemon Motors, Lemon Motors had no intent to defraud in this case.

POINTER: Remember that the law is not black and white and that there is not necessarily a right or wrong answer for every legal issue. If what you are analyzing is truly an issue, then good arguments can be made on both sides. Do not become overly frustrated if you are not certain about the resolution of an issue. Part of becoming a paralegal is learning how to cope with the ambiguity inherent in the law.

Now that we have examined the four parts of the IRAC method of legal analysis, it is time to look at Figure 8-2, which shows a completed sample IRAC analysis.

FIGURE 8-2 SAMPLE IRAC ANALYSIS

Issue Statutory rule	The first issue presented in this case is whether Lemon Motors had an intent to defraud when the car was sold to the Smiths. The applicable statute provides that any person who, with intent to defraud, gives a false statement as to the actual mileage of a motor vehicle upon transfer, shall be liable for three times the amount of actual damages sustained or $1,500, whichever is greater.
Describe the applicable case law	The meaning of the term "intent to defraud" was discussed in the case of *Kantorcyzk v. New Stanton Auto Auction*, 433 F. Supp. 889 (W.D. Pa. 1977). In *Kantorcyzk*, an automobile buyer brought suit against the dealer who sold him the car and against the auctioneer from whom the dealer had obtained the car. When the dealer purchased the vehicle at the auto auction, the dealer was told that the mileage was 50,006, when in actuality the mileage was 150,006. Given the condition of the car, it was reasonable for the dealer to believe that the lower figure was accurate. The court held that since the dealer lacked actual knowledge of the tampering, there was no fraudulent intent on the part of the dealer.
Application	Similarly, in the present case, the facts indicate that the odometer on the car was turned back before Tim Duncan traded in the car to Lemon Motors. It appears that Lemon Motors lacked actual knowledge of the tampering and believed that the mileage reflected on the odometer was correct. It further appears that this belief was reasonable based on the condition of the car.
Conclusion	Therefore Lemon Motors lacked an intent to defraud.

ORGANIZATION

Good organization is the key to effective legal writing. Legal documents must be tightly and logically organized and their arguments clear and easily understood. Paralegals write documents primarily for attorneys and judges, an audience that tends to be busy and overworked. If shoddy organization makes a document difficult to understand, attorneys and judges will not even bother to read it.

Good organization begins with an outline. Outlining allows you to think through the problem and develop logical arguments.

The IRAC method can provide a basic outline for any legal document in which rules of law are applied to the facts of a case. In addition to using this basic IRAC format, you should follow several other rules in order to ensure a well-organized document.

IRAC Each Issue Separately

When two or more issues need to be analyzed, always IRAC each issue separately. After reaching a conclusion on one issue, continue on to the next issue. Good organization is characterized by a clear and distinct separation of issues.

IRAC Each Subissue Separately

The issues we are analyzing in this chapter are relatively simple compared to the complex issues typically encountered in an actual case. Frequently, each issue contains several subissues, and each subissue contains its own applicable rule and set of facts. Your outline of a more complex case might look something like this:

I. Issue A
   A. Subissue 1
   B. Subissue 2
II. Issue B
   A. Subissue 1
   B. Subissue 2
   C. Subissue 3
III. Issue C

When analyzing more complex issues, always IRAC each subissue completely, and then move on to the next subissue. There should be a clear and distinct separation of subissues, just as there is a clear and distinct separation of main issues. Always IRAC the subissues under issue A before analyzing any part of issue B.

THE OFFICE MEMORANDUM

The office memorandum is a type of document that paralegals frequently prepare. It is variously referred to as a memo, an interoffice memorandum, an office memorandum of law, a memorandum of law, and a legal research memorandum.

Purpose

An **office memorandum** summarizes the law that is relevant to a case and predicts how the law will be applied to the facts of the case. The memo is prepared for the supervising attorney and may be used to advise the client or prepare a more formal legal document, such as a pleading or a brief.

A memo is not an advocacy document; that is, it does not promote a particular point of view. The purpose of a memo is to present objectively and honestly a balanced discussion of the facts and law involved in a case. When writing an office memorandum, you should present the strongest possible arguments on both sides of the dispute; you should never eliminate facts from consideration because they are harmful to your client's case. Such an omission could mislead your supervising attorney, who should be made aware of both the strengths and the weaknesses of the client's position.

Format

Although the format of an office memorandum may vary from law office to law office, most memos contain (1) a heading, (2) a statement of the questions presented, (3) a brief answer to each of the questions presented, (4) a statement of the facts, (5) a discussion section in which the law is applied to the facts, and (6) a conclusion.

FIGURE 8-3 SAMPLE OFFICE MEMORANDUM

MEMORANDUM

TO: Mark Samuel

FROM: Leslie Schermerhorn

SUBJECT: Dealer Liability with Respect to Odometer Tampering
Smith v. Lemon Motors, file number 123-456.

DATE: December 21, 1992

Question Presented

Is an automobile dealership liable for violation of the odometer disclosure requirements imposed by 15 U.S.C. Sections 1988-1989 when the dealership did not tamper with the odometer, but merely resold the vehicle without actual knowledge of the false odometer reading?

Brief Answer

Probably not. Without actual knowledge of odometer tampering, the dealership is not liable.

Statement of Facts

In September 1991, Tim Duncan purchased a new Allied Motors CS10 automobile from Valley Motors. On August 10, 1992, Duncan sold the car to Lemon as part of a transaction in which he purchased a new car from Lemon. On that date the odometer reflected the CS10's mileage to be 1,930. The tires on the car were in excellent condition, and the car was in such fine shape that it did not have to be detailed prior to resale.

On September 1, 1992, the Smiths purchased the CS10 from Lemon for $19,250. This purchase price included a premium for the low mileage. A Lemon agent signed an odometer mileage statement indicating that to the best of Lemon's knowledge the mileage on the car was 1,956.

In November 1992, the Smiths took the car to a mechanic for repairs. After a check of the warranty records maintained by the manufacturer, the Smiths learned that the actual mileage on the car substantially exceeded the mileage reflected on the odometer.

FIGURE 8-3 SAMPLE OFFICE MEMORANDUM (Cont.)

Discussion

Federal law addresses the issue of odometer tampering in one concise subchapter of the U.S. Code entitled Motor Vehicle Information and Cost Savings Act, 15 U.S.C. §§ 1981-1991. Section 1981 states that ''the purpose of this subchapter [is] to prohibit tampering with odometers on motor vehicles and to establish certain safeguards for the protection of purchasers with respect to the sale of motor vehicles having altered or reset odometers.'' (Emphasis added.)

Section 1988 outlines disclosure requirements on transfer of ownership of a motor vehicle. Any transferor, including a dealer, must disclose the actual cumulative mileage on transfer or indicate that the actual mileage is unknown. Subsection (b) states that to give a false statement to a transferee is a violation of the act. Section 1989 provides for civil actions to enforce liability for violation of the act:

> Section 1989. Civil actions to enforce liability for violations of odometer requirements; amount of damages; jurisdiction; period of limitation
>
> (a) Any person who, with intent to defraud, violates any requirement imposed under this subchapter shall be liable in an amount equal to the sum of --
>
> (1) three times the amount of actual damages sustained or $1,500, whichever is greater; and
>
> (2) in the case of any successful action to enforce the foregoing liability, the costs of the action together with reasonable attorney fees as determined by the court. (Emphasis added.)

Thus, to find liability on the part of the dealer, the plaintiff will have to show that the dealer acted ''with intent to defraud.''

A number of cases at the federal level address dealer liability in this situation. In Kantorcyzk v. New Stanton Auto Auction, 433 F. Supp. 889 (W.D. Pa. 1977), an automobile buyer brought suit against the seller (a dealer) and against the auctioneer from whom the dealer had obtained the automobile, alleging violations of the Motor Vehicle Information and Cost Savings Act. With respect to the dealer, the district court held that the evidence established that the dealer did not know that the actual mileage was greater than that

FIGURE 8-3 SAMPLE OFFICE MEMORANDUM (Cont.)

indicated on the odometer when he sold the auto, and that the dealer had not attempted to defraud the buyer. When the dealer purchased the vehicle at the auto auction, it was represented to him that the mileage was 50,006 when the actual figure was 150,006. The dealer had no way of knowing that the actual figure was different from the figure represented to him. Given the condition of the car, it was reasonable for the dealer to believe that the lower figure was accurate. Since the dealer lacked actual knowledge of the tampering, the court found he lacked the necessary intent to defraud and therefore was not liable. The auctioneer was found to have fraudulent intent; thus the plaintiff was able to collect from him.

The case of Shepherd v. Eagle Lincoln Mercury, Inc., 526 S.W.2d 92 (1976) similarly found that the dealer was not liable where he personally did not alter the odometer. The dealer had purchased the automobile from a party who represented on an odometer disclosure statement that the car had been driven 8,226 miles. The dealer merely passed on the representation, not knowing that it was false. Since the plaintiff was unable to show all of the elements of actionable fraud, the defendant dealer prevailed.

It seems clear, then, that in order to find liable a dealer who has merely resold a vehicle, the plaintiff must show that the dealer intended to commit fraud. A key issue in establishing this intent is the degree to which the dealer had knowledge of the false odometer reading. Must the dealer have actual knowledge of the false odometer reading, or will a lesser standard of constructive knowledge be applied?

In Mataya v. Behm Motors, 409 F. Supp. 65 (E.D.W.S. 1976), the court elaborated on this issue:

> If it is assumed that the intent to defraud required by Section 1989(a) may be presumed from a finding of actual knowledge of odometer alteration, a question would nevertheless remain as to whether an intent to defraud can be based solely upon a finding of constructive knowledge, which is all that seems to be required for a violation of Section 1988(b). The better view would seem to be that actual knowledge is necessary to support an inference of intent to defraud, and, correspondingly, recovery under Section 1989(a).

Since the defendant dealer in Mataya lacked actual knowledge of the tampering, he lacked the intent to defraud, and thus prevailed.

FIGURE 8-3 SAMPLE OFFICE MEMORANDUM (Cont.)

A case quite similar to ours is Pepp v. Superior Pontiac GMC, 412 F. Supp. 1053 (E.D. La. 1976). There the dealer received as a trade-in an auto with mileage quoted at 22,283. The dealer examined the car, and to him it seemed fine. The dealer sold the car to the buyer, who subsequently checked the car's records and determined that the odometer reading was inaccurate. There the court determined that

> Section 1989 makes it clear that a mere negligent violation, or even a knowing violation of the regulations does not give rise to a cause of action. That section imposes a civil liability only on a person who (a) violates any requirement imposed under this subchapter; (b) and does so ''with intent to defraud.'' 412 F. Supp. at 1054 (emphasis in original).

The court found the dealer merely negligent in not discovering the malfunctioning odometer and thus determined that he did not violate Section 1989.

However, not all courts accept the ''actual knowledge'' standard. Nieto v. Pence, 578 F.2d 640 (1978), is one case that imposed a reasonableness requirement on the dealer's actions. In Nieto, the dealer was trying to pass off a 10-year-old truck as having a mere 14,290 miles. The court held that ''if a transferor reasonably should have known that a vehicle's odometer reading was incorrect, although he did not know to a certainty the transferee would be defrauded, a court may infer that he understood the risk of such an occurrence.'' 578 F.2d at 642. Thus where the dealer fails to exercise reasonable care, Nieto suggests potential liability under Section 1989.

Nieto appears to be distinguishable on its facts. While it seems unreasonable for the dealer in Nieto to believe that the 10-year-old truck had been driven a mere 14,290 miles, it was reasonable for Lemon Motors to believe the CS10 had only 1,930 miles on it. Here the facts should be emphasized. For instance, it appeared that the CS10 had been equipped with new tires, and the car was in such fine shape that it did not have to be detailed prior to resale.

Delay v. Hearn Ford, 373 F. Supp. 791 (D.C.S.C. 1974) is often cited for the proposition that intent of the seller to defraud ''arises from proof of change in the odometer reading of the automobile sold and the seller's failure to disclose the change.'' This case, which seems to adopt a standard far short of actual knowledge,

FIGURE 8-3 SAMPLE OFFICE MEMORANDUM (Cont.)

should again be distinguished on its facts. In Delay it was readily apparent that the vehicle's odometer was rolled back while in possession of the dealer. In the case we are considering, the tampering was done prior to the acquisition by Lemon Motors.

The case of Jones v. Fenton Ford, Inc., 428 F. Supp. 1328 (D. Conn. 1977) also adopts a lesser standard, this time one of constructive knowledge. There the court stated:

> A widely accepted rule of fraudulent intent, applicable here, is that civil liability may be imposed where it is proved that a defendant's statements were made recklessly or carelessly, without knowledge of their truth or falsity, or without reasonable grounds for belief in their truth, especially in a case where (1) the defendant was under a duty to have the knowledge in question; (2) a relation of trust or expert reliance existed; (3) a statement was made to induce a business arrangement; or (4) the knowledge or information in question was within the special province of the defendant. 427 F. Supp. 1328, 1334.

Like Nieto and Delay, the Jones case should be distinguished on its facts. There the dealer was made aware of the defective odometer and its faulty reading, yet went ahead and represented the figure as being the true mileage. Note how the dealer in Jones had actual knowledge, yet the case is cited for the idea that a dealer can be found liable on some lesser standard.

Conclusion

Because Lemon Motors did not have actual knowledge of the false odometer reading at the time it sold the car, the dealership is most likely not liable under the federal statute. It appears that Lemon Motors did not act with the intent to defraud the Smiths. Even if the court adopts a standard less than ''actual knowledge'' in determining intent to defraud, the facts of our case indicate that Lemon Motors reasonably believed the odometer reading was correct.

Heading. The heading identifies to whom the memo was written, who wrote it, what it is about, and the date. For example:

MEMORANDUM

TO: Chris Redford

FROM: Pat Lippitt

SUBJECT: Mail Fraud
U.S. v. Schmuck, file number 234-567.

DATE: March 1, 1993

Questions Presented. The Questions Presented section contains a one-sentence statement of each legal question, or issue, that will be addressed in the memo. For example:

I. Where the defendant rolled back the odometers on used cars before selling them to retail dealers, and the retail dealers mailed in title application forms to the Department of Transportation on resale, is the mailing element of the crime of mail fraud satisfied?

Brief Answer. This section briefly answers each of the questions presented. Because the Brief Answer section immediately follows the Questions Presented section, the answer should respond directly to the question presented and then briefly explain the reasons for the answer. For example:

I. Yes. A mailing that is incident to an essential part of the scheme satisfies the mailing element of the crime of mail fraud.

Statement of Facts. This section is an objective description of the relevant facts in the case. These are the facts that will be analyzed in the Discussion section of the memo. The statement of facts must include those facts which are both favorable and unfavorable to your client's position. For an example, see Figure 8-3, Sample Office Memorandum.

Discussion. This section of the memo restates each of the questions presented and then applies the law to the facts in answer to each question. The Discussion section of the memo requires you to use many of the principles of legal writing discussed earlier in this chapter. For example:

- Analyze each issue (each question presented) and subissue separately.
- Reach a conclusion on each issue before moving on to the next issue.
- Explain the applicable law before applying the law to the facts and analyzing the facts.
- Explain how the facts of cases supporting your conclusions are similar to the facts of your own case.
- Distinguish the facts of cases inconsistent with your conclusions.

For an example of the Discussion section of a memo, see Figure 8-3.

Conclusion. The Conclusion section summarizes how each question presented was answered. The conclusion is slightly longer than the brief answer because it describes the reasoning supporting each conclusion. For an example, see Figure 8-3.

THE BRIEF OR MEMORANDUM OF LAW

A **brief** is a formal legal document submitted to a court for the purpose of convincing the court to adopt one party's position on the issues. While an office memorandum objectively discusses the issues, a brief advocates the client's position. The goal of brief writing is to present your client's position as strongly and forcefully as possible.

There are two kinds of briefs, trial briefs and appellate briefs. Trial briefs, which are submitted in connection with a trial, inform the trial court judge prior to the beginning of the trial about the facts that the party expects to prove at trial and how the law should be applied to those facts. A brief submitted in connection with a motion, although known by a variety of names, is most commonly referred to as a memorandum of points and authorities or a memorandum of law.

An appellate brief challenges or defends a trial court's decision. If you represent the appellant (the party appealing), then your appellate brief argues that the trial court committed errors that prejudiced the outcome of the case. If you represent the appellee (the party who prevailed in the lower court), then your brief argues that no prejudicial error was committed and that the trial court's decision should stand.

The most commonly used formats for trial briefs and appellate briefs are the following:

Trial Brief

1. Caption
2. Questions Presented (optional)
3. Statement of Facts
4. Argument
5. Conclusion

Appellate Brief

1. Cover Page
2. Table of Contents
3. Table of Authorities
4. Opinion(s) Below
5. Jurisdictional Statement
6. Constitutional Provisions, Statutes, Regulations, and Rules Involved
7. Questions Presented
8. Statement of Facts
9. Summary of Argument
10. Argument
11. Conclusion
12. Appendix(es)

POINTER: The format for trial and appellate briefs varies from jurisdiction to jurisdiction. A brief writer should check the local rules of court.

Figure 8-4 is an example of a trial brief. For an example of an appellate brief, see Appendix A.

THE CASE BRIEF

A **case brief** is a summary of the essential points of a court opinion. The purpose of briefing a case is to help you understand the case. In addition, briefing a case usually eliminates the need to read the entire case over again, since the brief should contain all of the basic information that you need to know about the case.

Briefing cases is primarily an activity of law students. In practice, lawyers and paralegals seldom take the time to actually write a case brief. However, sometimes a paralegal might brief the cases discovered when researching a particular legal problem. Occasionally, a supervising attorney might ask a paralegal to brief a case that the attorney does not have time to read in its entirety.

POINTER: As we have seen, the word ''brief'' has several meanings. While trial briefs and appellate briefs are formal written arguments submitted to a court in connection with a trial or an appeal, case briefs are informal documents intended for the writer's personal use.

There are many different ways to brief a case. In its simplest form, a case brief contains four separate parts: (1) the *facts* of the case, (2) the *issue* or legal controversy raised in the case, (3) the *holding* or rule of law announced in the case, and (4) the *rationale* or reasons why the court reached the decision it did. Figure 8-5 is a sample brief of the *Nieto v. Pence* case, which is reprinted at page 63.

Facts

When stating the facts, include only those facts that are crucial to the court's decision. In *Nieto v. Pence*, a crucial fact is that the 10-year-old truck had an odometer reading of only 14,736 miles. The court's decision in favor of the plaintiff is based on the belief that the auto dealer reasonably should have known that the odometer reading was incorrect. In contrast, the color of the truck (i.e., whether it was black or white) is irrelevant and would not be included in the statement of the facts.

Issue

The issue should always be stated in the form of a question. Sometimes the issue is whether the trial court understood the law correctly, or whether the law was applied to the specific facts of the case correctly. At other times, when a statute is the applicable law, the issue is whether the statute was interpreted correctly. For example, a statement of the first issue discussed in *Nieto v. Pence* might be this: Did the seller of the truck, who lacked actual knowledge that the odometer reading was incorrect, knowingly give a false statement within the meaning of 15 U.S.C. Section 1988?

FIGURE 8-4 SAMPLE TRIAL BRIEF

Mark Samuel
SAMUEL & JOSEPH
37 Sea Coast Highway
Seaside, CA 90277-2143
(310) 990-1234

Attorneys for Defendant and Cross-
Complainant Lemon Motors, Inc.

_______ COURT FOR THE _______ JUDICIAL DISTRICT
COUNTY OF _______, STATE OF _______

JOHN SMITH and MARY SMITH, Plaintiffs, v. LEMON MOTORS, INC., a California Corporation; TIM DUNCAN; and DOES 1 through 10, inclusive, Defendants. ______________________________ AND RELATED CROSS-ACTIONS. ______________________________	CASE NO. 123456 TRIAL BRIEF

1. STATEMENT OF FACTS

In September 1991, Duncan purchased a new Allied Motors CS10 automobile from Valley Motors. Allied Motors warranty records and independent mechanics' repair records indicate that Duncan had repairs performed on this car on several occasions. Most of these repairs were done by Seaside Motors. Two repair orders generated by Seaside Motors and dated February 9 and 10, 1992, indicate that the car's odometer reading as of the date those repairs were performed was 15,300. The same mileage is reflected in computerized records maintained by Allied Motors in connection with a warranty claim dated February 15, 1992. Two subsequent Seaside Motors repair orders, dated August 4, 1992, indicate that the car's odometer reading was 31,203 as of that date. This same mileage is reflected in Allied Motors' computerized warranty records.

FIGURE 8-4 SAMPLE TRIAL BRIEF (Cont.)

On August 10, 1992, Duncan sold the car to Lemon as part of a transaction in which he purchased a new car from Lemon. On that date the odometer reflected the CS10's mileage to be 1,930, and at the time of the sale Duncan signed an odometer mileage statement to that effect. It is the regular business practice of Lemon to prepare such statements on the basis of odometer readings at the time the statements are prepared.

On September 1, 1992, the Smiths purchased the CS10 from Lemon for $19,250.00. A Lemon agent signed an odometer mileage statement indicating that to the best of Lemon's knowledge the mileage on the car was 1,956.

In late November 1992, the Smiths took the car to a mechanic for repairs. After a check of the warranty records maintained by Allied Motors, this mechanic told the Smiths that the actual mileage on the car substantially exceeded the mileage reflected on the odometer.

The Smiths filed this lawsuit in February 1993.

2. DISCUSSION OF SELECTED LEGAL ISSUES AND RELEVANT EVIDENCE

A. The damages to which the Smiths are entitled are limited to the difference between the value of the car as represented and the actual value of the car.

Although it denies negligence, Lemon acknowledges its liability to the Smiths for breach of express warranty. However, it argues that the proper measure of the damages is the difference between the actual value of the car and the value of the car as warranted. Evidence to be introduced at trial will establish that the difference between the actual value and the value as warranted is, at most, $2,000.

The Smiths contend that they are entitled to treble their actual damages -- and to recover attorneys' fees -- by virtue of the Motor Vehicle Information and Cost Savings Act, 15 U.S.C. §§ 1981-1991.

Section 1988 outlines disclosure requirements on the transfer of ownership of a motor vehicle. Any transferor, including a dealer, must disclose the actual cumulative mileage on transfer, or indicate that the actual mileage is unknown. Section 1988(b) states that to give a false statement to a transferee is a violation of the act. Section 1989 provides for civil actions to enforce liability for violation of Section 1988. Section 1989 provides:

FIGURE 8-4 SAMPLE TRIAL BRIEF (Cont.)

(a) Any person who, with intent to defraud, violates any requirement imposed under this subchapter shall be liable in an amount equal to the sum of --

(1) three times the amount of actual damages sustained or $1,500, whichever is greater; and

(2) in the case of any successful action to enforce the foregoing liability, the cost of the action together with reasonable attorney fees as determined by the court.

(b) An action to enforce any liability created under subsection (a) of this section, may be brought in a United States district court without regard to the amount in controversy, or in any other court of competent jurisdiction, within two years from the date on which the liability arises. (Emphasis added.)

Thus to find liability on the part of a dealer such as Lemon, a plaintiff must show that the dealer acted ''with intent to defraud.'' As will appear from the proof at trial, only Duncan possessed the requisite intent to defraud. Duncan traded in the used CS10 after its odometer had been turned back. Lemon believed that the mileage reflected on the odometer was correct.

There are a number of cases on the federal level that address dealer liability in a situation similar to the one that is the subject of this case.

In Kantorcyzk v. New Stanton Auto Auction, 433 F. Supp. 889 (W.D. PA. 1977), an automobile buyer brought suit against the seller (a dealer) and against the auctioneer from whom the dealer had obtained the automobile, alleging violations of the Motor Vehicle Information and Cost Savings Act. With respect to the dealer, the district court held that the evidence established that the dealer did not know that the actual mileage was greater than that indicated on the odometer when he sold the auto, and that the dealer had not attempted to defraud the buyer. When the dealer purchased the vehicle at the auto auction, it was represented to him that the mileage was 50,006 when the actual figure was 150,006. The dealer had no way of knowing that the figure was different from the figure represented to him. Given the condition of the car, it was reasonable for the dealer to believe that the lower figure was accurate. Since the dealer lacked actual knowledge of the tampering, the court found he

FIGURE 8-4 SAMPLE TRIAL BRIEF (Cont.)

lacked the necessary intent to defraud. The auctioneer was found to have fraudulent intent, thus the plaintiff was able to collect from him.

The case of Shepherd v. Eagle Lincoln Mercury, Inc., 536 S.W.2d 92 (1976), similarly found that the dealer was not liable where he personally did not alter the odometer. The dealer had purchased the automobile from a party who represented on an odometer disclosure statement that the car had 8,226 miles on it. The dealer merely passed on the representation, not knowing that it was false. Since the plaintiff was unable to show all of the elements of actionable fraud, the defendant dealer prevailed.

It seems clear, then, that in order to find liable a dealer who has merely resold a vehicle, the plaintiff must show that the dealer intended to commit fraud.

A number of cases have attempted to define what is meant by an ''intent to defraud.'' In Mataya v. Behm Motors, 409 F. Supp. 65 (E.D. Wis. 1976), for example, the court elaborated on the issue of such intent:

> If it is assumed that the intent to defraud required by 1989(a) may be presumed from a finding of actual knowledge of odometer alteration, a question would nevertheless remain as to whether an intent to defraud can be based solely upon a finding of constructive knowledge which is all that seems to be required for a violation of 1988(b). The better view would seem to be that actual knowledge is necessary to support an inference of intent to defraud, and, correspondingly, recovery under § 1989(a).

Since the defendant dealer in Mataya lacked actual knowledge of the tampering, he lacked the intent to defraud and thus prevailed.

A case quite similar to the one at bar is Pepp v. Superior Pontiac GMC, 412 F. Supp. 1053 (E.D. La. 1976). There, the dealer received as a trade-in an auto with mileage quoted at 22,283. The dealer examined the car, and to him it seemed fine. The dealer sold the car to the buyer, who subsequently checked the car's records and determined that the odometer reading was inaccurate. There the court determined that

FIGURE 8-4 SAMPLE TRIAL BRIEF (Cont.)

> Section 1989 makes it clear that a mere negligent violation, or even a knowing violation of the regulations does not give rise to a cause of action. That section imposes a civil liability only on a person who (a) violates any requirement imposed under this subchapter; (b) and does so ''with intent to defraud.'' 412 F. Supp. at 1054 (emphasis in original).

The court found the dealer merely negligent in not discovering the malfunctioning odometer and thus determined that he did not violate Section 1989.

The evidence to be introduced at trial will demonstrate that Lemon had no actual knowledge of the incorrectness of the mileage shown on the odometer. Without a showing of such actual knowledge, the Smiths may recover only their actual damages.

B. Lemon is entitled to indemnification and recovery of three times its actual damages plus attorneys' fees from Duncan.

The evidence to be introduced at trial will demonstrate that, to the extent that the Smiths are able to recover actual damages from Lemon, Lemon is entitled to indemnification from Duncan. It is well established that when a defendant is sued for breach of contract, such defendant has a right of implied indemnity against any third person whose wrong was the ultimate cause of the defendant's breach. 14 Cal. Jur. 3d, Contribution and Indemnification, Section 41. As the Court of Appeal observed in Normelline Construction Co. v. Harris, 272 Cal. App. 2d 352, 359 (1969): ''A person who, in whole or in part, has discharged a duty which is owed by him but which as between himself and another should have been discharged by the other, is entitled to indemnity from the other.'' The theory of implied indemnity is, in essence, ''a shifting of the risk of loss from one upon whom it falls to the person who in justice should bear it.'' Muth v. Urricelqui, 251 Cal. App. 2d 901, 908 (1967). The theory applies in the context of negligence as well as breach of contract. Id. at 908-909.

Moreover, since Duncan defrauded Lemon when he misrepresented the car's mileage, Lemon is entitled to recover three times the amount of Lemon's loss plus its attorneys' fees in the action. As previously noted, 15 U.S.C. § 1988(b) provides that giving a false statement concerning the actual mileage of a car on its transfer is a violation of the federal statute. If the statement is given with

FIGURE 8-4 SAMPLE TRIAL BRIEF (Cont.)

intent to defraud, an injured party is entitled to three times the amount of actual damages (but not less than $1,500), plus its costs and attorneys' fees. 15 U.S.C. § 1989(a).

DATED: July 21, 1993. SAMUEL & JOSEPH

By: ______________________

Mark Samuel
Attorney for Defendant
and Cross-Complainant,
Lemon Motors, Inc.

FIGURE 8-5 SAMPLE CASE BRIEF

BRIEF OF *NIETO V. PENCE*, 578 F.2d 640 (1978)

Facts: Plaintiff Nieto purchased from defendant Pence, a used car dealer, a 10-year-old pickup truck with an odometer reading of 14,736 miles. The odometer reading was incorrect, although the defendant had no actual knowledge of this. The defendant, who had been in the business 12 years, was suspicious of the odometer reading, yet certified to the plaintiff that the odometer reading was correct. The trial court held that actual knowledge was required for liability under 15 U.S.C. Section 1989.

Issue: May the seller of a motor vehicle who lacks actual knowledge that the odometer reading is incorrect nevertheless be considered to have had an "intent to defraud" and thus be found liable for failure to disclose that the actual mileage is unknown?

Holding: Yes. The seller of a motor vehicle who lacks actual knowledge that the odometer reading is incorrect may still be considered to have had an intent to defraud, and thus be liable for failure to disclose that the actual mileage is unknown, if the seller reasonably should have known that the odometer reading was incorrect.

Rationale: The seller may not close her or his eyes to the truth.

Holding

The holding is usually the answer to the question posed by the issue. The holding is the most important part of the case because it is the rule of law that subsequent cases must follow. You do not really understand a case unless you can accurately state the holding.

Rationale

The rationale of a case is the reason why the court decided the case the way it did. A court will usually make several arguments in support of its decision. Often the arguments will be based on precedent. For example, the court in *Nieto v. Pence* cited five cases to support the proposition that "a transferor may have intended to defraud even if he lacked actual knowledge that the odometer reading was incorrect." (See page 65 of this text, section [20].)

In conclusion, a case brief should be just that—*brief.* You should try to summarize the essential points of the opinion in as few words as possible. A case brief will not serve its purpose if the brief is longer than the case.

ENDNOTES

1 Steve Barber, *Legal Writing for Paralegals* (Cincinnati: South-Western, 1993). Barber's book and several others provide in-depth coverage of the points made in this chapter. They include Charles R. Calleros, *Legal Method and Writing* (Boston: Little, Brown, 1990); Veda R. Charrow and Myra K. Erhardt, *Clear and Effective Legal Writing* (Boston: Little, Brown, 1986); and John C. Dernbach and Richard V. Singleton, *A Practical Guide to Legal Writing and Legal Method* (Littleton, CO: Fred B. Rothman, 1981).

2 15 U.S.C. § 1988(b) has been amended since the *Nieto* decision.

9 THE LITIGATION PROCESS: YOUR ROLE AS A PARALEGAL

MEMORANDUM

DATE: February 1, 1993

TO: Kim Starbard

FROM: Myrna Jackson

SUBJECT: Smith v. Lemon Motors

Mary and John Smith have decided to file suit against Lemon Motors and Tim Duncan. Please draft a complaint for (1) breach of contract against Lemon Motors, (2) negligence against Lemon Motors, and (3) fraud and misrepresentation against Tim Duncan.

As you learned in Chapter 1, litigation is the process through which disputes are settled in the courts. Many paralegals are involved in litigation matters on a daily basis, and all paralegals need a thorough understanding of the litigation process. Paralegals who specialize in real estate or business transactions, for example, endeavor to draft documents so as to *avoid* litigation, which sometimes results despite their efforts.

INTRODUCTION

This chapter highlights those stages of litigation in which paralegals are typically involved. Organized around the sample case of *Smith v. Lemon Motors*, it includes samples of documents frequently drafted by paralegals. Read the samples carefully because they are important learning tools.

The goals of this chapter are to build a litigation vocabulary, to develop a "feel" for the litigation process by following a case from beginning to end, and to begin to develop the skills necessary to draft litigation documents. The assignments in this chapter involve the actual drafting of litigation documents, which is the kind of work done by most practicing paralegals.

Because of the tremendous number of lawsuits filed in federal and state courts, detailed rules are needed to make the litigation process run smoothly. The Federal Rules of Civil Procedure (FRCivP) apply to all civil actions filed in the federal court system. State court systems have their own rules of civil procedure, most of which are modeled after the federal rules. This chapter uses the federal rules unless otherwise noted. The sample litigation documents generally use California rules and format.

POINTER: For civil actions filed in a state court, you must follow that state's rules of civil procedure. In addition, judicial districts within a state may have local rules of practice that must be followed.

THE COMPLAINT

A lawsuit is initiated by filing a **complaint** with the appropriate court.[1] A complaint is a document that contains three basic elements: (1) identification of the defendant(s) alleged to be responsible for the wrong; (2) a basic statement of the specific facts that led to the plaintiff being wronged; and (3) the remedies that the plaintiff seeks as compensation for the wrong. Figure 9-1 is a sample complaint.

Causes of Action

Chapter 3 introduced a cause of action as the legal theory that forms the basis of a lawsuit, the basis on which a plaintiff claims a right to recover. Every cause of action consists of certain factual elements, or constituent parts, that the plaintiff must establish in order to recover. For example, in a breach of contract cause of action, the plaintiff must establish among other things (1) the existence of the contract and (2) the type of contract entered into. These are essential elements. In the complaint the plaintiff must **allege**—that is, assert as true—those facts that, if proven, establish the essential elements of the cause of action and give the plaintiff a right to recover.

In the sample complaint (Figure 9-1), the plaintiffs' first cause of action is for breach of contract. In order to properly assert, or state, a cause of action for breach of contract, the plaintiffs must allege facts establishing the *existence* of the contract and the *type* of contract entered into. In paragraph 6 the plaintiffs allege that the contract was entered into on or about September 1, 1992 (existence), and that the contract was written (type).

Often there are numerous causes of action available to a plaintiff. In the complaint, the plaintiff will usually list all possible causes of action and allege the facts establishing each. At trial, the plaintiff must prove the facts that will establish the essential elements of each cause of action.

FIGURE 9-1 COMPLAINT

Myrna Jackson, Esq.
LAW OFFICES OF MYRNA JACKSON
1258 Coastline Drive
Seaside, CA 90277-2183
(310) 990-4321

Attorneys for Plaintiffs

__________ COURT FOR THE STATE OF __________
COUNTY OF __________, __________ JUDICIAL DISTRICT

JOHN SMITH and MARY SMITH, Plaintiffs, v. LEMON MOTORS, INC., a California Corporation; TIMOTHY A. DUNCAN; and DOES 1 through 10, inclusive, Defendants.	CASE NO. 123456 COMPLAINT FOR BREACH OF CONTRACT; NEGLIGENCE; FRAUD AND MISREPRESENTATION

PLAINTIFFS ALLEGE AS FOLLOWS:

FIRST CAUSE OF ACTION
(Breach of Contract Against Lemon Motors)

1. Plaintiffs are informed and believe and based on such information and belief allege that defendant Lemon Motors, Inc. (hereinafter "Lemon") is a corporation duly organized and existing under the laws of the State of __________.

2. Plaintiffs are informed and believe and based on such information and belief allege that defendant Timothy A. Duncan (hereinafter "Duncan") is a resident of this judicial district.

3. Plaintiffs are ignorant of the true names and capacities of the defendants sued herein as Does 1 through 10, inclusive, and therefore sue these defendants by such fictitious names. Plaintiffs will amend this complaint to allege their true names and capacities when ascertained.

4. Plaintiffs are further informed and believe and based on such information and belief allege that defendants Does 1 through 10, were at all times herein

FIGURE 9-1 COMPLAINT (Cont.)

mentioned, agents, servants, and employees of the other remaining defendants and in doing the things herein alleged were acting within the scope of their authority as such agents, servants, and employees, and with the permission and consent of their codefendants.

5. Plaintiffs are informed and believe and based on such information and belief allege that each such fictitiously named defendant is responsible in some manner for the occurrences herein alleged, and that plaintiffs' injuries as herein alleged were proximately caused by such defendant's actions.

6. On or about September 1, 1992, plaintiff and defendant Lemon entered into a written contract for the purchase and sale of a 1991 Allied Motors CS10 with mileage of 1,956 miles. A true and correct copy of said contract is attached hereto as Exhibit ''A'' and incorporated herein by reference.[2]

7. Defendant Lemon breached said contract by failing to deliver to plaintiff a 1991 CS10 with mileage of 1,956 miles. Plaintiff discovered in November 1992 that the automobile sold to plaintiff had approximately 30,000 miles instead of the 1,956 miles bargained for.

8. As a proximate result of defendant's breach as herein alleged, plaintiff has been damaged in a sum not yet ascertained.

9. The written contract between the parties attached hereto as Exhibit ''A'' provides the prevailing party shall be entitled to recover reasonable attorney's fees for any action brought to enforce the terms of this agreement.

10. As a proximate result of defendant Lemon's breach of the contract contained in the written agreement, plaintiffs have been required to retain the legal services of the Law Offices of Myrna Jackson, Esq., and have incurred and will continue to incur attorney's fees.

SECOND CAUSE OF ACTION
(Negligence Against Defendant Lemon)

11. Plaintiffs refer to paragraphs 1 through 10 of the First Cause of Action and by reference make the same a part hereof.

12. On or about September 1, 1992, defendant Lemon sold plaintiffs a 1991 Allied Motors CS10, which defendant Lemon represented had mileage of 1,956 miles at the time of sale.

13. Defendant Lemon owed plaintiffs the duty to use the reasonable care and skill of an automobile dealership in selling a used automobile to plaintiffs.

14. In November 1992, plaintiff discovered that defendant Lemon had breached said duty by representing to plaintiffs that the automobile that plaintiffs purchased had approximately 1,956 miles when it knew or should have known by inspecting the vehicle or examining records that the automobile in fact had approximately 30,000 miles on it at the time of sale to plaintiffs.

15. As a proximate result of defendant Lemon's actions as herein alleged, plaintiffs have been damaged in a sum not yet ascertained. Plaintiffs will amend this complaint to state the true amount thereof when ascertained.

FIGURE 9-1 COMPLAINT (Cont.)

THIRD CAUSE OF ACTION
(For Fraud and Misrepresentation Against Defendant Duncan)

16. Plaintiffs refer to paragraphs 1 through 15 and by reference make the same a part hereof.

17. Plaintiffs are informed and believe and thereupon allege that on or about August 10, 1992, defendant Duncan falsely and fraudulently represented to defendant Lemon that the automobile had been driven only 1,930 miles and that defendant Duncan had not altered, set back, or disconnected the odometer of said vehicle.

18. Plaintiffs are informed and believe and thereupon allege that the odometer had in fact been manipulated by defendant Duncan in such a manner as to show the mileage alleged in paragraph 17, and that the automobile had in fact been driven approximately 30,000 miles prior to its transfer to defendant Lemon.

19. Plaintiffs are informed and believe and thereon allege that at the time defendant Duncan made the foregoing representations with respect to mileage, he knew the representations were false, that the car had in fact been driven substantially in excess of 1,930 miles, and that the odometer had been set back in violation of the provisions of Section 28051 of the Vehicle Code. Defendant made these representations with the intent to induce defendant Lemon to purchase and/or accept the vehicle as a trade-in.

20. At the time that defendant Duncan made these representations to defendant Lemon, an automobile dealership, he knew or should have known that these representations would be relied on by a class of persons, such as plaintiffs, who would purchase the vehicle from defendant Lemon Motors.

21. At the time these representations were made, plaintiffs were ignorant of their falsity but believed them to be true. In reliance thereon, plaintiffs were induced to and did in fact purchase the 1991 CS10 automobile, which they would not have done had they known the fact that the odometer had been set back and that the car had been driven substantially in excess of 1,956 miles.

22. In November 1992, plaintiffs for the first time learned that these representations were in fact false, that the 1991 CS10 automobile had in fact been driven in excess of 30,000 miles at the time defendant Lemon purchased it from defendant Duncan, and that the odometer had been set back on at least one occasion prior to inspection of the car by plaintiffs.

23. As a proximate result of Defendant's fraudulent acts as herein alleged, plaintiffs have been damaged in a sum not yet ascertained. Plaintiffs will amend this complaint to state the true amount thereof when ascertained.

24. The representations made by defendant Duncan as herein alleged were willful, deliberate, malicious, and intended to oppress and defraud plaintiffs so that plaintiffs are entitled to exemplary and punitive damages in the additional sum of $5,000.

25. In addition, plaintiff is entitled to recover three times the amount of actual damages sustained or $1,500, whichever is greater, pursuant to Title 15, Section 1989 of the *United States Code*.

FIGURE 9-1 COMPLAINT (Cont.)

26. Title 15, Section 1989 of the *United States Code* provides that should plaintiffs prevail in this action they are entitled to reasonable attorney's fees and costs.

27. As a proximate result of defendant Duncan's fraudulent acts as herein alleged, plaintiffs have been required to retain the legal services of the Law Offices of Myrna Jackson, Esq., and have incurred and will continue to incur attorney's fees.

WHEREFORE, plaintiffs pray judgment against defendants, and each of them, as follows:

FIRST CAUSE OF ACTION:

1. For general damages according to proof;
2. For reasonable attorney's fees;
3. For costs of suit incurred herein; and
4. For such other and further relief as the court deems proper.

SECOND CAUSE OF ACTION:

1. For general damages according to proof;
2. For costs of suit incurred herein; and
3. For such other and further relief as the court deems proper.

THIRD CAUSE OF ACTION:

1. For general damages according to proof;
2. For damages pursuant to 15 U.S.C. Section 1989;
3. For punitive damages;
4. For costs of suit incurred herein;
5. For reasonable attorney's fees; and
6. For such other and further relief as the court deems proper.

DATED: February 10, 1993 LAW OFFICES OF MYRNA JACKSON

By: ______________________

Myrna Jackson
Attorney for Plaintiffs

Format of the Complaint

FRCivP 10 specifies the general format to be used in all pleadings filed in federal court. In state courts, the format used for a complaint varies from jurisdiction to jurisdiction. Consult your state and local rules for the proper format in your jurisdiction.

Caption. The complaint begins with the caption. The caption contains the name of the plaintiff's attorney, the name of the court, the names of all plaintiffs and defendants, the case number, the title of the pleading, and a list of the causes of action. The correct name and legal status (corporation, partnership, or the like) of all parties should be used. It is especially important to identify the defendant correctly because it may be difficult to collect on the judgment if a mistake is made.

Doe Defendants. **Doe defendants** are fictitiously named defendants. In some lawsuits, the names of all individuals who may be liable to the plaintiff are not known at the time the complaint is filed. When the names of these individuals become known, the complaint can be amended by substituting the actual names for the Doe defendants.

Many states do not require Doe allegations but allow the plaintiff to amend the complaint freely to include new defendants as they become known. Nor do the federal courts require Doe allegations; they allow the plaintiff to amend the complaint "when justice so requires."[3]

Body. Factual allegations form the body of the complaint. Each paragraph should allege a specific fact (or group of related facts) that helps establish the cause of action. When the plaintiff has no absolute or certain personal knowledge of the fact being alleged, but nonetheless has reason to believe the fact is true, then the fact is pled based on "information and belief." See paragraphs 1 and 2 of the sample complaint (Figure 9-1) for an example.

Prayer. The complaint ends with the **prayer**, which lists the remedies the plaintiff is requesting from the court. The prayer usually concludes by requesting "such other and further relief as the court may deem proper."

POINTER: Complaints can be difficult to draft. A common mistake is failure to allege facts establishing all of the essential elements that must be included in a particular cause of action. Furthermore, the language used in complaints (e.g., allegations "based on information and belief") is frequently unfamiliar. Therefore it is essential that a standard form complaint be used as a guide. Standard form complaints are found in form books, manuals, and practice guides. In addition, use as a model a sample complaint from your office case files whenever possible. If a complaint you are drafting alleges more than one cause of action, then locate a sample for each cause of action. Adapt the sample complaints to the specific facts of the case you are working on.

THE SUMMONS

The **summons** notifies the defendant that she or he has been sued; the defendant is literally being "summoned" to the courthouse. Usually the law office filing the complaint prepares the summons. The court "issues" the summons (usually by stamping it with the court's seal) at the same time that the complaint is filed. The summons and a copy of the complaint are then "served" on the defendant. **Service of process** is the delivery of the summons and complaint to the defendant. FRCivP 4 governs service of process in federal court.

The traditional manner of service is **personal service**, personal hand delivery to the defendant. The summons may be served by any person 18 years of age or older who is not a party to the action. If, after due diligence, personal service cannot be completed (three tries is usually sufficient), then **substituted service** may be performed by leaving a copy of the summons and complaint with a responsible adult at the defendant's residence or place of business.[4] The server must inform the person of the contents of the documents and mail a copy of the summons to the address at which the summons was left. Another method of service is by mailing (first-class) the summons, the complaint, an acknowledgment of receipt and a self-addressed stamped envelope to the defendant. If the defendant does not accept service and fails to return the acknowledgment, another method of service must be used. However, the defendant may be liable for the costs of completing another method of service.

In state court actions, the sheriff of the county in which the defendant lives frequently serves process. In some states, registered (licensed) process servers are used. A federal marshal may also be used in some circumstances. When the defendant has disappeared entirely, service by publication is used.

Figure 9-2 is a sample summons and proof of service.

ATTACKING THE COMPLAINT

Motions to dismiss or to strike are used to challenge the wording, the form, and/or the substance of a complaint. FRCivP 12(b) lists seven defenses that can be raised in a motion to dismiss, such as failure to state a claim upon which relief can be granted. A **motion to dismiss** asks the court to dismiss the entire complaint or at least one **count**—that is, one cause of action in the complaint.

A **motion to strike** asks the court to "order stricken from any pleading any insufficient defense or any redundant, immaterial, impertinent, or scandalous matter."[5] For example, the defendant might ask the court to strike unnecessary language that is inserted only to harass or humiliate the defendant. A motion to strike is used to strike a small part of the complaint. The court may either sustain (grant) or overrule (deny) the motions. If a motion to dismiss is sustained, the plaintiff is usually granted **leave to amend** the complaint, meaning the plaintiff may file a new complaint that attempts to state a cause of action properly. If the motion to dismiss is overruled, then the defendant is given a period of time to file an answer.

Other common grounds for attacking the complaint include lack of subject matter jurisdiction (when the complaint is not filed in the proper court), lack of capacity or "standing" to sue, and failure to file the suit in a timely manner. The **statute of limitations** fixes the time within which the lawsuit must be filed.

POINTER: The "standing to sue" doctrine focuses on the question of whether or not the plaintiff is the proper party to prosecute the lawsuit. The requirement of standing is satisfied if the plaintiff has a legally protectible and tangible interest at stake in the litigation.[6] For example, if John Smith's *mother* sued Lemon Motors for breach of contract, the case would be dismissed because she is not the proper party to prosecute the lawsuit.

FIGURE 9-2 SUMMONS AND PROOF OF SERVICE

SUMMONS
(CITACION JUDICIAL)

NOTICE TO DEFENDANT: ***(Aviso a Acusado)***

LEMON MOTORS, INC., a California Corporation; TIMOTHY A. DUNCAN; and DOES 1 through 10, inclusive

YOU ARE BEING SUED BY PLAINTIFF:
(A Ud. le está demandando)

JOHN SMITH and MARY SMITH

FOR COURT USE ONLY
(SOLO PARA USO DE LA CORTE)

You have *30 CALENDAR DAYS* after this summons is served on you to file a typewritten response at this court.

A letter or phone call will not protect you; your typewritten response must be in proper legal form if you want the court to hear your case.

If you do not file your response on time, you may lose the case, and your wages, money and property may be taken without further warning from the court.

There are other legal requirements. You may want to call an attorney right away. If you do not know an attorney, you may call an attorney referral service or a legal aid office (listed in the phone book).

Después de que le entreguen esta citación judicial usted tiene un plazo de 30 DIAS CALENDARIOS *para presentar una respuesta escrita a máquina en esta corte.*

Una carta o una llamada telefónica no le ofrecerá protección; su respuesta escrita a máquina tiene que cumplir con las formalidades legales apropiadas si usted quiere que la corte escuche su caso.

Si usted no presenta su respuesta a tiempo, puede perder el caso, y le pueden quitar su salario, su dinero y otras cosas de su propiedad sin aviso adicional por parte de la corte.

Existen otros requisitos legales. Puede que usted quiera llamar a un abogado inmediatamente. Si no conoce a un abogado, puede llamar a un servicio de referencia de abogados o a una oficina de ayuda legal (vea el directorio telefónico).

The name and address of the court is: *(El nombre y dirección de la corte es)*

CASE NUMBER: (*Número del Caso*)

______ Court for the State of ______
County of ______, ______ Judicial District
789 Seashore Dr.
Seaside, CA 90277-5678

The name, address, and telephone number of plaintiff's attorney, or plaintiff without an attorney, is:
(El nombre, la dirrección y el número de teléfono del abogado del demandante, o del demandante que no tiene abogado, es)

Myrna Jackson
1258 Coastline Dr.
Seaside, CA 90277-2183
(310) 990-4321

DATE:
(Fecha)

Clerk, by ______________________, Deputy
(Actuario) *(Delegado)*

(SEAL)

NOTICE TO THE PERSON SERVED: You are served

1. [X] as an individual defendant.
2. [ ] as the person sued under the fictitious name of *(specify)*:
3. [ ] on behalf of *(specify)*:

under:
[ ] CCP 416.10 (corporation)
[ ] CCP 416.20 (defunct corporation)
[ ] CCP 416.40 (association or partnership)
[ ] other:
[ ] CCP 416.60 (minor)
[ ] CCP 416.70 (conservatee)
[ ] CCP 416.90 (individual)

4. [X] by personal delivery on (*date*): February 15, 1993

(See reverse for Proof of Service)

SUMMONS

FIGURE 9-2 SUMMONS AND PROOF OF SERVICE (Cont.)

PROOF OF SERVICE — SUMMONS

(Use separate proof of service for each person served)

1. I served the
   a. [X] summons [X] complaint [ ] amended summons [ ] amended complaint
   [ ] completed and blank Case Questionnaires [ ] Other *(specify)*:
   b. on defendant *(name)*: TIMOTHY A. DUNCAN
   c. by serving [X] defendant [ ] other *(name and title or relationship to person served)*:
   d. [X] by delivery [X] at home [ ] at business
   (1) date: June 1, 1993
   (2) time: 9:00 a.m.
   (3) address: 4123 Del Mar Ave.
   Seaside, CA 90277-2112
   e. [ ] by mailing
   (1) date:
   (2) place:
2. Manner of service *(check proper box)*:
   a. [X] **Personal service.** By personally delivering copies. (CCP 415.10)
   b. [ ] **Substituted service on corporation, unincorporated association (including partnership), or public entity.** By leaving, during usual office hours, copies in the office of the person served with the person who apparently was in charge and thereafter mailing (by first-class mail, postage prepaid) copies to the person served at the place where the copies were left. (CCP 415.20(a))
   c. [ ] **Substituted service on natural person, minor, conservatee, or candidate.** By leaving copies at the dwelling house, usual place of abode, or usual place of business of the person served in the presence of a competent member of the household or a person apparently in charge of the office or place of business, at least 18 years of age, who was informed of the general nature of the papers, and thereafter mailing (by first-class mail, postage prepaid) copies to the person served at the place where the copies were left. (CCP 415.20(b)) ***(Attach separate declaration or affidavit stating acts relied on to establish reasonable diligence in first attempting personal service.)***
   d. [ ] **Mail and acknowledgment service.** By mailing (by first-class mail or airmail, postage prepaid) copies to the person served, together with two copies of the form of notice and acknowledgment and a return envelope, postage prepaid, addressed to the sender. (CCP 415.30) ***(Attach completed acknowledgment of receipt.)***
   e. [ ] **Certified or registered mail service.** By mailing to an address outside ________ (by first-class mail, postage prepaid, requiring a return receipt) copies to the person served. (CCP 415.40) ***(Attach signed return receipt or other evidence of actual delivery to the person served.)***
   f. [ ] Other *(specify code section)*:
   [ ] additional page is attached.
3. The "Notice to the Person Served" (on the summons) was completed as follows (CCP 412.30, 415.10, and 474):
   a. [X] as an individual defendant.
   b. [ ] as the person sued under the fictitious name of *(specify)*:
   c. [ ] on behalf of *(specify)*:
   under: [ ] CCP 416.10 (corporation) [ ] CCP 416.60 (minor) [ ] other:
   [ ] CCP 416.20 (defunct corporation) [ ] CCP 416.70 (conservatee)
   [ ] CCP 416.40 (association or partnership) [ ] CCP 416.90 (individual)
   d. [X] by personal delivery on *(date)*: February 15, 1993
4. At the time of service I was at least 18 years of age and not a party to this action.
5. Fee for service: $20.00
6. Person serving:
   a. [ ] Sheriff, marshal, or constable.
   b. [X] Registered process server.
   c. [ ] Employee or independent contractor of a registered process server.
   d. [ ] Not a registered process server.
   e. [ ] Exempt from registration under Bus. & Prof. Code 22350(b).
   f. Name, address and telephone number and, if applicable, county of registration and number:
   Alcala's Court and Courier Service, Inc.
   321 First St.
   Seaside, CA 90277-9721
   (310) 998-3162
   ________ County, Number 3421

I declare under penalty of perjury under the laws of the State of ________ that the foregoing is true and correct.

Date: February 15, 1993

▶ ________________________
(SIGNATURE)

(For sheriff, marshal, or constable use only)
I certify that the foregoing is true and correct.

Date:

▶ ________________________
(SIGNATURE)

ANSWER

If the attacks on the complaint are unsuccessful, or if no attacks are made on the complaint, then the defendant must file an **answer** either admitting or denying the allegations in the complaint. The answer may also include **affirmative defenses** in which the defendant alleges additional facts that, if proven, would excuse the defendant from liability. For example, suppose plaintiff alleges defendant committed a battery by throwing a ball that struck plaintiff on the head. Defendant might raise the affirmative defense of consent and allege that plaintiff and defendant were playing baseball according to the rules of the game at the time the accident occurred. The statute of limitations is another affirmative defense that is frequently raised.

If the complaint is a **verified complaint**—that is, if the plaintiff swears under penalty of perjury that everything in the complaint is true and correct—then the defendant must answer with a **specific denial**. In a specific denial, the defendant admits or denies paragraph by paragraph the allegations made in the complaint. The answer itself must be verified if the complaint is verified. If the complaint is not verified, the defendant may file a **general denial**. In a general denial, the defendant may deny each and every allegation in the complaint in a single statement of denial, even though some of the allegations may be true and would otherwise have to be admitted. Figure 9-3 is a sample answer.

SUBSEQUENT PLEADINGS

Pleadings are the formal allegations by the parties of their respective claims and defenses.[7] The complaint and the answer are both pleadings. Under the federal rules, subsequent pleadings may consist of a counterclaim and a reply to a counterclaim, a cross-claim and an answer to a cross-claim, and a third party complaint and third party answer.[8] A **counterclaim** is a claim made by the defendant against the plaintiff. The plaintiff's response to the counterclaim is called a **reply**. A **cross-claim** states a claim by one party against a coparty, such as a claim by a defendant against a codefendant. A **third party complaint** is a claim made by a defendant against a person who is not already a party to the action. The procedure by which additional parties are brought into the lawsuit is known as **impleader**.[9]

Some states use the term **cross-complaint** to refer to a claim by the defendant against either the plaintiff or another party. The cross-complaint is considered to be part of the original lawsuit, which allows the court to consider all the facts at the same time rather than in two or more separate lawsuits. The cross-complaint is usually filed at the same time as the answer, although it may be filed later with the court's permission. Appendix B contains a sample cross-complaint filed by Lemon Motors against Tim Duncan.

DISCOVERY

Discovery is the aptly named process by which the parties discover as much information as possible about the facts of the case. Most litigation paralegals spend most of their time on discovery matters.

FIGURE 9-3 ANSWER

Mark Samuel
SAMUEL & JOSEPH
37 Sea Coast Highway
Seaside, CA 90277-2143
(310) 990-1234

Attorneys for Defendant
Lemon Motors, Inc.

__________ COURT FOR THE __________ JUDICIAL DISTRICT
COUNTY OF __________, STATE OF __________

JOHN SMITH and MARY SMITH,	)	CASE NO. 123456
Plaintiffs,	)	ANSWER BY DEFENDANT LEMON MOTORS TO COMPLAINT
v.	)	
LEMON MOTORS, INC., a California Corporation; TIMOTHY A. DUNCAN; and DOES 1 through 10, inclusive,	)	
Defendants.	)	

Defendant Lemon Motors, Inc. (''Lemon'') answers the Complaint as follows:

FIRST CAUSE OF ACTION
(Breach of Contract Against Lemon Motors)

1. Answering paragraph 1, defendant admits that Lemon Motors is a corporation duly organized and existing under the laws of the State of __________.

2. Answering paragraph 2, defendant has no information or belief sufficient to answer the allegations thereof, and basing its denial on that ground, denies said allegations.

3. Answering paragraph 3, defendant has no information or belief sufficient to answer the allegation thereof, and basing its denial on that ground, denies said allegations.

4. Answering paragraph 4, defendant has no information or belief sufficient to answer the allegations thereof, and basing its denial on that ground, denies said allegations.

FIGURE 9-3 ANSWER (Cont.)

5. Answering paragraph 5, defendant has no information or belief sufficient to answer the allegations thereof, and basing its denial on that ground, denies said allegations.

6. Answering paragraph 6, defendant admits that on or about September 1, 1992, plaintiff and defendant entered into a written contract for the purchase and sale of a 1991 CS10. Defendant also admits that Exhibit ''A'' as amended is a document that purports to be an agreement between plaintiff and defendant, and refers to such document for the full and complete contents thereof.

7. Answering paragraph 7, defendant has no information or belief sufficient to answer the allegations thereof, and basing its denial on that ground, denies said allegations.

8. Answering paragraph 8, defendant denies the allegations thereof.

9. Answering paragraph 9, defendant has no information or belief sufficient to answer the allegations thereof, and basing its denial on that ground, denies said allegations.

10. Answering paragraph 10, defendant denies the allegations thereof.

SECOND CAUSE OF ACTION
(Negligence Against Defendant Lemon)

11. Answering paragraph 11, defendant has no information or belief sufficient to answer the allegations thereof, and basing its denial on that ground, denies said allegations.

12. Answering paragraph 12, defendant admits that it sold to plaintiff a 1991 CS10. Except as herein admitted, defendant has no information or belief sufficient to answer the allegations thereof, and basing its denial on that ground, denies said allegations.

13. Answering paragraph 13, defendant has no information or belief sufficient to answer the allegations thereof, and basing its denial on that ground, denies said allegations.

14. Answering paragraph 14, defendant has no information or belief sufficient to answer the allegations thereof, and basing its denial on that ground, denies said allegations.

15. Answering paragraph 15, defendant denies the allegations thereof.

FIGURE 9-3 ANSWER (Cont.)

THIRD CAUSE OF ACTION
(For Fraud and Misrepresentation Against Defendant Duncan)

16. With respect to the third cause of action, paragraphs 16-27, such cause of action is directed only against defendant Duncan. Therefore, defendant Lemon Motors refrains from answering said allegations.

FIRST AFFIRMATIVE DEFENSE
(Failure to State a Cause of Action
as to First and Second Causes of Action)

17. The complaint and each purported cause of action therein fails to state facts sufficient to constitute a cause of action against defendant Lemon.

DATED: March 1, 1993

SAMUEL & JOSEPH

By: ______________________
Mark Samuel
Attorney for Defendant
Lemon Motors, Inc.

Each party has the right to engage in discovery. Each party may obtain documents and other tangible evidence, the names of witnesses and what they will say at the trial, and admissions of fact from the other parties. Discovery enables all parties to gather a great deal of information about one another's cases.

Purposes of Discovery

The main purpose of discovery is to gather the facts needed to prevail at trial. Every cause of action and defense has certain factual elements that must be established if a party is to prevail. Discovery is the process of gathering those facts needed to establish the elements of each cause of action. The evidence gathered is then preserved for trial.

Discovery narrows the focus of the case. As additional information is discovered, certain issues may no longer be in dispute and need not be proven at trial.

Discovery also promotes pretrial settlement by enabling the parties to evaluate the strengths and weaknesses of each other's cases. By the completion of discovery, the parties have a good idea about the evidence that will be presented at trial, the likelihood of winning or losing the case, and the amount of the judgment that may be obtained. This provides a basis for settlement.

Scope of Discovery

What is discoverable and what is not? Federal Rule of Civil Procedure 26 (b)(1), which has served as the model for most states, provides for discovery regarding all matters relevant and not privileged.

Relevancy. Relevancy is the basic limitation on the right to discovery. However, the test for relevancy is a broad one: Is the discovery request reasonably calculated to lead to the discovery of evidence that would be admissible at trial? Note that the test is not whether the information sought would be admissible at trial, but whether the information sought would *lead to evidence* that would be admissible at trial. For example, a discovery request calling for hearsay would be relevant so long as the request was reasonably calculated to lead to evidence that was not inadmissible because of the hearsay rule.[10]

Privilege. **Privileged information** is information protected by law because of a special relationship which the law desires to foster. Examples include the attorney-client privilege, physician-patient privilege, clergyman-penitent privilege, and spousal communication privilege. Privileged information may not be discovered.

Under the **attorney-client privilege**, for example, a client has the right to refuse to disclose a confidential communication between the client and the attorney. The privilege exists as long as the communications are between the attorney and client, are confidential (not discussed with unnecessary third parties), and made with the purpose of giving or receiving legal advice. The privilege extends to all attorneys and employees of the firm, including paralegals and secretaries. The privilege may be claimed by either the client or the attorney.

A related privilege is the **attorney work-product privilege**. This privilege applies to any material that reflects the attorney's mental impressions, opinions, or legal research. The privilege extends to the work product of the paralegal.

Enforcing Discovery

If one party makes a discovery request seeking information that is irrelevant or privileged, the other party has the right to object to the discovery request. What happens if one party refuses to respond to discovery requests or makes objections to such requests with no basis or justification? The party seeking discovery may make a **motion to compel discovery**, such as a motion to compel answers to interrogatories. Monetary sanctions might be imposed against the party abusing discovery. If the abuse of discovery continues, then more serious sanctions might be awarded, such as dismissing the entire action or rendering a judgment by default.

Overview of Discovery Tools

The tools of discovery are the different methods through which information is obtained. These tools include interrogatories, depositions, requests for admissions, requests for production of documents, independent medical examinations, and exchange of expert witness lists.[11]

Interrogatories. **Interrogatories** are written questions propounded (asked) to another party to be answered in writing under oath. Interrogatories are a popular discovery tool because they are economical and easy to use. Drafting and answering interrogatories are important paralegal functions.

Figure 9-4 is an example of interrogatories that might be sent to defendant Duncan.

Drafting Interrogatories. There are two basic types of interrogatories, those seeking facts (identity of witnesses, relevant documents) and those seeking information supporting contentions. Sample questions 1 and 2 in Figure 9-4 seek to discover such basic background facts as the defendant's name and address. Sample questions 8 and 9 seek to discover a specific contention of the defendant and all facts supporting this contention.

When drafting interrogatories, phrase the questions concisely and precisely. Questions asking for specific information about people, places, and events are usually better than open-ended questions. Respondents will not (and are not required to) volunteer information not specifically requested. Here are some examples of POORLY DRAFTED interrogatories:

1. "*Did you discuss turning back the odometer with anyone?*" The question is worthless for two reasons. First, it assumes facts not in evidence. Respondent could object to the question on that ground. Second, even if the respondent had discussed this with someone, the respondent might simply answer, "Yes."
2. "*What prompted you to turn back the odometer?*" Again, the question assumes facts not in evidence. In addition, even if the odometer had been turned back, respondent might simply answer, "Nothing."
3. "*List the name, address, telephone number, and relationship to you of each and every person who was a passenger in your 1991 Allied Motors CS10 during the period you owned the car.*" The intent of the question is to discover the names of witnesses who might have information that the car had been driven in excess of 1,930 miles. The question does attempt to discover the names of specific people. However, there are several possible objections, including the fact that the question is overbroad, is unduly burdensome and oppressive, lacks relevance, and is an invasion of privacy. (These terms will be defined in the next section.) Could *you* compile this list for every person who has ever been a passenger in *your* car?

Responding to Interrogatories. A party may either answer an interrogatory or object to an interrogatory. When drafting an answer, a "good faith" effort must be made to answer the question as fully and completely as the available information permits. Do, however, read the question literally and provide only the information that is requested. Do not volunteer more information than is necessary to answer the specific question asked.

If an objection is raised to an interrogatory, the grounds for the objection must be clearly stated. Grounds for proper objections include lack of relevance

FIGURE 9-4 INTERROGATORIES

Mark Samuel
SAMUEL & JOSEPH
37 Sea Coast Highway
Seaside, CA 90277-2143
(310) 990-1234

Attorneys for Defendant and Cross-Complainant Lemon Motors, Inc.

__________ COURT FOR THE __________ JUDICIAL DISTRICT
COUNTY OF __________, STATE OF __________

JOHN SMITH and MARY SMITH, Plaintiffs, v. LEMON MOTORS, INC., a California Corporation; TIMOTHY A. DUNCAN; and DOES 1 through 10, inclusive, Defendants. AND RELATED CROSS-ACTIONS.	CASE NO. 123456 INTERROGATORIES

PROPOUNDING PARTY: CROSS-COMPLAINANT LEMON MOTORS, INC.

RESPONDING PARTY: DEFENDANT TIMOTHY A. DUNCAN

SET NUMBER: 1

1) State your full name and Social Security number.

2) State your present residence address, your residence addresses for the last five years, and the dates you lived at each address.

3) State:

(a) the name, address, and telephone number of your present employer or place of self-employment;

(b) the name, address, telephone number, and dates of employment for each employer or place of self-employment you have had for the last five years.

FIGURE 9-4 INTERROGATORIES (Cont.)

4) Have you ever been convicted of a felony? If so, for each conviction state:

(a) the city and state where you were convicted;
(b) the date of conviction;
(c) the offense;
(d) the court and case number.

5) State all facts on which you base your denial of paragraph 11 of the cross-complaint in which cross-complainant alleges that you breached the contract by delivering the automobile with approximately 30,000 miles instead of the 1,930 miles bargained for.

6) Identify each person having knowledge of any fact disclosed in the answer to the preceding interrogatory by stating the person's full name, business address, and residence address.

7) Describe each document, book, record, or other physical evidence which you believe supports the answer to Interrogatory 5.

8) Do you contend that Lemon Motors, Inc. is solely responsible for any damages suffered by plaintiffs?

9) If your answer to the preceding Interrogatory is other than an unqualified negative, then please:

(a) state each and every fact on which you base this contention;
(b) identify each and every document which supports this contention;
(c) state the name, address and telephone number of each and every witness who supports this contention.

DATED: April 1, 1993 SAMUEL & JOSEPH

By: ______________________

Mark Samuel
Attorney for Defendant
and Cross-Complainant
Lemon Motors, Inc.

(the information sought is not reasonably calculated to lead to the discovery of admissible evidence); violation of attorney-client privilege or attorney work-product privilege; unduly burdensome and oppressive question (indefinite as to time and scope, requires unreasonable effort to answer); overbroad question; vagueness and ambiguity; and ''asked and answered'' question (you need supply information only once).

Figure 9-5 is an example of how Duncan might answer the interrogatories.

FIGURE 9-5 ANSWERS TO INTERROGATORIES

Ann Diamond
LAW OFFICES OF ANN DIAMOND
589 Seashore Drive
Seaside, CA 90277-2168
(310) 990-1357

Attorney for Defendant and Cross-Defendant Timothy A. Duncan

IN THE __________ COURT OF THE __________ JUDICIAL DISTRICT
FOR THE COUNTY OF __________

JOHN SMITH and MARY SMITH, Plaintiffs, v. LEMON MOTORS, INC., a California Corporation; TIMOTHY A. DUNCAN; and DOES 1 through 10, inclusive, Defendants.	CASE NO. 123456 ANSWERS TO INTERROGATORIES

PROPOUNDING PARTY: CROSS-COMPLAINANT LEMON MOTORS, INC.

RESPONDING PARTY: DEFENDANT TIMOTHY A. DUNCAN

SET NUMBER: 1

TO CROSS-COMPLAINANT LEMON MOTORS, INC., AND TO ITS ATTORNEY OF RECORD:

PRELIMINARY STATEMENT

These answers are made solely for the purpose of, and in relation to, this action. Each answer is given subject to all appropriate objections (including, but not limited to, objections concerning competency, relevancy, materiality, propriety and admissibility) that would require the exclusion of any statement contained herein if the question were asked of, or any statement contained herein were

FIGURE 9-5 ANSWERS TO INTERROGATORIES (Cont.)

made by, a witness present and testifying in court. All such objections and grounds therefore are reserved and may be interposed at the time of trial.

Respondent has not completed an investigation of the facts relating to this matter, has not completed discovery, and has not completed preparation for trial. Consequently, the following answers are given without prejudice to cross-defendant's right to produce, at the time of trial, subsequently discovered evidence, relating to the proof of facts subsequently discovered to be material.

Except for any facts explicitly admitted herein, no admission of any nature whatsoever is to be implied or inferred. All responses must be construed as given on the basis of present recollection.

Cross-defendant objects to these interrogatories to the extent they seek information protected by the attorney-client privilege, the attorney work-product doctrine, and the right of privacy.

ANSWER TO INTERROGATORY NO. 1:

Timothy Alan Duncan
023-05-8967

ANSWER TO INTERROGATORY NO. 2:

Present address and address for last five years:
4123 Del Mar Ave.
Seaside, CA 90277-2112

ANSWER TO INTERROGATORY NO. 3:

(a) Wasco Manufacturing Company
97 River St.
Riverview, CA 91234-2179
(b) Same. Employee since 1982.

ANSWER TO INTERROGATORY NO. 4:

No.

ANSWER TO INTERROGATORY NO. 5:

Cross-defendant objects to Interrogatory No. 5 on the grounds that it is overbroad, vague and ambiguous, and burdensome and oppressive. Without waiving these objections, cross-defendant's denial is based on the following facts, among others:

FIGURE 9-5 ANSWERS TO INTERROGATORIES (Cont.)

(a) Cross-defendant rarely drove the automobile during the time that he owned it.

(b) Cross-defendant owned two other cars at the time he owned the automobile, which cars he drove almost exclusively.

ANSWER TO INTERROGATORY NO. 6:

Cross-defendant objects to Interrogatory No. 6 on the grounds that it is overbroad, vague and ambiguous, and burdensome and oppressive. Without waiving these objections, the following persons, among others, have notice of such facts:

(a) Kevin Roe
Business: 97 River St.
Riverview, CA 91234-2179

(b) Josephine Doe
Business: None
Residence: 312 Oak Drive
Woodville, CA 93456-7012

ANSWER TO INTERROGATORY NO. 7:

Cross-defendant objects to Interrogatory No. 7 on the grounds that it is overbroad, vague and ambiguous, and burdensome and oppressive. Without waiving these objections, the following physical evidence supports cross-defendant's answer to Interrogatory No. 5:

(a) The physical condition of the automobile.

(b) Documents evidencing cross-defendant's ownership and use of his other two automobiles, including, but not limited to, title documents, repair orders, and business mileage logs.

ANSWER TO INTERROGATORY NO. 8:

Yes.

ANSWER TO INTERROGATORY NO. 9:

(a) The automobile had only 1,930 miles on it when cross-defendant delivered it to Lemon Motors. Any odometer tampering that may have occurred must have occurred while the car was in Lemon Motors' possession.

(b) None are presently known to cross-defendant, except as already noted in answer to Interrogatory No. 7.

(c) None are presently known to cross-defendant, except as already noted in answer to Interrogatory No. 6.

DATED: April 15, 1993

LAW OFFICES OF ANN DIAMOND

By: ______________________________

Ann Diamond
Attorney for Defendant and Cross-Defendant Timothy A. Duncan

FIGURE 9-5 ANSWERS TO INTERROGATORIES (Cont.)

VERIFICATION

STATE OF __________, COUNTY OF __________

I am the cross-defendant in the above-entitled action.

I have read the foregoing Answers to Interrogatories and know the contents thereof. The same is true of my own knowledge, except as to those matters that are therein alleged on information and belief, and as to those matters, I believe them to be true.

I declare under penalty of perjury under the laws of the State of California that the foregoing is true and correct. Executed this 15th day of April, 1993, at Seaside, California.

____

Timothy A. Duncan

Depositions. In Chapter 1, you learned that a deposition is the questioning of a party or a witness under oath. The person who answers the questions is called the deponent. The attorney's questions and the deponent's answers are transcribed verbatim by a court reporter. Depositions are the favorite discovery tool of many attorneys because they provide an opportunity to meet face to face with the opposing party or a witness, obtain spontaneous testimony, and gauge the credibility of the witness. Figure 9-6 is an excerpt from a deposition transcript.

The Paralegal's Role in Depositions. Before a deposition, the paralegal may assist with the organization of documents that will be used at the deposition. If your client is being deposed, you may assist in preparing the client for the deposition by explaining what will take place and giving recommendations on how to answer questions. Deponents should be instructed to tell the truth but not to guess at questions to which they do not know or remember an answer. Paralegals may be asked to compile lists of possible deposition questions.

If you attend a deposition, take notes on the testimony. Organize any documents that the deponent produces.

Summarizing the Deposition. Summarizing, or digesting, the deposition transcript is a typical paralegal assignment. The testimony is summarized and organized to provide easy access to selected topics. The goal when summarizing is to distill the transcript into the least number of pages while still accurately conveying the essence of the testimony.[12]

There are many different types of deposition summaries. The most common is a chronological page-and-line summary in which topics are summarized

FIGURE 9-6 EXCERPTS FROM A DEPOSITION TRANSCRIPT

MRS. JACKSON: While you owned the CS10, did you ever have it serviced by a professional mechanic?

MR. DUNCAN: Yes.

Q. By whom?

A. I can't recall everyone who serviced the car.

Q. Who can you recall?

A. Let's see . . . Seaside Motors and a small shop somewhere on the north side of town.

Q. When did you have the car serviced by Seaside Motors?

A. I can't exactly recall. It wasn't too long before I sold the car to Lemon.

Q. Was that the only time?

A. There may have been another time as well, but I can't recall.

Q. What was done at Seaside Motors?

A. I think I had the oil changed.

Q. Can you remember the name of the small shop on the north side of town where you had the car serviced?

A. No.

Q. Can you remember when you brought the car in to be serviced there?

A. Not offhand.

Q. Do you remember what services were performed there?

A. No.

Q. Do you still have any of the service orders from the times you had the car serviced?

A. I doubt it. I'm pretty sure I threw all that stuff away after I sold the car to Lemon.

Q. Did you maintain a notebook in which you kept track of the occasions on which you had the car serviced?

A. No.

FIGURE 9-6 EXCERPTS FROM A DEPOSITION TRANSCRIPT (Cont.)

Q. While you owned the car, did you ever give rides to anyone on a regular basis?

A. No. Like I said, I hardly ever drove the car.

Q. Did you ever lend the car to anyone?

A. Never.

Q. Who, besides yourself, is familiar with your driving habits?

A. Let's see. My girlfriend, Josephine Doe. And my best friend from work, Kevin Roe. There are other people too, I suppose, but I can't think of any offhand.

Q. Did you ever use the car for business purposes?

A. Never.

page by page and line by line as they appear in the transcript. This chronological type of deposition summary is illustrated in Figure 9-7. Another method is the narrative summary, which is a simple essay summary. A narrative deposition summary is illustrated in Figure 9-8.

POINTER: Suggestions for summarizing a deposition:

1. Familiarize yourself with the case by reading the pleadings *before* you attempt to summarize the deposition.
2. Read the entire deposition transcript before summarizing.
3. Be concise, but accurate.
4. Exclude irrelevant and repetitive information.
5. Use the exact language of the witness.
6. Emphasize the purpose of the deposition. (In other words, what role does *this witness* play in the case?)
7. Never misstate testimony.
8. The summary should stand alone with no need to refer to the transcript.[13]

Requests for Admission. A **request for admission** is a written request to another party to admit or deny the truth of any relevant fact. The purpose of the request for admission is to conclusively establish certain facts and thereby narrow the issues that are in controversy.

When drafting requests for admission, the goal is not to uncover new facts, but rather to conclusively establish those facts that have already been discovered through the use of interrogatories and depositions. Figure 9-9 contains sample requests for admission.

FIGURE 9-7 CHRONOLOGICAL DEPOSITION SUMMARY

Page 18, lines 3–8	TD can't recall everyone who serviced the car while he owned it.
Page 18, lines 9–11	Seaside Motors and a small shop on the north side of town serviced the car.
Page 18, lines 12–18	The car was serviced at Seaside shortly before it was sold to Lemon, and possibly on one other occasion.
Page 18, lines 19–20	Seaside changed the oil.
Page 18, line 21 Page 19, line 3	TD can't recall any details about the shop on the north side of town.
Page 19, lines 4–10	TD doesn't have any service orders or a service notebook.
Page 19, lines 11–16	TD did not give rides to anyone on a regular basis, nor did he lend the car to anyone.
Page 19, lines 17–22	Josephine Doe, TD's girlfriend, and Kevin Roe, his best friend, are familiar with TD's driving habits.
Page 19, lines 23–24	TD never used the car for business.

FIGURE 9-8 NARRATIVE DEPOSITION SUMMARY

The car was serviced by Seaside Motors, a small shop on the north side of town, and possibly others. Seaside Motors changed the oil shortly before the car was sold to Lemon, and possibly on one other occasion. TD does not have any service orders or a service notebook.

TD did not give rides to anyone on a regular basis, nor did he lend the car to anyone or use the car for business. Josephine Doe, TD's girlfriend, and Kevin Roe, TD's best friend, are familiar with his driving habits.

Requests for Production of Documents. The discovery method used for gaining access to any document or other tangible thing in the possession of another party is a **request for production**. The method of gaining documents from a nonparty is through a subpoena or subpoena *duces tecum*. A **subpoena** is a command to appear at a certain time and place to give testimony upon a certain matter.[14] A **subpoena *duces tecum*** requires production of books, papers, and other documents that are pertinent to a lawsuit.[15] Figure 9-10 is a sample request for production of documents. Figure 9-11 is a sample subpoena *duces tecum*.

FIGURE 9-9 REQUESTS FOR ADMISSION

Myrna Jackson, Esq.
LAW OFFICES OF MYRNA JACKSON
1258 Coastline Drive
Seaside, CA 90277-2183
(310) 990-4321

Attorneys for Plaintiffs

IN THE __________ COURT OF THE __________ JUDICIAL DISTRICT
FOR THE COUNTY OF __________

JOHN SMITH and MARY SMITH,	)	CASE NO. 123456
	)	
Plaintiffs,	)	REQUESTS FOR ADMISSION
	)	
v.	)	
	)	
LEMON MOTORS, INC., a California Corporation; TIMOTHY A. DUNCAN; and DOES 1 through 10, inclusive,	)	
	)	
Defendants.	)	
	)	
________________________________	)	

REQUESTS FOR ADMISSION, SET NUMBER ONE, ARE HEREBY PROPOUNDED TO DEFENDANT LEMON MOTORS, INC., BY PLAINTIFFS JOHN AND MARY SMITH.

YOU ARE HEREBY REQUESTED TO ADMIT the truthfulness of each of the facts set forth below; and the genuineness of each document, a copy of which is attached to this Request.

EACH OF THE FOLLOWING FACTS IS TRUE:

1. On September 1, 1992, plaintiffs and defendant entered into a written contract for the purchase and sale of a 1991 Allied Motors CS10 with mileage of 1,956 miles.

2. Defendant failed to deliver to plaintiffs a 1991 Allied Motors CS10 with mileage of 1,956 miles.

* * *

FIGURE 9-9 REQUESTS FOR ADMISSION (Cont.)

EACH OF THE FOLLOWING DOCUMENTS IS GENUINE:

1. Agreement for Purchase and Sale of Automobile dated October 1, 1992.
2. Odometer Disclosure Statement dated October 1, 1992.

* * *

DATED: April 1, 1993 LAW OFFICES OF MYRNA JACKSON

By: ______________________________
Myrna Jackson
Attorney for Plaintiffs

FIGURE 9-10 REQUEST FOR PRODUCTION OF DOCUMENTS

Myrna Jackson, Esq.
LAW OFFICES OF MYRNA JACKSON
1258 Coastline Drive
Seaside, CA 90277-2183
(310) 990-4321

Attorneys for Plaintiffs

IN THE __________ COURT OF THE __________ JUDICIAL DISTRICT
FOR THE COUNTY OF __________

JOHN SMITH and MARY SMITH,	)	CASE NO. 123456
	)	
Plaintiffs,	)	REQUEST TO PRODUCE
	)	DOCUMENTS
v.	)	
	)	
LEMON MOTORS, INC.,	)	Date: May 1, 1993
a California Corporation;	)	Time: 10:00 a.m.
TIMOTHY A. DUNCAN; and	)	Place: 1258 Coastline Drive
DOES 1 through 10,	)	Seaside, CA 90277-2183
inclusive,	)	
	)	
Defendants.	)	
	)	
______________________________	)	
	)	
AND RELATED CROSS-ACTIONS.	)	
______________________________	)	

FIGURE 9-10 REQUEST FOR PRODUCTION OF DOCUMENTS (Cont.)

TO: DEFENDANT TIMOTHY A. DUNCAN AND HIS ATTORNEY OF RECORD:

PLEASE TAKE NOTICE that plaintiffs John Smith and Mary Smith request that Timothy A. Duncan produce items listed in Exhibit ''A,'' attached hereto and incorporated herein by this reference, for inspection and copying by Myrna Jackson on July 1, 1993, commencing at 10:00 a.m. at the Law Offices of Myrna Jackson, located at 1258 Coastline Dr., Seaside, CA, before a certified shorthand reporter or such other officer as may be present at said time and place.

The party on whom the request is served shall serve a written response subscribed under oath by such party, on or before April 21, 1993. The response shall identify the documents, papers, books, accounts, letters, photographs, objects, or tangible things falling within the category specified in the request, which are in the possession, custody, or control of the responding party, and shall state that inspection and related activities will be permitted as requested, unless the request is objected to, in which event the reason for objection shall be stated. If objection is made to part of an item or category, the part shall be specified.

In the event that you object to producing any document or thing herein sought by reason of any claim of privilege, said objection shall state the basis for the privilege, the general nature of the material claimed to be privileged, and in the case of letters and other documents which have been communicated from one person to another, all persons who have reviewed the original or received a copy.

DATED: April 1, 1993 LAW OFFICES OF MYRNA JACKSON

By: ______________________________

Myrna Jackson
Attorney for Plaintiffs

EXHIBIT ''A''

1. Any and all written documentation pertaining to, relating to, or describing, directly or indirectly, a 1991 Allied Motors CS10 License No. 1ABC123, Vehicle ID No. ABCDE1234A1234567, including, but not limited to, registration statements, Notices of Sale or Transfer of a Vehicle, mileage records, repair invoices, purchase agreements, and sales agreements.

2. Any and all writings or other documents relating to the transfer of the above referenced vehicle from defendant Timothy A. Duncan to defendant Lemon Motors.

FIGURE 9-11 SUBPOENA *DUCES TECUM*

ATTORNEY OR PARTY WITHOUT ATTORNEY (*Name and Address*): Myrna Jackson, Esq. Law Offices of Myrna Jackson 1258 Coastline Dr. Seaside, CA 90277-2183 — TELEPHONE NO.: (310)990-4321 — ATTORNEY FOR (*Name*): Plaintiffs John Smith and Mary Smith	CASE NUMBER: 123456
NAME OF COURT: Municipal Ct., Coast Jud. Dist. POST OFFICE and 789 Seashore Dr. STREET ADDRESS: Seaside, CA 90277-2183	**DEPOSITION SUBPOENA** For Production of Business Records
PLAINTIFF/PETITIONER: John Smith and Mary Smith DEFENDANT/RESPONDENT: Lemon Motors Inc., et al.	

THE PEOPLE OF THE STATE OF CALIFORNIA, TO (*name*): Custodian of Records
Allied Motors Corporation
321 Park Ave.
Detroit, MI 50932-1468

1. **YOU ARE ORDERED TO PRODUCE THE BUSINESS RECORDS described in item 3 as follows:**

Deposition Officer (*name*): Kim Collins
Date: May 1, 1993 Time: 10:00 a.m.
Address: 503 Coastline Dr.
Seaside, CA 90277-2183

a. [X] by delivering a true, legible, and durable copy of the business records described in item 3, enclosed in a sealed inner wrapper with the title and number of the action, name of witness, and date of subpoena clearly written on it. The inner wrapper shall then be enclosed in an outer envelope or wrapper, sealed, and mailed to the deposition officer at the address in item 1.

b. [ ] by delivering a true, legible, and durable copy of the business records described in item 3 to the deposition officer at the witness's address, on receipt of payment in cash or by check of the reasonable costs of preparing the copy, as determined under Evidence Code section 1563(b).

c. [ ] by making the original business records described in item 3 available for inspection at your business address by the attorney's representative and permitting copying at your business address under reasonable conditions during normal business hours.

2. *The records are to be produced by the date and time shown in item 1 but not sooner than 20 days after the issuance of the deposition subpoena, or 15 days after service, whichever date is later. Reasonable costs of locating records, making them available or copying them and postage, if any, are recoverable as set forth in Evidence Code section 1563(b). The records shall be accompanied by an affidavit of the custodian or other qualified witness pursuant to Evidence Code section 1561.*

3. The records to be produced are described as follows:

Any and all written documentation pertaining to, relating to, or describing, directly or indirectly, a 1991 Allied Motors CS10 automobile, License No. 1ABC123, Vehicle ID No. ABCDE1234A1234567, including, but not limited to, registration statements, Notices of Sale or Transfer of a Vehicle, mileage records, repair invoices, warranty claims, purchase agreements, and sales agreements.

[ ] Continued on attachment 3.

DISOBEDIENCE OF THIS SUBPOENA MAY BE PUNISHED AS CONTEMPT BY THIS COURT. YOU WILL ALSO BE LIABLE FOR THE SUM OF FIVE HUNDRED DOLLARS AND ALL DAMAGES RESULTING FROM YOUR FAILURE TO OBEY.

For Court Use Only

Dated: August 1, 1993

►
(Signature of Person Issuing Subpoena)

Myrna A. Jackson .... Attorney for Plaintiffs
(Type or print name) (Title)

(See reverse for proof of service)

DEPOSITION SUBPOENA—BUSINESS RECORDS

Independent Medical Examinations. If the physical or mental condition of a party is at issue, then a medical examination may be requested by another party. For example, suppose a plaintiff sues a grocery store for personal injuries suffered after slipping and falling on a banana peel. The grocery store may request an independent medical examination of the plaintiff in order to determine the extent of the injuries. Figure 9-12 is a sample demand for physical examination.

FIGURE 9-12 DEMAND FOR PHYSICAL EXAMINATION

HENDERSON, MORONES & NGUYEN
100 First Street
Merrimack, NH 03054-6170
(603) 424-2655
Richard Henderson
Attorney for the Defendant

__________ COURT FOR THE STATE OF __________
COUNTY OF __________, __________ JUDICIAL DISTRICT

JOE SEVERN,	)	CASE NO. 123456
Plaintiff	)	DEMAND FOR PHYSICAL EXAMINATION
v.	)	
GLADYS MONKS,	)	
Defendant.	)	

TO ALL PARTIES AND TO THEIR ATTORNEYS OF RECORD:

PLEASE TAKE NOTE that a demand is hereby made upon plaintiff JOE SEVERN to submit to a physical examination.

The examination shall take place on May 1, 1993, at 10:00 a.m. at the office of Dr. Joseph Paul, located at 2010 Main St., Nashua, NH.

The examination will be conducted by Dr. Paul, who is a certified specialist in pediatric neurosurgery.

DATED: March 20, 1993 HENDERSON, MORONES & NGUYEN

By: ______________________________
Richard Henderson
Attorney for the Defendant

Demand for Exchange of Expert Witness Lists. A party may discover the identity of all expert witnesses retained by the opposition who will testify at trial, as well as the reports and writings on which their testimony will be based. Figure 9-13 is a sample demand for exchange of expert witness lists.

FIGURE 9-13 DEMAND FOR EXCHANGE OF EXPERT WITNESS LISTS

Mark Samuel
SAMUEL & JOSEPH
37 Sea Coast Highway
Seaside, CA 90277-2143
(310) 990-1234

Attorneys for Defendant and Cross-Complainant Lemon Motors, Inc.

__________ COURT FOR THE __________ JUDICIAL DISTRICT
COUNTY OF __________, STATE OF __________

JOHN SMITH and MARY SMITH, Plaintiffs, v. LEMON MOTORS, INC., a California Corporation; TIMOTHY A. DUNCAN; and DOES 1 through 10, inclusive, Defendants. ______________________________ AND RELATED CROSS-ACTIONS. ______________________________	CASE NO. 123456 DEMAND FOR EXCHANGE OF LISTS, REPORTS, AND WRITINGS OF EXPERT WITNESSES

TO: DEFENDANT TIMOTHY A. DUNCAN AND HIS ATTORNEY OF RECORD:

You are requested to serve a list of the names of each person whose expert opinion you expect to offer at trial. Except as otherwise provided in Sections 2037-2037.9 of the Code of Civil Procedure, your failure to do so will constitute a waiver of your right to call unlisted expert witnesses at the trial.

FIGURE 9-13 DEMAND FOR EXCHANGE OF EXPERT WITNESS LIST (Cont.)

You are also requested to produce for inspection and copying all discoverable reports and writings of each identified expert witness's proposed testimony and preparations to testify. You are requested to produce such writings and reports on May 1, 1993, at the law office of Samuel & Joseph, 37 Sea Coast Highway, Seaside, CA, at 10:00 a.m.

DATED: April 1, 1993

SAMUEL & JOSEPH

By: ______________________

Mark Samuel
Attorney for Defendant and Cross-Complainant Lemon Motors, Inc.

Developing a Discovery Plan

What information and evidence must be discovered? Who can provide this information? How will it be discovered? You will need to analyze these questions before you actually begin discovery. Your discovery strategy should be outlined in the form of a **discovery plan**.

The first step in developing the discovery plan is to review all the pleadings. The following steps should be followed:

1. For each cause of action alleged in the complaint, list the facts alleged to establish that cause of action. For each fact listed, the plaintiff must discover the information and evidence needed to prove that fact at trial. The defendant will want to discover information to disprove the alleged fact.
2. Identify the person(s) who can provide information as to each fact alleged.
3. Identify which discovery tool(s) can be used to gather information about each fact alleged.

   For example, in our sample case of *Smith v. Lemon Motors*, plaintiff Smiths' third cause of action is for fraud and misrepresentation against defendant Duncan. To establish this cause of action, the plaintiffs allege that Duncan set back the odometer to read 1,930 miles rather than the 30,000 miles the car had actually been driven. (See Figure 9-1, Complaint, paragraphs 16–17.) Who might be able to provide information that the odometer was set back? Duncan himself, other people who rode in the car, mechanics who worked on the car, an Allied Motors dealership or other repair facility where the car may have been serviced or repaired, or Allied Motors headquarters, which might have the service history of the car. Which discovery tools could be used? Duncan could be sent interrogatories, sent requests for admissions, and/or deposed. Potential witnesses could be deposed. The repair facilities and Allied Motors could be served with requests to produce documents (such as the car's service records) that might tend to prove the odometer had been altered.

4. For each affirmative defense raised, list the alleged facts that establish the defense, identify sources of information, and determine how those facts can be discovered.
5. Follow the same procedure for any cross-pleadings (such as cross-complaints and answers to cross-complaints).

Figure 9-14 illustrates how to develop a discovery plan.[16]

FIGURE 9-14 DEVELOPING A DISCOVERY PLAN

ALLEGATIONS IN COMPLAINT	WHO CAN PROVIDE INFORMATION?	PROPOSED DISCOVERY
Third Cause of Action		
17. Odometer set back from approximately 30,000 to 1,930	Duncan	Interrogatories, Requests for Admission, Deposition
	Passengers	Deposition
	Mechanics	Deposition
	Dealership	Subpoena Documents (Service/Repair Records)
	Allied Motors	Subpoena Documents

After completing an analysis of the factual allegations made in the pleadings, it is good practice to review the jury instructions relevant to each cause of action. **Jury instructions** list the factual elements that must be established in order to prevail on a particular cause of action. Your review may suggest additional factual information that should be discovered. While formulating the discovery plan, remember that the plaintiff must be able to prove at trial facts establishing each element of the cause of action. The defendant must be able to establish the nonexistence of one element (or establish each element supporting an affirmative defense). Figure 9-15 is a sample jury instruction page.

PREPARING FOR TRIAL

Paralegals frequently play an important role in preparing a case for trial because they are familiar with most of the documents involved in the case. The goal when preparing for trial is to develop a logical system for organizing documents and an effective system to retrieve the documents quickly.[17] One organizational tool commonly used is the trial notebook.

Trial Notebook

A **trial notebook** is a three-ring binder in which the documents and other materials that will be needed at trial are organized. A defense attorney's trial notebook, for example, might be divided into such sections as jury selection, opening

FIGURE 9-15 SAMPLE JURY INSTRUCTION PAGE

FRAUD AND DECEIT—INTENTIONAL MISREPRESENTATION

1. The defendant must have made a representation as to a past or existing material fact;
2. The representation must have been false;
3. The defendant must have known that the representation was false when the defendant made it [or must have made the representation recklessly without knowing whether it was true or false];
4. The defendant must have made the representation with an intent to defraud the plaintiff; that is, the defendant must have made the representation for the purpose of inducing the plaintiff to rely on it and to act or to refrain from acting in reliance thereon;
5. The plaintiff must have been unaware of the falsity of the representation; the plaintiff must have acted in reliance on the truth of the representation and must have been justified in relying on the representation;
6. And, finally, as a result of that reliance on the truth of the representation, the plaintiff must have sustained damage.

statement, direct-examination questions, cross-examination questions, jury instructions, and closing argument. The trial notebook is basically an outline of the trial.

When preparing the trial notebook, a paralegal might perform such tasks as developing a detailed witness file that includes each witness who will be called at trial, drafting questions to ask prospective jurors, and writing jury instructions. Paralegals who assist in preparation of the trial notebook need to work closely with the attorney who is trying the case in order to make the notebook a useful tool.

Determining What Must Be Proved and How It Will Be Proved

The first step in trial preparation is to determine what must be proved at trial and how that proof will be accomplished. This is done by reviewing the pleadings. In the complaint, the plaintiff stated the causes of action and alleged the facts establishing each cause of action. At trial, the plaintiff must prove those facts that will establish the essential elements of each cause of action. The defendant must prove those facts that will establish the affirmative defenses raised in the answer.

For example, suppose a plaintiff's cause of action is for breach of an oral contract. At trial, the plaintiff must prove those facts that will establish the existence of the oral contract. How will this be accomplished? One or both parties will testify as to the existence of the contract; any witnesses to the making of the contract may testify; and any documents referring to the contract may be admitted into evidence. A paralegal must make sure that all the evidence needed to establish each cause of action has been gathered. If there are essential elements of a cause of action that cannot be established, then additional discovery must be done.

Preparation of Evidence

The next step is preparation of the evidence. Documentary evidence that will be needed at trial may not yet be in your possession. Documents may be obtained from nonparties by serving a subpoena *duces tecum*. Documents in the possession of the opposing party may be obtained through a notice to produce at trial. Every document that may be needed at trial must be indexed for easy access during the trial.

Exhibits such as documents and photographs that will be introduced at trial must be prepared and organized. The paralegal may also assist in the preparation of **demonstrative evidence**, which includes photographs, charts, or other visual aids that help the jury understand the case.

Preparation of Witnesses

Paralegals are frequently in charge of informing witnesses of the trial date, serving each witness with a subpoena before trial, and making sure witnesses are present at the proper time and place. The attorneys are usually in charge of actually preparing witnesses to testify. For instance, witnesses are usually instructed to always answer a question truthfully, but not to guess at an answer or provide more information than is needed to answer the question. Witnesses also need to be instructed on proper courtroom attire.

THE TRIAL

Although most litigation paralegals spend the bulk of their time on pretrial matters, many paralegals also assist at trial. This section explains the trial process.

The United States Constitution and most state constitutions provide the right to a trial by jury in many, but not all, types of lawsuits.[18] One of the parties must request a jury or the right is waived. In a jury trial, the jury is the trier of fact while the judge determines the issues of law. If the parties waive a trial by jury, or there is no right to a jury, then the judge determines both the questions of fact and the issues of law.

The first step in a jury trial is selecting the jury. Prospective jurors are questioned by the judge and both attorneys in a process called ***voir dire***.[19] If it is determined that a potential juror does not have the ability to be fair and impartial, then a party may **challenge** (the juror) **for cause** and the juror will be dismissed. Each party has an unlimited number of challenges for cause. In addition, each party may exercise a limited number of **peremptory challenges** in which no reason need be given to disqualify the juror. After the jury is sworn in, the trial is ready to begin.

The attorneys make **opening statements** to the jury about the facts that will be proven at trial. After this, the presentation of the evidence begins. The attorney for the plaintiff calls the first witness and begins the questioning. This is called **direct examination**. The opposing counsel then asks that witness questions in an attempt to disprove the testimony. This is called **cross-examination**. The attorney for the plaintiff may then conduct **redirect examination** to overcome the effect of the cross-examination, which may be followed by the defendant's attorney conducting **re-cross-examination**. Each succeeding witness is questioned in the same way.

The plaintiff has the burden of proof, which is the duty to produce evidence to substantiate the claims being made. This burden is met by establishing a case by a preponderance (greater weight) of the evidence.

After the examination of all of the plaintiff's witnesses has been concluded, the plaintiff "rests." The defendant may then move for a **nonsuit** on the grounds that the plaintiff has failed to present a **prima facie case**. A prima facie case is a case sufficient on its face, being supported by at least the minimum amount of evidence required.[20] Judges in jury trials will grant a motion for nonsuit only if they believe that a reasonable jury could not find in favor of the plaintiff.

If a motion for nonsuit is denied, the defendant's case is presented. Witnesses are again examined and cross-examined. After the defense rests in a jury trial, either party may move for a **directed verdict**. A directed verdict is a verdict ordered by the judge as a matter of law when the party with the burden of proof has failed to make a prima facie case.[21] If the motion for a directed verdict is denied, the attorneys then make **closing arguments**, in which each sums up the case in a light most favorable to that attorney's client.

In a jury trial, before the jury retires to the deliberation room, the judge instructs the jury as to the applicable law in the case. The attorneys have previously submitted a list of proposed jury instructions (sometimes called **charges**) that they want the judge to give to the jury. The jury is given those instructions approved by the judge. The jury then applies those rules of law to the facts as it determines them to be.

The jury (or the judge if there is no jury) reaches a **verdict** in favor of either the plaintiff or the defendant. If the verdict is for the plaintiff, then the amount of the damages will be specified.

After a jury trial, the losing party may file a motion for a new trial or a **motion for a judgment N.O.V.** (notwithstanding the verdict). The motion for a new trial will be granted if the judge determines that the jury was in error or the trial was not fair. The motion for a judgment N.O.V. will be granted if the judge determines that the verdict returned by the jury is clearly wrong as a matter of law (for example, the verdict was clearly the result of prejudice). In such a case, the court is empowered to disregard the jury verdict and enter a judgment contrary to the verdict.

If the motion for a new trial or motion for a judgment N.O.V. is denied, then the court enters a judgment conforming to the verdict. Usually the winning party will be awarded costs such as filing costs and statutory fees awarded to witnesses but not attorneys' fees unless an agreement between the parties allows them. In some cases, such as our sample case of *Smith v. Lemon Motors*, a statute may authorize payment of attorneys' fees to the winning party.[22] Figure 9-16 is a sample judgment.

FIGURE 9-16 JUDGMENT

Myrna Jackson, Esq.
LAW OFFICES OF MYRNA JACKSON
1258 Coastline Drive
Seaside, CA 90277-2183
(310) 990-4321

Attorneys for Plaintiffs

__________ COURT FOR THE __________ JUDICIAL DISTRICT
COUNTY OF __________, STATE OF __________

JOHN SMITH and MARY SMITH, Plaintiffs, v. LEMON MOTORS, INC., a California Corporation; TIMOTHY A. DUNCAN; and DOES 1 through 10, inclusive, Defendants. ______________________________ AND RELATED CROSS-ACTIONS. ______________________________	)	CASE NO. 123456 JUDGMENT

This cause came on regularly for trial on July 26, 1993, at 9:00 a.m., in Division 6, before the Honorable Sandra Fair. Plaintiffs JOHN SMITH and MARY SMITH appeared by Myrna Jackson of the Law Offices of Myrna Jackson; defendant and cross-complainant LEMON MOTORS, INC., appeared by Mark Samuel of Samuel & Joseph; and defendant and cross-defendant TIMOTHY A. DUNCAN appeared by Ann Diamond, attorney at law.

The Court, after having considered the evidence and oral argument, orders the following judgment:

IT IS ADJUDGED that on the Complaint, plaintiffs JOHN SMITH and MARY SMITH recover from defendants LEMON MOTORS, INC., and TIMOTHY A. DUNCAN, jointly and severally, actual damages in the sum of $1,500, plus attorney's fees in the sum of $10,000 and costs in the sum of $1,000.

FIGURE 9-16 JUDGMENT (Cont.)

IT IS FURTHER ADJUDGED that on the Complaint, plaintiffs JOHN SMITH and MARY SMITH recover from defendant TIMOTHY A. DUNCAN alone, additional damages in the sum of $3,000.

IT IS FURTHER ADJUDGED on the Cross-Complaint, that cross-complainant LEMON MOTORS, INC., is to be fully indemnified by cross-defendant TIMOTHY A. DUNCAN for any amount paid by LEMON MOTORS, INC., to plaintiffs JOHN SMITH and MARY SMITH pursuant to this judgment.

IT IS FURTHER ADJUDGED that on the Cross-Complaint, cross-complainant LEMON MOTORS, INC., recover from cross-defendant TIMOTHY A. DUNCAN attorneys' fees in the sum of $9,500 and costs in the sum of $150.

DATED: July 29, 1993

Sandra Fair
Judge, ____________ Court

THE PARALEGAL'S ROLE AT TRIAL

The paralegal assists in jury selection by keeping a chart of the names of prospective jurors and taking notes during *voir dire.* Once the trial begins, the trial exhibits must be ready for the attorney when needed. Witnesses need to be informed of the exact time they must be present in the courtroom. The attorney may want the paralegal to keep notes of the testimony given throughout the day. At the end of the day, the attorney and paralegal often meet to share observations about the day's events.

After the trial, the paralegal may assist with researching and drafting post-trial motions, such as a motion for judgment N.O.V. or a motion for a new trial. The paralegal may also assist in the preparation of an appeal.

APPEAL

The function of an appellate court is to review the proceedings of the trial court and determine whether any legal errors were made that prejudiced the outcome of the case. The appellate court does not hear evidence. It simply reviews the record on appeal, which includes the pleadings, the reporter's transcript of the oral proceedings at trial, the exhibits admitted into evidence, the jury instructions, rulings on motions, and the judgment from which the appeal is taken.

Appellate courts review for errors of law. Recall from Chapter 3 that a reversible error is an error of law that prejudiced the outcome of the case and entitles a party to a new trial. The case may be **remanded** (sent back to the trial court that originally heard the case) for a new trial. If no error was committed, or if the errors were harmless, the decision of the lower court is affirmed. A harmless error is an error that does not deprive the parties of a fair trial. The appellate court usually writes an opinion stating the reasons for its decision.

ENDNOTES

1 See Fed. R. Civ. P. 3.

2 This contract has been omitted.

3 Fed. R. Civ. P. 15 governs amended and supplemental pleadings.

4 The Federal Rules of Civil Procedure do not use the term ''substituted service.'' See Fed. R. Civ. P. 4(d)(1).

5 Fed. R. Civ. P. 12(f).

6 *Black's Law Dictionary*, Abridged Fifth Edition (St. Paul: West, 1983), p. 731.

7 Ibid., p. 601.

8 See Fed. R. Civ. P. 7.

9 See Fed. R. Civ. P. 14.

10 In-court evidence that asserts as the truth an out-of-court statement is hearsay evidence and inadmissible under the hearsay rule.

11 Fed. R. Civ. P. 26(a) lists only five methods of discovery; exchange of expert witness lists is not provided for under the federal rules.

12 Phillip J. Signey, *Litigation Paralegal* (Santa Ana: James Publishing Group, 1991), pp. 5–33.

13 Pat Medina, *Paralegal Discovery: Procedures and Forms* (Santa Ana: James Publishing Group, 1989), pp. 3–29 through 3–39; Signey, op. cit., pp. 5–32 through 5–36.

14 *Black's Law Dictionary*, p. 743.

15 Ibid.

16 Susan Burnett Luten, *California Civil Litigation* (St. Paul: West, 1989), pp. 142–143; Elizabeth C. Richardson and Milton C. Regan, *Civil Litigation for Paralegals* (Cincinnati: South-Western, 1992), p. 240.

17 Richardson and Regan, op. cit., p. 279.

18 Where equitable remedies are involved, for example, there generally is no right to a jury trial.

19 The judge does not participate in the questioning process in all states.

20 Steven H. Gifis, *Law Dictionary* (Woodbury: Barron's Educational Series, 1975), p. 160.

21 *Black's Law Dictionary*, p. 807.

22 See paragraph 26 of the sample complaint (Figure 9-1). See also Appendix A, Sample Appellate Brief.

10 LEGAL ETHICS: GUIDELINES FOR PROFESSIONAL CONDUCT

INTRODUCTION

Black's Law Dictionary defines **legal ethics** as "that branch of moral science which treats of the duties which a member of the legal profession owes to the public, to the court, to his professional brethren, and to his client."[1] This chapter examines some of the ethical duties of lawyers and paralegals.

The power to regulate lawyers and the practice of law rests with the individual states. Specifically, lawyers are licensed and regulated by an organization known as the state bar, which operates under the authority of the state's highest court. Each state has adopted a code of ethics for lawyers based largely on ethical rules promulgated by the American Bar Association. Lawyers are subject to discipline for violating the rules of professional conduct contained in the codes. Sanctions that can be imposed on lawyers for unethical conduct include disbarment (loss of the license to practice), temporary suspension from practice, or a public or private reprimand.

Because paralegals are not members of the state bar they are not directly subject to discipline for violation of a state's code of ethics. However, a paralegal's unethical conduct may result in the supervising attorney being disciplined. Under principles of agency law and rules governing the conduct of attorneys, lawyers are responsible for the actions and the work product of the paralegals they employ.[2] Therefore paralegals must have a thorough understanding of the ethical obligations imposed on lawyers.

When you begin working as a paralegal, you will face many difficult ethical decisions. For example, suppose you learn that a personal acquaintance who works as a paralegal at another firm is representing herself as an attorney and giving legal advice to clients. Should you report this unauthorized practice of law to the proper officials? For another example, suppose that after spending three hours working on an assignment, you discover that you misread the instructions and performed the work incorrectly. Should you bill the client for the three hours? The ethical rules presented in this chapter should serve as guidelines when making the difficult ethical decisions faced by paralegals.

SOURCES OF ETHICAL GUIDELINES

In this section we examine five sources of ethical guidelines that apply to paralegals:

1. State and federal laws, which are legally binding on everyone
2. State rules of professional conduct, which are legally binding on lawyers and ethically binding on paralegals
3. ABA-promulgated codes of ethics for lawyers, including the Model Code of Professional Responsibility, Model Rules of Professional Conduct, and Model Guidelines for the Utilization of Legal Assistant Services, which are ethically binding on lawyers and paralegals
4. ABA ethics opinions, which interpret the ABA codes and are ethically binding on lawyers and paralegals
5. Codes of ethics for paralegals promulgated by paralegal associations, which are ethically binding on paralegals only

The consequences of violating ethical guidelines, including the distinction between legally and ethically binding guidelines, will be examined later.

Requirements Imposed by Law on All Individuals

Like all citizens, paralegals are legally bound to follow state and federal laws. Paralegals must not commit any act that would constitute a crime under a criminal statute, such as theft or fraud. A paralegal may also be sued for committing a civil wrong such as defamation.

In addition, paralegals are legally obligated to avoid the unauthorized practice of law. Every state has laws that prohibit such practice; in most states it is a crime to engage in the unauthorized practice of law. For example, the California statute provides:

> Any person advertising or holding himself or herself out as practicing or entitled to practice law or otherwise practicing law who is not an active member of the State Bar, is guilty of a misdemeanor.[3]

Chapter 11 deals exclusively with the unauthorized practice of law.

State Rules of Professional Conduct

Because the power to regulate the legal profession rests with the individual states, each state has adopted its own code of ethics. Most state codes of ethics are based on the ABA Model Code or Model Rules. Consider, for example, Rule 2-100 of the California Rules of Professional Conduct:

> While representing a client, a member shall not communicate directly or indirectly about the subject of the representation with a party the member knows to be represented by another lawyer in the matter, unless the member has the consent of the other lawyer.

This California rule is based on ABA Model Rule 4.2:

> In representing a client, a lawyer shall not communicate about the subject of the representation with a party the lawyer knows to be represented by another lawyer in the matter, unless the lawyer has the consent of the other lawyer or is authorized by law to do so.[4]

If a California lawyer wrongfully communicates with a represented party, the lawyer is subject to discipline for violating the *state* rule (Rule 2-100). A lawyer is legally bound to obey all state rules of professional conduct, whereas the rules found in the ABA Model Code and ABA Model Rules are only ethically binding (unless, of course, they have been adopted as the state rules).

Many states have codified (put into statutory form) their ethical rules governing the conduct of lawyers. Rules that have not been codified can be found in pamphlets published by the state bar and in commercial publications, such as West's Rules of Court publications. *You must read and understand your state's rules.*

ABA-Promulgated Codes of Ethics for Lawyers

Formal codes of ethics for lawyers are another source of ethical guidelines that apply to paralegals.

Three important codes of ethics have been promulgated by the American Bar Association, a nationwide lawyers' organization in which membership is voluntary. One of the ABA's functions is to develop model codes of ethics, which are then used by the states to promulgate their own rules of professional conduct for lawyers. In 1969, the ABA promulgated the Model Code of Professional Responsibility (Model Code). In 1983, it rewrote the Model Code and named the new document the Model Rules of Professional Conduct (Model Rules). Although the Model Rules reflect the current position of the ABA, many states' ethics rules contain elements of both the Model Code and the Model Rules. Therefore it is important to be familiar with both.

In 1991, the ABA promulgated the Model Guidelines for the Utilization of Legal Assistant Services (Model Guidelines). The Model Guidelines specifically address the conduct required of attorneys who employ paralegals.

ABA Model Code of Professional Responsibility. The Model Code provides standards of professional conduct and rules to determine when a lawyer should be disciplined for failure to meet those standards. The Model Code consists of three basic components: Canons, Ethical Considerations (ECs), and Disciplinary Rules (DRs).

Canons. The Model Code contains nine **Canons**, which express in general terms the conduct expected of lawyers. The Canons are broad statements of ethical conduct from which the Ethical Considerations (ECs) and Disciplinary Rules (DRs) are derived. Figure 10-1 contains the nine Canons of the ABA Model Code.

Ethical Considerations (ECs). **Ethical Considerations** explain the general principle set forth in a Canon. The Ethical Considerations are aspirational in nature, setting forth objectives toward which lawyers should strive. The first part of Figure 10-2 is an Ethical Consideration (EC 4-1) accompanying Canon 4.

FIGURE 10-1 THE NINE CANONS OF THE ABA MODEL CODE

Canon 1	A Lawyer Should Assist in Maintaining the Integrity and Competence of the Legal Profession
Canon 2	A Lawyer Should Assist the Legal Profession in Fulfilling Its Duty to Make Legal Counsel Available
Canon 3	A Lawyer Should Assist in Preventing the Unauthorized Practice of Law
Canon 4	A Lawyer Should Preserve the Confidences and Secrets of a Client
Canon 5	A Lawyer Should Exercise Independent Professional Judgment on Behalf of a Client
Canon 6	A Lawyer Should Represent a Client Competently
Canon 7	A Lawyer Should Represent a Client Zealously Within the Bounds of the Law
Canon 8	A Lawyer Should Assist in Improving the Legal System
Canon 9	A Lawyer Should Avoid Even the Appearance of Professional Impropriety

Disciplinary Rules (DRs). Whereas Ethical Considerations are aspirational, **Disciplinary Rules** are mandatory in character. The Disciplinary Rules state the minimum level below which no lawyer's conduct can fall without subjecting the lawyer to disciplinary action. DRs are phrased in terms of what a lawyer "shall" and "shall not" do.

The second part of Figure 10-2 is a Disciplinary Rule (DR 4-101) accompanying Canon 4.

ABA Model Rules of Professional Conduct. Comprising the most widely used set of standards by which the conduct of lawyers is judged, the Model Rules of Professional Conduct relate more directly to specific conduct than do the broad, general principles found in the Canons of the Model Code. The fifty Model Rules are organized under eight topics: client-lawyer relationship, counselor, advocate, transactions with persons other than clients, law firms and associations, public service, information about legal services, and maintaining the integrity of the profession. Some rules are obligatory and stated in terms of "shall" or "shall not," while other rules are advisory and phrased in terms of "may." A series of **comments** follows each rule, helping to explain the meaning of the rule. Figure 10-3 illustrates Model Rule 5.3 and the comments following the rule.

In order to understand the difference between the older Model Code and the newer Model Rules, compare Canon 3 of the Model Code (Figure 10-1) with Model Rule 5.3 (Figure 10-3). Canon 3 states a broad, general principle: A Lawyer

FIGURE 10-2 SAMPLE ETHICAL CONSIDERATION (EC 4-1) AND DISCIPLINARY RULE (DR 4-101)

ETHICAL CONSIDERATION

EC 4-1 Both the fiduciary relationship existing between lawyer and client and the proper functioning of the legal system require the preservation by the lawyer of confidences and secrets of one who has employed or sought to employ him. A client must feel free to discuss whatever he wishes with his lawyer and a lawyer must be equally free to obtain information beyond that volunteered by his client. A lawyer should be fully informed of all the facts of the matter he is handling in order for his client to obtain the full advantage of our legal system. It is for the lawyer in the exercise of his independent professional judgment to separate the relevant and important from the irrelevant and unimportant. The observance of the ethical obligation of a lawyer to hold inviolate the confidences and secrets of his client not only facilitates the full development of facts essential to proper representation of the client but also encourages laymen to seek early legal assistance.

DISCIPLINARY RULE

DR 4-101 Preservation of Confidences and Secrets of a Client

(A) "Confidence" refers to information protected by the attorney-client privilege under applicable law, and "secret" refers to other information gained in the professional relationship that the client has requested be held inviolate or the disclosure of which would be embarrassing or would be likely to be detrimental to the client.

(B) Except when permitted under DR 4-101(C), a lawyer shall not knowingly:
- (1) Reveal a confidence or secret of his client.
- (2) Use a confidence or secret of his client to the disadvantage of the client.
- (3) Use a confidence or secret of his client for the advantage of himself or of a third person, unless the client consents after full disclosure.

(C) A lawyer may reveal:
- (1) Confidences or secrets with the consent of the client or clients affected, but only after a full disclosure to them.
- (2) Confidences or secrets when permitted under Disciplinary Rules or required by law or court order.
- (3) The intention of his client to commit a crime and the information necessary to prevent the crime.
- (4) Confidences or secrets necessary to establish or collect his fee or to defend himself or his employees or associates against an accusation of wrongful conduct.

(D) A lawyer shall exercise reasonable care to prevent his employees, associates, and others whose services are utilized by him from disclosing or using confidences or secrets of a client, except that the lawyer may reveal the information allowed by DR 4-101(C) through an employee.

FIGURE 10-3 SAMPLE ABA MODEL RULE (RULE 5.3)

RULE 5.3 Responsibilities Regarding Nonlawyer Assistants

With respect to a nonlawyer employed or retained by or associated with a lawyer:

(a) a partner in a law firm shall make reasonable efforts to ensure that the firm has in effect measures giving reasonable assurance that the person's conduct is compatible with the professional obligations of the lawyer;

(b) a lawyer having direct supervisory authority over the nonlawyer shall make reasonable efforts to ensure that the person's conduct is compatible with the professional obligations of the lawyer; and

(c) a lawyer shall be responsible for conduct of such a person that would be a violation of the rules of professional conduct if engaged in by a lawyer if:

(1) the lawyer orders or, with the knowledge of the specific conduct, ratifies the conduct involved; or

(2) the lawyer is a partner in the law firm in which the person is employed, or has direct supervisory authority over the person, and knows of the conduct at a time when its consequences can be avoided or mitigated but fails to take reasonable remedial action.

COMMENT:

Lawyers generally employ assistants in their practice, including secretaries, investigators, law student interns, and paraprofessionals. Such assistants, whether employees or independent contractors, act for the lawyer in rendition of the lawyer's professional services. A lawyer should give such assistants appropriate instruction and supervision concerning the ethical aspects of their employment, particularly regarding the obligation not to disclose information relating to representation of the client, and should be responsible for their work product. The measures employed in supervising nonlawyers should take account of the fact that they do not have legal training and are not subject to professional discipline.

Should Assist in Preventing the Unauthorized Practice of Law. Model Rule 5.3, in contrast, lists a lawyer's specific responsibilities regarding nonlawyer assistants.

ABA Model Guidelines for the Utilization of Legal Assistant Services. The single most important document concerning paralegal ethics is the newly promulgated ABA Model Guidelines for the Utilization of Legal Assistant Services (Model Guidelines). The Model Guidelines clarify the conduct required of attorneys who employ paralegals and explain the types of activities paralegals may or may not engage in.[5]

There are ten specific Model Guidelines. Each is followed by a commentary that identifies the basis for the guideline and explains any issues the guideline may present.[6] The most important guidelines will be discussed throughout the remainder of this chapter and in Chapter 11. The complete text of the Model Guidelines is reprinted in Appendix C.

Ethics Opinions

Lawyers who have a specific question concerning the ABA Model Code and Model Rules may submit the question to the ABA, which will publish an **Ethics Opinion** in answer. Courts look to the Model Code, Model Rules, Model Guidelines, and Ethics Opinions when determining the standard of conduct for the legal profession. Figure 10-4 is a sample Ethics Opinion.

Codes of Ethics Promulgated by Paralegal Associations for Paralegals

The National Association of Legal Assistants and the National Federation of Paralegal Associations have adopted paralegal-specific codes of ethics that provide important guidelines for determining the types of activities paralegals may or may not engage in. The NALA Code of Ethics and Professional Responsibility is reprinted in Figure 10-5. The NALA Model Standards and Guidelines for Utilization of Legal Assistants Annotated is reprinted in Appendix D. The NFPA Affirmation of Responsibility is reprinted in Appendix E.

CONSEQUENCES OF VIOLATING ETHICAL GUIDELINES

Lawyers are subject to discipline for violating the code of ethics adopted by the state in which they practice. The penalty imposed on a lawyer for violation of a state rule of professional conduct is called a **sanction**.

Sanctions for Lawyers

The ABA Model Code and Model Rules, which have been adopted in some form by most states, do not specify what sanction or penalty should be imposed for violation of a particular rule. Instead, the penalty imposed depends on the severity of the offense and the circumstances surrounding the offense. A relatively minor offense might result in a **private reprimand**, which is a letter warning the attorney about the unethical conduct. A more serious offense would lead to a **public reprimand** or **censure**, in which the warning is made public. A still more serious offense would result in a **suspension**, which means the lawyer would not be allowed to practice law for a designated period of time. Finally, a very serious ethical violation could result in **disbarment**, meaning the attorney would no longer be allowed to practice law in the state.

Application to Paralegals

Because paralegals are not members of the state bar, the state rules of professional conduct do not apply directly to them. This means that paralegals are not directly subject to discipline for violations of these rules. Similarly, the ABA Model Code, Model Rules, and Model Guidelines are directed specifically to lawyers, not paralegals. Why is it so important, then, for paralegals to follow these rules?

FIGURE 10-4 SAMPLE ETHICS OPINION

Informal Opinion 88-1526 **June 22, 1988**
Imputed Disqualification Arising from Change in Employment by Nonlawyer Employee

A law firm that employs a nonlawyer who formerly was employed by another firm may continue representing clients whose interests conflict with the interests of clients of the former employer on whose matters the nonlawyer has worked, as long as the employing firm screens the nonlawyer from information about or participating in matters involving those clients and strictly adheres to the screening process described in this opinion and as long as no information relating to the representation of the clients of the former employer is revealed by the nonlawyer to any person in the employing firm. In addition, the nonlawyer's former employer must admonish the nonlawyer against revelation of information relating to the representation of clients of the former employer.

The Committee is asked whether, under the ABA Model Rules of Professional Conduct, a law firm that hires a paralegal formerly employed by another lawyer must withdraw from representation of a client under the following circumstances. The paralegal has worked for more than a year with a sole practitioner on litigation matters. One of those matters is a lawsuit which the sole practitioner instituted against a client of the law firm that is about to hire the paralegal and wishes to continue to defend the client. The paralegal has gained substantial information relating to the representation of the sole practitioner's client, the plaintiff in the lawsuit. The employing firm will screen the paralegal from receiving information about or working on the lawsuit and will direct the paralegal not to reveal any information relating to the representation of the sole practitioner's client gained by the paralegal during the former employment. The Committee also is asked whether the paralegal's former employer must take any actions in order to comply with the Model Rules.

RESPONSIBILITIES OF EMPLOYING FIRM

The Committee concludes that the law firm employing the paralegal should not be disqualified from continuing to defend its client in the lawsuit, as long as the law firm and the paralegal strictly adhere to the screening process described in this Opinion, and as long as no information relating to the representation of the sole practitioner's client is revealed by the paralegal to any person in the employing firm.

* * *

It is important that nonlawyer employees have as much mobility in employment opportunity as possible consistent with the protection of clients' interests. To so limit employment opportunities that some nonlawyers trained to work with law firms might be required to leave the careers for which they are trained would disserve clients as well as the legal profession. Accordingly, any restrictions on the nonlawyer's employment should be held to the minimum necessary to protect confidentiality of client information.

* * *

FIGURE 10-5 NALA CODE OF ETHICS AND PROFESSIONAL RESPONSIBILITY

It is the responsibility of every legal assistant to adhere strictly to the accepted standards of legal ethics and to live by general principles of proper conduct. The performance of the duties of the legal assistant shall be governed by specific canons as defined herein in order that justice will be served and the goals of the profession attained. The canons of ethics set forth hereafter are adopted by the National Association of Legal Assistants, Inc., as a general guide and the enumeration of these rules does not mean there are not others of equal importance although not specifically mentioned.

Canon 1. A legal assistant shall not perform any of the duties that lawyers only may perform nor do things that lawyers themselves may not do.

Canon 2. A legal assistant may perform any task delegated and supervised by a lawyer so long as the lawyer is responsible to the client, maintains a direct relationship with the client, and assumes full professional responsibility for the work product.

Canon 3. A legal assistant shall not engage in the practice of law by accepting cases, setting fees, giving legal advice or appearing in court (unless otherwise authorized by court or agency rules).

Canon 4. A legal assistant shall not act in matters involving professional legal judgment as the services of a lawyer are essential in the public interest whenever the exercise of such judgment is required.

Canon 5. A legal assistant must act prudently in determining the extent to which a client may be assisted without the presence of a lawyer.

Canon 6. A legal assistant shall not engage in the unauthorized practice of law.

Canon 7. A legal assistant must protect the confidences of a client, and it shall be unethical for a legal assistant to violate any statute now in effect or hereafter to be enacted controlling privileged communications.

Canon 8. It is the obligation of the legal assistant to avoid conduct which would cause the lawyer to be unethical or even appear to be unethical and loyalty to the employer is incumbent upon the legal assistant.

Canon 9. A legal assistant shall work continually to maintain integrity and a high degree of competency throughout the legal profession.

Canon 10. A legal assistant shall strive for perfection through education in order to better assist the legal profession in fulfilling its duty of making legal services available to clients and the public.

Canon 11. A legal assistant shall do all things incidental, necessary or expedient for the attainment of the ethics and responsibilities imposed by statute or rule of court.

Canon 12. A legal assistant is governed by the American Bar Association Model Code of Professional Responsibility and the American Bar Association Model Rules of Professional Conduct.

The Preliminary Statement to the Model Code states that the rules "define the type of ethical conduct that the public has a right to expect not only of lawyers but also of their nonprofessional employees and associates in all matters pertaining to professional employment." Paralegals are legal professionals, and as such they have the obligation to follow the ethical guidelines established for the profession. The paralegal's own professional image, as well as the image of the legal profession in general, is at stake.

ABA Model Guideline 1 states that "a lawyer is responsible for all of the professional actions of a legal assistant performing legal assistant services at the lawyer's direction and should take reasonable measures to ensure that the legal assistant's conduct is consistent with the lawyer's obligations under the ABA Model Rules of Professional Conduct." The Kentucky Paralegal Code expresses the importance of paralegals following ethical guidelines in the following manner:

> While the responsibility for compliance with standards of professional conduct rests with members of the Bar, a paralegal should understand those standards. It is, therefore, incumbent upon the lawyer employing a paralegal to inform him of the restraints and responsibilities incident to the job and supervise the manner in which the work is completed. However, the paralegal does have an independent obligation to refrain from illegal conduct. Additionally, and notwithstanding the fact that the Code of Professional Responsibility is not binding upon lay persons, the very nature of a paralegal's employment imposes an obligation to refrain from conduct which would involve the lawyer in a violation of the Code.[7]

Therefore, although a paralegal is not directly subject to discipline for ethical violations, a paralegal's unethical conduct may result in the imposition of sanctions against the supervising attorney. Clearly, paralegals must follow their jurisdiction's ethics rules.

Because we have discussed several different codes of ethics applicable to attorneys and paralegals, it may be helpful at this point to summarize which rules *must* be followed and which rules are merely advisory. When are attorneys and paralegals liable for violating a particular ethical guideline?

1. *State rules of professional conduct.* The state rules of professional conduct are the most important in the sense that they *must* be followed by lawyers who practice in the state. Noncompliance will result in sanctions. Paralegals are not members of the state bar and thus are not directly subject to discipline for violating the state rules of professional conduct. However, if a paralegal violates a state rule, the supervising attorney is held responsible and is subject to discipline for the paralegal's unethical conduct.
2. *ABA Model Code, Model Rules, and Model Guidelines.* An attorney is not subject to discipline for violations of the Model Code, Model Rules, or Model Guidelines *unless they have been adopted as the state rules of professional conduct in the state in which the attorney practices.* Paralegals are not subject to discipline for violations of the Model Code, Model Rules, or Model Guidelines

even if they have been adopted as the state rules because paralegals are not directly subject to discipline for violations of the state rules of professional conduct.

3. *Codes of ethics adopted by NALA and NFPA.* Paralegals are not subject to discipline for violating any of the ethical rules adopted by the two national paralegal associations. NALA and NFPA are voluntary associations with no legal authority over paralegals.

SPECIFIC ETHICAL DUTIES OF LEGAL PROFESSIONALS

This section examines some of the specific ethical duties imposed on lawyers and paralegals, including (1) the duty to preserve confidential information, (2) the duty to avoid conflicts of interest, (3) the duty to represent clients competently, (4) duties regarding communication with a person represented by counsel, (5) duties regarding communication with an unrepresented person, (6) the duty of candor toward the tribunal, (7) the duty to avoid solicitation, and (8) the duty to report professional misconduct.

Duty to Preserve Confidential Information

> ABA Model Guideline 6: It is the responsibility of a lawyer to take reasonable measures to ensure that all client confidences are preserved by a legal assistant.

Both the ABA Model Code and the ABA Model Rules state that a lawyer has the responsibility to preserve confidential client information. The duty to preserve confidential information is a "fundamental principle in the client-lawyer relationship."[8] The purpose of the confidentiality rule is to encourage clients to communicate fully and frankly with the lawyer, even as to embarrassing and legally damaging information.[9] Only with full disclosure can the lawyer learn all the facts essential to proper representation of the client.

The duty not to disclose confidential information applies equally to the paralegal. The NFPA Affirmation of Responsibility states that "confidential information and privileged communication are a vital part of the attorney, paralegal and client relationship. The importance of preserving confidential and privileged information is understood to be an uncompromising obligation of every paralegal."

Consider the following example of what constitutes confidential client information: An attorney is representing a client on a murder charge. The client walks into the attorney's office and says, "I just returned to the scene of the crime and removed the gun from the place where I had hidden it. It's hidden in a much safer spot now." This communication between the client and the attorney during the course of the attorney-client relationship is privileged information. The attorney should not reveal to the prosecution the fact that the client removed evidence from the crime scene. If the attorney's paralegal was present at the meeting with the client, the paralegal would also have the duty not to disclose this confidential information.

Discussion of Confidential Information with Firm Personnel. The normal operation of a law office results in the exposure of confidential professional information to paralegals and other nonlawyer employees of the office.[10] A lawyer may share confidential information with firm personnel "when necessary to perform his professional employment."[11] As a paralegal who will be exposed to confidential client information, you have the ethical obligation to avoid indiscreet conversations regarding this information. In general, you should discuss a case no more than is necessary to provide adequate representation, and a case should be discussed with only those employees who are working with you on that particular case.[12]

Continuing Duty to Preserve Confidential Information. EC 4-6 of the Model Code states that a lawyer is obligated to preserve the confidences and secrets of a client after the file is closed and the employment is terminated, and even after the client dies.[13] This continuing duty to preserve confidential information applies to paralegals.

Exceptions to the Rule: When Confidential Information May Be Disclosed. A lawyer may reveal confidential client information (1) when the client consents to disclosure, (2) when a dispute arises regarding the lawyer's conduct, (3) to prevent the commission of a future crime, and (4) when other rules would permit or require the lawyer to disclose information.

Client Consent. Under Rule 1.6(a) and DR 4-101(C)(1), a lawyer may reveal information relating to representation of a client if the client consents. The attorney must fully inform the client of the consequences of disclosure.

In many cases, clients routinely consent to disclosure of confidential information. A client in a personal injury case may consent to disclosure of medical information; a client in an employment discrimination case may consent to disclosure of employment records.

Dispute Regarding Lawyer's Conduct. Rule 1.6(b)(2) and DR 4-101(C)(4) state that a lawyer may reveal confidential information in order to establish or collect the fee for the lawyer's services, to defend the lawyer or any employees against an accusation of wrongful conduct, or to respond to allegations concerning the representation of the client.

For example, suppose a client needs to have a will drafted. The client informs the attorney that there are very few assets and that it will be a simple will to prepare. The attorney and the client agree on a flat fee. The client actually has many different types of assets, and preparing the client's will is more complex and time-consuming than the attorney reasonably anticipated. The client refuses to pay any more money for the extra work. In such a case, the attorney may disclose confidential information in order to establish the attorney's fee.

For another example, suppose an attorney defends a client unsuccessfully in a criminal action. On appeal, the attorney's representation is found to fall below reasonable standards, and the client is awarded a new trial. The client subsequently sues the attorney in a civil action. The attorney may disclose confidential information in order to defend herself or himself, provided that the disclosures are limited to information that is relevant to the claim.

To Prevent Commission of Future Crime. Rule 1.6(b)(1) and DR 4-101(C)(3) permit an attorney to reveal both a client's intention to commit a crime and information necessary to prevent the crime. Rule 1.6(b)(1) limits disclosure to crimes that are "likely to result in imminent death or substantial bodily harm." Under the Model Code, an attorney may reveal the intention of a client to commit *any* crime.

Note that the exception applies to future crimes but not to past crimes. For example, if a client confesses to murdering someone in the past, the confession is confidential and may not be revealed. However, if the client says that she is going to murder her husband tomorrow afternoon, the attorney may reveal the information in order to prevent the murder.

When Permitted by Other Ethics Rules. Paragraph 20 of the Comments to Rule 1.6 and DR 4-101(C)(2) state that the Model Rules and the Disciplinary Rules may, in various circumstances, permit or require an attorney to disclose confidential information.[14] Rule 3.3(a)(2), for instance, states that a lawyer "shall not knowingly fail to disclose a material fact to a tribunal when disclosure is necessary to avoid assisting a criminal or fraudulent act by the client," and that this rule applies even if compliance requires disclosure of information otherwise protected by lawyer-client confidentiality.[15]

For example, suppose a defendant in a criminal case has posted bail. The defendant then fails to appear at the trial. Under such circumstances, the attorney's knowledge of the client's whereabouts is not privileged and must be disclosed to the proper authorities.

Duty to Avoid Conflicts of Interest

Model Guideline 7: A lawyer should take reasonable measures to prevent conflicts of interest resulting from a legal assistant's other employment or interests insofar as such other employment or interests would present a conflict of interest if it were that of the lawyer.

A lawyer has a mandatory duty to avoid conflicts of interest.[16] The ethical rules relating to conflicts of interest fall into three main categories: (1) the duty not to represent a client if that representation would be directly adverse to another client; (2) the duty to avoid conflicts with the interests of former clients; and (3) the duty not to represent a person when the lawyer's own financial, business, property, or personal interests can interfere with professional judgment.

The conflict of interest rules are based on the belief that the professional judgment of a lawyer should be exercised "solely for the benefit of his client and free of compromising influences and loyalties. Neither his personal interests, the interests of other clients, nor the desires of third persons should be permitted to dilute his loyalty to this client."[17] For example, suppose a lawyer represents Joyce in a breach of contract action against Carol. Carol then asks the lawyer to also represent her in the breach of contract action. The lawyer could not represent Carol because Carol's interests are directly adverse to Joyce's interests. Representing both Carol and Joyce would be a conflict of interest.

A paralegal may have a personal, business, or social interest that could conflict with the representation of the client. A paralegal should inform the supervising attorney of any interest that could result in a conflict of interest or even give the appearance of a conflict of interest.[18]

Paralegals need to be aware of situations that present possible conflicts of interest. When a paralegal changes jobs, for example, possible conflicts that may arise include working for both an insured and an insurer, a wife and a husband in a marital dissolution, or a buyer and a seller of real property.[19]

POINTER: When opening a new case file, it is important to ensure that representation of the new client will not create a conflict of interest. Office procedures used to screen for conflicts of interest vary. Some firms use a manual index system that contains an alphabetical list of past and present clients, as well as every party that is or has been adverse to the firm's clients in a lawsuit. Most large firms use a computer check for conflicts.

Competence

Lawyers have an ethical duty not to handle legal matters that they know they are not competent to handle unless they associate other lawyers who are competent to handle the matters.[20] For example, a lawyer in general practice might represent a corporate client in routine business matters such as drafting contracts. If the client becomes involved in a complex lawsuit involving alleged violations of securities laws, the lawyer should associate another attorney with expertise in this area of the law.

Lawyers also have the ethical duty not to neglect legal matters entrusted to them.[21] Model Rule 1.3 states that "a lawyer shall act with reasonable diligence and promptness in representing a client."[22] Model Rule 1.4(a) states: "A lawyer shall keep a client reasonably informed about the status of a matter and promptly comply with reasonable requests for information."[23] Many cases do not progress as rapidly as the clients would like, and the clients suspect that their legal matters are being neglected by the attorney. Paralegals frequently play an important role in alleviating this suspicion by maintaining communications with clients and informing them of recent developments in their cases. Settlement offers, in particular, must be promptly communicated to clients.

POINTER: If a case is going to last an extended period of time, the case file should be marked for review at least once a month. At that time, send the client a letter indicating the status of the case. This not only keeps the client informed, but also provides proof of diligence should the client accuse the attorney of neglect.[24]

Communication with a Person Represented by Counsel

Model Rule 4.2 states: "In representing a client, a lawyer shall not communicate about the subject of the representation with a party the lawyer knows to be represented by another lawyer in the matter, unless the lawyer has the consent of the other lawyer or is authorized by law to do so." Paralegals also must not communicate directly with an opposing party who is represented by counsel. If you receive phone calls from opposing parties, you must advise them that you cannot talk without the prior consent of their attorneys.

Communication with an Unrepresented Person

DR 7-104(A)(2) states that during the course of representing a client, a lawyer shall not give advice to a person who is not represented by a lawyer, other than the advice to secure a lawyer, if the interests of such person have a possibility of being in conflict with the interests of the lawyers's client. Model Rule 4.3 adds that a lawyer who is dealing on behalf of a client has a duty to inform the unrepresented person that the lawyer is not disinterested in the matter. These rules are intended to protect unrepresented persons from disclosing information that could be harmful to their cases.

Duty of Candor Toward the Tribunal

Model Rule 3.3 states the following:

> A lawyer shall not knowingly: (1) make a false statement of material fact or law to a tribunal; (2) fail to disclose a material fact to a tribunal when disclosure is necessary to avoid assisting a criminal or fraudulent act by the client; (3) fail to disclose to the tribunal legal authority in the controlling jurisdiction known to the lawyer to be directly adverse to the position of the client and not disclosed by opposing counsel; or (4) offer evidence that the lawyer knows to be false. If a lawyer has offered material evidence and comes to know of its falsity, the lawyer shall take reasonable remedial measures.

Paragraph (3) imposes a duty to disclose adverse law. Attorneys are considered officers of the court and must report both the favorable and unfavorable law that their legal research uncovers. For example, suppose an attorney is representing a client in an appeal in the state of Pennsylvania. The attorney's research uncovers two cases directly "on point" (the facts are similar to the client's case and the questions of law are the same). One case is from Pennsylvania, the other is from Ohio, and both are adverse to the client's position. The attorney *must* disclose the Pennsylvania case since it is legal authority from the controlling jurisdiction. The attorney is not ethically obligated to disclose the Ohio case. However, the better strategy is usually to cite all contrary law and then distinguish it.

POINTER: Always inform your supervising attorney of adverse law; never ignore it or try to hide it. You can then help to distinguish your case or challenge the soundness of the adverse case.

Duty to Avoid Solicitation

Model Rule 7.3 states: "A lawyer shall not by in-person or live telephone contact solicit professional employment from a prospective client with whom the lawyer has no family or prior professional relationship when a significant motive for the lawyer's doing so is the lawyer's pecuniary gain."[25] DR 2-104 provides that "a lawyer who has given in-person unsolicited advice to a layperson that he should obtain counsel or take legal action shall not accept employment resulting from that advice."[26]

Although lawyers are allowed to advertise,[27] Rule 7.3 prohibits in-person or live telephone solicitation. This is because there is a "potential for abuse inherent in direct contact,"[28] while advertising to the public is permitted because it is subject to scrutiny.

Because paralegals cannot perform work directly for the general public without engaging in the unauthorized practice of law, they are not allowed to advertise to the general public.[29] However, paralegals may advertise their services directly to attorneys.

Model Rule 7.2 states that "a lawyer shall not give anything of value to a person for recommending the lawyer's services . . ." Paralegals may not be paid for "signing up" clients for their employer's legal practice.[30]

POINTER: Most states have very specific rules concerning advertising and solicitation, and the rules vary from state to state. Be sure to read your state's rules concerning advertising and solicitation.

Duty to Report Professional Misconduct

Model Rule 8.3 states that "an attorney is required to inform the proper authorities if the misconduct [of another lawyer] raises questions as to that lawyer's honesty, trustworthiness or fitness as a lawyer."[31]

According to EC 1-4 of the Model Code, the integrity of the legal profession can be maintained only if unethical conduct is reported. EC 1-4 states that a lawyer should reveal voluntarily all unprivileged knowledge of conduct of lawyers that she or he believes clearly to be in violation of the Disciplinary Rules. The duty to report professional misconduct extends to the paralegal.

For example, suppose Attorney Wineman is an internationally known wine connoisseur who owns and operates a wine store in addition to practicing law. While negotiating a large sale, Attorney Wineman deliberately defrauds Minardi, the owner of a chain of Italian restaurants. Paralegal Honesto is present in the store and witnesses the fraud being committed. Paralegal Honesto must report the fraud to the appropriate authorities, even though the fraud was not committed while Wineman was practicing law. Attorney Wineman's conduct is in violation of DR 1-102(A)(4), which provides that "a lawyer shall not engage in conduct involving dishonesty, fraud, deceit, or misrepresentation."

ENDNOTES

1 *Black's Law Dictionary*, Abridged Fifth Edition (St. Paul: West, 1983), p. 465.

2 ABA Model Guidelines for the Utilization of Legal Assistant Services, Comment to Guideline 1.

3 California Business and Professions Code, Section 6126(a).

4 Model Rule 4.2. Copyrighted by the American Bar Association. All rights reserved. Reprinted with permission.

5 However, it should be noted that footnote 3 of the Model Guidelines states: ''While necessarily mentioning legal assistant conduct, lawyers are the intended audience of these Guidelines. The Guidelines, therefore, are addressed to lawyer conduct and not directly to the conduct of the legal assistant.''

6 Preamble to the ABA Model Guidelines for the Utilization of Legal Assistant Services.

7 Kentucky Paralegal Code (Rule 3.700); Kentucky has adopted this code, which governs lawyer conduct in relation to the use of paralegals, as part of its court rules of procedure.

8 Comments to Model Rule 1.6, Paragraph 4. Copyrighted by the American Bar Association. All rights reserved. Reprinted with permission.

9 Ibid.

10 EC 4-2. Copyrighted by the American Bar Association. All rights reserved. Reprinted with permission.

11 Ibid.

12 Elizabeth C. Richardson and Milton C. Regan, *Civil Litigation for Paralegals* (Cincinnati: South-Western, 1992), p. 40.

13 ABA Informal Opinion 1293.

14 For examples, see Rules 2.2, 2.3, 3.3, and 4.1.

15 Model Rule 3.3. Copyrighted by the American Bar Association. All rights reserved. Reprinted with permission.

16 See Model Rules 1.7 through 1.13, Canon 5, and DRs 5-101 through 5-107.

17 EC 5-1.

18 Comment to Guideline 7.

19 Deborah K. Orlik, *Ethics for the Legal Assistant* (Glenview, IL: Scott, Foresman, 1986), pp. 51–52.

20 DR 6-101. Copyrighted by the American Bar Association. All rights reserved. Reprinted with permission.

21 Ibid.

22 Model Rule 1.3. Copyrighted by the American Bar Association. All rights reserved. Reprinted with permission.

23 Model Rule 1.4(a). Copyrighted by the American Bar Association. All rights reserved. Reprinted with permission.

24 Richardson and Regan, op. cit., p. 48.

25 Model Rule 7.3. Copyrighted by the American Bar Association. All rights reserved. Reprinted with permission.

26 DR 2-104. Copyrighted by the American Bar Association. All rights reserved. Reprinted with permission.

27 See Model Rule 7.2.

28 See Comments to Rule 7.3.

29 Orlik, op. cit., p. 18.

30 Comment to Model Guideline 9.

31 Model Rule 8.3. Copyrighted by the American Bar Association. All rights reserved. Reprinted with permission.

11 PARALEGALS AND THE UNAUTHORIZED PRACTICE OF LAW

Paralegals have the legal and ethical obligation to avoid the unauthorized practice of law. But exactly what *is* the unauthorized practice of law? What activities may a paralegal legally and ethically perform? When does a paralegal cross the line and begin to practice law? This chapter examines these difficult questions.

PROHIBITING THE UNAUTHORIZED PRACTICE OF LAW

Both the ABA Model Code and the ABA Model Rules prohibit the unauthorized practice of law. Canon 3 of the Model Code states: "A Lawyer Should Assist in Preventing the Unauthorized Practice of Law." Model Rule 5.5 provides: "A lawyer shall not: (a) practice in a jurisdiction when doing so violates the regulation of the legal profession in that jurisdiction; or (b) assist a person who is not a member of the bar in the performance of activity that constitutes the unauthorized practice of law."[1]

In addition, all states have laws prohibiting the unauthorized practice of law. Slightly more than two-thirds of the states make the unauthorized practice of law a misdemeanor, while others treat it as contempt of court.[2]

The most common justification for limiting the practice of law to lawyers is the need to protect the public from those persons who might render legal services incompetently or unethically. For example, EC 3-1 of the Model Code states:

> The prohibition against the practice of law by a layman is grounded in the need of the public for integrity and competence of those who undertake to render legal services. Because of the fiduciary and personal character of the lawyer-client relationship and the inherently complex nature of our legal system, the public can better be assured of the requisite responsibility and

> competence if the practice of law is confined to those who are subject to the requirements and regulations imposed upon members of the legal profession.[3]

Similarly, the Comment to Model Rule 5.5 provides that "limiting the practice of law to members of the bar protects the public against rendition of legal services by unqualified persons."

DEFINING THE UNAUTHORIZED PRACTICE OF LAW

> Model Guideline 2: Provided the lawyer maintains responsibility for the work product, a lawyer may delegate to a legal assistant any task normally performed by the lawyer except those tasks proscribed to one not licensed as a lawyer by statute, court rule, administrative rule or regulation, controlling authority, the ABA Model Rules of Professional Conduct, or these Guidelines.

Although every state prohibits nonlawyers from practicing law, there is no universal definition of what actually constitutes the practice of law. The ABA Model Rules fail to define the practice of law, stating only that "the definition of the practice of law is established by law and varies from one jurisdiction to another."[4] And the Model Code takes the position that "it is neither necessary nor desirable to attempt the formulation of a single, specific definition of what constitutes the practice of law."[5]

What constitutes the practice of law, then, is a matter of state law. Some states take the same approach as the ABA and simply prohibit the unauthorized practice of law without defining it. Paralegals in these states are left in an unenviable position: while it is a crime for them to practice law, the practice of law is not defined, and the activities that constitute the practice of law are not listed.

Other states do attempt to define the practice of law. For example, a North Carolina statute defines the practice of law as follows:

> The phrase "practice law" as used in this Chapter is defined to be performing any legal service for any other person, firm or corporation, with or without compensation, specifically including the preparation or aiding in the preparation of deeds, mortgages, wills, trust instruments, inventories, accounts or reports of guardians, trustees, administrators or executors, or preparing or aiding in the preparation of any petitions or orders in any probate or court proceeding; abstracting or passing upon titles, the preparation and filing of petitions for use in any court, or assisting by advice, counsel, or otherwise in any such legal work; and to advise or give opinion upon the legal rights of any person, firm or corporation. . . .[6]

Even in those states that do attempt to define the practice of law, determining what activities are actually prohibited remains a problem. For example, one component of the North Carolina definition of the phrase "practice law" is "performing any legal service for any other person, firm or corporation." The term "*any legal service*" is so broad that it fails to give any practical guidance in terms of what activities may or may not be performed. The statute does go on to list certain activities that are prohibited—but what about the thousands of other activities that might constitute "performing a legal service" yet are *not* listed? The statute also defines the phrase "to practice law" as "to advise or give opinion upon the legal rights of any person, firm or corporation. . . ." But what does it mean to give legal advice, and how do paralegals know when they are giving legal advice? The following section will address this and other activities that potentially constitute the practice of law.

Finally, another difficulty in defining the unauthorized practice of law is that tasks that are specifically prohibited in some states may be delegated in others. For example, legal assistants may not supervise will executions or represent clients at real estate closings in some jurisdictions but may in others.[7]

AVOIDING THE UNAUTHORIZED PRACTICE OF LAW

This section examines some activities that may constitute the unauthorized practice of law, such as giving legal advice or preparing legal documents without the supervision of an attorney. This section should help you avoid unwittingly engaging in the unauthorized practice of law.

Giving Legal Advice

> Model Guideline 3: A lawyer may not delegate to a legal assistant . . . [r]esponsibility for a legal opinion rendered to a client.

The Comment to Model Guideline 3 attempts to explain what it means to "give legal advice" in the following manner:

> Clients are entitled to their lawyers' professional judgment and opinion. Legal assistants may, however, be authorized to communicate legal advice so long as they do not interpret or expand on that advice. Typically, state guidelines phrase this prohibition in terms of legal assistants being forbidden from "giving legal advice" or "counseling clients about legal matters." . . . Some states have more expansive wording that prohibits legal assistants from engaging in any activity that would require the exercise of independent legal judgment. Nevertheless, it is clear that all states, as well as the Model Rules, encourage direct communication between clients and a legal assistant insofar as the legal assistant is performing a task properly delegated by a lawyer. . . .

In general, paralegals are allowed to explain rules of law to a client, but they are not allowed to explain to the client how those rules apply to the facts of the client's case. This general rule is rooted in EC 3-5 of the Model Code, which states:

> The essence of the professional judgment of a lawyer is his educated ability to relate the general body and philosophy of law to a specific legal problem

of a client; and thus, the public interest will be better served if only lawyers are permitted to act in matters involving professional judgment.

Consider the following example. Suppose your supervising attorney asks you to interview a client who has been injured in an automobile accident. The client wants to sue the driver of the other car involved in the collision. In order to help you learn the pertinent facts regarding the accident, it would be permissible for you to explain the rules of law regarding negligence. You would be allowed to explain to the client that in order to recover for negligence, it must be proved that the other driver breached a duty of due care, and that the breach of the duty of due care was the actual and proximate cause of the client's injuries. However, if the client asked you whether or not the conduct of the driver of the other car constituted negligence, you would *not* be allowed to give your opinion. Such a statement would be giving legal advice. You are not allowed to advise a client concerning how the law applies to the facts of the client's case.[8]

POINTER: When a client asks you for legal advice or for your legal opinion on a particular matter, you should inform the client that only the lawyer can give legal advice. After the lawyer gives you an opinion on the matter, you may relay the information to the client. You should make it clear, however, that the information you are relaying is the lawyer's opinion and not your own.

Misrepresentations to the Public

Model Guideline 4: It is the lawyer's responsibility to take reasonable measures to ensure that clients, courts, and other lawyers are aware that a legal assistant, whose services are utilized by the lawyer in performing legal services, is not licensed to practice law.

As a paralegal, you have an affirmative duty to clearly identify your nonlawyer status. Misrepresenting yourself as an attorney constitutes the unauthorized practice of law.

Your duty to identify yourself as a paralegal can arise in a number of different situations. In any telephone conversation, for example, you should identify your nonlawyer status at the beginning of the conversation to avoid any possible confusion. When sending letters or other written communications to clients and others, you must make your nonlawyer status clear. (For an example of how a paralegal should sign a letter, see Figure 11-1.)

Letterhead. Model Guideline 5 provides that "a lawyer may identify legal assistants by name and title on the lawyer's letterhead and on business cards identifying the lawyer's firm." The Comment to Guideline 5 states that "the listing must not be false or misleading and must make it clear that the support personnel who are listed are not lawyers."[9] Some states, however, do not permit attorneys to list legal assistants on their letterhead.[10]

FIGURE 11-1 HOW A PARALEGAL SHOULD SIGN A LETTER

Your interview with Mrs. Lewis has been scheduled for 9:00 a.m. on May 1. We look forward to seeing you then.

Sincerely,

Monica A. Olden
Paralegal

Business Cards. Nearly all states allow paralegals to have business cards, and ABA Informal Opinion 1527 (1989) reiterates previous opinions that approve of legal assistants having business cards.[11] The paralegal's nonlawyer status must be clearly indicated and the card must not be used in a misleading way.[12]

People v. Miller. One of the more interesting cases involving misrepresentation is *People v. Miller*.[13] Miller, a law school graduate who had not passed the bar examination, was working in a law office as a paralegal. He was asked to accompany a client to a deposition because the supervising attorney had a scheduling conflict. During the deposition, the client became so upset by the questioning that she started to cry. Miller asked the opposing counsel if he could ask the client a few questions for the record, but the opposing counsel objected to this request. Miller asked her several questions anyway for the purpose of calming her down.

The California Bar Association claimed that Miller was holding himself out to the public as a lawyer and charged him with nine counts of the unauthorized practice of law. Miller was acquitted on eight counts and convicted on one: asking questions at the deposition constituted the unauthorized practice of law.

Representing a Client in Court

As a general rule, only lawyers are allowed to represent clients in court.[14] Paralegals are not allowed to appear on behalf of a client even at a hearing on a simple motion to continue a trial or hearing until a later date. Although a person has a constitutional right of self-representation, this does not generally include the right to be represented by a nonlawyer.

However, many administrative agencies at both the federal and the state level do provide for nonlawyer representation. For federal agencies, the Administrative Procedure Act states: "A person compelled to appear in person before an agency or representative thereof is entitled to be accompanied, represented, and advised by counsel or, if permitted by the agency, by other qualified representative."[15] Some agencies, such as the National Labor Relations Board, allow anyone to represent a person before the agency. Other agencies, such as the U.S. Patent Office, have established certain qualifications that an individual must meet in order to represent a person before the agency. Some agencies have even established certification programs. For example, immigration regulations provide that nonattorneys can become certified representatives before the Board of Immigration Appeals.

Preparing Legal Documents

Preparing legal documents such as pleadings, discovery documents, and motions is one of the most important functions of a paralegal. However, the preparation of legal documents can lead to the unauthorized practice of law when an attorney does not supervise the preparation. As previously noted, provided the lawyer maintains responsibility for the work product and supervises the work, paralegals are permitted to perform virtually any task.[16] EC 3-6 of the Model Code provides:

> A lawyer often delegates tasks to clerks, secretaries, and other lay persons. Such delegation is proper if the lawyer maintains a direct relationship with his client, supervises the delegated work, and has complete professional responsibility for the work product.[17]

Whenever a paralegal prepares a legal document, the attorney should review the document and make any necessary changes. The attorney—not the paralegal—should sign the document.

Florida Bar v. Furman. The most celebrated case involving a nonlawyer's preparation of legal documents is *Florida Bar v. Furman*.[18] Here are the facts: Rosemary Furman was a former legal secretary who started a business selling do-it-yourself divorce kits. She would sometimes interview the client in order to learn the information needed to complete the petition for dissolution of marriage. She would also prepare and type the documents that she considered necessary to secure the divorce, advise the client where to file the documents, explain trial procedure, and instruct the client as to what questions should be asked at the trial. She charged no more than $50 for this service. Furman always informed her clients of her nonlawyer status, and it was not alleged that her clients suffered any harm as a result of the services she rendered. The Florida Bar believed that Furman was engaging in the unauthorized practice of law and sought an injunction to stop her unlawful activity.

In a previously decided case,[19] the Florida Supreme Court had specified that a business like Rosemary Furman's could lawfully sell and type legal documents, so long as the typing service was limited to copying information provided in writing by the client. The court had emphasized that nonlawyers could not advise clients as to the various legal remedies available to them, or otherwise assist them in preparing the forms necessary for a divorce. More specifically, nonlawyers could not answer questions about which forms might be necessary, how to fill out the forms, where to file the forms, or how to present evidence at the court hearing. These were precisely the activities in which Rosemary Furman was engaging. Therefore the court found her guilty of the unauthorized practice of law and enjoined her from engaging in this illegal activity in the future.

When Rosemary Furman continued her business, the Florida Bar again alleged that she was engaging in the unauthorized practice of law. The trial court agreed and found her in contempt of court. She was ordered to serve 30 days in jail. The governor later suspended her jail sentence when she agreed to close her business.

Improper Division of Fees

> Model Guideline 9: A lawyer may not split legal fees with a legal assistant nor pay a legal assistant for the referral of legal business. A lawyer may compensate a legal assistant based on the quantity and quality of the legal assistant's work and the value of that work to a law practice, but the legal assistant's compensation may not be contingent, by advance agreement, upon the profitability of the lawyer's practice.

Model Rule 5.4 and Disciplinary Rule 3-102 of the Model Code provide that a lawyer or law firm shall not share legal fees with a nonlawyer. The purpose of this rule is to protect the lawyer's professional independence of judgment. A paralegal who improperly shares a legal fee with a lawyer is engaging in the unauthorized practice of law.

For example, suppose your supervising attorney is representing a client in a personal injury case on a contingency fee basis. In an attempt to motivate you to work harder, the attorney tells you that she or he will share one-half of any fee received from the case with you. Such an arrangement is an improper division of fees. By sharing legal fees with you, a nonlawyer, the supervising attorney's professional independence of judgment may be compromised.

The prohibition against fee splitting does not preclude a lawyer from paying a bonus to a paralegal following a particularly profitable period.[20] Similarly, a lawyer engaged in a particularly profitable law practice may compensate the paralegal more handsomely than the compensation paid to paralegals who work in law practices that are less lucrative.[21]

Improper Business Relationship

Model Rule 5.4 and Disciplinary Rule 3-10 of the Model Code provide that a lawyer shall not form a partnership with a nonlawyer if any of the activities of the partnership consist of the practice of law. For example, suppose a paralegal, a lawyer, and others form a limited partnership for the purpose of investing in real estate. This is a proper business relationship provided the partnership does not engage in the practice of law. If the partnership, in addition to investing in real estate, gives legal advice to other real estate investors, then the partnership is an improper business relationship. The paralegal would be engaging in the unauthorized practice of law.

SHOULD PARALEGALS BE ALLOWED TO PROVIDE ROUTINE LEGAL SERVICES DIRECTLY TO THE PUBLIC?

The rules prohibiting nonlawyers from practicing law are intended to protect the public from individuals who might provide incompetent services. But are these rules truly in the public's best interest? When low-income and even moderate-income people cannot afford to pay for a lawyer, should they be able to obtain legal services from nonlawyers who charge a significantly reduced fee? Or does the potential harm outweigh the benefits? Presently these questions are being asked throughout the country, and the answers may fundamentally change the future of the paralegal profession. Typical of the current heated debate are the following arguments made by paralegals and attorneys at a recent forum on this issue.[22]

Deborah Chalfie, Legislative Director of HALT:

> Study after study shows there is a national crisis in access to legal services. Eighty percent of low-income people's legal needs go unmet, and even middle-income consumers cannot afford legal help. Traditional solutions such as increasing pro bono assistance or funding for legal aid programs can barely make a dent in meeting the poor's needs, let alone address the needs of those with moderate incomes. The fact is, we now have a two-tiered system of justice, with the vast majority of citizens shut out of our legal system.
>
> Despite the ban on unauthorized practice of law (UPL), more than 5,000 independent paralegals—2,000 in California—have sprung up to meet this need. Not only have they proven that they can offer high-quality legal help with many everyday legal matters, they do so at a fraction of what lawyers charge. Consumers could save more than $1.3 billion annually by using paralegals for just four routine tasks—divorce, wills, bankruptcies and business incorporations.
>
> So, what is the problem with legalizing paralegals? Opponents say the public would be duped by incompetent and unethical providers. Despite speculations about public harm, experience shows there is little evidence of it. In the nearly 20 years paralegals have been in business in California, complaints about them have been "almost nonexistent." A California Bar survey found 76% of *pro se* litigants who had used legal technicians were satisfied and would use one again; only 64% of those who had used lawyers were satisfied. Nationally, the same relative absence of consumer complaints is found: less than 2% of all UPL cases alleged consumer harm.
>
> Contrast these statistics with the 40,000 complaints made against California lawyers in 1989. Obviously, lawyers' monopoly offers no "public protection" guarantee; yet, no one suggests the existence of these complaints is a reason to outlaw lawyers. Blanket UPL prohibitions can and should be replaced by less restrictive, more effective means of protecting consumers—means that balance consumers' interests in affordable access and meaningful public protection.[23]

Johnnie L. Cochran, Jr., Lawyer:

> I do not believe that nonlawyers should be licensed to practice law . . . primarily because of public protection issues. The public is already besieged with licensed lawyers who take advantage of the unsuspecting client. Independent licensed paralegals would only add to this growing scenario.

In addition, the proposed fields of law identified for nonlawyers involve some very complex substantive and procedural issues. At best it is difficult for a licensed lawyer to keep abreast of the complexities involved in these and other areas of law. To allow nonlawyers who have less education, training and supervision than licensed lawyers to enter this arena would be more of a disadvantage than an advantage to the public. An alternative might include providing some incentives for licensed lawyers to practice law in the areas of bankruptcy, family law, landlord/tenant law, and immigration.[24]

Honorable Melinda J. Lasater, San Diego County Superior Court Judge:

There presently exists an unmet need for legal services in certain limited areas of the legal system, and there is a large, but undetermined, number of people attempting to meet this need by practicing law without a license. The members of our community who seek these services are vulnerable and in actual need of legal services to maintain basic necessities of life. Those members of our community who are providing those services may or may not be trained, may or may not be providing actually needed services, may or may not be taking unfair advantage of their "clients," and may or may not be financially solvent and responsible. The legal community has not developed any other practical approach for meeting this need, and we are unable to effectively stop this unauthorized practice of law.[25]

Janice M. Kamenir-Reznik, past president of California Women Lawyers:

The ostensible aim of the various proposals which have promoted the concept of permitting "legal technicians" to render legal services, is to increase the availability of low cost representation to the public. While this ostensible aim is noble, the permitting of legal technicians will not only be ineffective in achieving that goal, but will in fact worsen the consumer's position. By virtue of the elaborate Code of Professional Responsibility which governs the activities of lawyers, the methods and manners in which lawyers can solicit business as well as conduct business are heavily regulated. Whatever restrictions, if any, might be imposed upon legal technicians, their access to the public vis-a-vis the direct solicitation of business and advertising will be much broader than the access afforded to lawyers under the Code. Concomitantly, the public's remedies against errant technicians will be much more limited than the remedies available to the public against lawyers.

Additionally, the institution of a system of "legal technicians" would have a disproportionately negative impact on women and minority lawyers as well as women and minority clients who are generally less affluent.[26]

Virginia Simons, independent paralegal and owner of TLC Divorce Service:

Having been in business for ten years as an independent paralegal, I know there is a great need for non-lawyer services. Studies have shown there is a great need for affordable legal services and that there is "no great harm" being done to the consumer by non-lawyer independent paralegals. The average consumer making from $4.25 to $20.00 per hour just simply cannot pay $125.00 to $300.00 per hour for an attorney.

I believe that independent paralegals/legal technicians should be licensed or regulated in some manner that will give the consumer protection, and that we should have continuing educational requirements. However, under no circumstances do I feel that attorneys should have any control over our services. We have already proven over a period of twenty years that we are capable of providing services to the consumer in an efficient and effective manner. The only reason for not licensing and recognizing us is that the legal community does not want to give up their monopoly.[27]

THE FUTURE OF THE PARALEGAL PROFESSION

The years ahead promise to be an exciting period of growth and expansion for the paralegal profession. Growth will most likely occur not only in the numbers of people entering the profession, but also in the activities that paralegals may legally and ethically perform. Because of the need to make the legal system more accessible to the average citizen, will paralegals soon be allowed to offer basic legal services directly to the public? If so, will paralegals be required to have a license? Will minimum educational standards be imposed? The answers to these and similar questions could radically change the future of the profession.

ENDNOTES

1 Model Rule 5.5. Copyrighted by the American Bar Association. All rights reserved. Reprinted with permission.

2 Deborah L. Rhode, The Delivery of Legal Services by Non-Lawyers, 4 *Georgetown Journal of Legal Ethics* (1990), pp. 209, 211; see also Deborah L. Rhode, Policing the Professional Monopoly: A Constitutional and Empirical Analysis of Unauthorized Practice Prohibition, 34 *Stan. L. Rev.* 1 (1981), p. 45, n. 134.

3 EC 3-1. Copyrighted by the American Bar Association. All rights reserved. Reprinted with permission.

4 Comment to ABA Model Rule 5.5.

5 EC 3-5. Copyrighted by the American Bar Association. All rights reserved. Reprinted with permission.

6 N.C. Gen. Stat. 84-2.1 (1988).

7 Comment to Model Guideline 2.

8 For an additional example of what constitutes giving legal advice, see Elizabeth C. Richardson and Milton C. Regan, *Civil Litigation for Paralegals* (Cincinnati: South-Western, 1992), p. 34.

9 Comment to Model Guideline 5; ABA Informal Opinion 1527 (1989).

10 See Comments to Model Guideline 5.

11 Comments to Model Guideline 5.

12 Comments to Model Guideline 5.

13 Bakersfield Municipal Court No. 238481; this case was never reported.

14 Local rules may permit nonlawyers to make court appearances in limited circumstances.

15 5 U.S.C.A. 555 (b) (1977).

16 Model Guideline 2.

17 EC 3-6. Copyrighted by the American Bar Association. All rights reserved. Reprinted with permission.

18 376 So. 2d 378 (Fla. 1979).

19 *Florida Bar v. Brumbaugh*, 355 So. 2d 1186 (Fla. 1978).

20 Comments to Model Guideline 9.

21 Comments to Model Guideline 9.

22 All of the statements presented here are from the handout entitled ''Biography and Statement of Panelists'' at the State Bar of California Annual Meeting, Legal Technician Forum, Sept. 14, 1991. Copyright © 1991, State Bar of California. Reprinted with permission.

23 Reprinted with permission of Deborah Chalfie.

24 Reprinted with permission of Johnnie L. Cochran, Jr.

25 Reprinted with permission of the Honorable Melinda J. Lasater.

26 Reprinted with permission of Janice M. Kamenir-Reznik.

27 Reprinted with permission of Virginia Simons.

APPENDIX

Appendix A Sample Appellate Brief

STATEMENT OF FACTS

This is an appeal by cross-complainant Lemon Motors, Inc. (''Lemon''), from an order denying recovery of attorneys' fees incurred by Lemon in conjunction with its execution of a judgment against cross-defendant Tim Duncan (''Duncan''). As part of the judgment, Lemon had been awarded its actual attorney's fees incurred through the end of trial,as well as estimated fees to be incurred after trial. Fees were awarded on the basis of a federal statute. Lemon subsequently brought a post-judgment motion to recover additional fees actually incurred by it in connection with enforcement of the judgment, which motion was denied on the grounds that there was no statutory authority for such an award. The question to be decided on this appeal, then, is a question of law: does the federal statute that provided authority for an award of attorneys' fees as part of the judgment also authorize an award of attorneys' fees incurred in conjunction with post-judgment enforcement proceedings?

This action originated with the filing of a complaint by plaintiffs John and Mary Smith (''the Smiths'') against Lemon and Duncan in February 1993. The complaint involved the purchase of a used automobile by the Smiths from Lemon, an automobile dealership. Lemon had obtained the used automobile from Duncan as a trade-in on a new automobile Duncan purchased from Lemon. Although the used automobile's odometer reading at the time of its purchase by the Smiths indicated that it had been driven only 1,956 miles, the Smiths subsequently concluded on the basis of service records maintained by the manufacturer and repair facilities that the car had in fact been driven in excess of 30,000 miles prior to its purchase by them. The Smiths accordingly sued Lemon for breach of contract and negligence and sued Duncan for fraud. Lemon in turn filed a cross-complaint against Duncan for indemnity, breach of contract, and fraud. Both the Smiths' complaint (paragraph 25) and Lemon's cross-complaint (paragraph 20) contained causes of action based on 15 U.S.C. Section 1989, a section of the Motor Vehicle Information and Cost Savings Act that creates a statutory cause of action against persons who fail to disclose a motor vehicle's mileage accurately on transfer of ownership. The statute also provides for recovery of attorneys' fees and costs incurred by a party who successfully prosecutes an action based on Section 1989.

After a court trial in July 1993, a judgment was entered on July 29, 1993. The judgment awarded the Smiths actual damages of $1,500, plus $11,000 in costs and attorneys' fees. Duncan and Lemon were made jointly and severally liable for this portion of the judgment. The Smiths were also awarded an additional $3,000 in exemplary damages against Duncan alone. The court further ruled that Duncan be required to indemnify Lemon for any amount that Lemon might pay to the Smiths by reason of the joint and several portion of the judgment. Lemon was also awarded $9,500 in attorneys' fees and $150 in costs from Duncan. Of the $9,500 in attorneys' fees awarded to Lemon, $8,000 represented fees actually incurred through the end of trial and $1,500 represented estimated fees to be incurred after trial. See Declaration of Mark Samuel, in Support of Award of Attorneys' Fees, filed July 28, 1993.

Following the trial, Lemon incurred attorneys' fees in the sum of $3,983 in connection with preparation of the cost bill and the declaration regarding attorneys' fees; correction of the written judgment; preparation and recordation of abstracts of judgment; documentation of Lemon's payment of the joint and several portion of the judgment to the Smiths; preparation of writs of execution and supporting documents; coordination of an asset search; preparation and service of an earnings withholding order; noticing, compelling an appearance at, rescheduling, and conducting a judgment debtor examination; coordinating levy on a stock broker account; and preparing a motion for recovery of post-judgment costs and attorneys' fees. See Declaration of Mark Samuel (paragraph 6) filed as part of the Application for Reconsideration of Order Denying in Part Motion for Costs of Enforcing Judgment, filed November 4, 1993.

On October 8, 1993, Lemon filed a motion seeking an order awarding costs incurred in enforcing its judgment pursuant to Code of Civil Procedure Section 685.080. A hearing on the motion was held on October 22, 1993. Lemon's request for recovery of miscellaneous costs on the basis of Code Civ. Proc. Section 685.080 was granted, but Lemon's request for recovery of $3,983 in attorneys' fees on the basis of 15 U.S.C. Section 1989(a)(2) was denied. See Minute Order filed October 22, 1993, and Order Allowing Judgment Creditor's Costs of Enforcing Judgment filed October 29, 1993. At the hearing, the court indicated that it was reluctant to grant the requested attorneys' fees due to confusion with respect to whether or not a credit had been given for the $1,500 in unincurred fees which had been awarded as part of the original judgment. The court also raised a question as to the availability of California authority supporting an award of attorneys' fees incurred after judgment. See Declaration of Mark Samuel (paragraph 3) filed as part of the Application for Reconsideration of Order Denying in Part Motion for Costs of Enforcing Judgment, filed November 4, 1993.

On November 4, 1993, Lemon filed an application for reconsideration of the portion of the October 22 order that denied recovery of attorneys' fees. The application included a declaration of counsel explaining that due to inadvertence the request for $3,983 in fees had not reflected a credit for the $1,500 in unincurred fees that had been awarded as part of the original judgment. See Declaration of Mark Samuel, paragraphs 4 and 5. The application also contained a memorandum of points and authorities citing California authorities supporting an award of fees. The application requested that fees in the amount of $2,483 be awarded.

At a hearing on the application for reconsideration conducted on November 21, 1993, the court refused to award the requested fees because it was not convinced that 15 U.S.C. Section 1989(a)(2) provided sufficient statutory authority for an award of fees, as required by Code Civ. Proc. Section 685.040. This basis for the court's ruling is specifically stated in the Minute Order filed on November 25, 1993.

SUMMARY OF ARGUMENT

Code Civ. Proc. Section 685.040 provides that attorneys' fees incurred in connection with enforcement of a judgment are recoverable if so provided by law. 15 U.S.C. Section 1989(a) provides that any person who violates the mileage disclosure requirements of 15 U.S.C. Section 1988 shall be liable for certain damages, as well as costs and reasonable attorneys' fees ''in the case of any successful action to enforce'' the liability imposed by Section 1989(a).

Federal courts interpreting Section 1989(a) have concluded that its provision for attorneys' fees reflects Congress's intent that attorneys be adequately compensated for their roles in cases involving claims based on Section 1989(a). Federal courts have awarded fees in connection with various post-trial proceedings on the basis of Section 1989(a). Although there are no reported cases involving the interpretation of Section 1989(a) by state or federal courts in California, California courts have, on several occasions, awarded fees incurred in conjunction with various post-trial activities designed to give effect to judgments. In view of these authorities, it is readily apparent that 15 U.S.C. Section 1989(a) provides sufficient authority for an award of attorneys' fees incurred in connection with enforcement of a judgment, as required by Code Civ. Proc. Section 685.040.

ARGUMENT

I. Attorneys' fees incurred in conjunction with enforcement of a judgment are recoverable if so provided by statute.

Code Civ. Proc. Section 685.040 provides:

> The judgment creditor is entitled to the reasonable and necessary costs of enforcing a judgment. Attorneys' fees incurred in enforcing a judgment are not included in costs collectible under this title unless otherwise provided by law.

This statute clearly authorizes an award of fees if so provided by statute. As the following discussion will demonstrate, in the present case such an award is authorized by 15 U.S.C. Section 1989(a)(2).

II. Federal statutory law authorizes recovery of attorneys' fees in conjunction with enforcement of the judgment in this case.

(a) Recovery of attorneys' fees is authorized by 15 U.S.C. Section 1989(a)(2).

15 U.S.C. Section 1989 provides:

> (a) Any person who, with intent to defraud, violates any requirement imposed under this subchapter shall be liable in an amount equal to the sum of -
>
> (1) three times the amount of actual damages sustained or $1,500, whichever is the greater; and
>
> (2) in the case of any successful action to enforce the foregoing liability, the costs of the action together with reasonable attorney fees as determined by the court.
>
> (b) An action to enforce any liability created under subsection (a) of this section, may be brought in a United States district court without regard to the amount in controversy, or in any other

court of competent jurisdiction, within two years from the date on which the liability arises.

At trial, Lemon was awarded damages on the basis of Duncan's violation of 15 U.S.C. Section 1988(b), which prohibits the transferor of an automobile from giving a false statement concerning the automobile's mileage to a transferee of the automobile. 15 U.S.C. Section 1989(a) provides that a person who violates Section 1988(b) is liable for, among other things, costs and reasonable attorneys' fees incurred in a successful action to enforce such person's liability for damages resulting from the violation. At trial, Lemon was awarded all of its attorneys' fees incurred up to the time of trial, plus estimated post-trial attorneys' fees, on the basis of this provision.

(b) In enacting 15 U.S.C. Section 1989(a)(2), Congress intended to ensure that attorneys be compensated adequately for their roles in aiding in enforcement of the Motor Vehicle Information and Cost Savings Act.

By creating a special statutory cause of action for victims of violations of the Motor Vehicle Information and Cost Savings Act (the ''Act''), Congress intended to deter would-be violators and to punish actual violators of the Act. Permitting an award of attorneys' fees further strengthens these goals of deterrence and punishment. See 15 U.S.C. Section 1981; Gimarc v. Neal, 417 F. Supp. 129, 131 n.4 (D.S.C. 1976). Beyond deterrence and punishment, however, it was Congress's goal by providing for an award of fees to ensure that attorneys would be adequately compensated, and therefore sufficiently motivated, to take cases involving violations of the Act. As the district court observed in Gimarc, supra:

> If this court sets a precedent awarding attorneys' fees in such a niggardly fashion as to discourage from handling this type of litigation the kind of lawyers we want in federal court, then we will have aborted the purpose of the Congress in passing the legislation. (417 F. Supp. at 131)

This understanding of Congress's intent is echoed in Kirkland v. Cooper, 438 F. Supp. 808, 812 (D.S.C. 1977) and Chapotel v. Bailey Lincoln-Mercury, Inc., 363 So. 2d 451, 454 n.8 (La. 1978).

The statute's language is broad. Attorneys' fees are to be awarded ''in the case of any successful action to enforce the foregoing liability.'' 15 U.S.C. Section 1989(a)(1) (emphasis added). The statute's intent in awarding fees is broad as well: deterrence and punishment of violations, and encouragement of attorney involvement in actions to enforce the Act. An award of fees incurred in conjunction with enforcement of a judgment rendered under the Act, then, is consistent with both the language and the intent of the statute.

(c) The federal courts have interpreted 15 U.S.C. Section 1989(a)(2) as authorizing an award of attorney fees incurred in conjunction with post-judgment activities.

In at least two reported cases, fees incurred for post-judgment activities have been awarded by federal courts on the basis of Section 1989(a)(2). In Gonzales v. Van's Chevrolet, Inc., 498 F. Supp. 1102, 1106 (D. Del. 1980), an award of fees incurred in preparing a petition for recovery of costs and attorneys' fees was based on Section 1989(a)(2). In Fleet Inv. Co. v. Rogers, 505 F. Supp. 522, 524 (D. Okl. 1980), Section 1989(a)(2) was interpreted to authorize an award of attorneys' fees incurred in defending an appeal of a judgment. Fees incurred in enforcing a judgment, like fees incurred in defending a judgment on appeal, are a necessary part of giving effect to that judgment. Accordingly, an award of fees incurred in enforcing the present judgment is both authorized and appropriate.

III. An award of attorneys' fees incurred in conjunction with enforcement of the judgment in this case is consistent with principles of California law.

Although there are no reported California cases interpreting Section 1989(a)(2), the same rationale applied by the federal courts in Fleet Investment Company and Gonzales, supra, has been applied in cases interpreting California statutes authorizing an award of attorneys' fees. For example, in Painter v. Estate of Painter, 78 Cal. 625 (1889), a California court affirmed a post-judgment award of attorneys' fees incurred in defending an appeal on the basis of a statute providing that a claimant who fails to recover must pay ''all costs, including defendant's reasonable attorneys' fees.'' (Former Code Civ. Proc. Section 1510, now Prob. Code Section 703.)

In Painter an attorney was appointed by the superior court to defend a claim against an estate. He succeeded in the trial and was awarded a $250 fee. He also successfully defended the judgment on appeal and was awarded an additional $1,000 for those services. The court reasoned that ''[i]t was not positively ascertained that the claimant did recover 'no judgment' until the appellate court acted on his appeal.'' 78 Cal. at 627. And, ''[t]he estate stood as much in need of an attorney in the appellate as in the lower court.'' Id. This same reasoning is applicable in the present case: Lemon stood as much in need of an attorney to enforce its judgment against Duncan as it did at trial when it obtained the judgment. Thus fees incurred for services rendered to enforce the judgment should be recoverable in addition to those fees incurred in an effort to obtain the judgment.

Serrano v. Unruh, 32 Cal. 3d 621 (1982), involved the question of whether a statutorily authorized fee award under the private attorney general doctrine (Code Civ. Proc. Section 1021.5) should include compensation to counsel for its efforts to secure its fee for the litigation. The Supreme Court affirmed the trial court's award of fees for services rendered in defending the fee award on appeal and remanded for reconsideration that portion of the trial court's order that denied compensation for preparing motions related to fees. Relying on federal precedent, the court held that ''absent circumstances rendering an award unjust, the fee should ordinarily include compensation for all hours reasonably spent, including those relating solely to the fee.'' 32 Cal. 3d at 624. In Serrano, then, the Supreme Court recognized that statutory authority for an award of fees can go beyond authorization for fees incurred in obtaining the judgment itself, to include authorization for fees incurred in connection with other matters related to the litigation, such as confirmation of a fee award. This is wholly consistent with appellant's contention that 15 U.S.C. Section 1989(a)(2) authorizes not only an award of fees incurred in obtaining a judgment, but also an award of fees incurred in connection with enforcing it.

CONCLUSION

For the foregoing reasons, appellant Lemon Motors, Inc., respectfully requests that this court reverse the lower court's order of November 25, 1993, and that the sum of $2,483 be awarded to appellant, along with the costs and attorneys' fees incurred by appellant in connection with this appeal.

Respectfully submitted,
SAMUEL & JOSEPH

By: ______________________________
Mark Samuel
Attorney for Defendant,
Cross Complainant, and
Appellant Lemon Motors, Inc.

Appendix B Cross-Complaint

Mark Samuel
SAMUEL & JOSEPH
37 Sea Coast Highway
Seaside, CA 90277-2143
(310) 990-1234

Attorneys for Defendant and Cross-Complainant Lemon Motors, Inc.

__________ COURT FOR THE __________ JUDICIAL DISTRICT
COUNTY OF __________, STATE OF __________

JOHN SMITH and MARY SMITH, Plaintiffs, v. LEMON MOTORS, INC., a California Corporation; TIMOTHY A. DUNCAN; and DOES 1 through 10, inclusive, Defendants.	CASE NO. 123456 CROSS-COMPLAINT BY DEFENDANT LEMON MOTORS AGAINST CROSS-DEFENDANTS TIMOTHY A. DUNCAN AND DOES 1 THROUGH 10, INCLUSIVE, FOR: INDEMNITY; BREACH OF CONTRACT; FRAUD
LEMON MOTORS, INC., a California Corporation, Cross-Complainant, v. TIMOTHY A. DUNCAN; and DOES 1 through 10, inclusive, Cross-Defendants.	

FIRST CAUSE OF ACTION
(Implied Indemnity Against All Cross-Defendants)

1. Cross-complainant is, and at all times herein mentioned was, a California corporation engaged in the business of selling new and used automobiles at 1984 Coastline Ave., Seaside, California.

2. Cross-complainant is informed and believes and based on such information and belief alleges that cross-defendant Tim Duncan (hereinafter ''Duncan'') is a resident at 4123 Del Mar Ave., Seaside, which is within the __________ Judicial District.

3. Cross-complainant is ignorant of the true names and capacities of cross-defendants sued herein as Does 1 through 10, inclusive and therefore sues these defendants by such fictitious names. Cross-complainant will amend this complaint to allege their true names and capacities when ascertained.

4. On or about August 10, 1992, cross-complainant Lemon Motors, Inc. (hereinafter ''Lemon'') and defendant and cross-defendant Tim Duncan (''Duncan'') entered into the sales agreement wherein Duncan agreed to sell Lemon a certain 1991 Allied Motors CS10, vehicle identification number ABCDE1234A1234567, (hereinafter the ''automobile''), which he represented had a total mileage of 1,930 miles. In return, cross-complainant Lemon agreed to provide Duncan with a credit in the sum of $15,000 toward the purchase of another automobile. A copy of this contract is attached as Exhibit ''A'' and incorporated herein.

5. On or about August 10, 1992, cross-defendant Duncan in connection with the sale of the automobile delivered to cross-complainant Lemon a document entitled ''Notice of Sale or Transfer of a Vehicle and Odometer Mileage Statement.'' Duncan affirmed therein that the automobile's odometer reading was 1,930 miles as represented in the notice. A copy of this notice is attached as Exhibit ''B'' and incorporated herein.

6. Cross-defendant failed to deliver an automobile with 1,930 miles as warranted. Lemon is informed and believes that the automobile had approximately 30,000 miles at the time of its sale to Lemon. Lemon subsequently sold the automobile to John and Mary Smith, plaintiffs in the original action.

7. On or about February 10, 1993, the Smiths brought an action against Lemon herein in __________ Court, __________ Judicial District, __________ County, ________________, Action No. 123456, to recover damages for cross-complainant's alleged breach of contract and negligence arising out of the sale of the automobile.

8. If cross-complainant is found liable to the Smiths in the original action in connection with the sale of the automobile, the cross-complainant is entitled to indemnity by the cross-defendant for any and all loss it may sustain in this matter, including all costs, attorneys' fees, or judgments, that might be entered against it, in that the Smiths' damages, if any, have been proximately caused by the actions of the cross-defendant in falsely representing that the automobile had only 1,930 miles on it at the time of its sale to Lemon.

SECOND CAUSE OF ACTION

(Breach of Contract Against Cross-Defendant Duncan)

9. Cross-complainant hereby incorporates by reference the allegations set forth in paragraphs 1 through 8 above.

10. On or about August 10, 1992, cross-complainant and cross-defendant entered into the sales agreement for the purchase by Lemon of the automobile with mileage of 1,930 miles.

11. Cross-defendant breached said contract by failing to deliver to cross-complainant the automobile with only 1,930 miles. Cross-complainant is informed and believes that the automobile had approximately 30,000 miles instead of the 1,930 miles it bargained for.

12. As a proximate result of Duncan's breach of the sales agreement, cross-complainant has suffered damage in a sum not yet ascertained. Cross-complainant will amend this complaint to state the true amount thereof when ascertained.

13. The sales agreement provides that the prevailing party shall be entitled to recover reasonable attorney's fees for any action brought to enforce the terms of the sales agreement.

14. As a proximate result of Duncan's breach of the contract contained in the sales agreement, cross-complainant has been required to retain the legal services of Samuel & Joseph and has incurred and will continue to incur attorneys' fees. Cross-complainant is therefore entitled to recover its reasonable attorneys' fees and costs.

THIRD CAUSE OF ACTION

(Fraud as Provided in 15 U.S.C.A. § 1989 Against All Cross-Defendants)

15. Cross-complainant hereby incorporates by reference the allegations set forth in paragraphs 1 through 14 above.

16. On or about August 10, 1992, with intent to deceive, cross-defendant entered into a contract with cross-complainant for the purchase by cross-complainant of the automobile with a total of 1,930 miles. Cross-defendant represented that only such mileage was then outstanding on the vehicle when in fact he knew such statement was false. Cross-defendant's misrepresentations were made with an intent to defraud cross-complainant.

17. Cross-defendant's misrepresentation violated 15 U.S.C.A. § 1988, which requires the accurate disclosure of a motor vehicle's mileage upon the transfer of ownership.

18. 15 U.S.C.A. § 1989 provides that any person who with intent to defraud violates odometer disclosure provisions such as § 1988 shall be liable in an amount of three times the amount of actual damages sustained or $1,500, whichever is the greater.

19. As a proximate result of cross-defendant's violation of 15 U.S.C.A. § 1988, cross-complainant has suffered actual damages in a sum not yet ascertained. Cross-complainant will amend this complaint to state the true amount when ascertained.

20. 15 U.S.C.A. § 1989(a)(2) provides that in the event a party is successful in enforcing liability under the odometer tampering provisions, such a party is entitled to recover reasonable attorneys' fees as determined by the court.

21. As a proximate result of cross-defendant Duncan's violation of 15 U.S.C.A. § 1988, cross-complainant has been required to retain the legal services of Samuel & Joseph and has incurred, and will continue to incur, attorneys' fees. Cross-complainant is therefore entitled to recover its reasonable attorneys' fees and costs.

Wherefore, cross-complainant prays for judgment against cross-defendants as follows:

ON THE FIRST CAUSE OF ACTION

1. For damages in the amount of any judgment obtained by plaintiff Smiths against the cross-complainant, including any costs or attorneys' fees awarded thereunder.

ON THE SECOND CAUSE OF ACTION

2. For general damages according to proof.

3. For reasonable attorneys' fees and costs.

ON THE THIRD CAUSE OF ACTION

4. For $1,500 or three times the actual damages according to proof, whichever is the greater, plus any costs and reasonable attorneys' fees incurred herein.

ON ALL OF THE CAUSES OF ACTION

5. For such other and further relief as the court may deem proper.

DATED: ______________________

SAMUEL & JOSEPH

By: ______________________

Mark Samuel
Attorney for Defendant and
Cross-Complainant Lemon
Motors, Inc.

Appendix C ABA Model Guidelines for the Utilization of Legal Assistant Services

Preamble

State courts, bar associations, or bar committees in at least seventeen states have prepared recommendations[1] for the utilization of legal assistant services.[2] While their content varies, their purpose appears uniform: to provide lawyers with a reliable basis for delegating responsibility for performing a portion of the lawyer's tasks to legal assistants. The purpose of preparing model guidelines is not to contradict the guidelines already adopted or to suggest that other guidelines may be more appropriate in a particular jurisdiction. It is the view of the Standing Committee on Legal Assistants of the American Bar Association, however, that a model set of guidelines for the utilization of legal assistant services may assist many states in adopting or revising such guidelines. The Standing Committee is of the view that guidelines will encourage lawyers to utilize legal assistant services effectively and promote the growth of the legal assistant profession.[3] In undertaking this project, the Standing Committee has attempted to state guidelines that conform with the American Bar Association's Model Rules of Professional Conduct, decided authority, and contemporary practice. Lawyers, of course, are to be first directed by Rule 5.3 of the Model Rules in the utilization of legal assistant services, and nothing contained in these guidelines is intended to be inconsistent with that rule. Specific ethical considerations in particular states, however, may require modification of these guidelines before their adoption. In the commentary after each guideline, we have attempted to identify the basis for the guideline and any issues of which we are aware that the guideline may present; those drafting such guidelines may wish to take them into account.

Guideline 1: A lawyer is responsible for all of the professional actions of a legal assistant performing legal assistant services at the lawyer's direction and should take reasonable measures to ensure that the legal assistant's conduct is consistent with the lawyer's obligations under the ABA Model Rules of Professional Conduct.

1. An appendix identifies the guidelines, court rules, and recommendations that were reviewed in drafting these Model Guidelines.
2. On February 6, 1986, the ABA Board of Governors approved the following definition of the term "legal assistant":

   A legal assistant is a person, qualified through education, training, or work experience, who is employed or retained by a lawyer, law office, governmental agency, or other entity in a capacity or function which involves the performance, under the ultimate direction and supervision of an attorney, of specifically delegated substantive legal work, which work, for the most part, requires a sufficient knowledge of legal concepts that, absent such assistant, the attorney would perform the task.

   In some contexts, the term "paralegal" is used interchangeably with the term legal assistant.
3. While necessarily mentioning legal assistant conduct, lawyers are the intended audience of these Guidelines. The Guidelines, therefore, are addressed to lawyer conduct and not directly to the conduct of the legal assistant. Both the National Association of Legal Assistants (NALA) and the National Federation of Paralegal Associations (NFPA) have adopted guidelines of conduct that are directed to legal assistants. See NALA, "Code of Ethics and Professional Responsibility of the National Association of Legal Assistants, Inc." (adopted May 1975, revised November 1979 and September 1988); NFPA, "Affirmation of Responsibility" (adopted 1977, revised 1981).

Comment to Guideline 1: An attorney who utilizes a legal assistant's services is responsible for determining that the legal assistant is competent to perform the tasks assigned, based on the legal assistant's education, training, and experience, and for ensuring that the legal assistant is familiar with the responsibilities of attorneys and legal assistants under the applicable rules governing professional conduct.[4]

Under principles of agency law and rules governing the conduct of attorneys, lawyers are responsible for the actions and the work product of the non-lawyers they employ. Rule 5.3 of the Model Rules[5] requires that partners and supervising attorneys ensure that the conduct of non-lawyer assistants is compatible with the lawyer's professional obligations. Several state guidelines have adopted this language. E.g., Commentary to Illinois Recommendation (A), Kansas Guideline III(a), New Hampshire Rule 35, Sub-Rule 9, and North Carolina Guideline 4. Ethical Consideration 3-6 of the Model Code encouraged lawyers to delegate tasks to legal assistants provided the lawyer maintained a direct relationship with the client, supervised appropriately, and had complete responsibility for the work product. The adoption of Rule 5.3, which incorporates these principles, implicitly reaffirms this encouragement.

Several states have addressed the issue of the lawyer's ultimate responsibility for work performed by subordinates. For example, Colorado Guideline 1.c, Kentucky Supreme Court Rule 3.700, Sub-Rule 2.C, and Michigan Guideline I provide: "The lawyer remains responsible for the actions of the legal assistant to the same extent as if such representation had been furnished entirely by the lawyer and such actions were those of the lawyer." New Mexico Guideline X states "[the] lawyer maintains ultimate responsibility for and has an ongoing duty to actively supervise the legal assistant's work performance, conduct and product." Connecticut Recommendation 2 and Rhode Island Guideline III state specifically that lawyers are liable for malpractice for the mistakes and omissions of their legal assistants.

Finally, the lawyer should ensure that legal assistants supervised by the lawyer are familiar with the rules governing attorney conduct and that they follow those rules. See Comment to Model Rule 5.3; Illinois Recommendation (A)(5), New Hampshire Supreme Court Rule 35, Sub-Rule 9, and New Mexico, Statement of Purpose; see also NALA's Model Standards and Guidelines for the Utilization of Legal Assistants, guidelines IV, V, and VIII (1985, revised 1990) (hereafter "NALA Guidelines").

The Standing Committee and several of those who have commented upon these Guidelines regard Guideline 1 as a comprehensive statement of general principle governing lawyers who utilize legal

4. Attorneys, of course, are not liable for violations of the ABA Model Rules of Professional Conduct ("Model Rules") unless the Model Rules have been adopted as the code of professional conduct in a jurisdiction in which the lawyer practices. They are referenced in this model guideline for illustrative purposes; if the guideline is to be adopted, the reference should be modified to the jurisdiction's rules of professional conduct.

5. The Model Rules were first adopted by the ABA House of Delegates in August of 1983. Since that time many states have adopted the Model Rules to govern the professional conduct of lawyers licensed in those states. Since a number of states still utilize a version of the Model Code of Professional Responsibility ("Model Code"), which was adopted by the House of Delegates in August of 1969, however, these comments will refer to both the Model Rules and the predecessor Model Code (and to the Ethical Considerations and Disciplinary Rules found under the canons in the Model Code).

assistant services in the practice of law. As such it, in effect, is a part of each of the remaining Guidelines.

Guideline 2: Provided the lawyer maintains responsibility for the work product, a lawyer may delegate to a legal assistant any task normally performed by the lawyer except those tasks proscribed to one not licensed as a lawyer by statute, court rule, administrative rule or regulation, controlling authority, the ABA Model Rules of Professional Conduct, or these Guidelines.

Comment to Guideline 2: The essence of the definition of the term legal assistant adopted by the ABA Board of Governors in 1986 is that, so long as appropriate supervision is maintained, many tasks normally performed by lawyers may be delegated to legal assistants. Of course, Rule 5.5 of the Model Rules, DR 3-101 of the Model Code, and most states specifically prohibit lawyers from assisting or aiding a non-lawyer in the unauthorized practice of law. Thus, while appropriate delegation of tasks to legal assistants is encouraged, the lawyer may not permit the legal assistant to engage in the "practice of law." Neither the Model Rules nor the Model Code define the "practice of law." EC 3-5 under the Model Code gave some guidance by equating the practice of law to the application of the professional judgment of the lawyer in solving clients' legal problems. Further, ABA Opinion 316 (1967) states: "A lawyer can employ lay secretaries, lay investigators, lay detectives, lay researchers, accountants, lay scriveners, nonlawyer draftsmen or nonlawyer researchers. In fact, he may employ nonlawyers to do any task for him except counsel clients about law matters, engage directly in the practice of law, appear in court or appear in formal proceedings as part of the judicial process, so long as it is he who takes the work and vouches for it to the client and becomes responsible for it to the client."

Most state guidelines specify that legal assistants may not appear before courts, administrative tribunals, or other adjudicatory bodies unless their rules authorize such appearances; may not conduct depositions; and may not give legal advice to clients. E.g., Connecticut Recommendation 4; Fla. EC 3-6 (327 So. 2d at 16); and Michigan Guideline II. Also see NALA Guidelines IV and VI. But it is also important to note that, as some guidelines have recognized, pursuant to federal or state statute legal assistants are permitted to provide direct client representation in certain administrative proceedings. E.g., South Carolina Guideline II. While this does not obviate the attorney's responsibility for the legal assistant's work, it does change the nature of the attorney supervision of the legal assistant. The opportunity to use such legal assistant services has particular benefits to legal services programs and does not violate Guideline 2. See generally ABA Standards for Providers of Civil Legal Services to the Poor, Std. 6.3, at 6.17-6.18 (1986).

The Model Rules emphasize the importance of appropriate delegation. The key to appropriate delegation is proper supervision, which includes adequate instruction when assigning projects, monitoring of the project, and review of the completed project. The Supreme Court of Virginia upheld a malpractice verdict against a lawyer based in part on negligent actions of a legal assistant in performing tasks that evidently were properly delegable. Musselman v. Willoughby Corp.,

230 Va. 337, 337 S.E.2d 724 (1985). See also C. Wolfram, Modern Legal Ethics (1986), at 236, 896. All state guidelines refer to the requirement that the lawyer "supervise" legal assistants in the performance of their duties. Lawyers should also take care in hiring and choosing a legal assistant to work on a specific project to ensure that the legal assistant has the education, knowledge, and ability necessary to perform the delegated tasks competently. See Connecticut Recommendation 14, Kansas Standards I, II, and III, and New Mexico Guideline VIII. Finally, some states describe appropriate delegation and review in terms of the delegated work losing its identity and becoming "merged" into the work product of the attorney. See Florida EC 3-6 (327 So. 2d at 16).

Legal assistants often play an important role in improving communication between the attorney and the client. EC 3-6 under the Model Code mentioned three specific kinds of tasks that legal assistants may perform under appropriate lawyer supervision: factual investigation and research, legal research, and the preparation of legal documents. Some states delineate more specific tasks in their guidelines, such as attending client conferences, corresponding with and obtaining information from clients, handling witness execution of documents, preparing transmittal letters, maintaining estate/guardianship trust accounts, etc. See, e.g., Colorado (lists of specialized functions in several areas follow guidelines); Michigan, Comment to Definition of Legal Assistant; New York, Specialized Skills of Legal Assistants; Rhode Island Guideline II; and NALA Guideline IX. The two-volume Working with Legal Assistants, published by the Standing Committee in 1982, attempted to provide a general description of the types of tasks that may be delegated to legal assistants in various practice areas.

There are tasks that have been specifically prohibited in some states, but that may be delegated in others. For example, legal assistants may not supervise will executions or represent clients at real estate closings in some jursidictions, but may in others. Compare Connecticut Recommendation 7 and Illinois State Bar Association Position Paper on Use of Attorney Assistants in Real Estate Transactions (May 16, 1984), which proscribe legal assistants conducting real estate closings, with Georgia "real estate job description," Florida Professional Ethics Committee Advisory Opinion 89-5 (1989), and Missouri, Comment to Guideline I, which permit legal assistants to conduct real estate closings. Also compare Connecticut Recommendation 8 (prohibiting attorneys from authorizing legal assistants to supervise will executions) with Colorado "estate planning job description," Georgia "estate, trusts, and wills job description," Missouri, Comment to Guideline I, and Rhode Island Guideline II (suggesting that legal assistants may supervise the execution of wills, trusts, and other documents).

Guideline 3: A lawyer may not delegate to a legal assistant:

(a) Responsibility for establishing an attorney-client relationship.

(b) Responsibility for establishing the amount of a fee to be charged for a legal service.

(c) Responsibility for a legal opinion rendered to a client.

Comment to Guideline 3: The Model Rules and most state codes require that lawyers communicate with their clients in order for clients to make well-informed decisions about their representation and resolution of legal issues. Model Rule 1.4. Ethical Consideration 3-6 under the Model Code emphasized that "delegation [of legal tasks to nonlawyers] is proper if the lawyer maintains a direct relationship with his client, supervises the delegated work and has complete professional responsibility for the work product." (Emphasis added.) Accordingly, most state guidelines also stress the importance of a direct attorney-client relationship. See Colorado Guideline 1, Florida EC 3-6, Illinois Recommendation (A)(1), Iowa EC 3-6(2), and New Mexico Guideline IV. The direct personal relationship between client and lawyer is necessary to the exercise of the lawyer's trained professional judgment.

An essential aspect of the lawyer-client relationship is the agreement to undertake representation and the related fee arrangement. The Model Rules and most states require that fee arrangements be agreed upon early on and be communicated to the client by the lawyer, in some circumstances in writing. Model Rule 1.5 and Comments. Many state guidelines prohibit legal assistants from "setting fees" or "accepting cases." See, e.g., Colorado Guideline 1 and NALA Guideline VI. Connecticut recommends that legal assistants be prohibited from accepting or rejecting cases or setting fees "if these tasks entail any discretion on the part of the paralegals." Connecticut Recommendation 9.

EC 3-5 states: "[T]he essence of the professional judgment of the lawyer is his educated ability to relate the general body and philosophy of law to a specific legal problem of a client; and thus, the public interest will be better served if only lawyers are permitted to act in matters involving professional judgment." Clients are entitled to their lawyers' professional judgment and opinion. Legal assistants may, however, be authorized to communicate legal advice so long as they do not interpret or expand on that advice. Typically, state guidelines phrase this prohibition in terms of legal assistants being forbidden from "giving legal advice" or "counseling clients about legal matters." See, e.g., Colorado Guideline 2, Connecticut Recommendation 6, Florida DR 3-104, Iowa EC 3-6(3), Kansas Guideline I, Kentucky Sub-Rule 2, New Hampshire Rule 35, Sub-Rule 1, Texas Guideline I, and NALA Guideline VI. Some states have more expansive wording that prohibits legal assistants from engaging in any activity that would require the exercise of independent legal judgment. Nevertheless, it is clear that all states, as well as the Model Rules, encourage direct communication between clients and a legal assistant insofar as the legal assistant is performing a task properly delegated by a lawyer. It should be noted that a lawyer who permits a legal assistant to assist in establishing the attorney-client relationship, communicating a fee, or preparing a legal opinion is not delegating responsibility for those matters and, therefore, may be complying with this guideline.

Guideline 4: It is the lawyer's responsibility to take reasonable measures to ensure that clients, courts, and other lawyers are aware that a legal assistant, whose services are utilized by the lawyer in performing legal services, is not licensed to practice law.

Comment to Guideline 4: Since, in most instances, a legal assistant is not licensed as a lawyer, it is important that those with whom the legal assistant deals are aware of that fact. Several state guidelines impose on the lawyer responsibility for instructing a legal assistant whose services are utilized by the lawyer to disclose the legal assistant's status in any dealings with a third party. See, e.g., Michigan Guideline III, part 5, New Hampshire Rule 35, Sub-Rule 8, and NALA Guideline V. While requiring the legal assistant to make such disclosure is one way in which the attorney's responsibility to third parties may be discharged, the Standing Committee is of the view that it is desirable to emphasize the lawyer's responsibility for the disclosure and leave to the lawyer the discretion to decide whether the lawyer will discharge that responsibility by direct communication with the client, by requiring the legal assistant to make the disclosure, by a written memorandum, or by some other means. Although in most initial engagements by a client it may be prudent for the attorney to discharge this responsibility with a writing, the guideline requires only that the lawyer recognize the responsibility and ensure that it is discharged. Clearly, when a client has been adequately informed of the lawyer's utilization of legal assistant services, it is unnecessary to make additional formalistic disclosures as the client retains the lawyer for other services.

Most state guidelines specifically endorse legal assistants signing correspondence so long as their status as a legal assistant is indicated by an appropriate title. E.g., Colorado Guideline 2; Kansas, Comment to Guideline IX; and North Carolina Guideline 9; also see ABA Informal Opinion 1367 (1976). The comment to New Mexico Guideline XI warns against the use of the title ''associate'' since it may be construed to mean associate-attorney.

Guideline 5: A lawyer may identify legal assistants by name and title on the lawyer's letterhead and on business cards identifying the lawyer's firm.

Comment to Guideline 5: Under Guideline 4, above, an attorney who employs a legal assistant has an obligation to ensure that the status of the legal assistant as a non-lawyer is fully disclosed. The primary purpose of this disclosure is to avoid confusion that might lead someone to believe that the legal assistant is a lawyer. The identification suggested by this guideline is consistent with that objective, while also affording the legal assistant recognition as an important part of the legal services team.

Recent ABA Informal Opinion 1527 (1989) provides that non-lawyer support personnel, including legal assistants, may be listed on a law firm's letterhead and reiterates previous opinions that approve of legal assistants having business cards. See also ABA Informal Opinion 1185 (1971). The listing must not be false or misleading and ''must make it clear that the support personnel who are listed are not lawyers.''

Nearly all state guidelines approve of business cards for legal assistants, but some prescribe the contents and form of the card. E.g., Iowa Guideline 4 and Texas Guideline VIII. All agree the legal assistant's status must be clearly indicated and the card may not be used in a deceptive way. New Hampshire Supreme Court Rule 7 approves the use of business cards so long as the card is not used for unethical solicitation.

Some states do not permit attorneys to list legal assistants on their letterhead. E.g., Kansas Guideline VIII, Michigan

Guideline III, New Hampshire Rule 35, Sub-Rule 7, New Mexico Guideline XI, and North Carolina Guideline 9. Several of these states rely on earlier ABA Informal Opinions 619 (1962), 845 (1965), and 1000 (1977), all of which were expressly withdrawn by ABA Informal Opinion 1527. These earlier opinions interpreted the predecessor Model Code and DR 2-102 (A), which, prior to Bates v. State Bar of Arizona, 433 U.S. 350 (1977), had strict limitations on the information that could be listed on letterheads. States which do permit attorneys to list names of legal assistants on their stationery, if the listing is not deceptive and the legal assistant's status is clearly identified, include: Arizona Committee on Rules of Professional Conduct Formal Opinion 3/90 (1990); Connecticut Recommendation 12; Florida Professional Ethics Committee Advisory Opinion 86-4 (1986); Hawaii, Formal Opinion 78-8-19 (1978, as revised 1984); Illinois State Bar Association Advisory Opinion 87-1 (1987); Kentucky Sub-Rule 6; Mississippi State Bar Ethics Committee Opinion No. 93 (1984); Missouri Guideline IV; New York State Bar Association Committee on Professional Ethics Opinion 500 (1978); Oregon, Ethical Opinion No. 349 (1977); and Texas, Ethics Committee Opinion 436 (1983). In light of the United States Supreme Court opinion in Peel v. Attorney Registration and Disciplinary Commission of Illinois, ___ U.S. _______, 110 S. Ct. 2281 (1990), it may be that a restriction on letterhead identification of legal assistants that is not deceptive and clearly identifies the legal assistant's status violates the First Amendment rights of the lawyer.

Guideline 6: It is the responsibility of a lawyer to take reasonable measures to ensure that all client confidences are preserved by a legal assistant.

Comment to Guideline 6: A fundamental principle underlying the free exchange of information in a lawyer-client relationship is that the lawyer maintain the confidentiality of information relating to the representation. "It is a matter of common knowledge that the normal operation of a law office exposes confidential professional information to non-lawyer employees of the office. This obligates a lawyer to exercise care in selecting and training his employees so that the sanctity of all confidences and secrets of his clients may be preserved." EC 4-2, Model Code.

Rule 5.3 of the Model Rules requires "a lawyer who has direct supervisory authority over the nonlawyer [to] make reasonable efforts to ensure that the person's conduct is compatible with the professional obligations of the lawyer." The Comment to Rule 5.3 makes it clear that lawyers should give legal assistants "appropriate instruction and supervision concerning the ethical aspects of their employment, particularly regarding the obligation not to disclose information relating to the representation of the client." DR 4-101(D) under the Model Code provides that: "A lawyer shall exercise reasonable care to prevent his employees, associates and others whose services are utilized by him from discharging or using confidences or secrets of a client . . . ."

It is particularly important that the lawyer ensure that the legal assistant understands that all information concerning the client, even the mere fact that a person is a client of the firm, may be strictly confidential. Rule 1.6 of the Model Rules expanded the definition of confidential information ". . . not merely to matters communicated in confidence by the client but also to all information relating to the representation, whatever its source."[6] It is therefore the lawyer's obligation to instruct clearly and to take reasonable steps to ensure the legal assistant's preservation of client confidences. Nearly all states that have guidelines for the utilization of legal assistants require the lawyer "to instruct legal assistants concerning client confidences" and "to exercise care to ensure that legal assistants comply" with the Code in this regard. Even if the client consents to divulging information, this information must not be used to the disadvantage of the client. See, e.g., Connecticut Recommendation 3; New Hampshire Rule 35, Sub-Rule 4; NALA Guideline V.

Guideline 7: A lawyer should take reasonable measures to prevent conflicts of interest resulting from a legal assistant's other employment or interests insofar as such other employment or interests would present a conflict of interest if it were that of the lawyer.

6. Rule 1.05 of the Texas Disciplinary Rules of Professional Conduct (1990) provides a different formulation, which is equally expansive:

> "Confidential information" includes both "privileged information" and "unprivileged client information." "Privileged information" refers to the information of a client protected by the lawyer-client privilege of Rule 503 of the Texas Rules of Evidence or of Rule 503 of the Texas Rules of Criminal Evidence or by the principles of attorney-client privilege governed by Rule 501 of the Federal Rules of Evidence for United States Courts and Magistrates. "Unprivileged client information" means all information relating to a client or furnished by the client, other than privileged information, acquired by the lawyer during the course of or by reason of the representation of the client.

Comment to Guideline 7: A lawyer must make "reasonable efforts to ensure that [a] legal assistant's conduct is compatible with the professional obligations of the lawyer." Model Rule 5.3. These professional obligations include the duty to exercise independent professional judgment on behalf of a client, "free of compromising influences and loyalties." ABA Model Rules 1.7 through 1.13. Therefore, legal assistants should be instructed to inform the supervising attorney of any interest that could result in a conflict of interest or even give the appearance of a conflict. The guideline intentionally speaks to other employment rather than only past employment, since there are instances where legal assistants are employed by more than one law firm at the same time. The guideline's reference to "other interests" is intended to include personal relationships as well as instances where a legal assistant may have a financial interest (i.e., as stockholder, trust beneficiary or trustee, etc.) that would conflict with the client's in the matter in which the lawyer has been employed.

"Imputed Disqualification Arising from Change in Employment by Non-lawyer Employee," ABA Informal Opinion 1526 (1988), defines the duties of both the present and former employing lawyers and reasons that the restrictions on legal assistants' employment should be kept to "the minimum necessary to protect confidentiality" in order to prevent legal assistants from being forced to leave their careers, which "would disserve clients as well as the legal profession." The Opinion describes the attorney's obligations (1) to caution the legal assistant not to disclose any information and (2) to prevent the legal assistant from working on any matter on which the legal assistant worked for a prior employer or respecting which the employee has confidential information.

If a conflict is discovered, it may be possible to "wall" the legal assistant from the conflict area so that the entire firm need not be disqualified and the legal assistant is effectively screened from information concerning the matter. The American Bar Association has taken the position that what historically has been described as a "Chinese wall" will allow non-lawyer personnel (including legal assistants) who are in possession of confidential client information to accept employment with a law firm opposing the former client so long as the wall is observed and effectively screens the non-lawyer from confidential information. ABA Informal Opinion 1526 (1988). See also Tennessee Formal Ethics Opinion 89-F-118 (March 10, 1989). The implication of this Informal Opinion is that if a wall is not in place, the employer may be disqualified from representing either party to the controversy. One court has so held. In re: Complex Asbestoses Litigation, No. 828684 (San Francisco Superior Court, September 19, 1989).

It is not clear that a wall will prevent disqualification in the case of a lawyer employed to work for a law firm representing a client with an adverse interest to a client of the lawyer's former employer. Under Model Rule 1.10, when a lawyer moves to a firm that represents an adverse party in a matter in which the lawyer's former firm was involved, absent a waiver by the client, the new firm's representation may continue only if the newly employed lawyer acquired no protected information and did not work directly on the matter in the former employment. The new Rules of Professional Conduct in Kentucky and Texas (both effective on January 1, 1990) specifically provide for disqualification. Rule 1.10(b) in the District of Columbia, which became effective January 1, 1991, does so as well. The Sixth Circuit, however, has held that the wall will effectively insulate the new firm from disqualification if it prevents the new lawyer-employee from access to information concerning the client with the adverse interest. Manning v. Waring, Cox, James, Sklar & Allen, 849 F.2d 222 (6th Cir. 1988). [As a result of the Sixth Circuit opinion, Tennessee revised its formal ethics opinion, which is cited above, and now applies the same rule to lawyers, legal assistants, law clerks, and legal secretaries.] See generally NFPA, "The Chinese Wall—Its Application to Paralegals" (1990).

The states that have guidelines that address the legal assistant conflict of interest issue refer to the lawyer's responsibility to ensure against personal, business or social interests of the legal assistant that would conflict with the representation of the client or impinge on the services rendered to the client. E.g., Kansas Guideline X, New Mexico Guideline VI, and North Carolina Guideline 7. Florida Professional Ethics Opinion 86-5 (1986) discusses a legal assistant's move from one firm to another and the obligations of each not to disclose confidences. See also Vermont Ethics Opinion 85-8 (1985) (a legal assistant is not bound by the Code of Professional Responsibility and, absent an absolute waiver by the client, the new firm should not represent client if legal assistant possessed confidential information from old firm).

Guideline 8: A lawyer may include a charge for the work performed by a legal assistant in setting a charge for legal services.

Comment to Guideline 8: The U.S. Supreme Court in Missouri v. Jenkins, 491 U.S.274 (1989), held that in setting a reasonable attorney's fee under 28 U.S.C. § 1988, a legal fee may include a charge for legal assistant services at "market rates" rather than "actual cost" to the attorneys. This decision should resolve any question concerning the propriety of setting a charge for legal services based on work performed by a legal assistant. Its rationale favors setting a charge based on the "market" rate for such services, rather than their direct cost to the lawyer. This result was recognized by Connecticut Recommendation 11, Illinois Recommendation D, and Texas Guideline V prior to the Supreme Court decision. See also Fla. Stat. Ann. § 57.104 (1991 Supp.) (adopted in 1987 and permitting consideration of legal assistant services in computing attorneys' fees) and Fla. Stat. Ann. § 744.108 (1991 Supp.) (adopted in 1989 and permitting recovery of "customary and reasonable charges for work performed by legal assistants" as fees for legal services in guardianship matters).

It is important to note, however, that Missouri v. Jenkins does not abrogate the attorney's responsibilities under Model Rule 1.5 to set a reasonable fee for legal services and it follows that those considerations apply to a fee that includes a fee for legal assistant services. Accordingly, the effect of combining a market rate charge for the services of lawyers and legal assistants should, in most instances, result in a lower total cost for the legal service than if the lawyer had performed the service alone.

Guideline 9: A lawyer may not split legal fees with a legal assistant nor pay a legal assistant for the referral of legal business. A lawyer may compensate a legal assistant based on the quantity and quality of the legal assistant's work and the value of that work to a law practice, but the legal assistant's compensation may not be contingent, by advance agreement, upon the profitability of the lawyer's practice.

Comment to Guideline 9: Model Rule 5.4 and DR 3-102(A) and 3-103(A) under the Model Code clearly prohibit fee "splitting" with legal assistants, whether characterized as splitting of contingent fees, "forwarding" fees, or other sharing of legal fees. Virtually all guidelines adopted by state bar associations have continued this prohibition in one form or another.[7] It appears clear that a legal assistant may not be compensated on a contingent basis for a particular case or paid for "signing up" clients for a legal practice.

Having stated this prohibition, however, the guideline attempts to deal with the practical consideration of how a legal assistant properly may be compensated by an attorney or law firm. The linchpin of the prohibition seems to be the advance agreement of the lawyer to "split" a fee based on a pre-existing contingent arrangement.[8] There is no general prohibition against a lawyer who enjoys a particularly profitable period recognizing the

7. Connecticut Recommendation 10; Illinois Recommendation D; Kansas Guideline VI; Kentucky Supreme Court Rule 3.700, sub-rule 5; Michigan Guideline III, part 2; Missouri Guideline II; New Hampshire Rule 35, Sub-Rules 5 and 6; New Mexico Guideline IX; Rhode Island Guideline VIII and IX; South Carolina Guideline V; Texas Guideline V.
8. In its Rule 5.4, which will become effective on January 1, 1991, the District of Columbia will permit lawyers to form legal service partnerships that include non-lawyer participants. Comments 5 and 6 to that rule, however, state that the term "nonlawyer participants" should not be confused with the term "nonlawyer assistants" and that "[n]onlawyer assistants under Rule 5.3 do not have managerial authority for financial interests in the organization."

contribution of the legal assistant to that profitability with a discretionary bonus. Likewise, a lawyer engaged in a particularly profitable specialty of legal practice is not prohibited from compensating the legal assistant who aids materially in that practice more handsomely than the compensation generally awarded to legal assistants in that geographic area who work in law practices that are less lucrative. Indeed, any effort to fix a compensation level for legal assistants and prohibit greater compensation would appear to violate the federal antitrust laws. See , e.g., Goldfarb v. Virginia State Bar, 421 U.S. 773 (1975).

Guideline 10: A lawyer who employs a legal assistant should facilitate the legal assistant's participation in appropriate continuing education and pro bono publico activities.

Comment to Guideline 10: While Guideline 10 does not appear to have been adopted in the guidelines of any state bar association, the Standing Committee on Legal Assistants believes that its adoption would be appropriate.[9] For many years the Standing Committee on Legal Assistants has advocated that the improvement of formal legal assistant education will generally improve the legal services rendered by lawyers employing legal assistants and provide a more satisfying professional atmosphere in which legal assistants may work. See, e.g., ABA, Board of Governors, Policy on Legal Assistant Licensure and/or Certification, Statement 4 (February 6, 1986); ABA, Standing Committee on Legal Assistants, "Position Paper on the Question of Legal Assistant Licensure or Certification" (December 10, 1985), at 6 and Conclusion 3. Recognition of the employing lawyer's obligation to facilitate the legal assistant's continuing professional education is, therefore, appropriate because of the benefits to both the law practice and the legal assistants and is consistent with the lawyer's own responsibility to maintain professional competence under Model Rule 1.1. See also EC 6-2 of the Model Code.

The Standing Committee is of the view that similar benefits will accrue to the lawyer and legal assistant if the legal assistant is included in the pro bono publico legal services that a lawyer has a clear obligation to provide under Model Rule 6.1 and, where appropriate, the legal assistant is encouraged to provide such services independently. The ability of a law firm to provide more pro bono publico services will be enhanced if legal assistants are included. Recognition of the legal assistant's role in such services is consistent with the role of the legal assistant in the contemporary delivery of legal services generally and is consistent with the lawyer's duty to the legal profession under Canon 2 of the Model Code.

THE STANDING COMMITTEE ON LEGAL ASSISTANTS OF THE AMERICAN BAR ASSOCIATION

May 1991

9. While no state has apparently adopted a guideline similar to Model Guideline 10, parts 4 and 5 of NALA Guideline VIII suggest similar requirements. Sections III and V of NFPA's "Affirmation of Professional Responsibility" recognize a legal assistant's obligations to "maintain a high level of competence" (which "is achieved through continuing education. . .") and to "serve the public interest." NFPA has also published a guide to assist legal assistant groups in developing public service projects. See NFPA, "Pro Bono Publico (For the Good of the People)" (1987).

Appendix D
NALA Model Standards and Guidelines for Utilization of Legal Assistants Annotated

INTRODUCTION

The purpose of this annotated version of the National Association of Legal Assistants, Inc. (NALA) Model Standards and Guidelines for the Utilization of Legal Assistants is to provide references to the existing case law and other authorities where the underlying issues have been considered. The authorities cited will serve as a basis upon which conduct of a legal assistant may be analyzed as proper or improper.

The Guidelines represent a statement of how the legal assistant may function in the law office. The Guidelines are not intended to be a comprehensive or exhaustive list of the proper duties of a legal assistant. Rather, they are designed as guides to what may or may not be proper conduct for the legal assistant. In formulating the Guidelines, the reasoning and rules of law in many reported decisions of disciplinary cases and unauthorized practice of law cases have been analyzed and considered. In addition, the provisions of the American Bar Association's Model Code of Professional Responsibility and the Model Rules of Professional Conduct, as well as the ethical promulgations of various state courts and bar associations have been considered in development of the Guidelines.

While the Guidelines may not have universal application, they do form a sound basis for the legal assistant and the supervising attorney to follow in the operation of a law office. The Model will serve as a definitive and well-reasoned guide to those considering voluntary standards and guidelines for legal assistants. If regulation is to be imposed in a given jurisdiction the Model may serve as a comprehensive resource document.

I PREAMBLE

Proper utilization of the services of legal assistants affects the efficient delivery of legal services. Legal assistants and the legal profession should be assured that some measures exist for identifying legal assistants and their role in assisting attorneys in the delivery of legal services. Therefore, the National Association of Legal Assistants, Inc., hereby adopts these Model Standards and Guidelines as an educational document for the benefit of legal assistants and the legal profession.

COMMENT

The three most frequently raised questions concerning legal assistants are (1) How do you define a legal assistant; (2) Who is qualified to be identified as a legal assistant; and (3) What duties may a legal assistant perform? The definition adopted answers the first question insofar as legal assistants serving attorneys are concerned. The Model sets forth minimum education, training, and experience through standards which will assure that one denominated as a legal assistant has the qualifications to be held out to the public in that capacity. The Guidelines identify those acts which the reported cases hold to be proscribed and give examples of services which the legal assistant may perform under the supervision of an attorney.

The three fundamental issues in the preceding paragraph have been raised in various cases for the past fifty years. In *Ferris v. Snively*, 19 P.2d 942 (Wash. 1933), the Court stated work performed by a law clerk to be proper and not the unauthorized practice of law required supervision by the employing attorney. The Court stated:

We realize that law clerks have their place in a law office, and we recognize the fact that the nature of their work approaches in a degree that of their employers. The line of demarcation as to where their work begins and where it ends cannot always be drawn with absolute distinction or accuracy. Probably as nearly as it can be fixed, and it is sufficient to say that it is work of a preparatory nature, such as research, investigation of details, the assemblage of data and other necessary information, and such other work as will assist the employing attorney in carrying the matter to a completed product, either by his personal examination and approval thereof or by additional effort on his part. The work must be such, however, as loses its separate identity and becomes either the product, or else merged in the product, of the attorney himself. (19 P.2d at pp. 945-46.) (See Florida EC3-6, infra at, Section IV.)

The NALA Guidelines constitute a statement relating to services performed by nonlawyer employees as approved by court decisions and other sources of authority. The purpose of the Guidelines is not to place limitations or restrictions on the legal profession. Rather, the Guidelines are intended to outline for the legal profession an acceptable course of conduct. By voluntary recognition and utilization of the Model Standards and Guidelines the legal profession will avoid many problems.

II DEFINITION

Legal assistants* are a distinguishable group of persons who assist attorneys in the delivery of legal services. Through formal education, training, and experience, legal assistants have knowledge and expertise regarding the legal system and substantive and procedural law which qualify them to do work of a legal nature under the supervision of an attorney.

*Within the occupational category some individuals are known as paralegals.

COMMENT

This definition has been used to foster a distinction between a legal assistant as one working under the direct supervision of an attorney and a broader class of paralegals who perform tasks of similar nature, but not necessarily under the supervision of an attorney. In applying the standards and guidelines it is important to remember that they in turn were developed to apply to the legal assistant as defined therein.

III STANDARDS

A legal assistant should meet certain minimum qualifications. The following standards may be used to determine an individual's qualifications as a legal assistant:

1. Successful completion of the Certified Legal Assistant certifying (''CLA'') examination of the National Association of Legal Assistants, Inc.;
2. Graduation from an ABA approved program of study for legal assistants;
3. Graduation from a course of study for legal assistants which is institutionally accredited but not ABA approved, and which requires not less than the equivalent of 60 semester hours of classroom study;
4. Graduation from a course of study for legal assistants, other than those set forth in (2) and (3) above, plus not less than six months of in-house training as a legal assistant;
5. A baccalaureate degree in any field, plus not less than six months of in-house training as a legal assistant;
6. A minimum of three years of law-related experience under the supervision of an attorney, including at least six months of in-house training as a legal assistant; or
7. Two years of in-house training as a legal assistant.

For purposes of these Standards, "in-house training as a legal assistant" means attorney education of the employee concerning legal assistant duties and these Guidelines. In addition to review and analysis of assignments the legal assistant should receive a reasonable amount of instruction directly related to the duties and obligations of the legal assistant.

COMMENT

The Standards set forth suggested minimum qualifications for a legal assistant. These minimum qualifications as adopted recognize legal related work backgrounds and formal education backgrounds, both of which should provide the legal assistant with a broad base in exposure to and knowledge of the legal profession. This background is necessary to assure the public and the legal profession that the one being identified as a legal assistant is qualified.

The Certified Legal Assistant ("CLA") examination offered by NALA is the only voluntary nationwide certification program for legal assistants. The "CLA" designation is a statement to the legal profession and the public that the legal assistant has met the high levels of knowledge and professionalism required by NALA's certification program. Continuing education requirements, which all certified legal assistants must meet, assure that high standards are maintained. Certification through NALA is available to any legal assistant meeting the educational and experience requirements.

IV GUIDELINES

These guidelines relating to standards of performance and professional responsibility are intended to aid legal assistants and attorneys. The responsibility rests with an attorney who employs legal assistants to educate them with respect to the duties they are assigned and to supervise the manner in which such duties are accomplished.

COMMENT

In general, a legal assistant is allowed to perform any task which is properly delegated and supervised by an attorney, so long as **the attorney is ultimately responsible to the client and assumes complete professional responsibility for the work product.**

The Code of Professional Responsibility of the American Bar Association, EC3-6 states:

ABA Model Rules of Professional Conduct, Rule 5.3 provides:

With respect to a non-lawyer employed or retained by or associated with a lawyer:

(a) a partner in a law firm shall make reasonable efforts to ensure that the firm has in effect measures giving reasonable assurance that the person's conduct is compatible with the professional obligations of the lawyer;

(b) a lawyer having direct supervisory authority over the non-lawyer shall make reasonable efforts to ensure that the person's conduct is compatible with the professional obligations of the lawyer; and

(c) a lawyer shall be responsible for conduct of such a person that would be a violation of the rules of professional conduct if engaged in by a lawyer if:

(1) the lawyer orders or, with the knowledge of the specific conduct ratifies the conduct involved; or

(2) the lawyer is a partner in the law firm in which the person is employed, or has direct supervisory authority over the person, and knows of the conduct at a time when its consequences can be avoided or mitigated but fails to take reasonable remedial action.

The Florida version of EC3-6 provides:

A lawyer or law firm may employ non-lawyers such as secretaries, law clerks, investigators, researchers, legal assistants, accountants, draftsmen, office administrators, and other lay personnel to assist the lawyer in the delivery of legal services. A lawyer often delegates tasks to such persons. Such delegation is proper if a lawyer retains a direct relationship with his client, supervises the delegated work, and has complete professional responsibility for the work product.

The work which is delegated is such that it will assist the employing attorney in carrying the matter to a completed product either by the lawyer's personal examination and approval thereof or by additional effort on the lawyer's part. The delegated work must be such, however, as loses its separate identity and becomes either the product or else merged in the product of the attorney himself.

The Kentucky Paralegal Code defines a legal assistant as:

. . . a person under the supervision and direction of a licensed lawyer, who may apply knowledge of law and legal procedures in rendering direct assistance to lawyers engaged in legal research; design, develop or plan modifications or new procedures, techniques, services, processes or applications; prepare or interpret legal documents and write detailed procedure for practicing in certain fields of law; select, compile and use technical information from such references as digests, encyclopedias or practice manuals; and analyze and follow procedural problems that involve independent decisions.

Kentucky became the first state to adopt a Paralegal Code, which sets forth certain exclusions to the unauthorized practice of law:

For purpose of this rule, the unauthorized practice of law shall not include any service rendered involving legal knowledge or advice, whether representation, counsel or advocacy, in or out of court, rendered in respect to the acts, duties, obligations, liabilities or business relations of the one requiring services where:

A. The client understands that the paralegal is not a lawyer;

B. The lawyer supervises the paralegal in the performance of his duties; and

C. The lawyer remains fully responsible for such representation, including all actions taken or not taken in connection therewith by the paralegal to the same extent as if such representation had been furnished entirely by the lawyer and all such actions had been taken or not taken directly by the attorney. Paralegal Code, Ky. S. Ct. R 3.700, Sub-Rule 2.

While the Kentucky rule is an exception, it does provide a basis for expanding services which may be performed by legal assistants.

There are many interesting and complex issues involving the use of legal assistants. One issue which is not addressed in the Guidelines is whether a legal assistant, as defined herein, may make appearances before administrative agencies. This issue is discussed in Remmer, *Representation of Clients Before Administrative Agencies: Authorized or Unauthorized Practice of Law?*, 15 Valparaiso Univ. L.Rev. 567 (1981). The State Bar of California Standing Committee on Professional Responsibility and Conduct, in opinion 1988-103 (2/8/89) has stated a law firm can delegate authority to a legal assistant employee to file petitions, motions and make other appearances before the Workers' Compensation Appeals Board provided adequate supervision is maintained by the attorney and the client is informed and has consented to the use of the legal assistant in such fashion.

In any discussion of the proper role of a legal assistant attention must be directed to what constitutes the practice of law. The proper delegation of work and duties to legal assistants is further complicated and confused by the lack of adequate definition of the practice of law and the unauthorized practice of law.

In *Davis v. Unauthorized Practice Committee*, 431 S.W.2d 590 (Texas, 1968), the Court found that the defendant was properly enjoined from the unauthorized practice of law. The Court, in defining the "practice of law," stated:

According to the generally understood definition of the practice of law, it embraces the preparation of pleadings and other papers incident to actions of special proceedings, and the management of such actions in proceedings on behalf of clients before judges in courts. However, the practice of law is not confined to cases conducted in court. In fact, the major portion of the practice of any capable lawyer consists of work done outside of the courts. The practice of law involves not only appearance in court in connection with litigation, but also services rendered out of court, and includes the giving of advice or the rendering of any service requiring the use of legal skill or knowledge, such as preparing a will, contract or other instrument, the legal effect of which under the facts and conclusions involved must be carefully determined.

The important distinguishing fact between the defendant in Davies and a legal assistant is that the acts of the legal assistant are performed under the supervision of an attorney.

EC3-5 of the Code of Professional Responsibility states:

It is neither necessary nor desirable to attempt the formulation of a single, specific definition of what constitutes the practice of law. Functionally, the practice of law relates to the rendition of services for others that call for the professional judgment of a lawyer. The essence of the professional judgment of the lawyer is his educated ability to relate the general body and philosophy of law to a specific legal problem of a client; and thus, the public interest will be better served if only lawyers are permitted to act in matters involving professional judgment. Where this professional judgment is not involved, non-lawyers, such as court clerks, police officers, abstracters, and many governmental employees, may engage in occupations that require a special knowledge of law in certain areas. But the services of a lawyer are essential in the public interest whenever the exercise of professional legal judgment is required.

There are many cases relating to the unauthorized practice of law, but the most troublesome ones in attempting to define what would or would not form the unauthorized practice of law for acts performed by a legal assistant are those such as *Crawford v. State Bar of California*, 355 P.2d 490 (Calif. 1960), which states that any act performed in a law office is the practice of law because the clients have sought the attorney to perform the work because of the training and judgment exercised by attorneys.

See also, Annot. "Layman's Assistance to Parties in Divorce Proceedings as Unauthorized Practice of Law," 12 ALR4 656; Annot. "Activities of Law Clerks as Illegal Practice of Law," 13 ALR3 1137; Annot. "Sale of Books or Forms Designed to Enable Layman to Achieve Legal Results Without Assistance of Attorney as Unauthorized Practice of Law," 71 ALR3 1000; Annot. "Nature of Legal Services or Law-Related Services Which May Be Performed for Others By Disbarred or Suspended Attorney," 87 ALR3 272. See also, Karen B. Judd, CLA, "Beyond the Bar: Legal Assistants and the Unauthorized Practice of Law," *Facts and Findings*, Vol. VIII, Issue 6, National Association of Legal Assistants, May-June, 1982.

V

Legal assistants should:

1. Disclose their status as legal assistants at the outset of any professional relationship with a client, other attorneys, a court or administrative agency or personnel thereof, or members of the general public;
2. Preserve the confidences and secrets of all clients; and
3. Understand the attorney's Code of Professional Responsibility and these guidelines in order to avoid any action which would involve the attorney in a violation of that Code, or give the appearance of professional impropriety.

COMMENT

Routine early disclosure of the legal assistant's status when dealing with persons outside the attorney's office is necessary to assure that there will be no misunderstanding as to the responsibilities and role of the legal assistant. Disclosure may be made in any way that avoids confusion. If the person dealing with the legal assistant already knows of his or her status, further disclosure is unnecessary. If at any time in written or in oral communication the legal assistant becomes aware that the other person may believe the legal assistant is an attorney, it should be made clear that the legal assistant is not an attorney.

The attorney should exercise care that the legal assistant preserves and refrains from using any confidence or secrets of a client, and should instruct the legal assistant not to disclose or use any such confidences or secrets.

DR 4-101(D), ABA Code of Professional Responsibility, provides in part that:

A lawyer shall exercise reasonable care to prevent his employees, associates, and others whose services are utilized by him from disclosing or using confidences or secrets of a client. . .

This obligation is emphasized in EC4-2:

It is a matter of common knowledge that the normal operation of a law office exposes confidential professional information to non-lawyer employees of the office, particularly secretaries and those having access to the files; and this obligates the lawyer to exercise care in selecting and training his employees so that the sanctity of all confidences and secrets of his clients may be preserved.

The ultimate responsibility for compliance with approved standards of professional conduct rests with the supervising attorney. *In the Matter of Martinez*, 107 N.M. 171, 754 P.2d 842 (N.M. 1988). However, the legal assistant should understand what he may or may not do. The burden rests upon the attorney who employs a legal assistant to educate the latter with respect to the duties which may be assigned and then to supervise the manner in which the legal assistant carries out such duties. However, this does not relieve the legal assistant from an independent obligation to refrain from illegal conduct. Additionally, and notwithstanding that the Code is not binding upon non-lawyers, the very nature of a legal assistant's employment imposes an obligation not to engage in conduct which would involve the supervising attorney in a violation of the Code. NALA has adopted the ABA Code as a part of its Code of Ethics.

VI

Legal assistants should not:

1. Establish attorney-client relationships; set legal fees, give legal opinions or advice; or represent a client before a court; nor
2. Engage in, encourage, or contribute to any act which could constitute the unauthorized practice of law.

COMMENT

Reported cases holding which acts can and cannot be performed by a legal assistant are few:

The legal assistant cannot create the attorney-client relationship. *DeVaux v. American Home Assur. Co.*, 444 N.E.2d 355 (Mass., 1983).

The legal assistant cannot make court appearances. The question of what constitutes a court appearance is also somewhat vague. See, for example, *People v. Alexander*, 53 Ill. App.2d 299, 202 N.E.2d 841 (1964), where preparation of a court order and transmitting information to court was not the unauthorized practice of law, and *People v. Belfor*, 611 P.2d 979 (Colo. 1980), where the trial court found that the acts of a disbarred attorney did not constitute an appearance and the Supreme Court of Colorado held that only the Supreme Court could make the determination of what acts constituted an appearance and the unauthorized practice of law.

The following cases have identified certain areas in which an attorney has a duty to act, but it is interesting to note that none of these cases state that it is improper for an attorney to have the initial work performed by a legal assistant. This again points out the importance of adequate supervision by the employing attorney.

Courts have found that attorneys have the duty to check bank statements, preserve a client's property, review and sign all pleadings, insure that all communications are opened and answered, and make inquiry when items of dictation are not received. *Attorney Grievance Commission of Maryland v. Goldberg*, 441 A.2d 338, 292 Md. 650 (1982). See also *Vaughn v. State Bar of California*, 100 Cal. Rptr. 713, 494 P.2d 1257 (1972).

The legal assistant cannot exercise professional legal judgment or give legal advice. In *Louisiana State Bar v. Edwins*, 540 So. 2d 294 (La. 1989) the court held a paralegal was engaged in activities constituting the unauthorized practice of law, which included evaluation of claims and giving advice on settlements. The attorney who delegated the exercise of these acts aided in the unauthorized practice of law. See also, *People of the State of Co. v. Gelker*, 770 P.2d 402 (Col. 1989).

Attorneys have the responsibility to supervise the work of associates and clerical staff. *Moore v. State Bar Association*, 41 Cal. Rptr. 161, 396 P.2d 577 (1964); *Attorney Grievance Committee of Maryland v. Goldberg, supra.*

An attorney must exercise sufficient supervision to insure that all monies received are properly deposited and disbursed. *Black v. State Bar of California*, 103 Cal. Rptr. 288, 499 P.2d 968 (1972); *Fitzpatrick v. State Bar of California*, 141 Cal. Rptr. 169, 569 P.2d 763 (1977).

The attorney must insure that his staff is competent and effective to perform the work delegated. *In Re Reinmiller*, 325 P.2d 773 (Oregon, 1958). See also, *State of Kansas v. Barrett*, 483 P.2d 1106 (Kansas, 1971); *Attorney Grievance Committee of Maryland v. Goldberg, supra.*

The attorney must make sufficient background investigation of the prior activities and character and integrity of his employees to insure that legal assistants have not previously been involved in unethical, illegal, or other nefarious schemes which demonstrate such person unfit to be associated with the practice of law. See *In the Matter of Shaw*, 88 N.J. 433, A.2d 678 (1982), wherein the Court announced that while it had no disciplinary jurisdiction over legal assistants, it directed that disciplinary hearings make specific findings of fact concerning paralegals' collaboration in nefarious schemes in order that the court might properly discipline any attorney establishing an office relationship with one who had been implicated previously in unscrupulous schemes.

VII

Legal assistants may perform services for an attorney in the representation of a client, provided:

1. The services performed by the legal assistant do not require the exercise of independent professional legal judgment;
2. The attorney maintains a direct relationship with the client and maintains control of all client matters;
3. The attorney supervises the legal assistant;
4. The attorney remains professionally responsible for all work on behalf of the client, including any actions taken or not taken by the legal assistant in connection therewith; and
5. The services performed supplement, merge with and become the attorney's work product.

COMMENT

EC3-6, ABA Code of Professional Responsibility, recognizes the value of utilizing the services of legal assistants, but provides certain conditions to such employment:

A lawyer often delegates tasks to clerks, secretaries, and other lay persons. Such delegation is proper if the lawyer maintains a direct relationship with his client, supervises the delegated work, and has complete professional responsibility for the work product. This delegation enables a lawyer to render legal services more economically and efficiently.

VIII

In the supervision of a legal assistant, consideration should be given to:

1. Designating work assignments that correspond to the legal assistants' abilities, knowledge, training and experience.
2. Educating and training the legal assistant with respect to professional responsibility, local rules and practices, and firm policies;
3. Monitoring the work and professional conduct of the legal assistant to ensure that the work is substantively correct and timely performed;

4. Providing continuing education for the legal assistant in substantive matters through courses, institutes, workshops, seminars and in-house training; and
5. Encouraging and supporting membership and active participation in professional organizations.

COMMENT

Attorneys are responsible for the actions of their employees in both malpractice and disciplinary proceedings. The attorney cannot delegate work to a legal assistant which involves activities constituting the unauthorized practice of law. See *Louisiana State Bar v. Edwins*, 540 So. 2d 294 (La. 1989), and *People of the State of Colorado v. Felker*, 770 P.2d 402 (Col. 1989). In the vast majority of the cases, the courts have not censured attorneys for the particular act delegated to the legal assistant, but rather, have been critical of an imposed sanctions against attorneys for failure to adequately supervise the legal assistants. See e.g., *Attorney Grievance Commission of Maryland v. Goldberg, supra.*

The attorney's responsibility for supervision of legal assistants must be more than a willingness to accept responsibility and liability for the legal assistant's work. The attorney must monitor the work product and conduct of the legal assistant to insure that the work performed is substantively correct and competently performed in a professional manner. This duty includes the responsibility to provide continuing legal education for the legal assistant.

Supervision of legal assistants must be offered in both the procedural and substantive legal areas in the law office.

In *Spindell v. State Bar of California*, 118 Cal. Rptr. 480, 530 P.2d 168 (1975), the attorney was suspended from practice because of the improper legal advice given by a secretary. The case illustrates that it is important that both attorneys and legal assistants confirm all telephonic advice by letter.

In all instances where the legal assistant relays information to a client in response to an inquiry from the client, the advice relayed telephonically by the legal assistant should be confirmed in writing by the attorney. This will eliminate claims if the client acts contrary to the advice given. It will establish that the legal advice given is in fact that of the attorney, not the legal assistant, and obviate any confusion resulting from transmission of the advice through the legal assistant.

The *Spindell* case is an example of an attorney's failure to supervise and educate his staff. Not only was the secretary uneducated as to the substantive provisions of the law, but more importantly, she was uneducated as to her duty and authority as an employee of the attorney.

IX

Except as otherwise provided by statute, court rule or decision, administrative rule or regulation, or the attorney's Code of Professional Responsibility; and within the preceding parameters and proscriptions, a legal assistant may perform any function delegated by an attorney, including but not limited to the following:

1. Conduct client interviews and maintain general contact with the client after the establishment of the attorney-client relationship, so long as the client is aware of the status and function of the legal assistant, and the client contact is under the supervision of the attorney.
2. Locate and interview witnesses, so long as the witnesses are aware of the status and function of the legal assistant.
3. Conduct investigations and statistical and documentary research for review by the attorney.

4. Conduct legal research for review by the attorney.
5. Draft legal documents for review by the attorney.
6. Draft correspondence and pleadings for review by and signature of the attorney.
7. Summarize depositions, interrogatories, and testimony for review by the attorney.
8. Attend executions of wills, real estate closings, depositions, court or administrative hearings and trials with the attorney.
9. Author and sign letters provided the legal assistant's status is clearly indicated and the correspondence does not contain independent legal opinions or legal advice.

COMMENT

The United States Supreme Court has recognized the variety of tasks being performed by legal assistants and has noted that use of legal assistants encourage cost effective delivery of legal services. *Missouri v. Jenkins*, 491 U.S. 274, 109 S. Ct. 2463, 2471, n.10 (1989). In Jenkins, the court further held that legal assistant time should be included in compensation for attorney fee awards at the prevailing practice in the relevant community to bill legal assistant time.

Except for the specific proscription contained in Section VI, the reported cases, such as *Attorney Grievance Commission of Maryland v. Goldberg*, supra, do not limit the duties which may be performed by a legal assistant under the supervision of the attorney. The Guidelines were developed from generally accepted practices. Each supervising attorney must be aware of the specific rules, decisions and statutes applicable to legal assistants within his jurisdiction.

Appendix E NFPA Affirmation of Professional Responsibility

PREAMBLE

The National Federation of Paralegal Associations, Inc. (NFPA) recognizes and accepts its commitment to the realization of the most basic right of a free society, equal justice under the law.

In examining contemporary legal institutions and systems, the members of the paralegal profession recognize that a redefinition of the traditional delivery of legal services is essential in order to meet the needs of the general public. The paralegal profession is committed to increasing the availability and quality of legal services.

NFPA has adopted this Affirmation of Professional Responsibility to delineate the principles of purpose and conduct toward which paralegals should aspire. Through this Affirmation, NFPA places upon each paralegal the responsibility to adhere to these standards and encourages dedication to the development of the profession.

I. PROFESSIONAL RESPONSIBILITY

A paralegal shall demonstrate initiative in performing and expanding the paralegal role in the delivery of legal services within the parameters of the unauthorized practice of law statutes.

Discussion: Recognizing the professional and legal responsibility to abide by the unauthorized practice of law statutes, NFPA supports and encourages new interpretations as to what constitutes the practice of law.

II. PROFESSIONAL CONDUCT

A paralegal shall maintain the highest standards of ethical conduct.

Discussion: It is the responsibility of a paralegal to avoid conduct which is unethical or appears to be unethical. Ethical principles are aspirational in character and embody the fundamental rules of conduct by which every paralegal should abide. Observance of these standards is essential to uphold respect for the legal system.

III. COMPETENCE AND INTEGRITY

A paralegal shall maintain a high level of competence and shall contribute to the integrity of the paralegal profession.

Discussion: The integrity of the paralegal profession is predicated upon individual competence. Professional competence is each paralegal's responsibility and is achieved through continuing education, awareness of developments in the field of law, and aspiring to the highest standards of personal performance.

IV. CLIENT CONFIDENCES

A paralegal shall preserve client confidences and privileged communications.

Discussion: Confidential information and privileged communications are a vital part of the attorney, paralegal and client relationship. The importance of preserving confidential and privileged information is understood to be an uncompromising obligation of every paralegal.

V. SUPPORT OF PUBLIC INTERESTS

A paralegal shall serve the public interests by contributing to the availability and delivery of quality legal services.

Discussion: It is the responsibility of each paralegal to promote the development and implementation of programs that address the legal needs of the public. A paralegal shall strive to maintain a sensitivity to public needs and educate the public as to the services that paralegals may render.

VI. PROFESSIONAL DEVELOPMENT

A paralegal shall promote the development of the paralegal profession.

Discussion: This Affirmation of Professional Responsibility promulgates a positive attitude through which a paralegal may recognize the importance, responsibility, and potential of the paralegal contribution to the delivery of legal services. Participation in professional associations enhances the ability of the individual paralegal to contribute to the quality and growth of the paralegal profession.

GLOSSARY

Acceleration The right of a lender to suspend an agreed-on payment schedule and declare the full amount of a loan immediately due and payable.

Acceptance A response to an offer that expresses an intention to be bound by all terms of the offer and is communicated to the party making the offer before the offer expires or is revoked.

Actus reus The particular physical act that must be done in order to commit a particular crime.

Administrative agencies Governmental bodies such as boards, bureaus, commissions, departments, divisions, or offices that have the power to make rules, enforce rules, and decide controversies arising under those rules.

Administrative law Rules, regulations, orders, and decisions made by administrative agencies.

Administrative law judge Judge who conducts hearings and makes decisions on an administrative agency's rules and policies.

Administrative Procedure Act (APA) Outlines the basic procedures to be followed in rulemaking and adjudication.

Administrator of the estate A personal representative for the estate of someone who dies intestate.

Admissible evidence Evidence that meets certain requirements laid down by the rules of evidence and may therefore be used in court.

Affidavit Written statement of facts signed by someone who has sworn under oath before a person authorized to administer oaths that the facts contained in the statement are true.

Affirmative defense A defense raised in the answer (to a complaint) in which the defendant alleges facts that, if proven, would excuse the defendant from liability.

Agency A form of representation by which an agent represents a principal with respect to the principal's dealings with third parties.

Agent A person who represents someone else, known as a principal, with respect to the principal's dealings with third parties.

Allege Assert as true.

Ancillary jurisdiction Federal jurisdiction over nonfederal matters that are factually related to a federal question.

Annotated code Contains statutory text plus valuable information including summaries of cases that have interpreted and applied the code.

Answer Pleading filed by the defendant in which the allegations in a complaint are either admitted or denied and affirmative defenses may be raised.

Antenuptial agreement A property division agreement entered into by prospective spouses prior to marriage; also called *prenuptial agreement.*

Appellate court Court of appeal, which reviews the record of what took place at trial.

Articles of incorporation The basic organizational documents of a corporation; also called *charter.*

Associate A lawyer employed by a private law firm.

Assumption of risk A defense to a claim involving negligence or strict liability that bars recovery by the injured party if the injured party knew of the risk involved in undertaking a particular activity and voluntarily proceeded in the face of such risk.

Attorney Another word for lawyer.

Attorney-client privilege Privilege that protects from disclosure confidential communications between client and attorney.

Attorney general Lawyer whose office provides legal services to a state government; also refers to the lawyer who heads the United States Department of Justice.

Attorney service Outside service provider hired by a law firm to file documents at the courthouse and to personally deliver summonses and other legal documents.

Attorney work-product privilege Privilege that protects from disclosure any material that reflects an attorney's mental impressions, opinions, or legal research.

Bankruptcy Legal proceeding that affords protection from creditors to a financially troubled individual or business.

Barrister In the United States, another word for lawyer; in the British legal system, a lawyer who presents oral arguments to the court.

Beneficiary One who benefits from a trust.

Beyond a reasonable doubt The burden of proof in a criminal action. The defendant is presumed innocent unless guilt is so clearly established that no reasonable doubt remains as to the defendant's guilt.

Billable hour An hour of work that can be billed to a client at a timekeeper's assigned hourly billing rate.

Board of directors The group of individuals who direct the activities of a corporation; also called *board of trustees.*

Board of trustees The group of individuals who direct the activities of a corporation; also called *board of directors.*

Breach A party's failure to perform in accordance with the terms of a contract.

Brief Formal legal document submitted to a court for the purpose of convincing the court to adopt one party's position on the issues.

Burden of proof The duty of proving the facts in dispute.

Bylaws Rules and regulations, especially those adopted by a corporation.

Canons Within the ABA Model Code of Professional Responsibility, the nine broad, general statements of the ethical conduct expected of lawyers.

Case brief A summary of the essential points of a court opinion.

Case of first impression Case that raises a question of law not previously decided.

Case reporters Volumes in which court decisions are published chronologically by date of issuance.

Cause in fact A cause "but for" which an injury would not have occurred.

Cause of action The legal claim on which the plaintiff is suing (e.g., a breach of contract).

Censure See *public reprimand.*

Certain loss A breach-of-contract loss that can be calculated fairly accurately in monetary terms.

Challenge for cause To dismiss a potential juror because it is determined the juror does not have the ability to be fair and impartial.

Charges Jury instructions.

Charter The basic organizational document of a corporation; also called *articles of incorporation.*

Chief counsel A senior lawyer who manages the legal department of a governmental entity.

Citation A method of legal shorthand used to identify authority, such as a case or statute.

Citators Sets of publications that provide the subsequent history and treatment of cases and statutes; e.g., *Shepard's Citations.*

City attorney A lawyer whose office provides legal services to a city government.

Civil law Defines a person's individual rights that are enforceable in a civil case.

Civil liability Liability that is determined in a civil (that is, noncriminal) proceeding brought by an injured party and is punishable by an award of damages to the injured party.

Closing argument After all the evidence has been presented at trial, the attorney's summary of the case in a light most favorable to the attorney's client.

Codification Legislative enactment into statute of existing common law.

Collateral Property subject to a lien.

Comments Within the ABA Model Rules of Professional Conduct, explanations that follow each rule.

Common law A system of law based on judicial precedent rather than legislative enactments.

Community property A method by which a husband and wife own a single estate in real property; also a term used in community property jurisdictions to describe all property acquired by either spouse during a marriage, with the exception of property acquired by gift or inheritance.

Comparative negligence A defense to a claim of negligence that reduces the injured party's recovery to the same extent that the injured party's own negligence is responsible for the injury.

Compensatory damages Money paid as compensation to an injured party by the party at fault.

Complaint The initial pleading filed in a lawsuit.

Condition concurrent An event that must occur at the same time a party is required to perform under a contract.

Condition precedent An event that must occur before a party is required to perform under a contract.

Condition subsequent An event that, if it occurs, will terminate a party's obligation to perform under a contract.

Consequential loss A loss that was actually caused by a breaching party's breach of a contract.

Consideration The bargained-for exchange that arises when each party to a contract agrees to incur an obligation in exchange for obtaining a right.

Constitution The fundamental law of a nation or state.

Contest Challenge the validity of a will.

Contingency fee A billing method in which the fee charged is a set percentage of the amount recovered in a lawsuit.

Contract An agreement between two or more parties by which each party undertakes to perform, or not to perform, one or more specific acts.

Contract attorney In a private law firm, an associate who is not on the partnership track; also called a *permanent associate*.

Contributory negligence A defense to a claim of negligence that precludes the injured party from recovering anything because the injured party's own negligence contributed to the injury.

Corporation A legal entity that is regarded by the law as having a completely separate existence from the individuals or entities who own it.

Co-tenants Two or more people who own a single estate in real property as tenants in common.

Counselor Another word for lawyer.

Count Cause of action.

Counterclaim A claim made by the defendant against the plaintiff.

Counter-offer A response to an offer that itself meets the requirements of an offer.

County counsel A lawyer whose office provides legal services to a county government.

Court A tribunal established by a government to settle disputes.

Covenant A promise regarding the use of a parcel of land.

Crime An act that is subject to punishment by the government acting on behalf of society as a whole.

Criminal law Defines offenses against society that are punishable by the government in a criminal action.

Criminal liability Liability determined in a criminal proceeding brought by the government and punishable by a fine or imprisonment or both.

Cross-claim States a claim by one party against a coparty, such as a claim by a defendant against a codefendant.

Cross-complaint A claim by the defendant against either the plaintiff or another party.

Cross-examination Questioning of a witness by an opposing attorney.

Cure The remedying of a default.

Damages A sum of money that must be paid to an injured party by the party responsible for the loss.

Declaration of trust A document that creates an inter vivos trust.

Declaration under penalty of perjury A written statement of facts signed by a person who declares in the statement "under penalty of perjury" that the facts contained in the statement are true.

Deed A document that evidences a transfer of title to real property.

Deed of trust A contract that documents a type of lien on real property consisting of the borrower's conditional conveyance of title to a third party for the benefit of the lender.

Default A breach of a contractual obligation.

Defense A circumstance that justifies a party's failure to perform in accordance with a contract or that reduces or voids the obligation of one who has committed a tort to compensate the injured party.

Deficiency judgment A judgment against a borrower for an amount equal to the difference between the amount borrowed and the amount received by the lender from the sale of collateral.

Demonstrative evidence Photographs, charts, or other visual aids that help the jury understand the case.

Deposition The questioning of a party or a witness under oath.

Digest Contains a series of one-paragraph summaries of court opinions organized by topic.

Directed verdict Verdict ordered by the judge as a matter of law when the party with the burden of proof has failed to make out a prima facie case.

Direct examination The first questioning of a witness by the party who calls the witness.

Disbarment Punitive action through which an attorney is no longer allowed to practice law in the state.

Disciplinary Rules Within the ABA Model Code of Professional Responsibility, statements indicating the minimum level below which no lawyer's conduct can fall without subjecting the lawyer to disciplinary action.

Discovery Process by which the parties discover as much information as possible about the facts of the case.

Discovery plan An outline of the discovery strategy in a case.

Dissolution First step in the termination of a partnership or corporation.

District attorney Lawyer who heads a prosecutors' office in a local government jurisdiction.

Diversity of citizenship jurisdiction A basis of federal court jurisdiction arising when plaintiff and defendant reside in different states and the amount in controversy exceeds $50,000.

Dividend A payment of corporate profits to a shareholder.

Doe defendants Fictitiously named defendants.

Duress Use of force or threats to compel a party to enter into a contract.

Easement A right to use a parcel of land for a particular purpose.

Employee A person hired by an employer to perform services under the direct control and supervision of the employer.

Encumbrance See *lien*.

Equitable servitude A promise not to perform specified acts on a parcel of land.

Escheat Process by which the government inherits the property of an intestate individual who dies without any living relatives.

Estate The property an individual owns at death.

Estate in real property A party's rights with respect to a parcel of land.

Estate planning The process by which a legal professional works with an individual to plan for the disposition of the individual's estate.

Ethical Considerations Within the ABA Model Code of Professional Responsibility, explanations of the general principles set forth in Canons; ECs are aspirational in nature, setting forth objectives toward which lawyers should strive.

Ethics Opinion The ABA's answer to a specific question concerning the ABA Model Code and Model Rules.

Eviction Physical removal of a tenant from the leasehold premises.

Excuse A circumstance that legally excuses a party from performing in accordance with a contract.

Execution The signing of a document.

Executive agencies Federal administrative agencies that are considered part of the executive branch of government.

Executor of the estate A personal representative who is named in a will.

Executory contract A contract in which any party promises to perform the terms of the contract at a future date.

Exemplary damages A sum of money awarded to an injured party for the purpose of punishing a wrongdoer and making an example of the wrongdoer to others; also called *punitive damages*.

Expert witness Someone who does not necessarily have first-hand knowledge of a particular event or transaction, but has an expert knowledge of events or transactions of the type that are in question.

Express contract Contract in which the parties' expressions of intention to be bound by the contract consist of words.

Express trust Trust created by means of a written or oral expression of an intention to create the trust.

Federalism System of government wherein power is divided between the central government (the federal government) and state governments.

Federal question jurisdiction A basis of federal court jurisdiction arising when a plaintiff's claim is based on the U.S. Constitution, a treaty, or a federal statute.

Fee simple The most comprehensive estate in real property, which consists of a largely unrestricted right to determine possession, occupancy, or use.

Felony An extremely serious crime, usually punishable by a term of imprisonment exceeding one year.

Fiduciary A person who has a duty to put the interests of another before her or his own interests.

Finding Decision of the court on a factual issue.

Flat fee An established charge for simple or routine services.

Foreclosure A legal proceeding to enforce the terms of a mortgage.

Foreseeable loss A loss that parties to a contract could have anticipated at the time they entered into the contract would likely result from a breach of the contract.

Forum state The state in which the lawsuit is filed.

Fraud An intentional tort involving the making of a false representation or a failure to disclose an important fact.

General counsel Senior lawyer who manages an in-house legal department.

General denial In the answer, the defendant denies each and every allegation in the complaint in a single statement of denial.

General jurisdiction Unlimited jurisdiction.

General partner A member of a general partnership, or a member of a limited partnership who has the rights and obligations of a general partner.

General partnership A partnership in which there is one class of partners, known as general partners.

General practice law firm A private law firm designed to meet the needs of clients who have relatively simple, routine legal problems.

General warranty deed Deed that contains extensive representations as to the executing party's authority and the status of title.

Government law office A law office whose only client is the federal government or a state or local government.

Heir An individual who is entitled to inherit property under the provisions of an intestacy statute.

Holding The rule of law announced by the court in a case.

Holographic will A signed will that is entirely in the testator's own handwriting.

Homicide The act of one human being killing another.

Hourly fee A billing method in which time expended by a timekeeper on individual projects is billed to the client at an established hourly rate.

Impleader A procedure by which additional parties are brought into a lawsuit.

Implied contract A contract in which the parties' expressions of intention to be bound by the contract consist of one or more actions.

Incorporate To organize a business or activity as a corporation under the laws of a state or other jurisdiction.

Independent agencies Federal administrative agencies that are separate from the executive branch of government.

Independent contractor Person hired by an employer to achieve a specified result using whatever means the contractor desires to achieve that result.

Infraction A minor crime, usually punishable by a fine.

In-house legal department A law office consisting of a separate department within a business that provides legal services to that business.

Injunction A court order requiring someone to perform, or to refrain from performing, certain acts.

***In rem* jurisdiction** Jurisdiction over property.

Installment sale contract A contract requiring a seller to convey title to real property to a buyer on the buyer's completion of a series of payments that constitute the purchase price.

Intentional tort A breach of the legal duty to refrain from committing intentional acts that cause injury to others.

Interrogatories Written questions propounded (asked) to another party to be answered in writing under oath.

Inter vivos trust A trust created by a trustor to become effective during the trustor's lifetime; also called *living trust.*

Intestacy statute A statute that prescribes how the property of an intestate individual is to be distributed.

Intestate Term used to describe an individual who has died without having made any legally valid arrangements for the disposition of the individual's estate.

Issue A point of law or fact disputed by the parties.

Joint and several liability A form of group liability by which each member of the group is fully liable to third parties for the debts of the group.

Joint tenancy A method by which two or more people, known as joint tenants, own a single estate in real property.

Joint tenants Two or more people who own a single estate in real property in joint tenancy.

Joint venture A partnership formed for a single business transaction or limited series of transactions.

Junior partner An owner of a private law firm who has been an owner or has practiced law for a relatively short period of time, or who has a relatively small ownership interest.

Jurisdiction A court's power to hear and determine a case.

Jury instructions Directions given by the judge to the jury before their deliberations listing the factual elements that must be established in order to prevail on a particular cause of action.

Landlord An owner of a parcel of land who grants another party a right to occupy and use the property; also known as *lessor.*

Law clerk A law student who works in a law office.

Lawyer A person who is licensed by a state or other jurisdiction to practice law.

Lease A written contract that documents a landlord-tenant agreement with respect to the rights and duties of each.

Leasehold An estate in real property by which the owner of a parcel of land grants another party the right to occupy and use the property.

Leave to amend Permission granted to a plaintiff to file a new complaint that attempts to properly state a cause of action.

Legal aid office A law office that provides legal services to clients who are unable to pay the fees that private law firms charge.

Legal analysis The process of applying legal rules to specific facts in order to find a logical solution to a legal problem.

Legal ethics According to *Black's Law Dictionary*, "that branch of moral science which treats of the duties which a member of the legal profession owes to the public, to the court, to his professional brethren, and to his client" (Abridged Fifth Edition, 1983, p. 465).

Legal issue A point of law disputed by the parties that must be resolved in order to determine the outcome of a legal dispute.

Legal periodicals Periodicals containing articles written by legal scholars analyzing a particular area of the law.

Lessee A party who is granted a right to occupy and use a parcel of land by the owner of the property; also known as *tenant*.

Lessor An owner of a parcel of land who grants another party a right to occupy and use the property; also known as *landlord*.

Lien An interest in property that allows its holder to order the sale of the property in order to raise money to pay off a debt owed the lienholder by the owner of the property; also called *encumbrance*.

Limited jurisdiction A court of limited jurisdiction is limited to hearing only particular types of cases, such as cases in which the amount in controversy is less than $50,000.

Limited partner A member of a limited partnership who has limited rights and limited obligations.

Limited partnership A partnership in which there are two classes of partners.

Liquidation The conclusion of a bankruptcy proceeding in which the debtor's assets are sold and the proceeds divided among the debtor's creditors in accordance with a system of priorities.

Litigation The process through which disputes are settled in the courts.

Litigation practice The practice of a lawyer who specializes in litigation.

Litigator A lawyer who specializes in litigation.

Living trust A trust created by a trustor to become effective during the trustor's lifetime; also called *inter vivos trust*.

Long-arm statute A state law giving courts within the state jurisdiction over nonresident defendants.

Malice A specific type of *mens rea* that implies the presence of either actual intention or wantonness, and the absence of justification, excuse, or a mitigating factor.

Malpractice The failure of a lawyer to provide the services a client needs, or to provide to a client services that meet professional standards of quality, or to provide services to a client on time.

Mandatory precedent A previous court decision that must be followed.

Mandatory primary authority Law that courts in a given jurisdiction must follow.

Marital dissolution The termination of a marriage, more commonly known as divorce.

Mens rea The particular mental state that must accompany the specific *actus reus* in order for the *actus reus* to constitute a crime.

Minor A person who has not reached the so-called age of majority, which is 18 years.

Misdemeanor A less serious crime, usually punishable by a term of imprisonment of one year or less.

Mortgage A contract that contains the terms governing a lender's right to sell real property collateral.

Motion for a Judgment N.O.V. Motion for a judgment notwithstanding the verdict; will be granted if the judge determines that the verdict returned by the jury is clearly wrong as a matter of law.

Motion to compel discovery Asks the court to order a party to comply with a discovery request.

Motion to dismiss Asks the court to dismiss the entire complaint or at least one count or cause of action in the complaint.

Motion to strike Asks the court to "order stricken from any pleading any insufficient defense or any redundant, immaterial, impertinent, or scandalous matter."

Negligence A breach of the legal duty to exercise reasonable care at all times and under all circumstances.

Nonbillable hours Hours a timekeeper spends on activities that benefit the law firm but cannot be billed to clients.

Non-suit A judgment against a plaintiff who fails to prove her or his case.

Notarization The process by which a document is executed or acknowledged in the presence of a public official known as a notary.

Notary A public official who has the authority to notarize documents.

Of counsel Term used to describe the status of a lawyer who is affiliated with a private law firm but who is neither an owner nor an employee of the firm.

Offer A proposal made by a party expressing the party's intention to enter into a contract with another party on such party's acceptance of the proposal.

Office memorandum Summarizes the law that is relevant to a case and predicts how the law will be applied to the facts of the case.

Officers Individuals who manage the day-to-day affairs of a corporation.

Official code The laws of the United States or an individual state, published by the government and containing only the actual text of statutes; *United States Code* (U.S.C.) is an official code.

On the partnership track Expression describing an associate who is expected to become a co-owner of a private law firm some day.

Opening statement An attorney's statement to the jury at the beginning of a trial about the facts that will be proven during the trial.

Outside counsel A private law firm retained by a business to provide legal services which exceed the capabilities of the business' in-house legal department.

Paralegal A professional who performs legal tasks while working under the supervision of a lawyer.

Parallel citations Two or more citations for the same case; the same case reported in a different place.

Parol evidence rule Rule providing that the parties to a written contract may not submit evidence in court concerning the terms of their contract that is inconsistent with the written contract itself.

Partition Physical division or sale of a parcel of land that is owned by tenants in common.

Partner A member of a partnership; also a term used to refer to a lawyer who is an owner of a private law firm.

Partnership An association of individuals or legal entities, known as partners, who are the co-owners of a business and who share the profits and losses generated by the business among themselves.

Percipient witness One who has first-hand knowledge of some fact related to an event or transaction.

Peremptory challenge Dismissal of a prospective juror without giving a reason.

Periodic tenancy A leasehold that continues in effect for successive periods of time until either party gives notice that the leasehold will terminate at the end of a specified period.

Permanent associate In a private law firm, an associate who is not on the partnership track; also called a *contract attorney.*

Personal jurisdiction The power of a court to enter a personal judgment against (i.e., impose personal liability on) a party to the action.

Personal property Property other than land and the improvements thereon (real property).

Personal representative Someone appointed by a court to put a deceased individual's affairs in order and distribute the assets of such person's estate.

Personal service Personal hand delivery of the summons and complaint to the defendant.

Persuasive precedent A previous court decision that may offer guidance but does not have to be followed.

Piercing the corporate veil Holding the shareholders of a corporation personally liable for its debts.

Plaintiff The party who brings the suit in a civil action.

Pleadings The formal allegations of the parties of their respective claims and defenses.

Pocket part See *pocket supplement.*

Pocket supplement A paperback supplement to a hardbound book, inserted in the book through a slit in its back cover, containing relevant cases decided after the hardbound book was printed; also called *pocket part.*

Power of sale The power given to a trustee under a deed of trust to sell real property collateral at auction if the borrower defaults on the loan secured by the deed of trust.

Practice of law Representing clients in court, giving clients legal advice, preparing documents of a legal nature for clients, and similar activities.

Prayer Lists the remedies the plaintiff is requesting from the court; ends the complaint.

Precedent A previously decided case used as authority when deciding a later case that is similar in facts or legal principles.

Prejudicial error See *reversible error.*

Prenuptial agreement A property division agreement entered into by prospective spouses prior to marriage; also called *antenuptial agreement.*

Preponderance of the evidence Greater weight of the evidence; the burden of proof in a civil action.

Prima facie case A case sufficient on its face, being supported by at least the minimum amount of evidence required.

Primary authority What the law *is*, such as cases, statutes, and administrative regulations.

Principal A person who is represented by someone else, known as an agent, with respect to dealings with third parties.

Private law firm A law office whose lawyers are in private practice.

Private practice The practice of a lawyer who provides legal services to the general public.

Private reprimand A letter warning an attorney about unethical conduct.

Privileged information Information protected by law because of a special relationship that the law desires to foster.

Probate A court proceeding by which a deceased person's estate is transferred to the persons entitled to it.

Pro bono The provision of legal services without pay.

Procedural law The rules by which justice is carried out in the legal system, including pleading rules, evidentiary rules, and practice rules; describes the manner in which the substantive law may be enforced.

Professional Someone whose work requires specialized knowledge.

Profit In the law of real property, a right to remove some natural resource, such as timber or minerals, from a parcel of land.

Promissory note A contract that contains the terms for repayment of a loan.

Prosecuting attorney A lawyer who heads a prosecutors' office in a local government jurisdiction.

Prosecutor A lawyer who is employed by the government to represent the interests of the general public in criminal proceedings.

Proximate cause A cause that is a "cause in fact" of an injury and is not accompanied by an unforeseeable intervening act.

Public defender A lawyer who is employed by the government to represent indigent criminal defendants; also refers to the lawyer who heads a public defenders' office in a local government jurisdiction.

Public interest law office A law office that serves large segments of the general public by filing test cases involving matters of public concern.

Public reprimand A public warning to an attorney about unethical conduct.

Punitive damages A sum of money awarded to an injured party for the purpose of punishing a wrongdoer and making an example of the wrongdoer to others; also called *exemplary damages*.

Quitclaim deed A deed that releases the executing party's ownership interest in a parcel of land.

Real property Land, along with the structures and other improvements constructed on it.

Re-cross-examination The second questioning of a witness by the opposing party.

Re-direct examination The second questioning of a witness by the party who called the witness; attempts to overcome the effect of the cross-examination.

Remand Send a case back for a new trial to the trial court that originally heard the case.

Removal jurisdiction If a plaintiff chooses to bring either a federal question case or a diversity of citizenship case in state court, the defendant usually has the right to remove (transfer) the case to federal court.

Reorganization The conclusion of a bankruptcy proceeding in which the debtor is allowed to remain in business while paying its creditors off, in whole or in part, in accordance with a plan approved by the bankruptcy court.

Reply The plaintiff's response to a counterclaim.

Request for admission A discovery method that consists of written requests to another party to admit or deny the truth of any relevant fact.

Request for production The discovery method used for gaining access to any document or other tangible thing in the possession of another party.

Rescission Termination of a contract and the return to each party of the consideration given by that party under the contract.

Respondeat superior The rule of liability by which a principal is held liable for torts committed by an agent who is an employee acting in the course of employment.

Retainer A deposit paid by a new client and placed in a law firm's trust account to secure payment for future services rendered; may also refer to a payment made in return for a lawyer's promise to remain available to handle a client's legal matters or to a nonrefundable fee charged by a lawyer in exchange for agreeing to accept a case.

Reversible error An error that prejudiced the outcome of a case and entitles a party to a new trial; also known as a *prejudicial error.*

Right of redemption A borrower's right to prevent or cancel a foreclosure sale by paying off the loan that is in default.

Rules of evidence Rules that prescribe the requirements evidence must meet in order to be submitted to a trier of fact for consideration.

Sanction A penalty imposed on a lawyer for ethical violations; may be a public or private reprimand, suspension, or disbarment.

Secondary authority Authority that comments on, interprets, or criticizes primary authority.

Senior associate A permanent associate, or an associate on the partnership track who has worked for a private law firm for several years.

Senior partner An owner of a private law firm who is a long-time owner of the firm, who has practiced law for a long period of time, or who is the owner of a substantial percentage of the firm.

Separate property A term used in community property jurisdictions to describe all property acquired by a spouse before marriage and all property acquired by a spouse by gift or inheritance during marriage.

Service of process The delivery of the summons and complaint to the defendant.

Settlor One who creates a trust; also called *trustor.*

Shareholders Individuals or entities who have purchased an ownership interest in a corporation in the form of shares of stock; also called *stockholders.*

Shepardize To find out subsequent treatment of cases, statutes, and other legal authorities by consulting the appropriate volumes of *Shepard's Citations.*

Sole practitioner A lawyer who practices law in a law office in which he or she is the only lawyer.

Sole proprietorship A business owned by one individual.

Solicitor In the United States, another word for lawyer; in the British legal system, a lawyer who advises clients and prepares written memoranda to assist barristers with their arguments.

Specialized practice law firm A private law firm designed to meet the needs of clients who have complex, specialized legal problems.

Specific denial In the answer, the defendant admits or denies paragraph by paragraph the allegations made in the complaint.

Specific performance A breach-of-contract remedy by which a court orders the breaching party to perform the terms of the contract.

Staff counsel A lawyer employed on a full-time basis by a legal aid office or public interest law office.

Stare decisis "To stand by that which was decided"; under this principle, the rule of law established in a case governs all future cases which involve substantially the same fact pattern.

Statute of frauds A collective term for the laws within a jurisdiction that require certain types of contracts to be in writing in order to be enforced by a court.

Statute of limitations Fixes the time within which a lawsuit must be filed.

Statute of wills A statute that prescribes the requirements that must be met by a legally valid will.

Statutes Laws enacted by state and federal legislatures.

Statutory codes The volumes in which federal and state statutes are compiled and published.

Stockholders Individuals or entities who have purchased an ownership interest in a corporation in the form of shares of stock; also called *shareholders.*

Strict liability The obligation to compensate others for injury regardless of one's intention or one's failure to exercise reasonable care.

Style manual A manual adopted by a law office that provides guidelines for the format of various types of documents.

Subject matter jurisdiction Refers to a court's power to hear and decide a particular *type* of case.

Sublease A leasehold arrangement between a tenant and a third party in which the tenant assumes the role of landlord.

Sublessee A party who has assumed the role of tenant under a sublease.

Sublessor A tenant who has assumed the role of landlord under a sublease.

Subpoena A command to appear at a certain time and place to give testimony on a certain matter.

Subpoena *duces tecum* A command to produce books, papers, and other documents that are pertinent to a lawsuit.

Substantive law Creates and defines duties, rights and obligations.

Substituted service Performed by leaving a copy of the summons and complaint with a responsible adult at the defendant's residence or place of business.

Summons Notifies the defendant that she or he has been sued.

Suspension Punitive action whereby a lawyer is not allowed to practice law for a designated period of time.

Tenancy at sufferance A leasehold that automatically arises when a tenant wrongfully refuses to relinquish possession of property on termination of a tenancy for years, periodic tenancy, or tenancy at will.

Tenancy at will A leasehold that continues in effect until notice of termination is given by either party.

Tenancy by the entirety A method by which a husband and wife own a single estate in real property.

Tenancy for years A leasehold that is scheduled to terminate on a fixed date.

Tenancy in common A method by which two or more people, known as cotenants, own a single estate in real property.

Tenant A party who is granted a right to occupy and use a parcel of land by the owner of the property; also known as *lessee.*

Testamentary intent The intention of an individual that a particular document serve as that individual's will.

Testamentary trust A trust created under the terms of a will to become effective on the trustor's death.

Testate Term used to describe an individual who dies leaving a will.

Testator The individual who made a will.

Third party complaint A claim made by a defendant against a person who is not already a party to the action.

Timekeeper A person in a law office who keeps track of the time she or he spends working on individual client projects.

Tort A breach of a duty imposed by law that results in injury to another.

Transactional practice The practice of a lawyer who specializes in activities other than litigation.

Treatises Commentaries written by legal scholars covering a particular area of law; may be multivolume and/or broad in scope.

Trial courts The courts in which lawsuits are commenced and actual trials are held.

Trial notebook A three-ring binder in which documents and other materials that will be needed at trial are organized.

Trier of fact Term used to describe a judge or jury charged with determining which version of the facts that underlie a particular dispute is correct.

Trust A relationship with respect to the ownership and management of specific property.

Trustee One who holds title to property under the terms of a trust.

Trustor One who creates a trust; also called *settlor.*

Unavoidable loss A loss that a party to a contract was unable to avoid by making reasonable alternative arrangements.

Unconscionable contract A contract the terms of which are so unreasonable, oppressive, or grossly unfair that the conscience of the court is shocked.

Undue influence Mental or physical coercion that has the effect of displacing the will of a testator with the will of the person responsible for the coercion.

Uniform Commercial Code (U.C.C.) Model code that covers several areas of business law and has been adopted in some form by almost all U.S. jurisdictions.

Unlawful detainer proceeding A special court proceeding in which the only issue is a tenant's right to possession of the leasehold premises.

Unlimited jurisdiction General jurisdiction.

Unofficial codes The laws of the United States or an individual state published by private publishers; *United States Code Annotated* (U.S.C.A.) and *United States Code Service* (U.S.C.S.) are unofficial codes.

Venue The geographic location where a lawsuit *should* be brought.

Verdict Decision made by the jury in favor of either the plaintiff or the defendant.

Verified complaint A complaint in which the plaintiff swears under penalty of perjury that everything in the complaint is true and correct.

Voidable contract A contract that imposes legal obligations on the parties, subject to the right of one of the parties to cancel the contract.

Void contract A contract that imposes no legal obligations on the parties and may not be enforced in court by any party.

Voir dire The questioning of prospective jurors.

Will Document in which an individual declares how she or he wishes her or his estate to be disposed of after death.

Winding up The second step in the termination of a partnership or corporation.

Writ of certiorari An order issued by the Supreme Court to a lower court commanding the lower court to send the record of a case to the Supreme Court for review.

INDEX